Fundamentals of
Learning

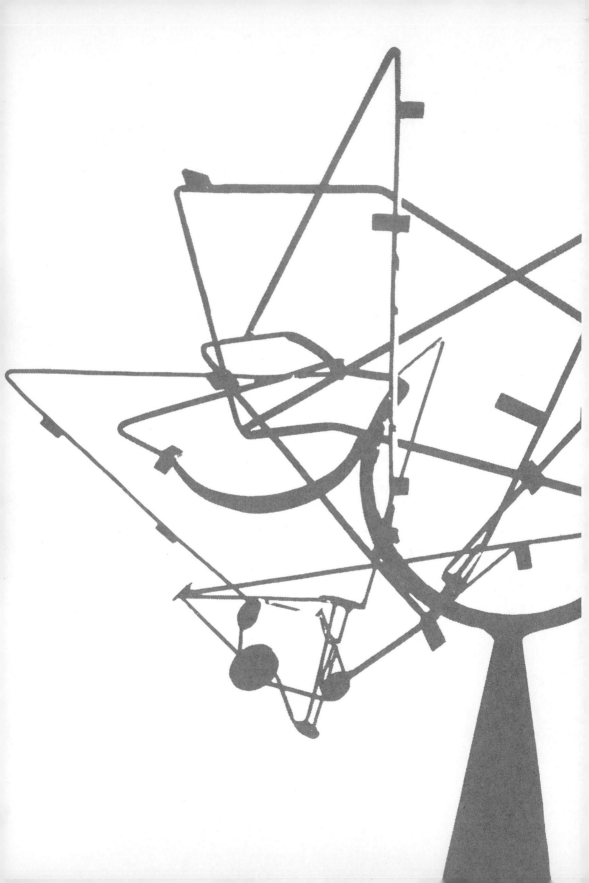

Fundamentals of Learning

John P. Houston

University of California, Los Angeles

ACADEMIC PRESS   New York   San Francisco   London

A Subsidiary of Harcourt Brace Jovanovich, Publishers

COPYRIGHT © 1976, BY ACADEMIC PRESS, INC.
ALL RIGHTS RESERVED.
NO PART OF THIS PUBLICATION MAY BE REPRODUCED OR
TRANSMITTED IN ANY FORM OR BY ANY MEANS, ELECTRONIC
OR MECHANICAL, INCLUDING PHOTOCOPY, RECORDING, OR ANY
INFORMATION STORAGE AND RETRIEVAL SYSTEM, WITHOUT
PERMISSION IN WRITING FROM THE PUBLISHER.

ACADEMIC PRESS, INC.
111 Fifth Avenue, New York, New York 10003

United Kingdom Edition published by
ACADEMIC PRESS, INC. (LONDON) LTD.
24/28 Oval Road, London NW1

Library of Congress Cataloging in Publication Data

Houston, John P
    Fundamentals of learning.

    Bibliography: p.
    1.   Learning, Psychology of.   2.   Learning and
scholarship.   I.   Title.   [DNLM: 1.   Learning.
2.   Psychology, Educational.   LB1051 H843f]
LB1051.H7925   153.1'5   75-26354
ISBN 0−12−356850−1

PRINTED IN THE UNITED STATES OF AMERICA

Contents

v

PART II. ACQUISITION

5 The Role of Contiguity in Learning   101

6 The Role of Practice in Learning   121

7 Reinforcement   151

PART III. TRANSFER

8 Generalization and Discrimination   187

9 Transfer of Training—The Impact of One Task upon Another   217

PART IV.   RETENTION

10 Interference: Data and Theory   239

11 The Information Processing Approach to Memory   259

12 How Many Memories?   281

13 Organization in Memory   307

PART V. EXTENSIONS AND APPLICATIONS

Preface

The aim of this text is to provide the reader with a broad, eclectic, well-referenced coverage of the expanding field of learning. In addition, it offers something that has been lacking in other texts—an integration of the fields of animal and human learning. The text addresses the wide range of issues and problems that reflect current, up-to-date thinking within the field, and evaluates data obtained from both animals and humans. It attempts, in a readable manner, to introduce the student to many of the complex similarities and differences between the subfields of animal and human learning. Traditional distinctions and similarities are challenged, and the student is invited to participate in this questioning process. By asking questions the text introduces the reader to the basic process of psychological investigation.

In a very basic sense the book is written for the student. It seems the field of learning is something many students pass through in order to concentrate on areas of more interest to them. Indeed, when compared with such wonderful topics as sex, insanity, love, hate, children, drugs, ESP, etc., rats pressing bars for food pellets does assume a rather pale quality. But much of what the field of learning has to offer is of value, and can be useful in understanding these other areas of psychology. As I see it, much of the problem stems from the manner in which the field is presented rather than from any inherent fault within the field itself. A consideration of learning can be light and informal and still remain accurate and informative. If the principles of learning are stated simply, lucidly, and with good examples then students do find them quite intriguing.

At the same time I have attempted to provide the serious preprofessional student with important, basic information and a good set of references, which will provide direction if he or she wishes to pursue some issue that has received cursory treatment. The coverage is broad. It ranges from basic conditioning paradigms through memory and retention processes. It includes some topics not normally covered in introductory texts (e.g., biological constraints on learning) and many standard, essential topics (e.g., reinforcement, memory).

As the investigation of learning progresses, it becomes apparent that the gap between efforts to understand animal and human learning processes remains, at best, a wide one. The reasons for the division are many. Not least of all, it has become increasingly difficult for a given individual to familiarize himself with a representative sample of the work being done within both these subfields. And yet to accept a dichotomy between animal and human learning processes would seem to belie the efforts of our predecessors who labored so mightily with the white rat in their efforts to understand the actions of man. It appears that there is much that is common to animal and human learning processes. Many of the differences seem to be more quantitative than qualitative. Accordingly, efforts are made in this text to bridge the gap between animal and human learning data and concepts. Sometimes parallel data in the two areas are not available. Sometimes a neat integration of the available data seems impossible. Still, whenever it seemed reasonable and fruitful, I have attempted to discuss issues and problems within the context of both animal and human data. The integration achieved in this text is clearly incomplete. At best, it can only be taken as a beginning. It is up to the reader to accept or reject such an approach, and to choose the approach which makes the most sense to her or to him.

The plan of the book is simple. It is based on the notion that the three basic areas of focus within the field of learning are acquisition, transfer, and retention. Part 1 deals with introductory methods, examples, and problems. Part 2 considers the processes of acquisition, including a detailed consideration of contiguity, practice, and reinforcement. Part 3 addresses the problems of transfer, with an emphasis on stimulus generalization and transfer of training. Part 4 includes an extensive discussion of problems, issues, and alternative theories within the field of retention.

I am indebted to the many students, friends, and colleagues who, directly and indirectly, aided in the writing of this book. Dr. Thomas Zentall and Dr. Paul W. Fox read the original manuscript and offered enormously helpful suggestions and criticisms. I feel fortunate in having had their assistance.

INTRODUCTION

This section introduces the reader to the language of the field of learning, and to many of the basic conditions and variables which are considered within the field. In addition, the significance of the differences among the many available learning tasks is considered. Finally, the constraints placed upon learning processes by the pressures of natural selection are discussed.

Chapter One is an attempt to bring the field of learning into focus for the reader in two ways. First, a word definition of learning is considered, and although such a definition is helpful, it is probably impossible to encompass all that is meant by "learning" in a single sentence. Accordingly, our second attempt to circumscribe the field of learning involves the brief description of a number of the different learning tasks employed and investigated by learning psychologists. These range from basic conditioning paradigms to more complex verbal tasks.

In Chapter Two *classical* and *instrumental conditioning* are examined in detail. The attention given to these two types of learning tasks is justified by the fact that they have been extremely important and influential throughout the field of learning. After having outlined a wide variety of learning tasks in Chapter 1 and having dealt with a pair of selected tasks in greater detail in Chapter Two, an important question is addressed in Chapter Three: Do all these various learning tasks represent fundamentally different learning processes or are they perhaps nothing more than different expressions of some common, unitary, underlying learning process? If it is eventually determined that these tasks do represent fundamentally different types of learning then we will be forced to develop theories and models that encompass each of the distinct learning processes. On the other hand, if it is eventually determined that some common underlying process accounts for all of these tasks then a single model should suffice. In Chapter Three, three representative learning tasks are examined in relation to one another. Both similarities and differences among the three are considered in detail. The conclusion drawn is that we are not yet ready to conclude with any degree of certainty that these tasks represent fundamentally different learning processes. The similarities among the tasks are strong enough to suggest that some unitary learning process may account for all of them.

Recent research has suggested that not all species are ready to learn all responses equally easily. Certain species seem *prepared* to learn certain responses but not others. Chapter Four examines the biological constraints on learning and deals with the emerging fact that each animal brings to every learning situation certain capabilities and predispositions to act and learn in certain ways. These predispositions may be formed by the pressures of natural selection.

What Is Learning?
A Word Definition and Some Examples

1

What do we mean by the word "learning?" It is a word we use all the time, and as a student, you must have some kind of special involvement with, or concern for, the learning process. But how would you define it? Stop for a moment and try to frame a word definition.

As you probably found, this is not an easy task. Psychologists have the same problem. They too are not sure how to define it. "Learning" is one of those words everyone uses, and seems to understand, but would be hard pressed to define. As a result, there are many different definitions floating about in the field of psychology. Some are very specific and concrete. Others are diffuse and general. Almost every learning text attempts a definition, and following suit, this text opens with a definition.

A WORD DEFINITION OF LEARNING

Gregory Kimble (1961, 1967) has developed a definition of learning that seems to encompass many of the elements contained in alternative definitions. Essentially the same definition has been proposed by others (for example, Logan, 1970). Hence it makes a good example. Kimble defines learning as A RELATIVELY PERMANENT CHANGE IN BEHAVIOR POTENTIALITY WHICH OCCURS AS A RESULT OF REINFORCED PRACTICE. Let us look at some of the terms in this definition. Why does Kimble include the term "permanent" in his definition? What kinds of behavior changes would he like to *exclude* by including the term "permanent?" Among others, he might want to exclude temporary changes in behavior due to shifts in motivation. For example, when we are tired, we sleep. The shift from the waking state to the sleeping state represents an enormous change in our behavior. But it does not represent new learning. It can be argued that changes in behavior due to fatigue should not be considered learned changes. Many other motivational factors, such as hunger, thirst, and the need for sex, can affect, or change, our behavior without involving new learning. For example, if we are hungry and a steak, a knife, and a fork are placed in front of us, we will probably eat the steak using the utensils. Our behavior changes. But does the change from not eating to eating represent new learning? Probably not. We utilize old, established habits (that is, the fundamentals of using a knife and fork), but we are not learning anything new. When we have finished eating and our hunger is reduced we will revert to our former mode of behavior (not eating). Hence *temporary* changes in behavior, due to fluctuations in motivational states, tend to be excluded from the category of learned changes.

What about the term "practice?" Why does Kimble include it in his definition? He seems to be arguing that only changes that occur as a result of practice are learned changes, and that unpracticed changes can occur, which we would not want to call learned changes. Among these are, for example, the effects of aging. There must be an enormous range of unlearned changes which occur as a result of aging. For example, as we grow older, our short-term memory may deteriorate. That is, we may have increasing difficulty remembering new materials for short periods of time. That is a big change. But such a change does not represent learning. We did not *learn* to be more forgetful. In addition, various physiological factors can produce unpracticed changes in behavior which are not considered learned changes. For example, disease and accidents can yield strong, permanent, unlearned changes in our behavior.

Why does Kimble consider learning to involve changes in "behavior potentiality" rather than in behavior? Why complicate the situation? An example may clear up the issue. At this moment, there resides within each of us, somewhere, somehow, the knowledge, or the learning, necessary to brush our teeth. But you are not brushing your teeth at this moment. We can say the capacity to brush is latent. It is in there somewhere, but it is not being expressed as overt behavior at this moment. We have acquired the capacity to brush, but that capacity is not always apparent, or expressed overtly.

Psychologists distinguish between "learning" and "performance." Performance refers to the TRANSLATION OF LEARNING INTO BEHAVIOR, USUALLY THROUGH THE INVOLVEMENT OF MOTIVATION. For example, if your mouth felt very unpleasant at this moment you would probably drop what you are doing and brush your teeth. You would be MOTIVATED to brush, and it would be the thrust of this motivation that would impel you to brush, or to translate the brushing potentiality into observable, overt behavior. Learning is invisible. It lies within us as a potentiality, and can only be observed when it interacts with motivation and is translated into, or expressed as, overt behavior.

The distinction between learning and performance is crucial, and we will return to it many times in future sections. Performance cannot always be taken as a measure of how much learning has occurred. For example, if one child spells all the words in a spelling test correctly and another child spells none of them correctly we cannot conclude that the first child has learned more than the second. The second child may *know* all the words but, for any number of reasons, he may refuse to reveal his learning. When we try to infer how much learning has occurred by looking at performance we *must* be aware of the fact that motivation as well as learning determines performance.

Finally, consider the term "reinforced practice," which Kimble includes in his definition. The concept of reinforcement is extremely complicated. For the moment, think of reinforcement as reward. According to Kimble's definition, an animal will not learn to do something unless it leads to, or is followed by a reward. A child will not learn to pick up his toys unless the behavior is followed by a reward. The reward may come in the form of parental praise and approval or it may be something the child likes or enjoys, such as candy or a trip to the zoo. The avoidance of punishment may also be rewarding. The child may even be able to reward himself by congratulating himself.

The question as to whether reinforcement is *necessary* for learning to occur is very controversial, and has been so for many years. Many psychologists feel it is essential, whereas others claim with equal conviction that it is not. Whether rewards will *facilitate* performance does not seem to be the question. If a child tells a joke, and the adults laugh, they may end up hearing that same joke to the point of tedium. Few psychologists would argue that reinforcements do not help to strengthen behaviors in one way or another. But some of them would argue that reinforcement is not *absolutely essential* for learning to occur. They feel learning can occur in the absence of reinforcement. For example, as we drive down the highway, caught up in our latest set of concerns, we pay very little attention to the passing scenery. Yet, at the end of our journey, if someone asks what we saw along the road, we may well be able to remember many events and objects. Where or what was the reinforcement for this incidental learning?

Consider the issue a little more closely. It seems the problem is to come up with a situation where everyone would agree learning occurs, but where there is no reward operating. Does the fact that we can remember the name of a stranger we met only briefly at a crowded party consitute learning without reward? The reinforcement theorist might argue that we rewarded ourselves in this case. We might pride ourselves on being able to remember names. Remember, rewards do not have to be food pellets or trips to Bermuda. They can be very subtle. What about the incidental highway learning just described? Is that learning without reinforcement? The reinforcement theorist might claim that the very acts of perceiving and processing information are reinforcing. Although the claim can be made that there is no proof that perceiving and processing information are rewarding, the reinforcement theorist can cite a long list of studies that seem to suggest we *will* learn responses that are rewarded by the opportunity to process information. For example, monkeys will learn to open little windows for nothing more than the opportunity for visual exploration (Butler, 1953). And so argument and counterargument go, and we begin to see the dilemma. Each time a new, reward-free learning situation is proposed, the reinforcement theorist is able to find some possible reinforcing event in it. The final step in the argument seems to come when it is proposed that the act of learning rewards itself. If we accept this, then it becomes impossible to conceive of a situation that involves learning without reward. Hence the issue, as interesting as it is, must be laid aside. We shall return to the concept of reinforcement many times, for, even though it may not be fully understood it is one of the most powerful variables in any learning situation.

So much for the word definition of learning. It is important to remember that psychologists have many different ideas about what would be an adequate definition. Kimble's definition merely represents one viewpoint.

EXAMPLES OF LEARNING

Another way to bring the field of learning into focus is to describe some of the learning tasks psychologists have used and studied in the laboratory. Obviously there are many different kinds of learning situations. We can learn to throw a ball; we can learn to stay out of trouble; we can learn to be a lawyer at night school; and we can learn the birds native to the western United States. These different learning situations may or may not represent fundamentally different types of learning. They may or may not require different theories to account for them. No one is quite sure how many truly different ways we can learn things. As you read about the different learning tasks described in what follows, keep in mind that, although they may seem quite distinct, they do not necessarily represent different underlying learning processes.

Classical Conditioning

Most people have heard of Pavlov's experiments with dogs, tones, and saliva, which represent something called CLASSICAL CONDITIONING. The experimental paradigm was as follows: Prior to the conditioning experiment (Anrep, 1920) the dog's salivary duct was surgically treated so that saliva flowed through a small opening to outside the dog's cheek, where it could be collected and measured accurately. The dog was then trained to stand in a harness as depicted in Figure 1.1. A tuning fork was sounded. Several seconds later, a small amount of dry meat powder was moved close to the dog's mouth and the dog was allowed to eat

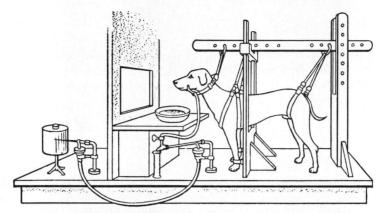

Figure 1.1. Pavlov's salivary conditioning apparatus. (Adapted from Yerkes, R. M. & Morgulis, S. The method of Pavlov in animal psychology. *Psychological Bulletin,* 1909, *6,* 257–273. Fig. 2, p., 264. Copyright 1909 by the American Psychological Association. Reprinted by permission.)

it. On the first trial (or pairing of the sound with the meat powder) the sound stimulated no salivation, but the food did. The procedure was to continue pairing the sound and the meat powder over a series of trials. After a number of pairings, the tuning fork was sounded alone. No meat powder was presented afterward. It was found that the sound alone elicited a salivary response. The salivary response had become conditioned to the sound of the tuning fork.

As we shall see, there are many different kinds of animals and responses that can be classically conditioned. But the Pavlovian situation allows us to identify the basic elements of all classical conditioning situations.

The Unconditioned Stimulus

The unconditioned stimulus (UCS) in the Pavlovian situation is the meat powder. It is a stimulus which, prior to the conditioning experiment, consistently and regularly elicits a response. *Every time* we present the meat powder the dog salivates. The capacity of the UCS to elicit a regular response can be innate or learned. It does not matter, so long as it elicits a response consistently.

The Unconditioned Response

The unconditioned response (UCR) is the consistent response to the UCS. In the Pavlovian situation the salivation in response to the meat powder is the UCR.

The Conditioned Stimulus

The conditioned stimulus (CS) is the sound of the tuning fork. The CS is a stimulus that does not initially elicit a learned response. We pair the CS (sound) with the UCS (meat powder) over and over again. With repeated pairings the CS will begin to elicit a salivary response when it is presented by itself.

The Conditioned Response

The conditioned response (CR) is the learned response elicited by the CS. That is, if we sound the tuning fork alone and the dog salivates then *that* salivary response is called the CR. If the dog salivates to the UCS alone then *that* response is a UCR, and not a CR. Students often ask if the CR and the UCR are the same thing. Saliva is saliva. A good point; but, strange as it may sound, the CR and the UCR may well differ in important ways. This problem will be considered in more detail at a later point.

Classical conditioning probably occurs in our everyday lives. For example, have you ever had an experience such as this? You find someone you think is very attractive. You approach, saying, "Why don't you stay awhile? Watch T.V., or something?" Very gentle. Very casual. The person gives you a flat, irritable look and says, "What in the world for?" You are humiliated, angry, and hurt, all at the same time, but you manage to live through it. A couple of days later one of your friends happens to mention the person in passing. You immediately feel a warm flush crawling up the back of your neck. That cringing is probably a CR. Many of our emotional reactions are probably classically conditioned. If we consistently experience strong emotions, either positive or negative, in a given situation, then anything that reminds us of the situation in the future may well trigger a conditioned emotional reaction. We cannot avoid it. It seems to be automatic.

There is an interesting demonstration that may be used in the classroom. Suppose your instructor should march into class one day, raise a pistol loaded with blanks above his head, shout "Boo!" and fire. Everyone feels something in this situation. The next day all your instructor need do is walk in, raise the pistol, and yell "Boo!" *without* firing. Almost everyone will experience a good CR.

Instrumental Conditioning

Imagine this situation. You are in a large, white, empty room. You do not know how you got there but you do know you are very hungry. Extremely hungry. There is a metal bar protruding from one of the walls of the room, and a little hole in the wall near the bar. There seems to be some kind of a ventilation grate up on the ceiling, but no windows and no doors. What would you do in this situation? You might explore, try to escape, sit down and cry, pound the walls, pace back and forth, or call for help. You might also investigate the metal bar and the small hole. At some point in your explorations you press the bar with your hand. As you do so it makes a clicking sound and you jump back, startled. As the click sounds, a small cracker rolls out of the hole beneath the bar. You eat the cracker. As you are still hungry, you give it another try; press the bar; eat the resulting food. You have discovered that the bar press and the delivery of food are related. You settle down, press the bar, and eat until your hunger is satisfied.

The situation just described demonstrates what psychologists call INSTRUMENTAL CONDITIONING. The probability of a particular response (the bar press) has been increased through the delivery of a reinforcement (the food) immediately following the response. The response was instrumental in obtaining something wanted and needed. As you probably know, psychologists often use the albino rat as a subject. Rats are creatures full of curiosity and ready to learn. They are inexpensive, small, and can be handled in ways that would outrage the average American undergraduate. A piece of equipment called a Skinner box is often used with rats (see Fig. 1.2). The hungry rat is placed in a box where it explores, discovers the bar, and learns to press it for rewards such as food pellets. If we can discover something about how these little animals learn then, by generalizing from the animal to the human situation, we may also discover something about how humans learn.

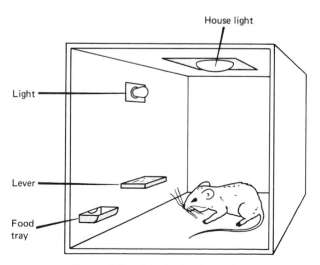

Figure 1.2. A typical Skinner box.

Discrimination Learning

Another learning task psychologists utilize is called DISCRIMINATION LEARNING. An example of this task would be one in which a hungry pigeon is placed in a Skinner box with two illuminated disks—a blue one on the right and a yellow one on the left—attached to the wall of the box. It is characteristic of hungry pigeons to engage in a good deal of pecking behavior. They peck the walls, the floor and the disks. The experimenter sets the situation up such that each time the pigeon pecks the blue disk, it is rewarded with a kernel of corn. Each time it pecks the yellow disk, it receives no reward. The blue disk is called the POSITIVE STIMULUS and the yellow is called the NEGATIVE STIMULUS. At first, the pigeon pecks the two disks about equally. But, as time goes on, it responds more and more often to the blue disk, the one that yields food. The pigeon discriminates between the colors. Or does it? Can we conclude, on the basis of the described situation, that the animal has learned a blue–yellow discrimination? No, we cannot, for it may have been learning a POSITION DISCRIMINATION. That is, it may have been ignoring the colors and attending to the positions of the positive and negative stimuli. If it pecks the one on the right it is rewarded. If it pecks the left disk nothing happens. We cannot be sure if the animal is discriminating color or position. How can we avoid this confusion and ensure that the pigeon is learning a color discrimination? One way to do it is to switch the positions of the colors on successive trials. Put the blue one on the left part of the time and put it on the right part of the time. Then the animal will be forced to utilize the color cues.

Figure 1.3 depicts a Lashley jumping stand. This is another piece of apparatus that may be used in discrimination learning. The rat must learn to jump to stimuli to gain access to the food table behind the stimuli, and to avoid falling into the net. If he leaps against the negative stimulus he bumps his nose and falls. If he jumps against the positive stimulus the card tips over easily, allowing the animal to reach the table.

It is reasonable to ask if discrimination learning is not just another kind of instrumental conditioning. It is in a way. It is a kind of instrumental conditioning in which the emphasis is upon the formation of a discrimination between two extremely salient cues. All instrumental conditioning involves discrimination learning. For example, a rat in a Skinner box must discriminate the bar from the rest of the box. It has to learn that pressing the wall, or its own foot, will not do any good. It is just that in discrimination learning tasks the *focus* of the study is upon the discrimination process. This is all part and parcel of the fact that we are merely describing different learning tasks, or situations, that psychologists have developed through the years. Although the tasks look different on the surface, there is no guarantee that they really repre-

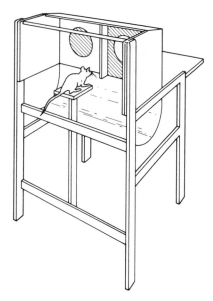

Figure 1.3. The Lashley jumping stand. If the animal leaps against the positive card it falls over easily, allowing the animal to reach the safety of the table. If the animal jumps against the negative card it bumps its nose and falls to the net below.

sent fundamentally different learning processes. There are many similarities among the various learning tasks. It is often difficult to separate them beyond distinctions that can be made on a superficial descriptive level.

The discrimination learning paradigm has definite counterparts in the real world. Discrimination learning is an essential part of everyday life. Imagine for a moment that you are, "The Person Who Lost the Ability to Discriminate." What would life be like if you could not discriminate? Most likely, it would be short. If you failed to discriminate red circles from green circles you would find it difficult to drive an automobile in the city. If you failed to discriminate female bodies from male bodies all sorts of peculiar things might happen to you. If you suddenly lost the ability to discriminate you would respond the same way to widely varying, and sometimes inappropriate, stimuli. We all learn to restrict our responses to stimuli that will yield rewards, and to inhibit our responses to stimuli that yield no reward or, worse yet, yield punishment.

Verbal Learning Tasks

Sometimes psychologists are specifically interested in human verbal learning. Accordingly there are a number of VERBAL LEARNING tasks used in the laboratory. Among them are serial learning, paried-associate learning, and free recall.

Serial Learning

In a typical serial learning situation, the subject is brought into the laboratory and is seated in front of a memory drum. Essentially, the memory drum is a metal box with a small window in front. Before the experiment begins the subject is told that a word, or some other type of verbal material, will appear in the window. A few seconds later this word will disappear and a second word will take its place. This pattern will be repeated until the subject has seen the entire list (for example, perhaps 15 words). The subject's task is to remember these words *and* to remember the order in which they occur. After the subject has seen the list once, all the way through, a blank space will appear in the window. This signals the subject that he is at the end of the list and that the drum is about to present the words again in exactly the same order. The subject's task is to anticipate which word will *next* appear in the window. Each time a word appears in the window the subject tries to recall, and say aloud, the word which will *next* appear in the window. This is called serial anticipation learning. The blank space at the end of the list is the subject's cue to recall the first word in the list.

Serial, or sequential learning seems to be an integral part of our everyday life. Some examples would include the memorization of phone numbers, the alphabet, poetry, and historical information. Language behavior, in general, possesses a strong sequential component. The hope is that our simple serial task will help us understand these more complicated serial behaviors. The serial learning task allows us to control, in a strict sense, any number of variables that we suspect might be important in determining serial learning. For example, Table 1.1 contains a serial

TABLE 1.1

**Serial List Composed
of Highly Emotional Words**

JOY
DEATH
ACID
SCREAM
FEEL
KISS
HATE
RAPE
LOVE
GRASS
SEX
KILL

---

list composed of highly emotional words. Do you feel this list might be more or less difficult to master than some less emotional list?

Paired-Associate Learning

Paired-associate (PA) learning is another of the many types of tasks available to the verbal learning psychologist. In this task subjects must learn to associate, or pair together, two items. In a typical experiment the subject will be faced with a memory drum containing two windows. A stimulus item (for example, a word) will appear in the left window for a couple of seconds. Then a response item will appear in the right window. These two words will be paired together throughout the experiment. Then the window will be cleared and a second pair, composed of two different words, will be exposed, first the stimulus word on the left and then the response word on the right. The subject's task is to recall and say aloud the correct response word each time he sees a stimulus word. To be correct he must say the correct response word aloud before it is actually exposed by the memory drum. Typically he has about 2 seconds to try to recall each response word. Lists vary in length. An average one contains eight or ten pairs. Table 1.2 contains a typical paired-associate list. The subject is usually asked to respond to the list until he has mastered it completely (that is, until he can recall correctly each response item given the stimulus items). Sometimes, depending upon the experimenter's purpose, all subjects are given a set number of trials rather than asked to master the list completely. The stimuli and responses may be almost anything, including words, syllables, shapes, numbers, and colors.

The pairs in a PA list are almost always rearranged from trial to trial for a very simple reason. If the order of the items were kept constant

TABLE 1.2

A Typical Paired Associate List Involving Syllables as Stimuli and Words as Responses

Stimuli	Responses
TUM	SINCERE
JAK	POTENT
BAV	FURTHER
GOG	BASHFUL
WIF	MIGRANT
DEX	IMMENSE
LOH	ACUTE
PEC	GALLANT

from trial to trial the subject could learn the responses in a serial fashion and totally ignore the stimulus components. If the order of the items were kept constant we would not know whether the subject was learning a serial list composed of the response units or a PA list composed of both stimulus and response units.

Paired-associate learning was developed with the idea that a very simple learning situation, in which discrete stimulus units are associated with discrete response units, would ultimately help us in our attempts to understand more complicated learning events, such as concept formation and problem solving. As it turns out, PA learning is not simple at all. It seems the more psychologists learn about PA learning the more complicated it becomes. The discussion of some of these complexities will be reserved for a later section.

Our lives are filled with learning situations that have something in common with PA learning. Associating names with faces, telephone numbers with people, and Spanish words with English equivalents all seem to approximate PA learning. The entire process of giving verbal meaning to the world, through labeling, seems to be related to the laboratory paradigm.

Free Recall

There is another interesting verbal task that has been utilized with increasing frequency in recent years. In a free-recall task, the subject is given a list of verbal items and is then asked to recall the items in any order he wishes. Since the subject is free to recall the items in any order this task allows us to tap into, or learn about, what the subject does with, or how he organizes, the materials he is trying to learn. For example, from a long list of randomly presented nouns the subject might first recall all the nouns that have something to do with people, and then move on to all the nouns which have something to do with animals, and so on. The subject CLUSTERS his responses according to categories. It seems that recalling the nouns by category makes the job easier. Not surprisingly, this suggests that some complicated organizational processes are going on inside the subject. The materials are not spit out in the same order they were fed in. The subject actively processes the materials, seeking ways to make his task easier.

If someone asks us to recall all our known blood relatives we may search through some hierarchical scheme. For example, we might start with our maternal grandparents and trace down through the generations. Or we might try to recall all cousins first, then uncles, and so on. But we would probably not recall the materials randomly, we would utilize some scheme, or structure, or outline to make the search and retrieval processes easier and more efficient. Free recall is one of the tasks that allow us to peek into these enormously complicated and individualized organizational activities.

Words and Nonsense Syllables

Psychologists use a variety of verbal materials in the learning tasks we have been discussing. Although words are often employed they are not the only verbal unit utilized in serial, paired-associate and free-recall learning. For example, nonsense syllables are often employed. Typically, a nonsense syllable is a three letter sequence, such as ZXB or JAX, which is presumed to possess little meaning. (CCCs are consonant, consonant, consonant sequences, and CVCs are consonant, vowel, consonant sequences). The idea behind their development was that if we could utilize verbal units which are relatively free from preexperimentally established meaning then we would be in a better position to study pure, new learning unencumbered by previously established habits. (Unfortunately, nonsense syllables are never really devoid of meaning. For instance, VUL, NAP, and even REZ, probably elicit some kind of responses as you read over them. It may be impossible to come up with a truly nonsensical syllable.)

In addition to words and nonsense syllables psychologists utilize, depending upon their purposes, a wide range of additional materials (for example, geometric shapes, colors, phrases, sentences, digits, and numbers). Thus, the array of usable materials plus the variety of available tasks provide the investigator with a flexible set of tools to use in his study of learning processes.

Problem Solving

Although it does not exhaust the types of learning tasks investigated by psychologists, problem solving will serve as a final example in this section. Table 1.3 contains some sample problems. Give them a try. Once you have tried to solve these problems you will be able to reflect upon the complexity of the mental activities associated with their solution. It is interesting that one of the learning situations that concerns us most in the real world (problem solving) is also one of the most complicated and difficult to study. There is little doubt that we would rather understand problem solving than paired-associate learning. And yet, the PA task seems to receive more attention in the field of learning than does the more complicated, relevant problem solving situation. It is as though psychologists hoped that an eventual understanding of the problem solving situation would follow, or evolve, from a thorough understanding of more limited, simplified learning situations. It was hoped that an analysis of the basic building blocks, involving simple associations between simple

TABLE 1.3

Sample Problems

1. By moving only two matches make four boxes out of these five boxes (using all matches in the solution).

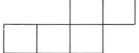

2. Complete this meaningful sequence.

O T T F F S S __ N

3. You are on the way to the city and you meet a man at a fork in the road. You do not know which fork to take. You know that the man is one of two brothers who live in the area. One of these brothers always tells the truth while the other never tells the truth. You don't know which one you are facing. You can ask him one question, which he can answer with a yes or no, which will assure you of taking the correct fork. What is that question?

4. Nine steel balls all look alike. Eight of the balls weigh the same amount while one is heavier than the rest. You are given a pan balance and allowed two weighings of any combination or number of these balls to discover which one is the heavy one.

5.

Without lifting your pencil from the paper, draw four straight lines through all nine points.

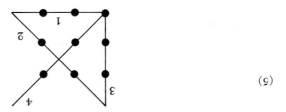

(5)

(4) Weigh any three against any other three. If one group of three is heavier than the other then it contains the heavy ball. If not then the remaining unweighed group of three contains the heavy ball. To determine which of three balls is the heavy one, weigh any one against any other one.

(3) Point to either fork and ask the man if his brother would say this was the correct fork. If he says "No," then it is the correct fork. If he says "Yes," it is the wrong fork.

(2) O T T F F S S E̅ N

These are the first letters of the numbers one through nine.

stimuli and responses, would lead to an understanding of more complex situations. Unfortunately, this aim has not been clearly achieved. If anything, it appears that the so-called simple learning situations are not at all simple, and that they will require a good deal more study before we can successfully utilize our knowledge of them in our attempts to understand more complex learning events.

SUMMARY

Learning may be defined in many ways. According to a sample definition learning refers to a relatively permanent change in behavior potentiality which occurs as a result of reinforced practice. This definition excludes from consideration changes in behavior due to motivational fluctuations, maturation, and various physical and physiological factors. It argues that a distinction between learning and performance must be made. In addition, it proposes that reinforcement is necessry for learning to occur.

A second effort was made to bring the field of learning into focus. Selected examples of learning tasks employed by psychologists in their laboratories were examined. These included classical conditioning, instrumental conditioning, discrimination learning, serial learning, paired-association learning, free recall, and problem solving. Two points should be kept firmly in mind. First, these are only a few of the many learning paradigms employed by psychologists. Second, psychologists are uncertain about whether these tasks represent many different, distinct types of learning or merely different varieties of some common underlying process.

Classical and Instrumental Learning 2

This chapter is devoted to a more detailed consideration of classical and instrumental conditioning. They deserve special consideration because more has been done with these two learning situations than most of the others. The discussion will take the following form: Classical conditioning will be considered first; examples, procedures, and basic phenomena will be presented. The same kind of consideration will then be given to instrumental conditioning.

In the next chapter, the following kinds of questions will be asked. What are some of the differences and similarities among our available learning tasks? Are we capable of learning in more than one way? Are instrumental and classical conditioning different from one another? What about PA learning? Is PA learning an example of instrumental or classical conditioning, or does it represent an entirely different kind of learning?

OPERANT AND RESPONDENT CONDITIONING

Sooner or later students run into, and are sometimes confused by, the terms OPERANT CONDITIONING and RESPONDENT CONDITIONING. For our purposes, OPERANT CONDITIONING IS THE SAME AS INSTRUMENTAL CONDITIONING, and RESPONDENT CONDITIONING IS IDENTICAL TO CLASSICAL CONDITIONING. The terms "operant" and "respondent" conditioning were developed by B. F. Skinner, and are currently used by a large number of psychologists. Although some investigators attempt to distinguish between operant and instrumental conditioning, and between respondent and classical conditioning (Ellis, 1972), this text will not.

CLASSICAL CONDITIONING

Examples

Classical conditioning is not limited to situations wherein dogs salivate and bells ring. If it were, we would not give it a second thought.

The phenomenon is, in fact, widespread. It occurs across a large number of animals, responses, and situations. There are even reports in the literature claiming success with classically conditioning plants.[1] Let us look at a few selected examples of classical conditioning, which should provide some idea of the diversity of classical conditioning situations.

Eyelid Conditioning

One of the most widely used classical conditioning situations is the one in which an eye blink is conditioned to some neutral stimulus, such as a sound or a light. In these situations a puff of air (the UCS) is directed toward the subject's eyeball. As one would imagine, the air puff causes the subject, often a human, to blink (the UCR). At, or very nearly, the time the air hits the eyeball a CS, such as a bell, tone, or light, is presented. Successive pairings of the UCS (air) and the CS (bell, tone, or light) eventually lead to the situation wherein the CS alone is capable of eliciting a blink (the CR). Because eyelashes are sometimes thin, and eyeblinks occur so rapidly, they are not always easy to see. One technique used to ensure the detection of the slightest movement of the eyelid involves a false eyelash. A strip of paper or aluminum foil is pasted to the eyelash and allowed to flutter up and down.

Conditioning of Planaria

Another example of classical conditioning involves planaria. This small, simple, freshwater flatworm seems capable of acquiring conditioned responses. Thompson and McConnell (1955) placed these creatures in dishes of water. Then, at the same time they shocked the animals by passing electrical current through the water, they changed the illumination in the experimental situation (CS). The UCS (shock) caused the animals to, among other things, contract their bodies (see Figure 2.1). After a number of pairings of the CS (illumination change) and UCS (shock) the authors noted an increase in the tendency of the CS to elicit contractions.

Aversive Conditioning Using Sickness as the Unconditioned Response

In another interesting example Garcia, McGowan, and Green (1972) describe conditions in which the drinking of a saccharin solution (CS) was paired with X-irradiation (UCS), which makes rats sick. Later the subject rats showed a definite aversion to the taste of saccharin. The

---

[1] Although stranger things have happened, you might want to be skeptical about reported instances of vegetable learning. Actual events, unfortunately, may not be as interesting as the products of our imagination.

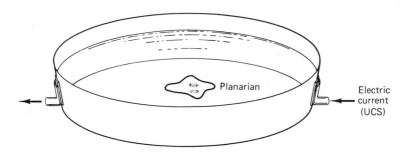

Figure 2.1.   Classical conditioning of a planarian.

notion here is that the taste of saccharin (CS) produced a CR composed of an unpleasant sensation similar to the original UCR (sickness). You know, after you've been deeply inebriated the sight of a gin bottle makes you feel ill all over again.

Additional Examples

Scores of animals and responses have been involved in classical conditioning. Chick embryos (Hunt, 1949) and human fetuses (Spelt, 1948) have undergone conditioning; heart rates (Black, 1965) and pupillary dilation (Gerall, Sampson, & Boslov, 1957) have been classically conditioned; the list goes on and on. The point here is that classical conditioning is not restricted to the Pavlovian situation. It is pervasive in the animal kingdom and it is pervasive in our lives.

The Temporal Spacing of the CS and the UCS

We already know that classical conditioning will occur when the CS and the UCS occur simultaneously and when the CS precedes the UCS. But what about when the CS follows the UCS? Will classical conditioning occur then? For example, if your instructor walked into your classroom, fired a pistol, and then shouted "Boo!" would conditioning occur? If it did at all, the conditioned response to the CS would be very weak. Thus we can see that the TEMPORAL SPACING of the CS and the

UCS is critical in classical conditioning. Names have been given to the various temporal patterns.

Delayed Classical Conditioning

In delayed procedures, the onset of the CS always precedes the onset of the UCS. The CS is then left on *at least until the beginning* of the UCS. It may then be terminated or continued into, and even beyond, the duration of the UCS.

Simultaneous Classical Conditioning

In simultaneous conditioning, the onset of the CS occurs at the same time as the onset of the UCS. In addition, the two stimuli are usually terminated together.

Trace Classical Conditioning

In trace conditioning, the CS is presented *and terminated* before UCS onset.

Backward Classical Conditioning

In this situation, the CS follows the UCS. Generally speaking, very poor conditioning occurs with this pattern.

Figure 2.2 is a graphic representation of the four types of classical conditioning. The delayed procedures are best and the backward proce-

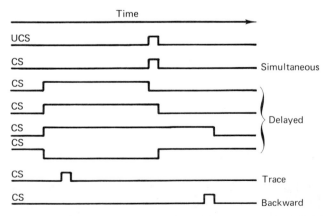

Figure 2.2.   Temporal arrangements of the CS and the UCS used in the various conditioning procedures. The upward movement of a line represents the onset of a stimulus while the downward movement of a line represents the offset of a stimulus.

dures are least effective (see Keith-Lucas & Guttman, 1975). The simultaneous and trace procedures tend to be of intermediate effectiveness.

How Does One Go About Observing a CR?

Let us assume your instructor has given you several delayed classical conditioning trials using his pistol and the "Boo!" Of course, the class is startled and alarmed each time the stimuli are presented. But is the startle response a CR or a UCR? Since both the CS and the UCS are presented we cannot be sure. The observed startle response may be a mixed response, possessing both learned and unlearned components. A good way to differentiate a CR from a UCR is to leave out the UCS on a given trial. Any response which then occurs must be a CR.

There is a problem with this procedure for observing a CR. If we leave out the UCS on a given trial we have instituted what is called an EXTINCTION trial. In classical conditioning, extinction refers to the fact that presentation of the CS alone, without the UCS, will lead to a cessation of the response. That is, your instructor cannot put his pistol away and say, "Boo!" every day for the rest of the semester and expect you to respond each time. You would extinguish, or stop responding after a time. If we try to observe a CR by occasionally leaving out the UCS we are slipping extinction trials into the learning situation. We are diluting the learning situation and will obtain a false picture of the increasing strength of the CR. It is a dilemma. We want to know if CRs are occurring, but we do not want to leave out the UCS for fear of partially extinguishing, or weakening, whatever CR strength we already have. The more we leave out the UCS the more checks we have on the developing CR. But an increase in the number of such checks also increases the number of unwanted extinction trials.

Fortunately, nature comes to the rescue. As it turns out, after delayed training has progressed for a while the CR begins to *precede* the onset of the UCS. That is, the CR will occur, or begin, *after* the onset of the CS but *before* the onset of the UCS. In our example, the instructor would call out, "Boo!" Then, *before* the gun went off, the class's conditioned startle response would begin. The CR occurs *in anticipation* of the UCS. Thus, in delayed procedures, there is no need to leave out the UCS. The CR begins in that little delay between the CS and the UCS. If the experimenter observes a response occurring *before* the onset of the UCS he calls it a CR. It could not be a UCR because, by definition, a UCR is a response to the UCS. The fact that the CR eventually just precedes UCS onset is sometimes called INHIBITION OF DELAY.

Inhibition of delay helps us when we want to observe CRs in delayed classical conditioning, but it does not help us in simultaneous procedures. Of course, it does not even occur in simultaneous situations, where both

CRs and UCRs begin after the onset of both stimuli. Thus, to observe the CR in a simultaneous classical conditioning paradigm, the UCS must occasionally be left out.

Is the CR the Same as the UCR?

An eye blink is an eye blink, right? Perhaps not. Classical conditioning has sometimes been thought of as the simple *transfer* of a given response from one stimulus (UCS) to another (CS), but additional research has revealed that the CR is not identical to the UCR (see Kimble, 1961). There are two views of the nature of the CR.

The CR as a Component of the UCR

One view holds that the CR is a *component* of the UCR. For example, in the salivary conditioning situation the UCS (meat powder) elicits a very complicated pattern of reactions, including salivation, tongue smacking, and licking, etc. But the CS (tone) elicits only the salivary response. The same effect appears in other conditioning situations. For example, when your instructor shouts, "Boo!" without firing the pistol you will experience a startle reaction, but it will not be as complete, or dramatic, as the one that follows the actual firing of the gun.

The CR as a Preparatory Response

A second view holds that the CR is a response that *prepares* the animal for the UCS. For example, in delayed eyelid conditioning the CR may begin after the onset of the CS but before UCS onset. It is as though the CR is preparing the animal for the UCS (air puff). One way to think about it is that the CR may actually allow the animal partially to avoid the noxious air puff.

These two views, the preparatory and the component positions, are not mutually exclusive. THE CR MAY WELL BE A PARTIAL RESPONSE AND PREPARE THE ANIMAL FOR THE UCS.

Responses Beyond the CR and UCR

Another interesting discovery is that, in delayed eyelid situations, there are many different kinds of blinks occurring, not just CRs and UCRs. For example, random blinks often occur. They are a potential source of confusion in eyelid conditioning experiments. If the subject happens to blink randomly, immediately before the onset of the UCS, then there is the danger that the experimenter will mistakenly call that blink a CR. In addition, some subjects are more than helpful in eyelid conditioning situations. They blink voluntarily. The experimenter does not want to count these VOLUNTARY RESPONSES as true CRs. Fortunately, voluntary responses tend to begin earlier in the CS–UCS interval than true CRs and to last longer. But they are a problem. Finally, there is something called an ALPHA RESPONSE, which may appear in classical conditioning situations. This is a small blink which occurs immediately after the onset of the CS. It can easily be confused with a true CR even though it occurs earlier in the CS–UCS interval and is smaller than the typical CR. The Alpha Response is a UCR to the CS, or a small STARTLE RESPONSE. The bell alone occasionally causes the subject to blink a little. The Alpha Response is not a learned response. It is a reflex response to the CS.

We can begin to see that classical conditioning is quite complicated (see Holland & Rescorla, 1975). What began as a simple situation, in which one response was supposed to be transferred from one stimulus to another, turns out to involve many different responses.

Some Selected Phenomena and Areas of Research in Classical Conditioning

Pseudoconditioning

Pseudoconditioning is an interesting phenomenon in which the UCS is first presented alone for a series of trials. Then the CS is presented alone. Upon this very first presentation of the CS, which has never been paired with the UCS, something resembling a CR is elicited. For example, 50 successive solitary puffs of air may be directed toward the subject's eye. Then a bell may be sounded by itself. The subject will blink. The effect is called pseudoconditioning because the CS and the UCS have never been paired together. The argument is that there has been no opportunity for learning to occur. Pseudoconditioning has been observed in humans (Prokasy, Hall, & Fawcett, 1962), cats (Harlow & Toltzein, 1940), goldfish (Harlow, 1939), and many other species.

Pseudoconditioning may be demonstrated in the classroom. Suppose your instructor fired his blank pistol on 20 successive mornings without ever saying, "Boo!" Then, on the twenty-first day, he said, "Boo!" instead of firing the gun. Pseudoconditioning would be demonstrated if you, as a subject, reacted to the verbalization in a manner similar to your response to the report of the gun.

There have been several different interpretations of pseudoconditioning. One of them argues that the response to the CS is a result of generalized excitement. The implication is that, after a series of UCS presentations, we are so excited, and ready to respond, that we will respond to anything, even a neutral stimulus, such as a tone. Another interpretation argues that pseudoconditioning may actually be true classical conditioning, and not "pseudo" at all. How could that be? Where is the pairing of a CS and a UCS which is essential to the classical conditioning paradigm? The trick is to find the CS. We are looking for something which is common to the presentation of the UCS alone (air puff) and to the presentation of the CS alone (bell). One possibility is A CHANGE FROM NOTHING TO SOMETHING, OR A CHANGE FROM NO STIMULATION TO STIMULATION. This change is common to the presentation of the air puff and the bell. During the series of trials when the UCS is being presented our newly discovered CS (change from no stimulation to stimulation) is present. It is "paired" with the air puff. Then, when the bell alone is presented our subtle CS (change from no stimulation to stimulation) is also present (see Wickens & Wickens, 1942). Thus pseudoconditioning may actually be true classical conditioning in which the CS is a subtle energy change.

The CS–UCS Interval

The amount of time between CS onset and the onset of the UCS has long been one of the major concerns in the field of classical conditioning. Generally speaking, a CS–UCS interval of about .5 second has proven to be optimal in many situations. Although the data suggest that this is true, the reasons for it are not at all clear. Studies that have varied the CS–UCS interval suggest that either longer or shorter intervals are less effective in the development of conditioned responses (see Figure 2.3) (Kimble & Reynolds, 1967; Spooner & Kellogg, 1947; Wolfle, 1930, 1931).

The CS–UCS Interval and CS Complexity

The relationship between conditioning and the CS–UCS interval is not a simple one. Although the optimal CS–UCS interval is, in general, around .5 second there are cases where this rule does not hold. For example, Ross and Ross (1972) present data which suggest that, at least in some situations, the optimal interval is strongly affected by the complexity of the CS. In some of their studies longer CS–UCS intervals were needed for optimal conditioning when a complex CS was being used.

The CS–UCS Interval and CS Intensity

The intensity of the CS is another factor that seems to interact with the CS–UCS interval. Ross and Ross (1972) summarize data which suggest

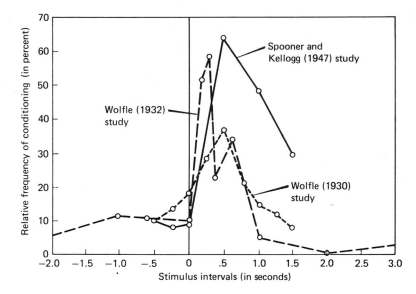

Figure 2.3. Relationship between conditioning and the CS–UCS interval. Note that the maximum frequency of conditioned responses occurs when the CS–UCS interval is approximately .5 second (Adapted from Spooner, A., & Kellogg, W. N. The backward conditioning curve. *American Journal of Psychology*, 1947, *60*, 321–334. Fig. 2, p. 327.)

that a more intense CS will strengthen conditioning when the CS–UCS interval is around .5 second, but that variations in CS intensity will have little effect upon conditioning when longer intervals are used.

Without going into great detail the point here is that the relationship between conditioning and the CS–UCS interval is extremely complicated and is probably affected by many different aspects, or characteristics, of the CS itself.

Multiple Response Measures

A recent trend in the study of classical conditioning focuses upon the fact that classical conditioning involves many different, and perhaps related, changes within the organism (Black & Prokasy, 1972). For example, in eyelid experiments, the experimenter has traditionally focused upon the eye blink as a specific CR to a specific CS. As it turns out, the eye blink is not the only response that can be elicited by the CS. Concurrently there may be important changes in such things as heart rate and skeletal activity. The new trend in the field is to examine the relationships among these various response systems, to look at the actions of the whole organism in response to the CS, and to avoid looking at a simple CR, such as the eye blink, in isolation. The questions being asked are: How are the different response systems related? Can changes in one be predicted from changes in the others? The goal is the understanding of the overall pattern of behaviors involved in classical conditioning.

Latent Inhibition

Repeated presentation of the CS, prior to the presentation of the paired CS and UCS, will sometimes lead to poorer conditioning than if the CS is paired with the UCS from the outset. For example, if a tone is sounded alone for 150 trials, and is then paired with an air puff, the resulting eye blink conditioning will be slower than if the tone had not been presented alone. The phenomenon is called LATENT INHIBITION. Some workers have felt that the preconditioning exposure to the CS reduces the subject's attention to, or orientation toward, the CS. In other words, if someone rings a bell endlessly, we will adapt to it, or pay less attention to it, and its effectiveness as a cue in learning will be reduced accordingly. Much of the work on latent inhibition has been done in the Soviet Union, but its appeal has been spreading in the United States and Europe.

Adaptation

Adaptation refers to the situation wherein the UCS, rather than the CS, is presented alone for a series of trials before the CS and UCS are paired together. When this is done conditioning is again slowed. MacDonald (1946) has shown that a series of 50 air puffs, given prior to the pairing of the CS and UCS, will reduce the number of CRs obtained when the CS and UCS are paired together.

At this point one might ask about the relationship between adaptation and pseudoconditioning. Both procedures involve the same manipulation. The UCS is presented alone for a series of trials. Yet in pseudoconditioning something like a CR is obtained on the very first presentation of the CS, whereas in adaptation conditioning is slowed over a series of CS–UCS pairings. It seems the difference between the two phenomena may lie in the fact that the pseudoconditioning effect appears on the very first presentation of the CS, and is a transitory effect. That is, its impact will not be observed over a long series of CS–UCS pairings. Adaptation, on the other hand, refers to a decrement which occurs over a long series of CS–UCS pairings. Pseudoconditioning may actually occur in adaptation experiments, on the first trial or two, but it is neither strong enough nor lasting enough to affect, or counteract, the decrement in conditioning that appears over a long series of CS–UCS pairings.

SELECTED EXAMPLES OF
INSTRUMENTAL CONDITIONING

Instrumental Reward Training

The rat learning to press the bar for food in a Skinner box is a straightforward example of REWARD TRAINING. In reward training the animal is REWARDED IF HE MAKES A PARTICULAR RESPONSE. Children learning to tie their shoes for parental approval, adolescents learning a paper route for spending money, college students absorbing course materials for a grade, athletes mastering their particular sport for money and recognition, and college professors learning to publish experiments for promotions all represent reward training. The essential characteristic of the situation is that the animal, or human, must first make a particular response before it receives something it wants or needs.

Avoidance Training

Examples

In AVOIDANCE TRAINING the animal is PUNISHED IF IT FAILS TO MAKE A PARTICULAR RESPONSE. The apparatus depicted in Figure 2.4 may be used to demonstrate avoidance training. One side of the box is painted black. The other side, painted white, has a metal grid floor. Electric current may be passed through this grid. A hurdle, or fence, separates the black from the white side./ When a rat is placed in the white side it engages in normal rat behavior, nosing about and exploring the box. The apparatus is set up such that the current will be turned on in 15 seconds. If, by that time, the animal has not climbed over the barrier, removing himself from the white box, it will be shocked. If it does move into the black box before the 15 seconds have elapsed it will not be shocked. When the rat is first placed in the box it will typically wander about. When it receives the first shock it squeaks, leaps about, and soon

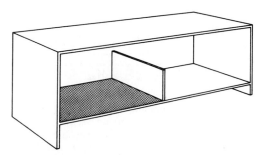

Figure 2.4.   Drawing of apparatus that may be used in avoidance conditioning.

scrambles into the black box. The experimenter begins another trial. This means he picks up the rat and places it back in the white box. The rat again has 15 seconds to jump the fence or be shocked. You can easily see what will happen in this situation. Over a series of trials the rat learns to jump the fence promptly when placed in the white box. No question about it. He's leaving, thank you very much. After a series of trials the rat no longer receives any shock at all. It has learned to avoid the shock.

Figure 2.5 contains some typical avoidance training data obtained from a single dog (Solomon & Wynne, 1953). In this experiment, the dog was shocked 10 seconds after the beginning of a trial if it failed to jump across the barrier separating the two compartments. As training progressed the number of avoidance responses (leaping the barrier before shock) increased. In addition, as can be seen in Figure 2.5, the latency of the avoidance response decreased. That is, the time between the beginning of a trial and the occurrence of the avoidance response decreased.

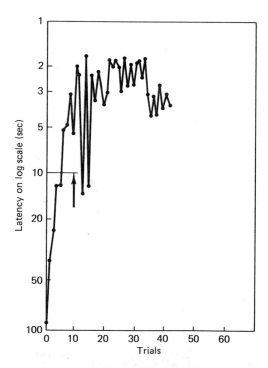

Figure 2.5. Typical avoidance conditioning data involving response latency on successive trials for a single dog. (Adapted from Solomon, R. L., & Wynne, L. C. Traumatic avoidance learning: Acquisition in normal dogs. *Psychological Monographs,* 1953, 67. [Whole no. 354]. Fig. 4, p. 6. Copyright 1953 by the American Psychological Association. Reprinted by permission.)

The Permanence of the Avoidance Response

In the reward training situation, it is easy to imagine what will happen if the reinforcement is removed from the situation. If a rat is no longer given food for bar pressing it will stop pressing quite quickly. This is called EXTINCTION of the response. Similarly, if a high hurdles man jumps hurdles 10 hours a day and never makes the team he will probably stop practicing (unless some other form of reward keeps him going). But what about the avoidance situation? What do you think the rat will do if the shock is permanently removed from the situation? No more shock. Just a white box and a black box. Interestingly enough, he keeps right on jumping even though there is no need for it. He never waits long enough to find out he will not be shocked. If left to his own devices the rat will maintain his avoidance response for a very long time.

There are ways to ensure extinction of avoidance responses. For example, one way to do it is to make the barrier so high the rat cannot jump over it. He is forced to stay in the white box and discover he will no longer be shocked. The rat is rather unhappy for awhile but, sooner or later, the escape response drops out.

The Two-Factor Theory of Avoidance Conditioning

One particular theory of avoidance conditioning has been very influential (Mowrer & Lamoreaux, 1942, 1946). According to this interpretation, avoidance conditioning involves both instrumental conditioning *and* classical conditioning. When a rat is placed in the white box and shocked a kind of classical conditioning occurs. The rat's reaction to the shock becomes classically conditioned to the white box. Mowrer and others have called this conditioned reaction FEAR. One can think of the rat's reaction to the shock as something else if one wishes, but fear is close enough for our purposes. The white box is the CS. The shock is the UCS. The fear elicited by the shock is the UCR. The fear elicited by the white box is the CR. Thus, the first factor in the two-factor theory is the classical conditioning of a fear reaction. The second factor refers to the notion that the rat will learn to *escape* from the fear producing situation in an *instrumental* fashion. When the rat finds itself in the white box, it experiences conditioned fear. It then leaps the barrier. The termination of the fear-producing stimuli, and consequently the fear itself, is the reward, or reinforcement, for the escape behavior.

In summary, the two-factor theory holds that a negative emotional reaction becomes classically conditioned to a particular set of stimuli. The animal then instrumentally learns to escape from these circumstances, and is reinforced by the reduction in the conditioned emotional reaction. The reader is referred to Bolles (1970), Rescorla and Solomon (1967), and Wahlsten and Cole (1972) for discussions of the two-factor theory.

Learned Helplessness

One interesting development in the field of avoidance conditioning has been the discovery of the LEARNED HELPLESSNESS phenomenon (Maier, 1970; Maier, Seligman, & Solomon, 1969). If, prior to normal avoidance training a dog has experienced *inescapable* shock, it will sometimes fail to learn the avoidance response. For example, if a dog is shocked repeatedly in a Pavlovian harness, without any opportunity for escape, and is then placed in an avoidance situation where shock may be avoided by leaping a barrier, the dog will sometimes remain relatively silent and motionless during the shock periods. It will fail to learn the escape response. After unavoidable shock the dog somehow operates as though action would be fruitless. It is without "hope."

Similar kinds of reactions have been observed in humans. Sometimes prisoners of war adopt an aggressive stance, and attempt to subvert the purposes of their captors. Others become apathetic, listless, and without the will to escape or resist (Strassman, Thaler, & Schein, 1956). The difference between the two types of prisoners seems to be in their attitude about the effectiveness of their own actions. The active, resisting prisoners believe they can improve the situation through action, whereas the "helpless" prisoners believe there is no hope. They feel any action on their part would be futile or perhaps dangerous.

Escape Training

Another variety of instrumental conditioning is called ESCAPE TRAINING. In this situation, INEVITABLE PUNISHMENT IS CONTINUED UNLESS THE SUBJECT MAKES A PARTICULAR RESPONSE. For example, imagine the avoidance learning situation just described, but with one slight change. In escape training the current is *always* on in the white box. The rat is dropped into the white box and is, obviously, shocked when he lands on the grid. It quickly learns to escape by leaping the barrier. The difference between avoidance and escape training is that in escape training the animal can never completely avoid the shock. No matter how hard it tries it is always shocked at the beginning of every trial.

When an enthusiastic father tosses his screaming, 4-year-old non-swimmer into the family pool, the child is undergoing escape training.

Swim or sink. No matter how hard he tries the child hits that unpleasant water every time, just as the rat hits the electrified grid on every trial. (It is true that the child's dislike of the water may lessen with exposure, but those first few tosses into the water surely represent escape training.)

The Relationship between Escape and Avoidance Training

If you think back to the discussion of avoidance training you can see that avoidance training really involves classical conditioning of the fear reaction and instrumental *escape* training. In other words, the animal learns to escape the unavoidable fear that has been classically conditioned to the white box. It can learn to avoid the shock completely, but it cannot avoid the fear completely. It can only *escape* that unpleasant emotion, as it is elicited every time he is placed in the white box, no matter how quickly he jumps the barrier.

Punishment Training

In PUNISHMENT TRAINING, the animal is PUNISHED IF IT MAKES A PARTICULAR RESPONSE. For example, suppose a cat has been trained to run from a start box, through a maze, and into a goal box where it is rewarded with food. If the situation is suddenly changed to one in which the animal is shocked in both the maze and the goal box it will stop running, and will spend most of its time in the safe start box. If a child has had a lot of rowdy fun in the first grade but is routinely punished for such disruptive behavior by his new second grade teacher he will probably drop the offensive action. Solomon (1964) argues that the essence of punishment training is that the animal is being taught *what not to do*, whereas in escape and avoidance training the animal is being taught *what to do*.

The effects of punishment are complicated, and tricky. Some of the factors that determine the effectiveness of punishment include the intensity of the punishment, the strength of the response to be punished, and the species of the subject. Many of the important variables influencing punishment are discussed by Solomon (1964).

In any case, our application of punishment may not always work out as planned. If, for example, you wish to stop your dog from escaping through a hole in the backyard fence you may wait patiently by the hole until the dog attempts to go through. As it passes through the opening you may swat it with a newspaper. That is punishing a particular response, or is it? Maybe not. Your dog may well avoid you for 2 weeks, and continue to use the hole in the fence.

*The Relationship between Avoidance
and Punishment Training*

Mowrer (1960) has argued that punishment training is not that different from avoidance training. He states that in both cases fear is classically conditioned and then instrumentally escaped. As we already know, in avoidance conditioning fear is classically conditioned to the white box. The rat then learns instrumentally to escape from that situation. In punishment training, the fear is classically conditioned to the *punished response itself*. The response itself is then avoided. It is as though the *thought* of making the punished response makes us afraid to do it.

Keep in mind that, although distinctions have been made between reward, avoidance, escape, and punishment training, these distinctions are operational and descriptive. A little thinking has led us to the position that the four types possess a good deal in common.

The Distinction between Positive and Negative Reinforcement

POSITIVE REINFORCEMENT usually refers to anything which, if *presented* to the organism following a response, will increase the probability of that response occurring. For example, if a hungry rat presses a bar and is then given food then that reinforcement is called a positive one. Things such as food, water, sex, and the opportunity to explore are usually considered to be positive reinforcers.

NEGATIVE REINFORCEMENT usually refers to something which, if *taken away* from the animal, will increase the probability of a response occurring. For example, if an animal leaps a barrier and shock is *removed* then the probability of the escape response will have been strengthened. Generally speaking, noxious stimuli such as shock are considered to be negative reinforcers. They must be removed to obtain the reinforcing effect.

Now, having made this neat distinction between positive and negative reinforcers, can we argue that it might be a superficial one? Consider the rat pressing the bar for food. Does this situation involve a positive or negative reinforcer? We are tempted to say positive, because we are presenting something to the animal following his response. Is it possible, though, that the reinforcing factor in this situation is the *removal of hunger pangs* and not the mere presentation of the food? Is it possible that this situation involves a negative reinforcer? It is as though the psychologist has distinguished between positive and negative reinforcers, not on the basis of what is important to the animal, but what he, as an experimenter, does in the experimental situation. Positive and negative reinforcers may be opposite sides of the same coin. So far as the animal is concerned the presentation of food may normally be the same as taking away hunger pains. The removal of shock may be the same as presenting the state of not being shocked.

If we entertain the possibility that positive and negative reinforcers may be opposite sides of the same coin then we must entertain such thoughts as the possibility that reward and escape training are identical. In reward training the rat may merely be learning to escape from the unpleasant state of being hungry or otherwise deprived. In escape training the rat may be reinforced by the presentation of the state of nonshock. The two processes may well coincide. For example, when we are hungry and seek food we may well be reinforced by the presentation of food *and* the removal of hunger pangs. It is difficult to separate the presentation of pleasant factors and removal of unpleasant ones.

There are some interesting experiments which bear upon this issue. They suggest that both the presentation of food *and* the removal of hunger reinforce behavior. A discussion of these studies will be delayed until a later section.

The Distinction between Responding and Not Responding

If an animal is punished for making a particular response, and ceases to make that response, it is customary to say we have taught the animal what not to do. A response has been eliminated. But is that the case? Is it not possible to think of the act of not responding as an actual response in some cases? When we try not to be rude to others, because we know it will lead to punishment, are we not actually engaging in some kind of response? If we think of the act of not responding, or inhibiting a response, as an active response then punishment training and reward training become closely related. Punishment training may be thought of as reward training in which the response of not responding is rewarded by the absence of punishment. Before we accept the psychologist's distinctions we should think carefully about the meaning of his terms. They are not as clean and crisp as we would like them to be.

SUMMARY

Classical Conditioning

1. In an attempt to underline the fact that classical conditioning is a widespread phenomenon several selected examples were outlined. These included *eyelid conditioning, conditioning of planaria,* and *aversive conditioning using sickness as the UCR.*

2. The temporal spacing of the CS and the UCS is an important variable in the study of classical conditioning. Typical CS–UCS patterns include *delayed, simultaneous, trace,* and *backward procedures.*

3. A CR may be observed by leaving out the UCS occasionally or, in the case of delayed and trace procedures, by observing the development of the CR prior to the onset of the UCS.

4. The CR is not the same as the UCR. The CR has been viewed as a component of the UCR and as a response which prepares the organism for the UCS.

5. Responses within the typical conditioning situation are not limited to CRs and UCRs. For example, random blinks, voluntary responses, and UCRs to the CS (Alpha Responses) have been identified in eyelid conditioning.

6. Pseudoconditioning refers to the fact that a CS, when presented alone following a long series of solitary UCS presentations, will often elicit a response resembling a CR. Pseudoconditioning has been interpreted in terms of generalized excitement, and as a case of true classical conditioning.

7. The length of the CS–UCS interval is a critical variable in classical conditioning. In many cases a CS–UCS interval of about .5 sec. seems to be optimal, but this optimal interval interacts with other variables, such as CS complexity and intensity.

8. A recent trend in the field (multiple response measurement) has focused on the fact that classical conditioning involves many different, and perhaps related, changes within the organism.

9. Latent inhibition refers to the fact that repeated presentations of the CS alone, prior to the paired presentation of the CS and UCS, will sometimes lead to poor conditioning.

10. Adaptation refers to the finding that repeated presentations of the UCS, prior to the paired presentation of the CS and the UCS, will also lead to poor conditioning.

Instrumental Conditioning

1. Instrumental reward training refers to the situation wherein the animal is rewarded if it makes a particular response.

2. In avoidance training the animal is punished if it fails to make a particular response.

3. Relative to reward trained responses, avoidance trained responses are extremely durable under conditions of extinction.

4. The two-factor theory of avoidance conditioning argues that "fear" is classically conditioned to the punishment situation and that the animal then learns, in an instrumental fashion, to escape from this fear. The reduction in fear is the reinforcer.

5. Learned helplessness refers to the fact that avoidance learning, following inescapable shock, will sometimes be very poor.

6. In escape training inevitable punishment is continued unless the animal makes a particular response.

7. In punishment training the animal is punished if it makes a particular response.

8. Mowrer argues that punishment and avoidance training are essentially the same thing. In avoidance training "fear" is classically conditioned to the external situation while in punishment training "fear" is somehow classically conditioned to the punished response itself.

9. Positive reinforcement usually refers to anything which, if presented to the animal, will increase the probability of a response occurring. Negative reinforcement usually refers to anything which, if taken away from the animal, will increase the probability of a response occurring.

10. The distinction between positive and negative reinforcers may be a superficial one. The presentation of something positive may not be different from the removal of something negative.

11. It is possible that the act of not responding is, in some situations, an actual response. If this position is taken then many of the distinctions among the different types of conditioning become blurred.

Learning Tasks: 3
Some Similarities and Differences

In view of the fact that we have a number of different learning tasks commonly utilized in research, we may examine some of the important similarities and differences among these tasks. Although these tasks (e.g., classical and instrumental conditioning, and verbal learning tasks) appear to be quite distinct on a procedural level, there may be important similarities among them. It is the intent of this chapter to explore some of these similarities and to attempt to evaluate them in relation to the apparent differences among the same tasks. In other words, are we sure these different tasks reflect different underlying learning processes or is it possible that they represent different expressions of some common, unitary underlying learning process? In a general sense we are asking the following questions. Do we possess the ability to learn in more than one way? How sure are we that our operationally distinct learning tasks truly represent different kinds of learning processes?

The discussion will take the following form. Three representative varieties of learning have been selected (other examples could have been chosen, but these will suffice). They include instrumental conditioning, classical conditioning, and PA learning. First, PA learning will be examined in relation to the other types: Is PA learning more like instrumental conditioning, or is it more closely related to classical conditioning? Does it clearly represent a totally separate kind of learning? Second, differences between classical and instrumental conditioning will be examined: Are the traditional differences between these two types of learning valid, or might they be superficial differences that do little to substantiate the claim that classical and instrumental conditioning are fundamentally different? Third, the range of common phenomena obtained with these three learning tasks will be outlined.

This exercise is limited in that it considers only three selected learning tasks. If it can be shown that these three types are closely related there is no guarantee that all other types of learning (e.g., problem solving, sequential learning) will also be closely tied together. But the weight of the evidence would suggest that such a possibility should be taken seriously.

The implications of these kinds of questions are far-reaching. *If it is found that humans possess the capacity to learn in several different ways, perhaps utilizing different levels or aspects of the nervous system, then theories, laws, rules, models, and generalizations governing each of these learning capacities will have to be developed. If, on the other hand, it is eventually determined that some common, underlying process can account for all the disparate types of learning situations then some single, fundamental explanatory system may suffice.*

It is not the intent of this chapter to *prove* that some underlying, unitary learning process exists. Neither is it intended that a comparison of instrumental, classical, and paired-associate learning is uniquely important. What the chapter does intend to suggest is that there may be important similarities among these, and other tasks, which are sometimes ignored.

At the same time we should be aware of another danger. A lack of precision in our thinking about learning tasks may also lead us to "find" similarities among tasks when they do not really exist. Thus we must be careful not to overemphasize similarities when those similarities may be superficial. We seek neither to accept unwarranted similarities nor to dismiss legitimate ones. Rather we wish to grasp all the possible interpretations of some fairly complicated situations.

IS PAIRED-ASSOCIATE LEARNING RELATED TO EITHER CLASSICAL OR INSTRUMENTAL CONDITIONING?

Paired-associate learning is essentially a human task, which requires the subject to associate pairs of verbal units. Does this learning task definitely represent some new, unique form of learning, or is it possible that it may be subsumed under some other heading, such as classical or instrumental conditioning?

Paired-Associate Learning as Instrumental Learning

It may be argued that PA learning is an instance of instrumental reward training. For example, suppose a subject is required to associate the nonsense syllable BEV with the nonsense syllable JAX. When the memory drum exposes JAX the subject's task is to recall and say aloud "BEV." The reward, or reinforcement for making the correct response, comes in the form of response confirmation. The memory drum, by exposing BEV, informs the subject that he was correct in saying "BEV." Making correct responses is definitely rewarding for the average subject in this situation. Thus the PA situation contains many of the elements of the typical Skinner box situation. The human sees the stimulus word, makes a response and is rewarded. The rat sees the bar, presses it and is rewarded.

That subjects find satisfaction in correctly responding is unquestionable. The PA learning situation is quite often a tense one. The subject's self-concept is, in a mild way, on the line. The subjects often interpret the situation as one in which their intelligence level will be revealed. There are no tricks the subject can use. There are no avenues of escape. If he can learn the list easily he tends to think of himself as bright. If he has trouble with the list he often feels anxious, and doubts his ability level. College students (the customary subjects), already caught up in the process of proving themselves in an academic setting, readily interpret the PA task as one more test of their ability. Hence success in PA learning is highly rewarding.

Careful debriefing is needed after PA tasks, for the subject may easily receive a distorted picture of his own ability. For example, lists can be constructed that are very simple to master or extremely difficult. Table 3.1 contains two PA lists. One is easily learned, whereas the other is next to impossible to master. If you were asked to learn the difficult list, and were not informed of its extreme nature, you might well walk out of the experimental situation believing you were less intelligent than you had hoped.

In summary, PA learning may be thought of as an instance of instrumental conditioning wherein the subject perceives a stimulus and responds to it. Correct responses are followed by rewards (response confirmations), whereas incorrect responses are not rewarded. This does not mean we have *proved* that we learn paired-associates in exactly the same manner that the rat learns to press a bar. Our mental activities (e.g., organizing, testing hypotheses) are (hopefully) quite a bit more complicated than the rat's mental operations. But it does suggest that the essential observ-

TABLE 3.1

Difficult and Easy Paired-Associate Lists

Easy		Difficult
HOUSE	→ HOME	XQKZ → QKZX
TABLE	→ CHAIR	QXKZ → KQXZ
DARK	→ LIGHT	QZKX → KQZX
NOW	→ THEN	KZXQ → ZXQK
MOTHER	→ FATHER	XZQK → QZXK
UP	→ DOWN	KQZX → XZKQ
RIVER	→ WATER	ZKXQ → ZXKQ
SPIDER	→ WEB	ZXQK → XKQZ

able qualities of the two situations (*stimulus, response, and reinforcement*) are duplicated. In other words, it would seem premature to conclude that instrumental conditioning and PA learning represent clearly different types of learning.

Paired-Associate Learning as Classical Conditioning

Paired-associate learning may be understood in different ways. For example, it may be, and has been, thought of as an instance of classical, rather than instrumental learning (Fig. 3.1). Consider the JAX–BEV pair. Assume, for the sake of argument, that JAX is a CS, and that the printed syllable BEV is a UCS. In the PA learning situation JAX (the CS) is presented just before the presentation of BEV (the UCS). This corresponds to a delayed classical conditioning procedure. When the printed syllable BEV is presented the subject reacts to it. That is, he thinks, or perhaps even says, "BEV." The saying or thinking of "BEV" may be considered the UCR. It happens every time the printed syllable BEV is presented. At first JAX (the CS) does not elicit the thought or the verbalization "BEV" (unless the subject has had an unusual childhood). As JAX (CS) and BEV (UCS) are paired together, over and over, JAX (CS) begins to elicit the thought or verbalization "BEV." When JAX (CS) elicits "BEV" we call *that* "BEV" a CR. Note that, as conditioning progresses, "BEV" (CR) begins to occur in *anticipation* of the UCS (BEV). It corresponds to the pattern obtained in classical conditioning where the CR follows the CS and precedes the UCS.

It seems PA learning may be thought of as *either* classical or instrumental conditioning. At this point many people begin to argue that PA learning is closer to instrumental than classical conditioning because classical conditioning seems to involve involuntary reflexive responding, whereas PA learning and instrumental conditioning seems to involve complicated, voluntary processes. In response it must be admitted that subjects often use enormously complicated schemes for storing and retrieving paired-associate items, and that these activities do not resemble what we normally think of as involuntary classical conditioning activities. For example, subjects will make up stories or images relating paired-asso-

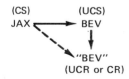

Figure 3.1. Schematic representation of paired-associate learning as an instance of classical conditioning.

ciate stimuli and responses. JAX might remind one subject of the familiar childhood game. He might store the pair by remembering that *BEV*erly cleaned out the neighborhood in a couple of fast games. On the other hand, subjects sometimes report that the paired-associate stimulus causes the response to "pop into" their minds in an involuntary manner. Hence, at least in some situations, PA learning does seem to possess the automatic, involuntary quality of the classically conditioned response.

Interpretations of PA learning have not been limited to classical and instrumental learning. Many investigators have begun to think of human learning and retention in terms of information processing, wherein the emphasis is upon storage and retrieval mechanisms (Lindsay & Norman, 1972). A detailed consideration of the information processing approach will be discussed in later sections.

In summary, PA learning cannot clearly be distinguished from classical and instrumental conditioning. It may or may not represent a distinct learning process. Probably the most scholarly stance to assume is one in which we are aware of the many alternative ways of thinking about PA learning, and human learning in general.

Why the Distinction?

If PA learning may be thought of as either classical or instrumental then why has it traditionally been kept distinct from these two forms of conditioning? How is it that there is an enormous body of literature involving PA learning and another, separate and distinct, involving classical and instrumental conditioning? One reason is that, although PA learning is essentially a human task, much of the classical and instrumental work has been done with animals. It is very difficult to compare, and to integrate, nonverbal animal activity with human verbal action. Psychologists are forced to use different tasks to study nonverbal animal and human verbal activity. For example, a rat in a Skinner box struggles to master a single response (the bar press), while a human in a paired-associate situation is *simultaneously* connecting ten different responses to ten different stimuli. If the human were asked to learn a single association, such as JAX–BEV, he would learn it instantly. Psychologists are forced to complicate the human learning situation in order to slow us down enough so the course of learning may be observed. If an animal were required to master a task as difficult as a paired-associate list, it would not be able to do it. Thus we can see that the tasks in animal and verbal learning are so different that it has been difficult to compare results.

Another factor that has contributed to the separation of the fields is that animals may be manipulated in ways that would be unacceptable with humans. For example, in studying the effects of motivation, psychologists sometimes starve rats down to 80% of their body weight. Can you imagine what would happen if psychologists tried this manipulation with college sophomores? And even if we did starve a human in one of our experiments could we be sure he would be acting out of hunger? He might, at that late point, be more interested in injecting confusion and doubt into the experimenter's results. In other words, if we deprive a rat of food we can be fairly sure he will be operating in the service of that need. Who knows what a college sophomore would be doing at that point? Human motivation is subtle, and uncontrollable, when compared to that of animals. Rats have also had electrodes implanted in their brains (Olds, 1956). Obviously this procedure cannot be routinely used with introductory psychology students. Because of these kinds of differences, there are all sorts of results obtained with animals that have not been replicated with humans.

Because psychology has grown in leaps and bounds a single person can no longer master all the different fields. As a result, different investigators, using different vocabularies and subjects, concentrate on their own specialties. Curiously, a given phenomenon, which may well appear in both animal and human behavior, is sometimes given different labels by animal and human psychologists. It is not recognized as a common phenomenon. Several examples of this kind of isolation will be examined in this text. The intent will be to bridge the gap between animal and human learning, for animal research will be of little interest if it does not ultimately contribute to our understanding of human behavior.

CLASSICAL AND INSTRUMENTAL CONDITIONING COMPARED

Now that it has been suggested that PA learning may be thought of as either classical or instrumental conditioning the question of the relationship between classical and instrumental conditioning may be addressed. Are they related forms of some underlying process? The answer to this question has been shifting slowly. Fifteen years ago, it was assumed that instrumental and classical conditioning represented two distinct learning systems. More recent research has suggested that this traditional distinction may have to be abandoned, or at least modified. The discussion will take the following course. First, some of the problems inherent in trying to compare the two types of conditioning will be presented. Second, some of the attempts to condition the same response both classically and instrumentally will be examined in detail. Finally, an attempt will be made to point out the ways in which these differences, so firmly held for so many years, are beginning to be questioned.

Problems Inherent in the Comparison of Classical and Instrumental Conditioning

It may well be that we never have a case of pure classical conditioning or a case of pure instrumental conditioning. Instrumental conditioning may always involve classical conditioning and classical conditioning may always possess attributes of the instrumental paradigm.

Instrumental Conditioning in Classical Conditioning

In classical eyelid conditioning, the CR may reduce the impact of the noxious UCS. By blinking, the subject partially avoids the air puff. To the extent that the CR does avoid the air puff it becomes instrumental in the animal's life. It affects his future well-being. Hence this classical situation possesses attributes of the instrumental paradigm. Other types of classical conditioning also involve reinforced instrumental learning. In the salivary conditioning situation, meat powder (UCS) eaten after salivation may be more pleasant than dry meat powder eaten without preliminary salivation. Hence the conditioned salivary response may be reinforced. Similarly, in the conditioning of planaria, a constricted body (CR) may lessen the impact of the shock (UCS), just as bracing against a blow seems to lessen the severity of the blow. It is difficult to be certain about these sorts of things, but the idea that classical conditioning may involve instrumental conditioning has been emphasized by a number of authors (D'Amato, Fazzaro, & Etkins, 1968; Hilgard & Marquis, 1940).

Classical Conditioning in Instrumental Conditioning

Just as classical conditioning never seems to be quite pure, so instrumental conditioning never seems to be completely free from classical conditioning elements. The case of instrumental avoidance learning has already been examined wherein there may be classical conditioning of "fear" followed by instrumental escape from that "fear." Even more interesting is the fact that classical conditioning has been implicated in simple reward training (Trapold & Overmeir, 1972). If a rat is trained to press a bar in a Skinner box, and is reinforced for doing so, then he experiences the pairing of the Skinner box (CS) with the food (UCS). The positive reaction to the food, whatever you want to call it, becomes conditioned to the situation such that, when the rat is placed in the Skinner box in the future, he will experience a CR. This CR has been called, among other things, "hope," conditioned excitement, and incentive motivation. A rough counterpart of this kind of CR would be what you might experience when you are very, very hungry and approach your favorite restaurant. You can almost taste the food. The closer you get, the more excited you become. The conditioned excitement seems to pull you toward your goal. It somehow interacts with your instrumental behaviors.

In summary, even if classical and instrumental conditioning are different, they are so inextricably bound into one another that, for all practical purposes, attempts to separate them may finally prove to be futile.

Attempts to Condition the Same Response both Classically and Instrumentally

Early experimenters assumed the way to separate classical and instrumental conditioning would be to isolate one response, and then condition that response both classically and instrumentally. If one or the other of the conditioning procedures yielded better conditioning of that given response then it could be argued that the two procedures do differ, and that one of them is superior to the other. Although the approach makes sense, the results have been equivocal. Sometimes instrumental conditioning leads to faster conditioning (Brogden, Lipman, & Culler, 1938) and sometimes classical conditioning is superior (Logan, 1951). In the Brogden, Lipman, and Culler study, guinea pigs were shocked (the UCS) in a revolving exercise wheel. The shock produced running (the UCR). A buzzer (CS) was paired with the shock. In the classical, or nonavoidance, condition the animal was shocked whether he ran or not. In the instrumental, or avoidance, condition the animal was not shocked if he ran, but would be shocked if he failed to run. The group that could avoid the shock (instrumental conditioning) did a lot more running over a series of trials than did the group that received the shock no matter what they did. This study seems to suggest that instrumental conditioning is superior to classical conditioning. On the other hand, in the Logan (1951) study an eyeblink (CR) either avoided an air puff (instrumental conditioning) or did not avoid an air puff (classical conditioning). In this study the nonavoidance, or classical, group yielded faster conditioning than did the avoidance, or instrumental, group. Thus one study suggests that classical is superior whereas the other suggests that instrumental conditioning is superior. Obviously, there are all kinds of problems with this type of comparison experiment, and they have occupied psychologists for many years. Hellige and Grant (1974a,b) provide a recent treatment of this approach.

Traditional Differences between Instrumental and Classical Conditioning

If you had taken this course a number of years ago you might well have read that instrumental and classical conditioning are clearly distinct and that there are several obvious differences between the two types of conditioning. Things were relatively simple then. But matters have become a bit more complicated. Psychologists have begun to question the validity of these traditional differences.

Distinction 1: Contiguity and Reinforcement

Many psychologists believe that instrumental conditioning involves reinforcement while classical conditioning does not. According to this position all instrumental responses, such as bar pressing, are firmed up or acquired through the application of reinforcements. If the animal is not reinforced the response will not be acquired. On the other hand, classically conditioned responses are presumed to be acquired without the aid of reinforcement. If a response (such as an eyeblink) occurs in the presence of a stimulus (such as a buzzer) then that response will be connected to that stimulus automatically and without reinforcement. According to this position temporal contiguity of the stimulus and response is supposed to be sufficient for classical conditioning to occur. (Two things are *contiguous* if they are adjoining, or near one another.) Temporal contiguity is assumed to be *necessary* for instrumental conditioning but not *sufficient*. For instrumental conditioning to occur both contiguity and reinforcement are required.

We already know where this distinction begins to break down. Classical conditioning may well involve subtle types of reinforcement. For example, in eyelid conditioning a conditioned eye blink may be reinforced in that it partially avoids the noxious air puff. Similarly, in planaria conditioning, the conditioned constriction of the body may be reinforcing in that it lessens the impact of the shock. This is not to say that it has been clearly established that classical conditioning always involves reinforcement. But it is a possibility, and to the extent that we feel it is a valid interpretation we will want to reject the notion that classical conditioning does not involve reinforcement. Classical and instrumental conditioning cannot be distinguished with any certainty on this basis, for reinforcing qualities may be identified in both situations. Kimmel (1965) has considered this argument in detail.

Distinction 2: The Effect of Classical and Instrumental Responses upon the Animal's Future

What happens to an animal in an instrumental conditioning situation is strongly affected by whether it responds or not. If it responds it receives a reinforcement. If it fails to respond it gets nothing. On the other hand, events in the classical conditioning situation are often presumed to be independent of the animal's actions. If the animal fails to respond to the CS it receives the UCS. If it responds to the CS he *still* receives the UCS. The CS and UCS are delivered in the same manner each time, regardless of the animal's actions. Hence many psychologists have concluded that, in classical conditioning, the animal's future is unaffected by its actions while, in instrumental conditioning, the animal's actions strongly affect his future.

This argument is specious. As we have seen, the animal's future is indeed affected by its conditioned response in a classical situation. For example, receiving an air puff against a partially closed eye is probably not the same as receiving one against a fully opened eye.

This so-called distinction is closely tied in with the previous one. To the extent that an animal's conditioned response is followed by a reinforcer (e.g., air puff avoidance), then that conditioned response is clearly affecting the animal's future (Estes, 1969; Wahlsten & Cole, 1972).

Distinction 3: Voluntary versus Involuntary Responding

This is the most commonly cited of all the distinctions between instrumental and classical conditioning. It involves the notion that classical conditioning is a simpler type of learning, and that *involuntary* responses can only be modified by this type of conditioning. On the other hand, instrumental conditioning is presumed to be a more complicated type of learning. It is argued that only *voluntary* responses can be modified by this technique.

The distinction seems to make sense, in some intuitive way, when one surveys the kinds of responses discussed in previous sections. Involuntary responses such as eye blinks, heart rate, and salivation, have been modified by classical procedures. Complicated voluntary responses, such as bar pressing and leaping over barriers, have been modified by the instrumental procedures. The assumption behind this distinction is that the two types of conditioning involve different levels, or aspects, of the total nervous system, with the classical procedures involving involuntary response systems and the instrumental procedures modifying more advanced voluntary responses. As we shall see, there is growing doubt about the validity of this distinction.

Neal Miller's Work

Against all traditional thought, Neal Miller has asked an intriguing question. Can involuntary responses be conditioned instrumentally? Can the strength of an involuntary response be increased if it is followed by a reinforcement? Over a number of years Miller (1973) and his colleagues have conducted a series of experiments that seems to suggest that involuntary responses may actually be conditioned instrumentally.

Miller has concentrated on visceral responses (e.g., heart rate and intestinal contraction), which are mediated by the autonomic nervous system. The basic design of their experiments is as follows: The skeletal muscles of a rat are paralyzed with curare. (As these muscles are voluntarily controlled by the animal, paralysis removes them as a source of possible contamination in the experiment.) Paralysis with curare does not affect the involuntary responses under consideration. Next, the visceral response (e.g., heart rate) is recorded accurately. A rat's heart rate is not constant. Sometimes it increases a little, sometimes it decreases. Each time the experimenter observes one of those little, spontaneous increases he rewards the animal. One problem Miller had to face was how to reward a paralyzed rat. He solved the problem by using escape from mild shock to the tail as one reinforcement. The animal had to increase its heart rate to escape from the shock. Miller found that rats will increase their heart rate from 5 to 20% in order to escape from shock. (Miller has also used brain stimulation as a reinforcer. This technique will be discussed in a later section.)

It is possible that in the situation Miller used (the animal in paralysis and being shocked) that the heart rate would go up due to fear, excitement, tension or general arousal. Miller recognized this possibility, so he rewarded some animals when they showed a decrease in heart rate. These animals decreased their heart rate over a series of sessions. Hence the effect canot be attributed to excitement or arousal.

Figure 3.2 indicates that animals rewarded for increases or decreases in their heart rate will show increases and decreases, respectively. But animals rewarded for intestinal contraction or relaxation will not alter their heart rate (even though they will alter their intestinal activities). This *specificity* of the learning is further evidence for the notion that the experiment is not just increasing the general arousal level of the animal.

In addition to his work with heart rate and intestinal contraction Miller has been able to condition urine formation. He has also reported being able to train a rat to blush in one ear, but not the other. Keep in mind that the instrumental training of so-called involuntary responses argues *against* the position that instrumental and classical conditioning may be distinguished on the basis of a voluntary–involuntary split.

The Problem of Voluntary Mediation

Some investigators have suggested that these kinds of experiments do not clearly demonstrate instrumental conditioning of involuntary responses. They argue that the effect upon the involuntary system is medi-

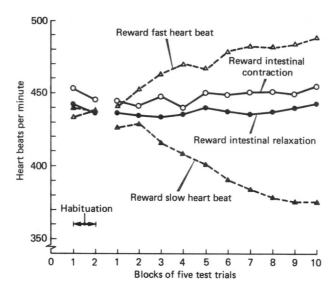

Figure 3.2. Heart rate changes in rats rewarded for increases and decreases in heart rate, and heart rates for rats rewarded for intestinal contraction and relaxation. (After Miller, N. E., & Banuazizi, A. Instrumental learning by curarized rats of a specific visceral response, intestinal or cardiac. *Journal of Comparative and Physiological Psychology,* 1968, **65,** 1–17. Fig. 4, p. 5. Copyright 1968 by the American Psychological Association. Reprinted by permission.)

ated by, or affected by, voluntary responses. For example, if you were offered $5 for every increase you could produce in your pulse rate you would quickly earn a lot of money by running around the block. The *voluntary* running response would cause the increase in the involuntary pulse rate.

Although the voluntary mediation of changes in involuntary systems remains a serious problem in the field, Miller's use of curare has silenced many critics. The curare paralyzes the voluntary skeletal muscles so that they are incapable of mediating anything at all. If you were offered money for pulse rate increases and paralyzed at the same time you would not be able to increase your pulse rate by running. If your pulse rate *did* increase under these conditions then that would be evidence for the position that the reward somehow acted *directly* upon the so-called involuntary pulse rate (unless, of course, you were mediating the increase by thinking about exciting or frightening factors).

The Problem of Replication

Another problem in this area of research has been the progressive decline in results obtained by Miller over the past few years (see Figure 3.3). Miller acknowledges this decline, describes it as a vexing phenome-

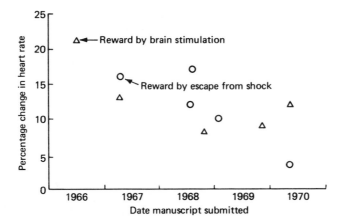

Figure 3.3. Progressive decline in amount of learned change in heart rate obtained in 10 experiments over a 5-year period. (Adapted from Miller, N. E. Interactions between learned and physical factors in mental illness. *Seminars in Psychiatry,* 1972, 4, 239–254. Fig. 8, p. 247. By permission of Grune & Stratton, Inc., New York, N.Y.)

non, and speculates about its causes. He wonders if it might be due to some subtle form of contamination in our environment, or by changes in the rats themselves due to extensive breeding practices and/or antibiotic treatment.

Whatever the outcome, Miller has suggested that so-called involuntary responses may well be affected by the procedures we normally describe as instrumental. This argues against the voluntary–involuntary distinction between instrumental and classical conditioning.

The Burgeoning Field of Biofeedback

Miller's work, and the development of biofeedback training procedures, represent some of the most intriguing events of the past decade (Shapiro, Barber, DiCara, Kamiya, Miller, & Stoyva, 1973). This material is almost like science fiction, and once you read about it you will be able to understand why there has been such an enormous increase in the amount of attention given to these procedures. In biofeedback training, a human is given information about involuntary changes within his own body (e.g., changes in his heart rate or blood pressure). The subject is not normally aware of these changes. They are often thought to be beyond voluntary control. For example, if you try to increase your blood pressure, you will probably decide that it is beyond your control. In the biofeedback procedure, the experimenter rewards the subject for responses of a certain amplitude or duration. Just as was the case with Miller's rats, the human subject alters his so-called involuntary responses.

For example, a subject may hear a click each time his heart beats. The experimenter may then reward increases or decreases in the click rate. The heart rate varies a little, spontaneously. The experimenter watches these fluctuations, and rewards the ones he chooses to reward. The reward may be just about anything (money, praise, avoidance of shock). Over time the subject's heart rate moves in the rewarded direction.

This kind of *experimental* investigation of the control of involuntary systems was predated by many practices observed in Eastern cultures. There have been many reports which suggest that meditation, as practiced by yoga and Zen meditators, can have strong effects on physiological activities presumed to be beyond voluntary control. For example, Wallace and Benson (1972) describe studies in which Zen meditators dramatically decreased their oxygen consumption and carbon dioxide output during meditation. Green (1973) reports a case in which a Swami caused his heart to cease pumping blood for 17 seconds. It is as though Western science and technology is just beginning to explore events which have long been known to Eastern meditators.

Quite a few so-called involuntary responses have been brought under instrumental control in man. They include, among others, heart rate, blood pressure, electrical activity of the brain, skin temperature, salivation, vomiting, and electrodermal activity (Blanchard & Young, 1974; Shapiro & Schwartz, 1972).

Application of Biofeedback Techniques

If the research pays off, biofeedback techniques may be used in many different ways. Consider psychosomatic illnesses wherein physical symptoms appear when there are no identifiable underlying physical causes. For example, imagine an individual in a state of constant gastric distress, with physicians unable to find any physical basis for the disorder. Biofeedback research suggests that the symptoms may be learned. The gastric distress symptoms may be "involuntary" responses that have been instrumentally rewarded: Every time the gastric symptoms appear the patient is allowed to stay home from the office. A child may instrumentally acquire a fever if that fever is consistently rewarded by attention from a set of worried parents. A soldier may develop a true paralysis if the condition avoids having to engage in combat. Without knowing it, these individuals may have undergone biofeedback training. Their so-called involuntary illnesses may have been brought under instrumental control.

Although there is little hard evidence to support it at present, it is hoped that these kinds of responses may be extinguished by removing the reinforcers, just as a rat ceases to press the bar when reinforcement is removed. If the child with the fever is not given reinforcing attention, the fever may well subside.

It is possible that such conditions as high blood pressure and tension headaches may sometimes be alleviated through the use of biofeedback techniques (Shapiro & Schwartz, 1972). The possibilities are almost unlimited. When reading in this new and controversial field one will discover a wide range of concerns from the scientific to the mystical. Whatever the eventual outcome of all this activity, the field does represent a new and challenging arena.

Summary of the Comparison of Instrumental and Classical Conditioning

The three distinctions mentioned in the preceding pages are not the only ones that have been proposed. But they are perhaps the most important ones. The clarity of these distinctions has begun to fade, and as new thinking and research appear it seems that the very least one must conclude is that instrumental and classical conditioning are very closely related. Some of the more recent thinkers (Bindra, 1972) have gone so far as to claim that classical and instrumental conditioning are the outcomes of some common, fundamental underlying process.

Procedural Comparisons

In attempting to make sense of the array of learning tasks it is useful to distinguish three ways in which learning tasks may be compared. If we merely look at the *procedures* involved in the various learning tasks it is clear that they do differ. No one would deny that classical procedures differ from instrumental procedures. In instrumental conditioning, a reward is given only if the animal responds, whereas in classical conditioning, the experimenter presents the CS and UCS whether the animal responds or not. But we have already seen that what the experimenter thinks is important may or may not be important to the animal. Despite the insistence that events are independent of the animal's response in classical conditioning we have seen that they are not. Thus, if we are to discover true differences between the various learning situations we must look beyond these superficial procedural differences.

Comparisons at the Neurological Level

Learning tasks may be compared in terms of their location in the nervous system. If one task involves, or is associated with, action in one part of the nervous system, then it may be distinguished from other types of learning that are to be found in other levels of the nervous system. Yet it has proven difficult to separate learning tasks on this basis. The traditional distinction between involuntary classical conditioning and voluntary instrumental conditioning has broken down. Instrumental conditioning has been heavily implicated in those aspects of the nervous system (e.g., the autonomic nervous system) which were once presumed to be the domain of classical conditioning alone.

Behavioral Comparisons

In view of the fact that procedural distinctions may be superficial, and neurological distinctions are difficult to maintain, we must look for other ways to try to compare various learning tasks. For example, we could see if the various learning tasks react in similar ways to the same manipulations. Say we are faced with two children, and we want to find out how similar they are. We might begin by taking something away from both of them. If they both scream and yell, or if they both look hurt, or if they both react with scorn, then we have some evidence for the idea that, at least in some ways, the children are similar. The more similarities we can find, the more common responses the two children have in similar situations, the more likely we are to believe they are similar in some fundamental ways.

The same kind of comparison technique may be applied to learning tasks, in an effort to answer the following types of questions: How do the various tasks react to the same important variables (e.g., amount of practice and external distractions)? Do they all show similar increases, or decreases, in performance? Or are they totally different in their responses to a given variable? To the extent that they react similarly to a wide range of variables we have some evidence for the conclusion that they are similar, or operate according to the same behavioral laws.

SIMILARITIES AMONG PAIRED-ASSOCIATE LEARNING, CLASSICAL CONDITIONING, AND INSTRUMENTAL CONDITIONING

Acquisition

What happens to performance as practice continues? The simplest answer is that performance increases as practice increases. But further questions may be asked. For example, what is the specific form of the relationship between practice and performance? Does performance increase slowly at first and then more rapidly as practice increases? Or does performance start out rapidly and then level off? Figure 3.4 suggests some of the kinds of relationships, both reasonable and fanciful, that might exist between practice and performance.

Without some advance knowledge it is difficult to decide which of these curves represents the general relationship between performance and practice.

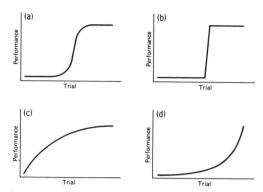

Figure 3.4. Performance curves, real and fanciful.

One might also wonder if the relationship might differ for different types of learning tasks. For example, are PA learning, classical conditioning, and instrumental conditioning represented by the same curve? Figure 3.4c represents the curve that is most often obtained with all three of these tasks. As practice, or the pairing of the CS and the UCS, increases in classical conditioning the probability of the CR increases quite rapidly and then levels off. In PA learning the probability of a correct response increases and then levels off. Similarly, the most common finding in instrumental learning is that the response builds up rapidly and then levels off.

The characteristic form is termed a NEGATIVELY ACCELERATED PERFOR-MANCE CURVE, which means that increases in performance start out rapidly and then level off. The fact that the negatively accelerated per-formance curve is characteristic of all three selected learning tasks is a tiny bit of evidence for the conclusion that the tasks are similar.

Looking back it is easy to accept the fact that all three display nega-tively accelerated curves. Yet it need not have been that way. No one would have been particularly surprised if PA learning had shown a curve like that of Figure 3.4d, whereas instrumental and classical conditioning displayed curves like that of Figure 3.4a. That they yield similar curves in response to the same variable (practice) suggests that they might possibly operate according to the same behavioral laws.

Three points should be kept in mind. First, the negatively accelerated curve is only characteristic of these tasks. That is, it does not *always* appear. It is the most commonly observed curve, but it is not the only one that can be obtained. For example, a PA list can be constructed which is so easy it will be learned on the first trial (e.g., composed of pairs such as hi–ho, one–two, and black–white). On the other hand, PA lists may be developed which are next to impossible to master (e.g., com-posed of such pairs as XZKQZZKXQ–QKQXQXZKX, QZKXKZXQX–QXKKZQZKX, and XZKZQKZXQ–XKKQXZQKQ). Figure 3.5 contains

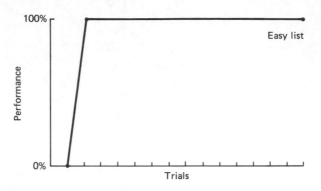

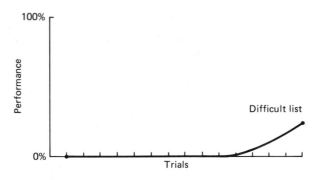

Figure 3.5 Hypothetical curves that might be obtained with very difficult and very simple paired-associate lists.

the curves that might be obtained with these two lists. Second, keep in mind that these are not learning curves. They are performance curves. If you will recall, performance refers to the translation of learning into behavior through the involvement of motivation. All we can observe is performance, or behavior, and this is affected by motivation as well as learning. Third, remember that we are being very selective in comparing only three learning tasks. If it is found that they react in similar ways to a wide range of variables we must be careful about wanting to conclude, on the basis of this limited kind of comparison, that *all* types of learning tasks are similar.

Extinction

Extinction refers to a DECREASE IN RESPONSE STRENGTH WITH REPEATED NONREINFORCEMENTS. For example, if food is no longer given to a rat after he presses a bar, he will gradually cease to press. A similar effect will also appear in classical conditioning and PA learning. One of the most common findings in classical conditioning is that if the UCS is removed from the situation the CR will fade. If a bell (CS) is presented over and over again, without an air puff (UCS), the blink (CR) will lessen, and finally cease altogether. The extinction effect in PA learning is a little more complicated, but it is there. It will be discussed in detail in Chapter Ten. For now, accept the fact that if a subject has first connected BAV to JAX, and is then no longer reinforced for giving BAV as the response, then the probability of JAX eliciting BAV will decrease.

Thus, extinction-like effects appear in all three tasks. Again, in hindsight, this is far from astounding. But things might have turned out differently. Classically conditioned responses might have been permanent. Instrumentally conditioned responses might have been obliterated by the mere passage of time rather than through this active extinction process. There are any number of things that might have been true. But the fact that all three show similar extinction effects adds to the argument that they are all operating according to the same laws.

Extinction is an interesting and controversial effect. What it says, in a sense, is that things are not forgotten passively. If the bar pressing rat is left alone in his home cage, away from the bar, he will retain the bar pressing behavior for long periods of time. The mere passage of time does little to reduce the response. For it to be erased the animal must make the response over and over again, and not be reinforced. This view is difficult to reconcile with our subjective feelings about how we forget things. Our memories seem just to fade away as time passes. But the extinction literature suggests that humans may not forget things passively. Our memories may not just decay with the passage of time. For something to be forgotten it may have to undergo an active extinction process wherein the responses are made, but not reinforced. This proposition is extremely controversial. But there is evidence suggesting that much of our forgetting is not passive. There may be a good deal of correspondence between experimental extinction, as observed in the Skinner box, and normal human forgetting. The relationship between animal extinction and human forgetting will be discussed in a later section, where alternative views of human memory will be presented.

Extinction as Acquisition

Extinction may be thought of as nothing more than an acquisition process. For example, when the rat's bar pressing response is extinguished, one may envision this situation as one in which the animal actually learns not to respond, or acquires the response of not responding. The human may have to learn not to say BAV when he sees JAX. According to this interpretation, the organism's response is not just dropped out due to nonreinforcement. The animal is actually learning something new. It is learning not to make the response.

Spontaneous Recovery

Spontaneous recovery (see Boakes & Halliday, 1975) refers to the fact that an extinguished response will, with rest, recover *some* of its strength. The general procedure for demonstrating spontaneous recovery involves four steps (Fig. 3.6). First, the animal learns a particular response. Second, that response is extinguished through nonreinforcement. Third, the animal is allowed to rest. Fourth, the strength of the response is tested following the rest interval. If the response is stronger at the end of the rest phase than it was at the end of the extinction phase, then spontaneous recovery is said to have occurred. After the response has recovered it may be brought back to full strength through further reinforcement or it may be reextinguished through nonreinforcement.

This phenomenon appears in PA learning, classical, and instrumental conditioning situations. Pavlov (1927) reports experiments of the following sort. Dogs were classically conditioned to salivate. Then the CS was presented alone for a series of extinction trials. These extinction trials reduced the number of drops of saliva secreted in response to the CS from ten to three. The animal was then allowed to rest for approximately half an hour. At the end of the rest interval the CS was presented alone, and six drops of saliva were secreted. The salivary response had spontaneously recovered some of its strength. Characteristically, recovery is not complete. The response does not usually return to the highest level obtained during the acquisition phase.

Lewis (1956) has demonstrated spontaneous recovery of an instru-

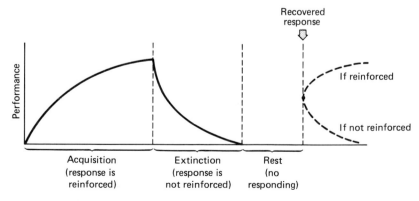

Figure 3.6. Schematic representation of the course of acquisition, extinction, and spontaneous recovery.

mentally conditioned response. He first trained rats to run down a straight alley to food. He extinguished the response and then allowed the rats to rest. At the end of the rest interval Lewis observed that the extinguished running response had spontaneously recovered some of its strength.

Spontaneous recovery in PA learning has been a little more difficult to obtain (Birnbaum, 1965; Houston, 1966; Slamecka, 1966), but it has been done. The general procedure has been to extinguish a learned list and then to observe whether the extinguished, or forgotten, list will recover some of its strength with time (Postman, Stark, & Frazer, 1968; Saltz, 1965; Silverstein, 1967). The details of this procedure will be considered in a later section. For now, it is sufficient to say that the "forgotten" associations do seem to recover some of their strength with rest.

In summary, acquisition, extinction, and spontaneous recovery all seem to be common to our three selected learning tasks. This suggests that, at least on a behavioral level, the three tasks are closely related.

External Inhibition

External inhibition refers to the fact that a new stimulus introduced during acquisition, along with the CS, will slow the acquisition process. For example, if a buzzer is suddenly sounded along with the CS in eye blink conditioning, the conditioning will be slowed. The same kind of effect can be obtained in instrumental conditioning. For example, Winnick and Hunt (1951) trained rats to run down an alley to obtain food at the end. A buzzing sound introduced at the beginning of a trial slowed the rat's performance dramatically. It is difficult to find PA learning studies that parallel this effect exactly, but you might imagine what would happen if someone, out of the clear blue, sounded a buzzer while you were trying to connect FXZG to ZKLG. You would be externally inhibited, to say the least.

External inhibition may be thought of as a distraction effect. Any change in the conditioning situation that distracts the subject from the task will reduce performance accordingly.

Subjects tend to adapt to external inhibitors. The disruptive quality of an external inhibitor is temporary. After a number of trials in which the buzzer is presented along with the CS, performance returns to its original level.

Stimulus Generalization

Stimulus generalization refers to the fact that a response conditioned to one stimulus will tend to be elicited by other similar stimuli. The greater the difference between the conditioned stimulus and the test stimulus the less the tendency for the test stimulus to elicit the response.

For example, we have all learned to stop our cars when we see nice, round, red lights. Suppose we were faced with a red light that was not quite as bright, and not quite as red, as the ones we were used to? We would probably stop anyway. Suppose the light were very dim, or square? Our stopping response might not be so salient. Suppose the light were pink and oblong? Suppose it were purple and 1 foot off the ground? We can see that AS THE SIMILARITY BETWEEN THE NEW, TEST STIMULI AND THE ORIGINAL, ROUND, RED STIMULUS DECREASES, OUR GENERALIZED TENDENCY TO STOP WOULD DECREASE. This relationship can be summed up in a stimulus generalization gradient (see Figure 3.7).

Stimulus generalization has been one of the main concerns in the field of learning, and thousands of studies have been published concerning it. The importance of stimulus generalization in our own lives is undeniable. Suppose for the moment that you are "The Man Who Cannot Generalize." If you connect a response to a given stimulus then *only* that stimulus will elicit that response. Similar stimuli will *not* elicit the response. Your life would probably be dangerous and confusing. We need to generalize to get along in the world. Otherwise we would be doing things like running red lights in strange towns, and having trouble identifying strangers as people.

Stimulus generalization has often been demonstrated in classical conditioning (Moore, 1972). In general, a two-step experimental procedure is used. First, a CR is connected to a particular CS (e.g., a given tone). Second, after learning is completed, similar stimuli (e.g., varying tones) are presented. It is usually found that the probability of the response

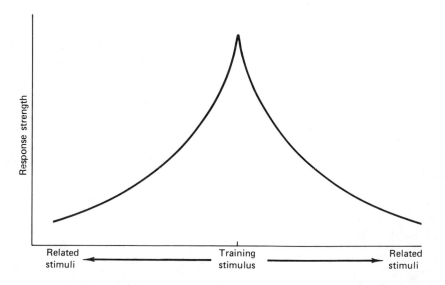

Figure 3.7. Idealized stimulus generalization gradient.

to the varying test stimuli increases as the similarity between the test stimuli and the original stimulus is increased.

Guttman and Kalish (1956) have demonstrated stimulus generalization in instrumental conditioning. Their general procedure has been one in which pigeons are trained to peck a colored disk. The pecking response is rewarded with food. After the response is well established the pigeons are tested with other colors. As the similarity between the training and the test stimuli increases the response to the test stimuli increases.

Morosko and Baer (1970) describe an interesting case of stimulus generalization. Alcoholic subjects were shocked upon the ingestion of small cups of alcoholic beverages. They learned to avoid the shock by refraining from drinking the alcoholic beverages. Follow-up work indicated that the avoidance behavior generalized across alcoholic beverages. If a subject was shocked for drinking vodka then he showed a decreased interest in drinking other varieties as well. But, as we would expect from our knowledge of stimulus generalization gradients, the effect was only partial. That is, the trained variety was the most aversive. If the subject was shocked for drinking vodka then he would continue to drink such beverages as beer, but in reduced amounts.

These studies indicate that stimulus generalization appears in both classical and instrumental conditioning, but says nothing about PA learning. Within the field of verbal learning, which will be considered in detail later, there is something that seems to be closely related to the stimulus generalization effect. In these experiments subjects first learn a given PA list. They then learn a second PA list. The responses in the two lists are identical. The stimuli in the second list vary in terms of their similarity to the first-list stimuli. Some second-list stimuli are identical to some of the first-list stimuli. Some of the second-list stimuli are moderately similar to some of the first-list stimuli, and so on. For example, if a given first-list item was JAX–BAV then the second-list item might also be JAX–BAV (identical stimuli). Or the second-list item might be JEX–BAV (similar stimuli), or QKX–BAV (highly dissimilar stimuli). The results of these studies support the conclusions obtained in studies of stimulus generalization. THE DIFFICULTY OF LEARNING THE SECOND LIST DECREASES AS THE SIMILARITY BETWEEN THE FIRST AND SECOND LIST STIMULI INCREASES (Dallett, 1962; Hamilton, 1943; Yum, 1931).

There is another interesting kind of experiment, which suggests that stimulus generalization operates in connection with verbal materials. In SEMANTIC GENERALIZATION studies, a response is connected to a verbal item (e.g., a word). Varying test words are then presented to the subject. It is usually noted that the response is elicited by similar test stimuli. In one experiment, Lang, Geer, and Hnatiow (1963) presented 12 very hostile words (e.g., annihilation) along with some neutral ones (e.g., abstract). Each time a hostile word was presented the subject was shocked. The shock yielded a change in the GALVANIC SKIN RESPONSE (GSR). (The GSR is an index of the electrical conductivity of the surface of the skin. In other words, if we are shocked we perspire a little. The perspiration conducts electricity.) Following the training period subjects were presented with *new* test words that were highly hostile, hostile, of low hostility, or neutral. The authors found the higher the hostility of the test words, the greater the change in the GSR. The GSR had generalized from the hostile training words to the similar hostile test words.

We will return to stimulus generalization in Chapter Eight. For now, realize that it is a phenomenon that occurs in all three of our selected learning tasks. It is one more bit of evidence for the conclusion that the tasks are behaviorally related.

Discrimination

One of the discrimination learning situations described earlier involved a hungry pigeon and two disks of different colors. One disk was called the positive stimulus and the other the negative stimulus. If the pigeon responded to the positive stimulus by pecking it, it received a reward. If it pecked the negative stimulus it received no reward. The bird gradually discriminated between the colors, and gradually restricted its response to the postive stimulus. These events constitute an instance of discrimination learning in an instrumental conditioning situation. The same kind of discrimination formation occurs in classical conditioning. If one stimulus (i.e., buzzer) is consistently paired with a UCS while another stimulus (i.e., a light) is presented but not accompanied by the UCS, then a CR gradually develops in connection with the buzzer but not the light. The animal discriminates between the two potential CSs, and only responds to the one that is paired with the UCS.

Of course, PA learning also involves discrimination formation. In fact, many discriminations are required before a PA list can be mastered. Suppose the stimuli in a PA list were very similar to one another (e.g., QZKL, KLZQ, QZLK, KLQZ, KZQL, and QLZK). Before the subject can connect the proper responses to these stimuli he must distinguish one from another. They all look pretty much alike at first, but continued exposure allows the subject to discriminate them. Thus, just as in classical and instrumental conditioning, discrimination formation is an integral part of the PA learning process.

Summation

Assume a given response is separately connected to two different stimuli. If the two different stimuli are then presented together, the strength of the response is often greater than it is to either of the stimuli alone. This effect is called SUMMATION and it may be demonstrated in PA learning, classical conditioning, and instrumental conditioning. Pavlov ran experiments in which a salivary response was first connected to a given CS. The salivary response was then conditioned to a second, different CS. When the two CSs were presented together the amount of saliva produced was greater than that produced by either CS alone. The same kind of effect may be obtained in instrumental conditioning situations. For example, one might run an experiment in which a rat is trained in a T-maze. The rat might first be required to run right for food if a buzzer is sounded, and left if no buzzer is sounded. He might then be trained to turn right if a light is turned on, and left if the light is not turned on. In the final step, both the light and the buzzer would be presented. If the tendency to turn right in response to both the stimuli was greater than it was to either stimulus alone then we would conclude that summation had been demonstrated. Hill and Wickens (1962) ran an experiment which demonstrated summation in PA learning. In part of their study, subjects first learned PA lists in which the stimuli were nonsense syllables and the responses were words. They then learned a second list in which the responses were the *same words* but the stimuli had been changed to colors. In the final phase both the colors and the nonsense syllables were presented together. The authors noted that a definite advantage had been gained by having been trained with each of the different stimuli alone.

CONCLUSION

Even with all this discussion of similarities and differences it has not been conclusively demonstrated that these and other types of learning tasks represent fundamentally distinct learning processes. It is probably premature to conclude either that they do or that they do not represent truly different kinds of learning.

Eventually it may be possible to develop a unitary model that will account for all these task variations. Obviously, the problem is that there are so many different learning situations that it is extremely difficult to imagine a single model that would encompass them all. In addition, the similarities we have discussed may be more apparent than real—they may be the result of a lack of precision in our language rather than any identity of basic process. But it has not been the intent of this chapter to prove that the many learning tasks definitely represent different forms or expressions of some unitary, underlying process. Rather, we have attempted to suggest that such a unitary process is a possibility, and that this possibility should be given serious consideration before we expend considerable amounts of energy building new and distinct models for every new task we invent (see Tarpy, 1975).

SUMMARY

1. It is important to consider whether or not our various learning tasks reflect truly different learning processes. If they do, then theories and models governing each learning capacity must be developed. If it is determined that some common, underlying process accounts for all the various learning tasks then a single model should suffice.

2. An attempt was made to point out some of the difficulties in trying to decide if the various learning tasks represent different kinds of learning.

3. Paired-associate learning may be thought of as either classical or instrumental conditioning. Despite this correspondence, the investigation of paired-associate learning has been kept separate from the analysis of conditioning phenomena.

4. A comparison of classical conditioning and instrumental conditioning is hampered by the fact that classical conditioning always seems to possess characteristics, or elements, of the instrumental paradigm. Similarly, instrumental conditioning situations never seem to be free of classical conditioning elements.

5. Attempts to distinguish between classical and instrumental conditioning by instrumentally and classically conditioning the *same* responses have been relatively unfruitful.

6. The notion that instrumental conditioning involves reinforcement whereas classical does not is challenged by the fact that potentially reinforcing events may be identified in all classical paradigms.

7. The notion that the animal's future is affected by his response in instrumental conditioning but not in classical conditioning also seems to be untrue. Classically conditioned responses do appear to affect the animal's future.

8. The notion that involuntary responses can only be classically conditioned is challenged by biofeedback research, which suggests that so-called involuntary visceral responses may be instrumentally conditioned. But the field of biofeedback is not without its own problems. Replication is a problem. In addition, some involuntary responses may be mediated by voluntary responses. Biofeedback research, which was predated by Eastern practices, may prove to be fruitful in an applied sense.

9. Comparisons of learning tasks at a procedural level yield distinct, but superficial, differences.

10. Distinctions among the various learning tasks at a neurological level have proven difficult to maintain.

11. Behavioral comparisons of the various learning tasks reveal a wide range of similarities. The various tasks respond in similar ways to many sorts of manipulations. Similar performance and extinction curves appear in many different tasks. Spontaneous recovery, external

inhibition, stimulus generalization, discrimination, and summation also appear in the various tasks.

12. At present, it would seem to be premature to draw definite conclusions concerning the existence of multiple learning processes. Although there do seem to be a good number of similarities among a number of learning tasks, the significance of these similarities remains to be seen.

Biological Constraints on Learning 4

THE "INTERCHANGEABLE-PARTS" CONCEPTION OF LEARNING

American psychologists have spent the better part of this century developing what may be termed the "interchangeable-parts" conception of learning. According to this model there are certain laws and generalizations that govern the development of associations between all stimuli and all responses. The nature of the stimuli, the nature of the responses, and the nature of the animal doing the learning are not considered to be particularly important.

Stimulus Interchangeability

According to the "interchangeable parts" conception the specific nature of the stimulus is relatively unimportant in determining the course of learning. So long as the animal can perceive the cue he can utilize it. For example, if we are training a dog to respond to a signal it does not make much difference whether the cue is a light, a bell, or a mild shock. The notion is that, so long as we reinforce the animal when he responds to the stimulus, learning will occur in pretty much the same fashion, regardless of the nature of the stimulus. So long as they are clearly perceived and are relatively equal in terms of salience, stimuli are interchangeable. Curiously, this American belief in the equivalence of stimuli can be traced back to the Russian physiologist Pavlov (1928) who stated that *any stimulus* chosen at will, such as a visual stimulus, a sound, an odor, or a touch, can become a conditioned stimulus.

Response Interchangeability

The same kind of thinking has been applied to the responses. For example, suppose a dog is confined in a box, and wants to escape. In one condition he must bark to gain release. In another condition he must roll over to escape. According to the kind of thinking we have been discussing it should not make much difference which of these two responses is required. Learning should progress at about the same rate in either case. The responses should be interchangeable.

A Challenge to the Interchangeability Concept

Unfortunately, this simple, elegant model does not really fit the facts of nature. There has been, and is, a growing body of literature which suggests that such a conception vastly oversimplifies the nature of reality. For example, Garcia and Koelling (1966) showed that, if a specific flavor, a certain sound, and a particular light are all paired with an aversive stimulus, rats will associate the flavor but not the sound or the light with the aversive stimulus. In other words, the three stimuli are differentially effective as stimuli. They are not interchangeable.

As Lockard (1971) puts it:

Pick any animal species at random, study its behavior in its normal habitat throughout its life cycle, and you will discover an intricate set of behaviors, many of them of almost incredible matching relationships to demands of the environment, like a lock and a key. . . . You may also find that natural selection has produced special learning abilities such that some ecologically relevant task is learned at a much faster rate than an arbitrary task, or natural stimuli are much more effective than artificial stimuli [p. 172].

We are faced with the notion that each animal brings to every learning task certain capabilities and predispositions to act in certain ways. These distinct capabilities may well be the result of natural selection, as well as the result of the individual animal's past life experiences. The animal comes prepared to act through the use of a limited set of specific responses.

THE CONTINUUM OF PREPAREDNESS

Seligman (1970) has defined a continuum of preparedness, which may help us grasp the significance of these facts. According to Seligman animals may be differentially prepared to associate certain responses with certain stimuli. Preparedness may exist in any degree, from completely prepared to completely unprepared. The relative preparedness of an animal to connect a given response to a given stimulus is operationally defined by Seligman in terms of the NUMBER OF PAIRINGS OF THE STIMULUS AND RESPONSE REQUIRED FOR LEARNING TO OCCUR.

This is one of several somewhat circular definitions we will find. Preparedness is defined in terms of the number of pairings required for learning to occur. Ease of learning, on the other hand, is indexed by degree of preparedness. One would have to develop an independent measure of preparedness to break this circularity. But the concept of preparedness does have some heuristic value. Animals may be extremely prepared to associate certain events, somewhat ready to associate others, and totally unprepared to associate still others. Seligman's hypothesis challenges the traditional American position.

A note of caution should be sounded at this point. Our emphasis in this chapter will be upon the notion that preparedness reflects innate, genetically determined predispositions to associate certain elements more easily than others. Although natural selection may often account for the fact that animals may be differentially prepared to associate certain responses with certain stimuli, we should not lose sight of the fact that some instances of preparedness may well be due to *prior experience* rather than to innate, genetic factors.

For example, Thorndike's (1964) work suggests that cats are more prepared to learn to escape using pulling or pressing responses than they are to learn to escape using licking or scratching responses. Although it is entirely possible that these differences are innate, it is also conceivable that they are acquired. The cat may well have had a good deal of experience attempting to "escape." He may have already learned, before his experience in Throndike's apparatus, that pulling and pushing responses are better than scratching and licking responses in effecting an escape.

Hence, as we explore the idea that differences in preparedness are innately or genetically determined we should keep in mind that not all instances of preparedness will be attributable to such factors. It must be recognized that prior experience is a powerful factor in determining what will and what will not be learned in a given situation.

Evidence for a Preparedness Continuum

Preparedness in Instrumental Conditioning

Although few would argue with the fact that many diverse kinds of responses and stimuli may be associated in roughly comparable ways, there is a wide array of data which suggests that the notion of equivalent associability must be tempered by a consideration of genetic and evolutionally determined factors and predispositions which animals, including man, bring to the learning situation.

Let us begin with some examples of UNPREPARED INSTRUMENTAL CONDITIONING. Konorski (1967) attempted to reinforce yawning in dogs with food. Konorski reports that, whereas other responses are easily trained, it is extremely difficult, if not impossible, to train a dog to yawn for food. The animal is unprepared to associate these events. Using monkeys, Bolles and Seelback (1964) reinforced various responses with noise offset and punished others with noise onset. Some responses, such as exploratory behavior, could be strongly affected by both noise onset and offset, but grooming behavior was relatively unaffected by either event.

In exploring PREPARED INSTRUMENTAL CONDITIONING, Brown and Jenkins (1968) ran an interesting experiment that represents an instance of extreme preparedness. Pigeons were exposed to a lighted key. Grain was presented each time the key was lit regardless of what the bird did. The pigeon was not required to do anything. It was free to stand there and eat the grain as it was delivered. But the pigeon began to peck the lit key despite the fact that no response was required for the delivery of food. The key-pecking behavior was maintained, even though it had no effect on food delivery. This unique effect has been called "autoshaping," and we shall discuss it in some detail in Chapter Seven. For now, think of it as an example of extreme preparedness in an instrumental situation.

Preparedness in Discrimination Learning

Discrimination learning involves the presentation of two stimuli, a positive one and a negative one. If the animal responds to the positive stimulus it is reinforced. If it responds to the negative stimulus it is not reinforced. Several investigators (Dobrzecka & Konorski, 1967, 1968; Lawicka, 1964; Szwejkowska, 1967) have found that dogs are quite ready to discriminate certain types of stimuli in certain situations, but not others. For example, they attempted to teach dogs to go and receive food, or to stay, based on verbal commands. One voice tone from the experimenter was the positive stimulus whereas a different voice tone from the same experimenter was the negative stimulus. The animals mastered this discrimination easily, going in response to one tone and staying in response to the other. But when the positive and negative stimuli were changed, quite different results were obtained. If a given voice tone came from *above* the dog it represented the positive stimulus. If the same voice tone, from the same experimenter, came from *below* the dog it represented the negative stimulus. In this case the dogs had a great deal of trouble learning the discrimination. They did not seem prepared at all to use the *location* of the voice as a cue in deciding whether to go or stay.

At this point you may be thinking that the dogs' failure to learn may have been due to their inability to perceive differences in the location of the voice source. A tone from above and a tone from below may have sounded the same to the dogs. As it turns out, this is not the case. This same group of experimenters have shown that dogs can use location differences in learning other kinds of discriminations (e.g., voice from above means go left, voice from below means go right). It seems the dogs were just not prepared to use location as a cue in the go–no-go situation. Interestingly, it was also found that when two voice tones located in the same position were used as the cues in the go-left–go-right discrimination the dogs had a good deal of trouble mastering the task.

Human Preparedness

Are we prepared to associate certain events and unprepared to associate others? It is an interesting question but, unfortunately, we do not have much information yet. Much of what we do have is anecdotal and speculative. Lenneberg (1967) has argued that we are very much prepared to learn an important class of materials—language. We seem to learn language without a great deal of elaborate training. Human children acquire language with ease, and they seem to do it in all cultures in roughly the same manner. Adult humans do not have to set up elaborate training procedures to ensure that their children will acquire language. It is accomplished efficiently. The child seems prepared to acquire language. On the other hand, every parent knows only too well how difficult it is to teach children to be polite, to share, and to brush their teeth.

Most of the experimental work concerning biological constraints on learning has been done with animals, but humans may well prove to be subject to similar constraints. For example, all humans learn to suckle and to walk at an early age without elaborate training procedures. Humans seem ready to learn these behaviors. On the other hand, consider biofeedback training. If you will recall, an example of this might involve a human learning to increase or decrease some internal "involuntary" process such as heart rate. This learning process is gradual, difficult, and sometimes almost impossible. It requires complicated and exacting experimental training procedures. The human seems relatively unprepared to learn to control his internal "involuntary" responses.

You might spend a moment thinking about your own behavior and its relationship to the concept of preparedness. Does the concept make any intuitive sense to you? Are there classes of events which seem more or less associable to you? Do you feel the concept of preparedness is, when compared to "lower" animals, more or less applicable to the human situation?

Bait-Shyness

Exterminators, or those who poison animals for commercial purposes, are familiar with the fact that if a given animal eats poisoned bait, and survives, he develops an aversion for the flavor of that particular bait. In some sense the flavor becomes a danger signal. It is similar to what a human will experience when he becomes leery of a particular delicacy that has made him ill.

Psychologists have brought this phenomenon into the laboratory and have discovered some interesting things about it. They have shown that rats will quickly learn to avoid distinctively flavored solutions when the ingestion of these solutions is followed by gastrointestinal distress or some other type of malaise (Garcia, Ervin, & Koelling, 1966; Garcia, Ervin, Yorke, & Koelling, 1967; Mitchell, Kirschbaum, & Perry, 1975; Nachman, 1970; Rozin, 1967, 1968, 1969). In a typical experiment, rats are given saccharin flavored water and simultaneously exposed to X rays. X irradiation makes rats sick after an hour or so. It has been found that, after drinking and becoming ill, the rats subsequently show a distinct aversion for the saccharin flavor. They somehow associate the flavor with the illness. The aversion can persist through many weeks of preference testing.

A great deal of work has been done with these kinds of taste aversions. Garcia, Hankins, and Rusiniak (1974) point out that similar effects have been obtained with rats, mice, cats, monkeys, ferrets, coyotes, birds, fish, and reptiles. Flavors have included sweet, sour, bitter, salty, coffee, fruit juice, and milk. Malaise has been caused by ingested toxins, injected drugs, X rays, gamma rays, neutron bombardment, transfusion of blood from irradiated donor animals, and motion sickness. Garcia, Hankins, and Rusiniak (1974) also report some unpublished data indicating that humans find foods distasteful if they are coincidentally followed by sickness. Thus we can see that the bait-shyness effect is not limited. Many different flavors, animals, and noxious elements have been utilized.

Garcia, Hankins. and Rusiniak (1974) summarize some of the general principles that have evolved from all this research. They report that, all other things being equal, the stronger the flavor the greater the aversion. In addition, the more severe the illness the stronger the aversion. Finally, the strength of the aversion decreases as the time between ingestion and illness is increased. This is all as we might expect. Strongly flavored foods followed by immediate, severe illness will yield the greatest aversion.

The Relationship between Bait-Shyness and Avoidance Conditioning

We can see that the bait-shyness phenomenon possesses many, but perhaps not all of the qualities of the avoidance conditioning paradigm. If you will recall, Mowrer conceived of avoidance conditioning as a two-step process. "Fear," or some other emotional response, is first classically conditioned and then instrumentally avoided. In the bait-shyness situation we can think of the flavor as a CS. The UCS is the noxious agent. The

UCR is the illness caused by the UCS. We pair the flavor (CS) with the UCS (noxious agent). Through this pairing the CS (flavor) comes to elicit a CR which in some sense approximates the UCR (illness). The presentation of the flavor (CS) elicits a "conditioned illness." The animal then avoids, or escapes from, the CS and its associated unpleasantness. In a sense, the bait-shyness effect is similar to that of the rat jumping a barrier to escape from a distinctive compartment which has been associated with shock.

But there is at least one important difference between bait-shyness and the typical avoidance conditioning situation. In the bait-shyness learning situation, there is often a long delay (sometimes hours) between presentation of the CS (flavor) and occurrence of the illness. Most of the conditioning situations described to this point involve CS–UCS intervals of no more than a few seconds. And CS–UCS intervals of more than a few seconds usually result in very poor conditioning. No one knows for sure why conditioning can be obtained in the bait-shyness situation with these long delays. Some feel bait-shyness represents a different kind of learning altogether. Others feel that some *trace* of the CS (flavor) is brought forward in time such that it does occur, or exist, at the time the illness occurs. This latter position holds that bait-shyness involves ordinary trace classical conditioning and does not represent a new or different variety. A detailed consideration of this interesting issue will be presented in the next chapter, when the general issue of stimulus–response contiguity will be discussed.

Preparedness and Bait-Shyness

Garcia and Koelling (1966) ran an experiment in which several things happened to rats, all at once. While they drank saccharin flavored water they were X irradiated. In addition, lights flashed and a noise sounded at the same time. The question was which of the CS elements (flavor, sound, or light) would become aversive. Interestingly, only the flavor became aversive. The animals showed no aversion at all to the flashing light or sound. The argument is that the rats were *unprepared* to associate lights and noise with illness, but they were prepared to associate flavor with illness. The investigators ran another experiment in which flavor, noise and flashing lights were paired with foot shock rather than X irradiation. In this case the light and noise became aversive but the flavor did not.

All this seems to fit into some kind of logical schema, probably because all of it is adaptive. Natural selection would favor animals that were prepared to associate illness with taste, and not with other external environmental events. Natural selection would favor animals predisposed to associate foot pain with external events, rather than with what they have eaten. Turn it around and it becomes ridiculous and maladaptive from an evolutionary point of view. Animals predisposed to avoid the flavors they experienced when their feet hurt probably would not last very long.

This kind of experimentation has led to the generalization that some animals, such as the rat, are phylogenetically prepared to associate internal events (e.g., illness) with internal cues (e.g., taste sensations) but not with external cues (e.g., noises). The interested reader is referred to Best, Best, and Mickley (1973) for a good treatment of these issues.

Bait-Shyness and the Control of Predation

Aside from its theoretical implications, bait-shyness has some relevance in a practical sense. As is widely known, there is an ongoing conflict between conservationists and stockmen concerning the coyote and its undeniable tendency to eat little lambs. Naturalists argue that the coyote should be preserved, and that it occupies an important niche in the ecology of our lands. Stockmen, on the other hand, think of the coyote as a pest and a killer, which should be eliminated. The stockmen's view is that the coyote must go so the sheep may remain. As a result coyotes are hunted and poisoned in enormous numbers.

The bait-shyness phenomenon may offer a solution that will allow both the prey and the predator to survive. Gustavson, Garcia, Hankins, and Rusiniak (1974) tested the effectiveness of predation control through the use of bait-shyness under quite natural conditions. They fed coyotes lamb flesh dosed with lithium chloride. Lithium chloride causes the coyote to be extremely ill. After several of these meals, and subsequent illnesses, the coyotes were offered the opportunity to attack live lambs and live rabbits. The coyotes refused to attack the lambs. They, in fact, ran from them. Their misguided predatory habit had been effectively curbed. But they were more than willing to attack rabbits after having eaten treated lamb flesh. The aversion was specific to lamb flesh. Further experimentation indicated that the consumption of treated rabbit's flesh would inhibit attacks on rabbits but not on lambs.

Garcia, Hankins, and Rusiniak (1974) have noted that this kind of research could easily lead to reasonable predation control programs. Bait which smells and tastes like lamb, and has been treated with lithium chloride, could be scattered about the countryside. Coyotes would consume the bait, experience the illness, and refrain from attacking lambs. They would restrict their attacks to rabbits and other natural prey, thereby protecting both ranchers' stock and the balance of the ecosystem. This kind of predation control program seems especially hopeful when one considers that it may well be applicable to many different types of prey and predators.

Bait-Shyness and Aversion Therapy in the Human

There is a kind of treatment used with humans that resembles the bait-shyness effect. In aversion therapy, humans are stimulated with some strong noxious event while they are engaging in the behavior to be controlled (e.g., smoking, drinking, eating). The most popular kinds of noxious events are electric shock and drugs that induce illness (Sherman, 1973). By being paired with a noxious event the "bad habit," or the object of the habit, becomes aversive in much the same manner that the flavor of a particular food becomes aversive in the bait-shyness effect. Wolpe and Lazarus (1966) describe typical procedures using electric shock. Electrodes are attached to the subject's arm. The level of shock employed as a noxious stimulus is often just beyond the point where the subject describes it as being distinctly unpleasant. The level used varies from individual to individual, as some people are more sensitive to shock than others. The shock is presented either while the subject is actually engaged in the unwanted behavior (e.g., smoking) or when he is *imagining* that he is engaged in it.

The technique wherein the subject imagines rather than engages in the behavior seems to be particularly useful when the target behavior cannot easily, or practically, be brought in to the treatment situation. For example, Lazarus (1960) reports a case in which a 10-year-old boy had developed the habit of waking in the middle of the night and going to his mother's bed. Needless to say, this behavior, which occurred regularly each night, began to put some strain on the family relationships. No amount of parental bribery, punishment, or reward seemed to help. Aversion therapy finally terminated the behavior. Electrodes were attached to the boy's arm and he was asked to imagine he was in his mother's bed. When he felt he had a good strong image of the requested situation he was to say, "mother's bed." At that moment the experimenter turned on the current. When the patient could no longer tolerate the shock (typically after a few seconds) he was to say, "my bed." At that point the shock was terminated. The treatment appears to have been very successful. The child regularly slept in his own bed thereafter. The point is that the child did not actually have to be shocked in his mother's bed. An image of the situation was sufficient.

Kolvin (1967) reports another example in which a 14-year-old boy had been charged with indecent assaults upon three women. Success was obtained in this case by administering a noxious stimulus when the patient experienced a vivid, exciting, erotic image associated with assault.

Although aversive conditioning with humans appears to be a rough counterpart of the bait-shyness phenomenon there is obviously no guarantee that the two are identical effects. For instance, we have seen that in bait-shyness certain events are more easily associated than others.

Whether these kinds of differences hold true in aversive conditioning remains to be seen. Sherman (1973) argues that there may well be preparedness differences in human aversive conditioning. He suggests that drug-induced nausea may be appropriate when the unwanted behavior involves oral consumatory activities (e.g., eating, drinking), whereas shock may be better suited for other types of problems.

Finally, it should be pointed out that aversive therapy may not cure anything in a direct fashion. It may have little or no direct effect on the *causes* of such symptomatic behaviors as overeating, or drinking. If a man is drinking himself to death because he cannot tolerate his wife, his job, his children, his relatives, and himself, then shocking him while he is drinking would seem to involve the elimination of a symptom of a more basic problem. At the same time, the elimination of the drinking behavior might free the individual to cope with the underlying problems in a more successful manner.

Preparedness and Species-Specific Defense Reactions

We have been speaking as though a continuum of preparedness exists, but we have said little about why it exists, or what accounts for the fact that certain events are more easily associated than others. We have noted, in a very general fashion, that the pressures of natural selection probably contribute to its existence. But Bolles (1970) has gone a bit further in attempting to explain at least some differences in preparedness. He has presented a very persuasive argument concerning the nature of avoidance conditioning. The problem he addressed is that some avoidance responses are easily learned by certain species, whereas others are not. For instance, rats will learn to jump or run to avoid shock (Baum, 1969; Miller, 1951). But they have a difficult time learning to press levers to avoid shock (D'Amato & Fazzaro, 1966; Fantino, Sharp, & Cole, 1966). The same is true of pigeons; They will learn to fly away to avoid something unpleasant (Bedford & Anger, 1968), but it is difficult to train them to peck a key to avoid negative stimuli (Azrin, 1959; Rachlin & Hineline, 1967). Why these differences? Bolles (1970) argues that animals have SPECIES-SPECIFIC DEFENSE REACTIONS (SSDRs) such as running, flying, freezing, or fighting. These are innate, automatic behaviors that occur in response to any novel or sudden stimulus event. He argues that it is these innate defense reactions which are the ones that are easily established in avoidance conditioning experiments. Arbitrary responses, such as the bar press, which have been selected for the psychologist's convenience, are not easily acquired. Bolles states that if a particular response is easily acquired then it *must necessarily* be an SSDR.

He illustrates his case with a little fable. A furry little animal ran about the forest eating and copulating as much as possible. One day it was attacked by a large predator. Luckily, it escaped. It was hurt and frightened, but nothing more. Some time later, while running through the forest again, it perceived a conditioned stimulus. That is, it heard, or saw, or smelled something that had preceded the first attack. It was frightened by this sign, or cue, and ran for safety. From that day on the little animal successfully avoided attacks by the bad predator. The fable fits the ordinary conception of avoidance learning. Based upon Mowrer's two-factor theory, one would argue that fear had been classically conditioned to the cues preceding the first attack. Later these cues produced fear, which was instrumentally avoided. Fear reduction reinforced the escape response.

Bolles argues that this reasoning is "utter nonsense." First, predators do not present cues just before they attack. Owls do not hoot $2\frac{1}{2}$ seconds before they hit their prey. Coyotes do not consistently give recognizable signs before they pounce. The whole idea, we must assume, is for the predator to minimize such telltale signs. They might occasionally slip up, but Bolles points out that *predators do not allow their prey enough trials for ordinary avoidance conditioning to occur*. Mice do not generally escape from owls dozens of times. Bolles suggests that the little animal stays alive, not because of laboratory type avoidance conditioning, but because of his innate SSDRs. Whenever the animal is faced with novel or sudden stimuli it *innately* and automatically flies, or freezes, or runs. It has not learned these responses through narrow escapes. They are automatic responses to novel or sudden stimulus situations. As Bolles points out, gazelles do not run from lions because they have been bitten by lions. They automatically run from any large object that approaches them (see also Blanchard, Mast, & Blanchard, 1975). Prey will react with an SSDR to the sudden presentation of a harmless stimulus, as well as to the sudden appearance of a truly dangerous predator.

One can see how Bolles's hypothesis might account for our laboratory data. Rats may well come in to our experiments neurally wired, or prepared, to run in response to danger or any other sudden stimulus change. Bar pressing, on the other hand, is not one of their SSDRs and is therefore difficult to establish.

Obviously Bolles's hypothesis does not answer all our questions. It is an interpretation of the limited avoidance-conditioning situation and does not account for other types of preparedness. But it is provocative and does suggest that we must consider the innate survival mechanisms that the animal brings to our mechanized, arbitrary, laboratory learning situations.

Instinctive Drift

Instinctive drift is an interesting concept developed by Breland and Breland (1961, 1966). It is relevant to our consideration of preparedness, and an example or two should clarify its meaning. The Brelands attempted to train a raccoon to pick up coins and place them in a 5-inch metal box. Raccoons have the reputation of being tractable, eager, and quite intelligent. Hence the Brelands expected little difficulty in establishing this particular response sequence. At first things went along pretty well. Each time the raccoon dropped the coin in the box it was reinforced with food. But after a while, the raccoon, instead of promptly dropping the coins in the box, would spend seconds, and sometimes minutes, rubbing the coins together and dipping them in the box. All it had to do was let go to be reinforced. But it seemed to have difficulty letting go at all. As time went on, the rubbing and holding and dipping behavior became stronger and stronger even though it resulted in fewer and fewer reinforcements. It was as though the raccoon's innate "washing behavior" crept into the conditioning situation. Parenthetically, the Brelands suggest that the so-called washing behavior may help raccoons break away the exoskeleton of their natural prey, the crayfish. In another situation Breland and Breland attempted to train pigs to pick up large wooden coins and place them in a bank. At first the pigs eagerly performed the correct responses, picking up, carrying, and depositing the coins without hesitation. But, over a period of weeks, the reinforced behavior deteriorated. The pigs began to drop the coins, root them, pick them up, drop them again, and root them again. In some instances the pigs finally required 10 minutes to carry four coins a distance of six feet. The pigs natural food-gathering responses appeared to intrude into the learning situation. These "disruptive" behaviors seemed to violate what is typically thought to be true of learning situations. That is, they used more energy than the simple, required responses. In addition, they resulted in fewer reinforcements.

In attempting to account for this type of "misbehavior" Breland and Breland (1961) state,

> It seems obvious that these animals are trapped by strongly instinctive behaviors, and clearly we have here a demonstration of the prepotency of such behavior patterns over those which have been conditioned.
> We have termed this phenomenon "instinctive drift." The general principle seems to be that whenever an animal has strong instinctive behaviors in the area of the conditioned response, after continued running the organism will drift toward the instinctive behavior to the detriment of the conditioned behavior and even to the delay or preclusion of the reinforcement. In a very boiled-down, simplified form, it might be stated as "learned behavior drifts toward instinctive behavior." [p. 69].

The Brelands conclude that all this is not to disparage the use of learning principles. It merely suggests that the assumptions underlying what we have termed the "interchangeable-parts" conception of learning must be tempered by a consideration of the animal's instinctive apparatus. The Brelands state that the animal does not come to the laboratory as a tabula rasa, that species differences are important, and that all responses are not equally conditionable to all stimuli.

IMPRINTING

In its simplest form imprinting includes the fact that a newly hatched bird will approach, or form a social attachment to, the first moving object it encounters, whether it be the real parent or some parent surrogate. The longer the bird is exposed to the target object the stronger the filial tendency becomes (Bateson, 1966; Sluckin, 1965). Lorenz (1937) noticed that if the first object a gosling encounters is a human then the gosling will approach that human. In the future the gosling will approach that human in preference to its real mother. After the egg cracks and the bird struggles out, it straightens up, dries out, takes a little time to get organized, and looks about. It approaches the first moving object it encounters and becomes imprinted on it.

Many different kinds of stimuli will serve as a "mother." Objects that have been successfully used as parental surrogates include balloons and electric trains (Fabricius, 1951, 1955; Fabricius & Boyd, 1954), footballs (Ramsay, 1951), moving lines (Smith & Hoyes, 1961), animals of a different species (Baer & Gray, 1960), and colored boxes (Salzen & Sluckin, 1959), to mention a few. Most of the experimental work has been done with various sorts of birds, but some authors argue that imprinting occurs to one degree or another in animals such as dogs, primates, and even humans (Hoffman & Ratner, 1973). We shall return to the question of imprinting in humans in a later section.

We can see how this phenomenon might be adaptive. Those birds which wander off rather than stay close to their parent would probably be less likely to survive. But is imprinting a kind of learning, or is it innate and unlearned behavior? Does it represent some combination of learned and innate behaviors? No one quite knows, but these are the questions psychologists and ethologists address. Our discussion of imprinting will take the following form. First, we shall take a look at some sample equipment and procedures. Second, we shall consider the possibility that imprinting is an innate type of behavior. Third, we shall take the opposite view and discuss the possibility that imprinting is a type of learning. Fourth, we shall look at imprinting in terms of the position it holds in our preparedness continuum.

Sample Apparatus and Procedures

Hess (1958, 1959, 1964, 1972) has done a good deal of influential experimental work with imprinting. A description of his procedures should provide a good example of the kind of experimental rigor obtainable in connection with the imprinting process. Hess's (1959) apparatus is depicted in Figure 4.1. It consists of a circular walkway enclosed with plexiglas walls. The decoy, or object upon which the duckling will be imprinted, is a model of a male Mallard duck. It is equipped with a loudspeaker which will emit a human voice saying, "gock, gock, gock, gock." The decoy also contains a heating unit. Mallard ducklings are hatched in incubators and immediately placed in small cardboard boxes until they are used in the experiments. The notion here is that they will not be able to imprint on anything in their dim little compartments. In the imprinting procedure, the ducklings are released into the apparatus by remote control. The decoy begins to move and emit the "gock" sound. The little duck follows, round and round, presumably being imprinted upon the decoy. When the experimenter wishes to terminate the imprinting procedure, the duckling is tumbled through a little trap door.

As a test of the strength of the imprinting the experimenter then places two decoys in the apparatus. One is the male decoy they were imprinted on while the other might be a model of a female Mallard emitting the recorded sounds of a real female duck. The duckling is reintroduced into the apparatus and the experimenter observes which decoy attracts him. During these kinds of tests most ducklings respond to the male decoy, thereby demonstrating the imprinting effect. Small blocks, or barriers, placed between the ducklings and the male model do not deter the little ducklings. They clamber over these obstacles to be near their "mother."

The experimenter can vary any number of factors in this apparatus. For instance, he can vary the nature of the decoy and/or the sound it emits. He can vary the time spent in the apparatus and/or the speed

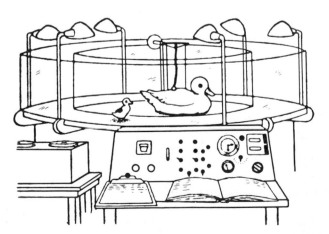

Figure 4.1. The imprinting apparatus. (Adapted from Hess, E. H. Imprinting. *Science,* 1959, *130,* 133–141. Fig. 1, p. 134.)

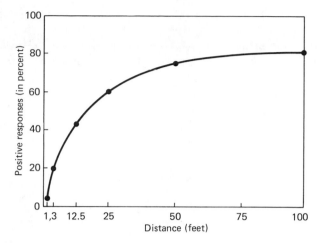

Figure 4.2.   Strength of imprinting as a function of the distance traveled, with exposure time held constant. (Adapted from Hess, E. H. Imprinting. *Science*, 1959, *130*, 133–141, Fig. 6, p. 137.)

of the decoy. In one set of experiments Hess wanted to know if it was the *time* the duckling spent with the decoy or the *distance* he traveled following the decoy which was important in determining the imprinting effect. Accordingly, in one condition Hess kept the time spent in the apparatus constant while varying the speed of the decoy. This allowed him to vary the distance traveled by the obliging little ducks in a given time period. Figure 4.2 contains the results of this experiment. Imprinting clearly increased in strength as the distance the duckling followed the decoy increased. In a companion experiment Hess varied the time the duckling spent in the presence of the decoy while keeping the distance traveled constant. In this case imprinting did not vary as a function of time. Thus Hess concluded that distance traveled is more important than time of exposure in determining the strength of the imprinting effect.

Imprinted Behavior as Innate Behavior

Ethological Interpretations

It is not difficult to imagine the controversy surrounding the nature of imprinting. Although they sometimes disagree (cf. Hess, 1970; Thorpe, 1956), ethologists have argued that imprinted behavior is genetically determined. That is, when the young bird perceives the appropriate moving stimulus it automatically, and in a predetermined fashion, approaches and follows that object. It is as though the behavior pattern is already there, waiting to be released to the appropriate stimulus.

Ethologists speak of "releasers" and "fixed-action patterns." Releasers are a certain limited range of critical stimuli which, when perceived, will automatically release a fixed-action pattern (e.g., approach and follow). According to this position, imprinting is a built-in mechanism. Whenever one of the critical releasers is perceived, the fixed-action pattern is triggered or unblocked. There is no learning in this interpretation. Practice is unnecessary and reinforcement is unnecessary.

Rajecki (1973) has argued against this interpretation on two grounds. First, he challenges the concept of a limited range of releasers. According to the ethologists themselves not all stimuli are releasers. Only a certain set of stimuli are supposed to be effective in unblocking the fixed-action pattern. But Rajecki points out that an enormous range of stimuli have been found to be effective "releasers" (e.g., blinking lights, James, 1959, 1960; and live hawks, Melvin, Cloar, & Massingill, 1967). It may be that all of these varied stimuli are included in some range, but the range is so wide and so diverse that the concept of a *limited* set of releasers is of little value. It does not help us understand what is going on. Second, Rajecki (1973) questions the notion that the fixed-action pattern is really all that fixed. It seems the ethologists wish to conclude that the pattern consists of a limited set of prescribed behaviors (e.g., approach and follow and nothing more). But Rajecki notes a case in which a domestic chick not only imprinted on a swan goose but copied its feeding habits and some of its calls as well. The fixed-action pattern seems to be less fixed than the ethologists would have us believe.

Thus, although the "releaser–fixed-action pattern" sequence is appealing, and does account for a good deal of the data, it seems there is more to imprinting than this simple concept would imply. The concept of a limited set of releasers and fixed behaviors cannot easily account for the variability in both imprinting stimuli and imprinted responses.

The Concept of a Critical Period

As the "releaser–fixed action" pattern is unsatisfactory we need to find something else that would suggest that the imprinting process is different from ordinary learning. Very early observations (Heinroth, 1911; James, 1890; Lorenz, 1935, 1937; Spalding, 1873) led to the conclusion that birds will form social attachments with moving objects but that such attachments will only be formed during a very brief period of their lives, soon after hatching. It seems as though it takes a little time before imprinting can occur, presumably because the very young bird is still a little shaky and disorganized. Then there ensues a brief period during which imprinting readily occurs. Following this "critical period" there seems to be a lessening of the tendency to imprint, and an increase in the tendency to flee from any novel stimulus.

These early field observations have been substantiated in the laboratory. Hess (1959) and Hess and Schaefer (1959) varied the ages of ducklings to be imprinted. That is, the ducklings were kept safely in their cardboard containers for varying amounts of time before they were exposed to the male Mallard decoy. The results depicted in Figure 4.3 indicate that 13–16 hours old seems to be the best age to obtain the imprinting phenomena. Older and younger ducks seemed to imprint less readily.

The point Hess wishes to make is that ordinary learning is not restricted to a critical period. It can occur more or less readily at any age level. Clearly it is not restricted to a time span of several hours early in the organism's life. Hess (1964) argues that the critical period is one of several characteristics that sets imprinting apart from most learned behavior.

Unfortunately the notion of critical period also does not set imprinting apart from ordinary learning. Hess himself (Hess, 1959) sets the stage for a rejection of the notion. He argues that the rise and fall in the effectiveness of the imprinting procedures is due to two interacting factors. First, the initial rise in imprinting may be due to the ducks' growing locomotor capacity after hatching. That is, the very young duck may want to imprint but his little legs are so wobbly that he cannot get up on them and get the job done. Initially he cannot follow, which, according to Figure 4.2, is a critical factor in imprinting. Second, the *decrease* in imprinting after the 13- to 16-hour period seems to be due to the ducks growing capacity to experience fear, and the resulting unwillingness to follow novel stimuli. Thus the duck may possess the *capacity* to imprint beyond the critical period but it does not normally do so be-

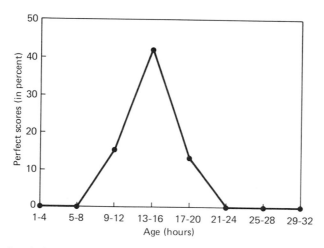

Figure 4.3.   Imprinting as a function of age. (Adapted from Hess, E. H. Imprintin⌐ *Science*, 1959, *130*, 133–141. Fig. 2, p. 135.)

cause it has gradually developed the capacity to fear novel objects and does not follow them after a certain age.

Several experiments suggest that fear does, in fact, block imprinting beyond the "critical period." The rationale behind these experiments is that if an older bird's fear of an unfamiliar stimulus can be *reduced* then imprinting beyond the so-called critical period should occur (Bateson, 1964, 1969; Hoffman, Ratner, & Eisener, 1972; Sluckin & Salzen, 1961). Basically, all these studies use the same simple technique for reducing fear in older birds. They merely expose the bird to the harmless but fear producing novel stimulus for a prolonged period of time. They do not allow the bird to flee. As time goes on the bird discovers the stimulus will not harm him. His fear is reduced. Once fear is reduced these older birds begin to form social attachments to the stimuli. In a nutshell, imprinting may not be limited to a critical period. It may merely be blocked by a normal pattern of developing fear reactions. If the fear is removed then imprinting occurs beyond the so-called critical period. Thus IMPRINTING MAY NOT BE DISTINGUISHABLE FROM ORDINARY LEARNING ON THE BASIS OF THE CONCEPT OF A CRITICAL PERIOD. Learning blocked by fear is commonplace. Many humans, for example, fail to learn certain responses, not because they are incapable of learning, but because they are afraid (e.g., dancing, sky diving).

We can see how Lorenz (1937), working in the field, would be led to conclude that birds never imprint beyond a certain critical age. In the field, the fear reaction would always lead to escape. Each time a novel stimulus is perceived, an unrestricted, older bird will flee. Thus, imprinting will never occur. In the laboratory, on the other hand, the birds can be arbitrarily confined in the presence of a particular stimulus until the fear of that stimulus is reduced. Then, and only then, do filial bonds begin to appear in older birds.

The Effects of Noxious Stimuli upon Imprinting

Is there anything else which might be taken as evidence for the notion that imprinting is somehow fundamentally different from learning? Hess and his associates (Hess, 1964; Kovach & Hess, 1963) have proposed that there is, and that it has to do with the effects of noxious stimulation. Hess points out that, in normal learning, noxious stimulation presented in the presence of a particular object will result in a definite tendency to avoid that object. For instance, if a rat is shocked in a black box it will escape into an adjoining white box. Similarly, if a cat is shocked each time it eats food in one corner of its cage it will quickly begin to avoid that corner. Hess claims that the effects of noxious stimuli are exactly the opposite in the imprinting situation. To support this claim Kovach and Hess (1963) ran an experiment in which birds were shocked during the imprinting process, and in the presence of the decoy. Hess argues that a learning interpretation would predict that the birds would avoid the decoy. But the birds actually increased their following behavior. The shocked birds imprinted more strongly than nonshocked controls.

If we examine the Kovach and Hess (1963) experiment a little more closely we can see where Hess's position may begin to unravel. The problem with the experiment is that the shocks were not made contingent upon the following response. The bird was merely placed near the decoy. The decoy was then moved intermittently around the track. The bird was free to walk or to stand still. Shock was presented intermittently, but no effort was made to ensure that the duck was shocked only while it was in the act of following the decoy. Thus the bird could receive shock as it stood still. It could receive shock as the decoy began to recede around the track. The bird may have been unshocked while following the decoy closely. We can see where the confusion comes in here. Part of the time the bird may actually have been learning to escape *to* the safe decoy and *away* from the shocked state of standing still. Thus the effect of shock on imprinting is inconclusive in this experiment because the shock was not consistently applied during the following response. This is like shocking the cat all over its cage, sometimes while it eats, sometimes while it walks about, and sometimes while it is in the far corners. The cat would probably show no more aversion for the food corner than any other part of the cage.

This explanation may account for the fact that the shocked birds did not actually *avoid* the decoy, but we must now try to account for the fact that they actually *approached it*. Hoffman and Ratner (1973) have argued that these intermittent shocks merely raised the general arousal level of the bird. More shock yields more fear, more excitement, and more motivation. These authors argue that the shock raised the overall performance level of the shocked birds, thereby accounting for their superiority as compared to the nonshocked controls.

In any case, it has not been clearly demonstrated that the effects of noxious stimuli are different in learning and imprinting situation. There is enough confusion surrounding this type of experiment to preclude such a conclusion. A telling experiment by Barret, Hoffman, Stratton, and Newby (1971) comes as close as any to clearing up the issue. Ducklings were *explicitly punished for following behavior*, and not merely for standing about. In this case, the ducklings quickly *stopped* following the decoy. This result would seem to cement the conclusion that the effects of noxious stimuli are at least similar in learning and imprinting situations. If the noxious stimulus is made contingent upon the following response then that response decreases and does not, as Hess implies, increase.

Hess and others have proposed additional differences between imprinting and learning but they also suffer from a degree of ambiguity. For instance, Hess (1964) has argued that imprinting is much more resistant to extinction than ordinary learning. Things are not quite that simple. Being resistant to extinction does not distinguish imprinting from learned behavior for many types of learned behavior also show extreme resistance to extinction (e.g., avoidance conditioning, partially reinforced responses, human actions based upon acquired motivation).

Imprinted Behavior as Learned Behavior

Let us now attempt to look at imprinting as though it involves ordinary learning. Given that it is difficult to defend the position that imprinted behavior is purely innate, or genetically determined, can we conclude that it is learned? There have been a number of attempts to explain imprinting in terms of conditioning (Fabricius, 1962; James, 1959; Moltz, 1963).

In an early attempt Moltz (1960) argued this way. When *first* exposed to a novel decoy at the age of 8 to 10 hours Peking ducklings showed no emotionality, presumably because they had not yet matured sufficiently. They were, at this age, in a "low anxiety" state. This low anxiety, or sense of tranquility, was classically conditioned to the moving decoy, such that, in the future, the decoy should elicit this conditioned low-anxiety state. When the duckling was returned to the same situation the next day it was no longer in a low-anxiety state. Its tranquility had evaporated, and it now expressed high anxiety. According to Moltz, the reason for this change is that the bird had matured to the point where it could perceive new aspects of the test situation, and react to them with fear. In addition, it had become accustomed to the rearing area and the test situation now seemed, by contrast, unfamiliar and frightening. At this point, the frightened bird perceived the decoy which had been previously associated with a low-anxiety state. The decoy elicited the conditioned sense of low anxiety. Any response that would be instrumental in bringing the duckling closer to the decoy would reduce anxiety. And there you have it. The duckling ran over to the decoy because he felt just fine last time he was near it. Imprinting, or the approach response, was reinforced by anxiety reduction.

This interpretation runs into one difficulty right away. It is dependent upon the idea that the first exposure to the decoy occurs when the animal is in a low-anxiety state. To the contrary, many studies have shown that imprinting is stronger if the first exposure occurs under noxious conditions. For instance, Salzen (1970) found that chicks will imprint strongly upon a flat board after having been hit lightly by that board. Pitz and Ross (1961) found that imprinting was enhanced when a loud noise was introduced while the animal was first observing the decoy. These and other studies argue against Moltz's conditioning interpretation.

Hoffman and Ratner (1973) have presented another conditioning interpretation. Actually, their model contains a "little bit of both." They suggest that imprinted behavior is partly innate and partly learned. The first assumption they make is that certain classes of stimuli (e.g., moving objects) *innately* elicit filial responses. If a stimulus drawn from this critical class is presented to the immature bird it will approach the stimulus in an innate fashion, with no learning necessary. Now, if the authors left their model at this point we would have to predict that the bird would run about following *any* moving stimulus. But we know this is not the case. The bird does not become imprinted on the whole class of stimuli but rather on one particular stimulus drawn from that class. This is where the authors bring in the notion of classical conditioning. Assume the decoy is a moving, green football. The critical aspect of the decoy (e.g., the fact that it is a moving object) is the UCS. This UCS innately elicits a UCR (approach and follow). The CS is composed of those *initially neutral* aspects of the decoy which distinguish it from other moving objects (e.g., green, small, etc.). Initially it is only the moving quality of the object that elicits filial responses. The other attributes of the decoy (e.g., green, small) are, at first, neutral or ineffective in eliciting filial responses. But by presenting the ball to the duck *the filial responses are classically conditioned to those initially neutral attributes*. Thus, in the future, the presentation of the ball will elicit filial behavior because of both the innate UCS (moving object) → UCR (approach) relationship, and because of the conditioned CS (green, small) → CR (approach) connection. When presented a choice between a man and the football the combination of the innate and conditioned filial tendencies would ensure a preference for the football.

Hoffman and Ratner (1973) point out, as others have, that there appears to be a maturationally based increase in the tendency for maturing young birds to fear novel or unfamiliar stimuli. They argue that their model accounts for the fact that the birds do not come to fear the imprinted object as well. The exposure process, and the resulting classical conditioning, has rendered *all* elements of the decoy familiar to them.

The final fate of their model remains to be seen, but Hoffman and Ratner (1973) have attempted to clarify the ambiguous status of the imprinting concept by accounting for both innate and learned elements within the process. According to these authors it is not an all-or-none question but rather one of attempting to untangle the simultaneous involvement of both innate behaviors and those which may be modified or acquired through the process of conditioning. But their model is not free of difficulties. For instance, it is dependent upon the notion of a *limited* set of releasers. We have seen that this concept may be difficult to justify.

Imprinting and the Preparedness Continuum

Let us return to the main thread of the chapter. Not all responses are equally easily connected to all stimuli. How does imprinting relate to this theme? We have seen that it is difficult, if not impossible, to resolve the question of whether imprinted responses are innate or learned. After reviewing the status of imprinting, many students, to say nothing of researchers in the field, are left with a certain sense of dissatisfaction. One way to lessen this uneasy feeling, or to gain perspective on the issue, is to think about imprinting in relation to other behaviors on the preparedness continuum. We may think of the preparedness continuum presented in Figure 4.4 as a dimension of survival mechanisms. All of the behaviors encompassed by the dimension are designed, or somehow function, to ensure the survival of the species. Some are more fixed, or predetermined, than others. Figure 4.4 contains a few sample behaviors. The reader may consider for himself where additional behaviors might fall on the dimension.

Purely instinctive behavior represents one extreme end of the dimension. Present a stimulus to the animal and the response will occur automatically. Neither practice nor reinforcement is necessary to establish this association. It is as though the connection is already there, or built into the animal's nervous system. The fighting behavior of the stickleback fish will serve as an example of instinctive behavior (Tinbergen, 1937, 1952). During the mating season the throat and belly of the male stickleback turn red. The male instinctively attacks the color red. The color

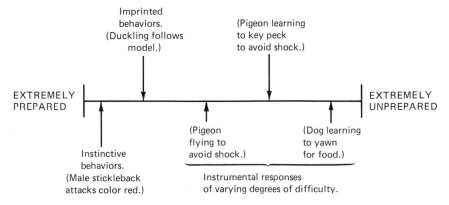

Figure 4.4. The preparedness continuum as a dimension of survival mechanisms, with some selected behaviors included.

red automatically releases attack behavior, it does not have to be practiced or reinforced. Tinbergen (1952) relates one instance in which a red mail truck driving past the window at a distance of approximately 100 yards released attack behavior in the male stickleback.

At the other end of the continuum, we would find events that just do not seem to be learnable, no matter how much practice or reinforcement is involved. As noted, for instance, it is almost impossible to teach a dog to yawn for food (Konorski, 1967).

Imprinting may be considered an instance of highly prepared learning. It does not require much practice at all, nor is much, if any, reinforcement necessary for it to be established. The little duckling is *ready* to associate his filial responses with certain kinds of stimuli. The very fact that imprinting is so prepared actually leads to the confusion about whether it is innate or learned. By thinking of it as prepared behavior one can avoid some of this confusion. Rather than worrying about whether it is or is not learned behavior we may merely think of it as very prepared behavior. As Seligman (1970) puts it, learning and instinct may be continuous, rather than dichotomous. They merely represent different degrees of preparedness. Ethologists have traditionally examined behavior near the prepared end of the dimension, whereas learning psychologists have looked at less prepared behaviors. The controversy over innate versus learned behaviors may be a matter of degree rather than kind.

It should be kept in mind that the preparedness continuum does not really explain anything. It is merely a frame of reference that allows us to put certain behaviors in perspective, to consider them in relation to one another, and to sort out our thoughts about how they might or might not differ. It is, in a sense, a convenient holding pattern, which we may maintain until we know more about the behaviors in question.

Humans and Imprinting

Do humans imprint or is the concept one that only makes sense in reference to "lower" organisms? Certainly tiny children do not pad along in single file behind their parents. But very young children obviously do form strong social attachments to their parents or caretakers. They do tend to straggle after a moving parent; they sometimes react with fear when a strange adult approaches; and they approach their parents when offered a choice between their parents and a stranger. We will now try to determine whether these behaviors represent some type of imprinting, or whether they are more complicated, less prepared, learned behavior.

We tend to think of ourselves as possessing survival mechanisms which, when compared to the so-called "lower" animals, fall somewhere near the unprepared end of the dimension. That is, we tend to think of ourselves as more adaptive, more flexible, and less in the grip of rigid behavior patterns. But some authors have argued that we do possess characteristics reminiscent of instinctive, or at least highly prepared, behaviors. For example, early human socialization has been assumed by some to possess attributes of the imprinting process. Bowlby (1969) argues that human infants develop attachment behavior in a manner that is quite similar to the imprinting process observed in other mammals and in birds

Unfortunately, we really have little more than speculation and opinion concerning the existence of imprinting in humans. But the question is an exciting one, and it should generate a good deal of interesting research in the years to come.

IMPLICATIONS FOR GENERAL LEARNING THEORY

This chapter began with a discussion of the "interchangeable-parts" conception of learning, which has evolved gradually in American psychology. We then traced through a number of areas of research that contradict this model of learning. Some events are more easily associated than others. RESPONSE PREPAREDNESS refers to the fact that an animal may be more prepared to connect one response over another to a given stimulus. STIMULUS PREPAREDNESS refers to the idea that an animal may be more prepared to connect a given response to one stimulus over another in a given situation (see Foree & Lolordo, 1975).

These findings call into question the very notion that we may be able to arrive at a unified, general theory of learning. The questions we might ask are these: Do different degrees of preparedness require different laws, or different principles, of learning? Does learning occur in a different manner at different points on the preparedness continuum?

Our principles of acquisition, extinction, spontaneous recovery, stimulus generalization, and the like, have been obtained in the learning laboratory. Laboratory learning experiments typically involve behaviors drawn from a very restricted segment of the preparedness continuum: They tend to involve relatively unprepared kinds of events. The question is whether our laboratory-based laws and principles will hold for all points on the preparedness continuum. For example, does a highly prepared phenomenon such as imprinting operate according to the principles that govern traditional learning experiments? We have already seen how difficult it is to answer this question.

Seligman (1970) speculates that the laws of learning may very well vary with the continuum of preparedness. He states, "Detailed studies which compare directly the delay of reinforcement gradients, extinction functions, etc., for prepared versus unprepared associations are needed.

It would be interesting to find that the extinction and inhibition functions for prepared associations were different than for unprepared associations [p. 416]."

We are on a frontier of sorts. We have taken the issue of learning into the laboratory and have established, with some rigor, a set of general principles that seem to govern the establishment of associations between stimuli and responses in that setting. Now we are challenged by the notion that our rules and laws, developed under restricted laboratory conditions, may not apply to, or completely account for, learning accomplished by varied animals in the world outside the laboratory. Our laboratory-based principles must be tested in more natural settings. If our principles prove to be adequate, and generally applicable, then our laboratory strategy has been successful. If they fail to account for naturally occurring behaviors then our task is clear. Our existing laws must be recognized as limited and only applicable to the laboratory niche. New rules and laws will have to be developed for more diverse species, behaviors, and environmental settings.

SUMMARY

1. During the better part of this century many American psychologists have adopted a concept of learning in which it is assumed that all responses are about equally conditionable to all stimuli.

2. This position is challenged by a growing body of literature, which indicates that the rule of equivalent associability is inadequate.

3. Seligman has proposed a continuum of preparedness, which suggests that animals may be differentially prepared to associate certain events.

4. Animal studies supporting the notion of a preparedness continuum come from, among others, the fields of instrumental conditioning, discrimination learning, and avoidance conditioning.

5. There is some speculation that humans, as well as other animals, are prepared to associate some events and unprepared to associate others.

6. Bait-shyness refers to the fact that if an animal eats poisoned bait, and survives, it will develop a shyness for the flavor of that bait.

7. Although bait-shyness possesses many of the characteristics of avoidance conditioning, one apparent difference is that the bait-shyness effect may be established with extremely long intervals (e.g., hours) between consumption and illness.

8. Bait-shyness supports the notion of a preparedness continuum because it has been found that an aversive reaction will only be associated with certain aspects of the bait (e.g., flavor). The animal is unprepared to associate illness with other aspects of the bait situation (e.g., visual aspects).

9. It has been suggested that at least some animals are phylogenetically prepared to associate internal events (e.g., illness) with internal cues (e.g., taste sensations) but not with external cues (e.g., lights or sounds).

10. Preparedness differences may well be related to the pressures of natural selection.

11. In a practical sense, bait-shyness may be useful in the control of predation.

12. Bait-shyness resembles aversion therapy in humans. In aversion therapy the human is stimulated with a noxious agent while engaging in or imagining the unwanted behavior (e.g., smoking, overeating).

13. Species-specific defense reactions (SSDR) are innate reactions animals automatically produce in response to sudden or novel stimuli. Bolles argues that if an avoidance response is easily acquired in the laboratory then it must necessarily be an SSDR.

14. Instinctive drift refers to the fact that, after continuous conditioning, innate behaviors sometimes begin to intrude into conditioning situations.

15. Imprinting refers to the fact that a newly hatched bird will approach and follow the first moving object it encounters. The longer the exposure the greater the attachment. The distance the bird follows the object seems to be more important than the time of exposure in determining the strength of imprinting.

16. Some authors have argued, without total success, that imprinted behavior is completely innate.

17. The concept of a critical period refers to the idea that imprinted social attachments will only be formed during a very brief period of the bird's life, soon after hatching.

18. Additional experimentation has shown this to be a false assumption. Once fear is removed older birds will form social attachments. Imprinting is not limited to a critical period and cannot be distinguished from learning on this basis.

19. Some authors have argued that imprinting and learning respond differently to the presentation of a noxious stimulus. Analysis of the experimental work indicates that this distinction between imprinting and learning is also difficult to maintain.

20. Some authors have taken the opposite view, and claimed that imprinted behavior is learned behavior. Currently, there is no conditioning model of imprinting that is entirely satisfactory.

21. If we think of innate behavior and learned behavior as continuous rather than dichotomous then much of the confusion concerning the nature of imprinting evaporates. Imprinting may be thought of as highly prepared behavior falling somewhere near the innate end of the preparedness continuum.

22. Some authors have speculated that the early human socialization process is similar to the imprinting phenomenon.

23. Psychologists have taken learning into the laboratory and have established, with some rigor, a set of laws and principles that seem to govern behavior in that limited setting. The areas of research described in this chapter represent a challenge to that set of laws. Whether our laboratory based laws will be sufficient to account for the diverse behaviors of diverse species in diverse environmental settings remains to be seen.

2

ACQUISITION

The preceding
chapters were concerned primarily
with the various learning tasks employed
by psychologists. We explored the
relationships among these tasks, and
the possibility of a general learning
theory. The following chapters
deal more with specific issues and
concerns within the learning process
than with the general nature of
learning as a whole. There are several
ways to present the field of learning.
One way is to consider, in a sequential
fashion, the works of influential
theoreticians within the field. Good
examples of this reasonable approach
are provided by Hilgard and Bower
(1975) and Hill (1971). We will
take an alternative tack in which
issues and problems, rather than
theories, are considered sequentially.
We will trace the issues that have
been of concern to all major thinkers
in the field, and refer to their works
when relevant. Hulse, Deese, and
Egeth (1975) provide another example
of the approach we will adopt. See
also Peterson (1975).

The next three sections are labeled
Acquisition, Transfer, and *Retention.* A
few comments concerning this breakdown of the field are in order. When
first faced with the field of learning,
students are often perplexed by the
masses of data and interrelated issues.

They have difficulty grasping the limits
of the field, or somehow ordering it in
such a way as to make it comprehensi-
ble and manageable. One way to ensure
some grasp of the field is to think of
it as being reducible to these three subprocesses. Almost any study we run
across, whether animal or human, can
be included in one of these categories.
The major thrust of each investigation
is usually concerned with one or the
other of these processes.

ACQUISITION refers to those processes and events which occur during
the establishment of an S–R association.
When we are concerned with acquisition, we are concerned with events relating to the *building* of associations, presumably through practice and reinforcement. For instance, if we study how a
rat increases its lever-pressing behavior
for food, we are focusing on the acquisition process. If we study the relationship
between a child's increasing ability to
read and the amount of praise we give
him for each success, then we are primarily concerned with the acquisition
process.

TRANSFER refers to the effects of
one learned task upon subsequent attempts to learn, or perform, additional
tasks. Positive transfer refers to the situation in which the learning of one task

facilitates the learning of additional tasks. For example, if we observe that a child's ability to memorize one set of vocabulary words is facilitated by the fact that he had previously learned another set of words then we have demonstrated positive transfer. Negative transfer refers to the situation in which prior learning hinders present performance. If the child's previous learning upsets, or inhibits, his present learning then we are dealing with negative transfer. We can see how important the concept of transfer must be in the field of education. Educators want to be able to arrange classroom materials and procedures so that positive transfer is obtained. Obviously, negative transfer is what everyone wants to avoid.

RETENTION refers to what happens to associations, or learning, after practice has ceased. After associations have been acquired, and they are no longer being rehearsed, what happens to them? Do they "remain within us" forever? Do they fade away? How quickly? What factors determine the rate at which things are forgotten? If we ask these kinds of questions, and focus our attention on the fate of learned associations, then we are primarily concerned with the retention process.

Two notes of caution should be sounded about our approach. First,

some studies are obviously, and legitimately, concerned with more than one of these processes. For instance, a given study may easily be concerned with the establishment of associations *and* with their eventual fate once practice has ceased. Second, and more importantly, the distinctions among acquisition, transfer, and retention are, in a very real sense, arbitrary and superficial. They should be taken as convenient, but not necessarily crystal clear, distinctions. For instance, acquisition is probably never free from retention effects. Consider a paired-associate learning situation. The subject acquires the list by repeatedly rehearsing it. Although the emphasis here is upon the acquisition process, the situation is obviously not free from retention effects. The subject must remember the materials from trial to trial. To the extent that he utilizes what he learned on the last trial the retention process is intertwined with the acquisition process. Similarly, transfer experiments always involve the retention process. For one task to affect performance on a second task, either positively or negatively, it must be remembered. Furthermore, retention experiments involve transfer processes. In fact, retention experiments may represent a special case of transfer; the one in which the two successive tasks are identical. The subject learns a list of word pairs on Day 1. On Day 2 he is given the stimulus words and asked to recall the response words. We are looking at the effects of one list upon the subsequent performance of the very same list, or, in other words, a transfer situation in which the two successive tasks are as identical as we can make them.

Without reviewing all the possibilities, we can see that the acquisition, transfer, and retention processes all involve one another. You might take a moment and pursue some of the combinations. In what way do acquisition experiments almost always involve transfer effects? How is the acquisition process involved in retention experiments? How is retention involved in transfer studies?

Section Two considers some of the major issues within the area of acquisition. Traditionally, the issues of CON-TIGUITY, PRACTICE, and REIN-FORCEMENT have maintained central positions in this arena. In fact, these three issues, or variables, may be the ones about which major theoreticians most often disagree. Their roles in the acquisition process are controversial. We shall see what is known about each of them by drawing upon both animal and human research.

The CONTIGUITY issue is taken up in Chapter Five. Must a response occur in the presence of a stimulus for learning to occur? Or can an association be established if the stimulus occurs at Time 1 and the response does not occur until Time 2?

Chapter Six deals with the role of PRACTICE in learning. Is practice, or rehearsal, necessary for learning to occur? What is the relationship between amount of practice and strength of learning? The answer seems obvious. The more we practice, the more we learn; but it is not quite so simple as it might appear. For instance, some argue that increasing practice does not increase the strength of learning. They argue, and quite persuasively, that learning occurs in an all-or-none fashion. According to this controversial position learning is either complete, or it does not occur at all in a given trial.

Chapter Seven deals with the role of REINFORCEMENT in acquisition. Is reinforcement necessary for learning to occur? What happens to learning when we vary such factors as the amount and kind of reinforcement we deliver to the animal? What are some of the current models, or conceptions, of reinforcement?

The Role of Contiguity in Learning

5

THE CONCEPT OF CONTIGUITY

One of the oldest assumptions in the field of learning is that temporal contiguity of the stimulus and response is necessary for learning to occur. It has generally been assumed that THE RESPONSE MUST OCCUR IN THE PRESENCE OF, OR VERY SOON AFTER, THE STIMULUS FOR AN ASSOCIATION TO BE ESTABLISHED. Another way to phrase it is to say that events that occur together in time may be associated. Events that are separated by any substantial amount of time will not be associated. In referring to the law of contiguity Robinson (1964) argues that many psychologists feel that it embodies the very essence of the associative process.

Intuitively, it seems extremely unlikely that an association will be formed between two events if they are separated by any considerable length of time unless, of course, the subject somehow brings them together, either mentally or physically. For example, there is no intuitive reason to assume that an event experienced today (e.g., the sound of a hand clap) will in any way be associated with a particular response made tomorrow (e.g., speaking the word "table"), unless, of course, the two are somehow brought together, or linked in time, in which case the learning would be contiguous. The fact that noncontiguous learning seems so unlikely may account for the fact that the contiguity principle is so universally and uncritically accepted. Few seem to doubt it. But believing something to be true is not the same as knowing it to be true, so we shall revisit this issue. We shall challenge the law of contiguity by attempting to discover instances of noncontiguous learning in the experimental literature. If we can find some examples of noncontiguous learning then the contiguity principle must be modified.

The Lack of Experimentation

An acceptance of the law of contiguity is inherent in most existing theories of learning (Hilgard & Bower, 1975). In fact, of our three critical factors (contiguity, practice, and reinforcement) it is the least controversial, and the most widely accepted. Interestingly, it is also the least documented. A review of the literature reveals relatively few studies concerned with this basic and very critical assumption. Although thousands of studies relate to the controversial issues of practice and reinforcement, the importance of the contiguity principle seems to have been accepted without a lot of hue and cry.

Aside from the intuitive appeal of the contiguity principle, there is another reason for this lack of experimentation. Very simply, it is difficult to do this type of research. It is difficult to envision experiments that could disprove the contiguity principle. Suppose, for example, we wished to discover if the words "table" and "dog" can be connected, or associated if they are separated by a 24-hour interval. On Day 1 we read the word "dog" to our group of subjects, and then dismiss them with instructions to return the next day. On Day 2 we read the word "table." We then test to see if the word "dog" will elicit the word "table," and it does. The two are somehow related. But this probably does not demonstrate noncontiguous learning. The subjects probably *thought* of the word "dog" on Day 2, while we were in the process of presenting "table." The subjects established a contiguous relationship by bringing a trace of the stimulus and the response together in time. This is not noncontiguous learning. It is contiguous learning where the time gap has been bridged by the subject's memory.

In any experiment where the stimulus and the response are separated in time there remains the constant possibility that the stimulus, or an "image" of it, will be brought forward in time such that it does "exist" at the time the response occurs. We may imagine various ways to avoid this possibility. For instance, we might try to keep the subject from knowing what the stimulus is. We might conceal our stimulus word "dog" in some rambling discourse, or in a poem. In that way we might make it highly unlikely that the subject would carry a trace of the stimulus forward in time. The trouble is that learning probably would not occur in this case. We would not be any closer to finding noncontiguous learning than we were before.

There is another way in which our attempts to disprove the contiguity principle may be short-circuited. Rather than bringing a stimulus trace forward in time the subject may mediate time intervals between stimuli and responses with long strings of associations. For instance, suppose we present the word "table" at Time 1 and the word "stand" at Time 2. Suppose we found, in a test, that an association had been formed between "table" and "stand." This association also may not demonstrate noncontiguous learning. Many psychologists have argued that such an association may be mediated by a string of associations. "Table" causes the subject to think of "chair" which, in turn, leads to "sit." Finally, "sit" elicits "stand." That these kinds of PREEXPERIMENTAL CHAINS exist is undisputed (Cramer, 1967). They are based upon our past experiences in a linguistic world, and the subjects bring them to the experiment. Each of these individual links (e.g., sit → stand) is presumed to have been established through a contiguous relationship (Spear, Ekstrand, & Underwood, 1964). Thus, what appears to be noncontiguous learning (table → stand) is, according to this analysis, merely the result of a string of contiguously established associations (table → chair → sit → stand).

All of this says that a general acceptance of the contiguity principle is not surprising. First, it is intuitively appealing, and appears to coincide with what we perceive about us. Second, it is very difficult to disprove experimentally. Mediators always lurk about our experiments, and subjects are more than capable of moving a trace of the stimulus forward in time.

But these are not very good reasons for accepting such an important principle. At one time it was intuitively appealing to accept the notion that the world was flat. It was also difficult to disprove the notion that the world was flat (man had not yet developed the technology necessary for an adequate test). But the assumption was not a good one. Similarly, the assumption of the contiguity principle may not be a good one. Hence we will spend some time looking for experiments that demonstrate learning in the absence of S–R contiguity.

Contiguity: Necessary or Sufficient?

We have seen that most psychologists accept the notion that S–R contiguity is *necessary* for learning to occur. But we wish to investigate whether S–R contiguity is a *sufficient* condition for learning to occur. If a response occurs in the presence of a perceived stimulus, will learning occur automatically, without further practice, and without reinforcement? This is the point at which psychologists begin to disagree. In fact, many of the most heated controversies in the field of learning center around the questions of what are and what are not the necessary and sufficient conditions for learning. It is interesting to note, as an example, that two of the most influential, early theoreticians in the field, Clark Hull and Edwin Guthrie, disagreed over the roles of contiguity, reinforcement, and practice in learning. Hull (1943, 1952) felt that contiguity was necessary, that reinforcement was necessary, and that reinforced practice gradually increased amount of learning. Guthrie (1935, 1952), on the other hand, believed S–R contiguity was a sufficient condition for learning to occur, reinforcement was unnecessary, and practice did not add to learning. According to Guthrie, if a response occurs in the presence of a stimulus then the association between the two events will be completely and automatically established. Thus both Hull and Guthrie accepted the importance of contiguity in learning, but they disagreed concerning the importance of practice and reinforcement. We shall return to these theories, and their more recent offspring (Estes, 1959, 1964; Spence, 1956, 1960), in Chapter Six. For now, we should realize that these three factors (contiguity, reinforcement, practice) have formed cornerstones of some of the more important theories of learning.

What is a Stimulus? What is a Response?
What is an Association?

Before we begin searching for examples of noncontiguous learning we should consider the nature of stimuli and responses a little more closely. We have referred to learning as a relatively permanent change in behavior potentiality that occurs as a result of reinforced practice. In addition, we have adopted what is usually referred to as an S–R, or behaviorist, language. According to this particular way of speaking and thinking, learning refers to an increase in the tendency to behave, or respond, in a particular fashion when confronted with a particular stimulus situation. We refer to this increasing tendency to respond as the building, or strengthening, of an association between that particular response and that particular stimulus situation. The S–R language is not the only way to speak of learning. But it is convenient, and it has been widely adopted. In later chapters we shall review some of the alternative languages (e.g., information processing). It is important to keep in mind that we use the S–R language because it helps us order and structure our thinking about very complicated events. We do not use it because we believe it represents the only way to understand the learning process. Like any language, it has its limitations and its use must be kept in perspective.

The three basic elements of an S–R language are the stimulus (S), the response (R), and that little dash between them that we refer to as an association between the S and the R (Fig. 5.1).

The S–R Association

The strength of an association may be revealed by the probability of a particular response occurring in a particular stimulus situation. As an association between a stimulus and a response increases, the probability of that response occurring in the presence of that stimulus increases. So far, this sounds like a circular definition. The strength of an association determines response probability, and response probability determines strength of association. Fortunately, we can break this circularity by considering additional factors that *independently* index the strength of an association. Although not all agree, some of the more commonly accepted independent determinants of strength of association are practice, contiguity, and reinforcement. Thus, if a situation involves a large amount of S–R contiguity, practice, and reinforcement we assume associative strength is increasing. In turn, we can predict an increase in response probability. The S–R scheme is a predictive system. We predict changes in dependent variables (response probability, latency, magnitude, etc.) through a consideration of changes in our independent variables (reinforcement, contiguity, practice, etc.). The S–R association is a construct; it is not something we can directly observe. In fact, it is not an absolutely essential part of the predictive system. For instance, we could predict response probability without ever evoking the notion of an association. All we would have to do is apply our knowledge of how our independent variables affect our dependent variables. But the concept of the S–R association has heuristic value. Even though it may not be absolutely essential it seems to help us order and structure our thinking about learning.

The Stimulus

Logan (1970) defines a stimulus as "any adequate change in energy falling upon an appropriate sensory receptor [p. 8]." In other words, any detected energy change may serve as a stimulus. For example, lights, sounds, tastes, odors, and shock may serve as stimuli. Offset of any of these may be as effective as their onset. Relationships may serve as stimuli. An animal can learn to respond to the brighter of two stimuli, regardless of their absolute values. Being to the left, or being later in time, can serve as effective stimuli. Any detected event, which is distinguishable from other events, may serve as a stimulus.

However, it should always be kept in mind that not all energy changes are equally effective as stimuli. For instance, the pigeon, quite a visual creature, will easily associate illness with visual stimuli, but not so readily with taste. Rats, on the other hand, readily associate illness with taste, but not with visual stimuli. What is an effective stimulus for one species may not be for another. Humans are quite ready to use verbal units as stimuli, presumably because we are prepared to, and have, utilized them as stimuli.

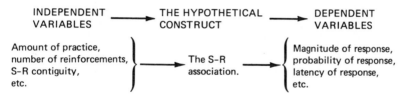

Figure 5.1   The concept of an S–R association.

Psychologists are just beginning to tease out these species differences. The psychologist's ability to predict which stimulus will be effective is fairly limited. At present, we almost have to try out a potential stimulus before we can be sure about how effective it will be in a given learning situation.

Obviously, if an energy change is not impinging upon, and firing, suitable receptors then it cannot serve as a stimulus. In addition, if we are not *paying attention* to a particular energy change then it tends not to be used as a stimulus. Attention is an important, but poorly defined, concept in psychology. At any given moment our sensory receptors are being bombarded by a large number of energy changes, each of which has the potential to be a stimulus. But, somehow, we are not aware of all of them at any given moment. We channel our attention, or focus on only a few of these many potential stimuli. For instance, as you read these words you are attending to the print. You are probably not attending to your hands even though they are part of the total stimulating pattern. You may attend to them if you wish. Without moving your eyes away from the printed words you can be aware of their position, their color, and their movement. Similarly, think about your left leg for a moment. You can feel all sorts of things going on down there when you pay attention to it. But before we drew your attention to it you were probably unaware of such things as the pressure of cloth upon your leg. To be effective as a stimulus, our attention must be directed toward an energy change.

Responses as Stimuli

Responses sometimes act as stimuli. For instance, when we speak, and hear ourselves, the sounds can serve as stimuli for further responses. If we detect that we are speaking too loudly we may respond by speaking more softly. In addition, we use the sound of our own voices to keep track of where we are in our sentences. This is dramatically demonstrated by the following type of experiment (Thurlow, 1971). The subject speaks into a microphone and the sound of his voice is played back to him through earphones after a delay of a fraction of a second. The experimenter asks the subject to read a simple passage. He has difficulty reading, stutters, and reads in bursts. The subject becomes confused and loses track of where he is in the passage. He talks more and more loudly, as if trying to drown out the interfering sound of his own voice. An experience like this is very peculiar indeed, and one that demonstrates how important the stimulus qualities of our own voices are in guiding further speech.

Presumably other types of actions are equally affected by the stimulus qualities of our responses. For instance, if a gymnast did not receive sensory input from his body as he went through his complicated routine he would probably lose track of what he was doing. Visual cues and the like would help, but they would not be sufficient. We would hardly expect a top notch performance from an athlete who was dependent upon *seeing* his legs go over the bar without also *feeling* it happen.

Thinking probably represents another case in which responses serve as stimuli. One "thought" leads to another. One cognitive action, or response, serves as a cue for the next.

Contextual Stimuli

We have been speaking as though the stimulus in a given learning situation is a distinct, easily identifiable unit, such as a particular color, tone, or level of shock, and as though all the other potential stimuli in the learning situation (e.g., the surrounding room, the temperature level, the condition of the subject's digestive tract, the sounds coming through the windows of the laboratory) are of little importance. Such is not the case; the other stimuli are important. The effective, or functional, stimulus may be the *total* stimulus complex, and not just the particular subset of stimuli chosen and isolated by the psychologist. Clearly, some aspects of the total stimulus complex are more important than others, but there is evidence suggesting that these lesser stimuli also affect the probability of a response occurring.

Two areas of research will illustrate the importance of contextual stimuli. First, in STATE DEPENDENT LEARNING studies, subjects learn a set of materials in one particular state (e.g., under the influence of alcohol). They are then tested either in that same state or in some other state (e.g., completely sober). Although the results are controversial, some studies have shown that retention is better when the learning and test states are the same (e.g., under the influence while learning *and* recalling, or sober while learning *and* recalling). Mixing the states (e.g., learning while sober and recalling while under the influence) can result in poorer retention. The same kind of effect has been obtained with amphetamines. The correct responses seem to be associated with the cues offered by the general condition of the body, as well as with the cues presented and manipulated by the psychologist (Devietti & Larson, 1971).

Another kind of experiment suggests that if a person masters a task in one particular classroom, then his ability to perform that task will be reduced if he is moved to another room for the retention test. In some sense, the responses seem to be associated with the surrounding room. Aside from illustrating the importance of contextual cues, this type of result may have some relevance in the real world. Suppose an instructor splits his large class into two sections for the final examination. Half the class reports to the lecture hall occupied during the semester, and the other half is required to take the exam in a new room. The instructor may well be short changing the half required to move. The more closely the learning conditions approximate the testing conditions the better the student may do. In fact, the student's position *within* a large lecture hall may be important. Thus if a student spends the entire semester taking notes in the last row, and then moves to the very first row for the final exam he may be hurting his own performance. Logan (1970) suggests that students would be well advised to arrange their study environment to be as similar as possible to the classroom environment. Advice such as Logan's may be a little optimistic. The research on this issue is much too spotty and contradictory to draw any such conclusions (Bilodeau & Schlosberg, 1951; Greenspoon & Ranyard, 1957; Strand, 1970). But it does suggest that contextual stimuli may be important not only in the laboratory, but also in the world outside the laboratory.

The notion of contextual stimuli ties in with one of the main criticisms of general S–R language. It has been argued that it is impossible to identify the effective stimulus in a learning situation. What, for example, is the stimulus for laughing at a joke? What is the stimulus for dreaming about one's past? What is the stimulus for reaching a creative solution to a problem? What is the stimulus for learning to swim? Some feel that the S–R conception, with its emphasis upon discrete, identifiable stimuli, is simple-minded. It may well be. Life is obviously a good deal more complicated than a lot of stimuli and responses. The criticism is a just one, and it is not easily brushed aside.

Yet several points may be made in defense of the S–R position. First, just because we cannot *always* identify the functional stimulus does not mean we *never* can. There are very many situations in which the most important stimuli can be identified easily. Second, just because we cannot always observe the effective stimuli directly does not necessarily mean there are no such stimuli. It may merely be beyond our technical ability to measure, or observe, them at the present time. Third, the S–R language, although imperfect, does provide a structure within which to think of the complicated world of learned events.

The Stimulus Trace

In its simplest form the stimulus trace notion implies that the *continuation* of a stimulus is not dependent upon the continued stimulation of sensory receptors by some outside energy source. Once an external stimulus has activated sensory receptors the message is "taken into" the organism and maintained therein. Traces of external stimuli, or the neural remainders of external stimuli, may take various forms and may persist for varying amounts of time.

The term STIMULUS TRACE has been used in several ways. On the one hand, it has been used to refer to essentially sensory phenomena. For instance, we are all familiar with afterimages. As children we discovered that if we stared at a lit light bulb for some time, and then looked away, we could still see something that resembled the bulb. This afterimage, or trace, fades rather quickly. It represents one instance in which a terminated external stimulus "lives on" within the organism.

The afterimage represents a stimulus trace which decays rather rapidly, but there are some kinds of traces that may persist indefinitely. Consider what you might do if some attractive person gave you a phone number in a crowded, noisy situation. You desperately rehearse it, hoping to preserve the trace until you can write it down, or until it becomes part of your permanent memory. The entire field of memory and retention is, in a sense, concerned with stimulus traces. When we remember something we are often dealing with the trace of a long gone external stimulus.

Because its usage has been so diverse, the concept of the stimulus trace is difficult to define. The inner, or neurological, nature of the stimulus trace is, at present, beyond our grasp. Presumably we will eventually be able to identify it on a neurological level. We have learned all we know now in just a few hundred years, so one can only imagine how much we will know in 2000 years. Current psychological thinking will probably seem primitive. Be that as it may, the important thing to remember now is that energy changes in the world about us are transformed into stimulus traces, which persist within us well beyond the termination of the external stimulus.

What Is a Response?

It is as difficult to define the response as it is to define a stimulus in our S–R language. Let us say a college student, wanting to get acquainted with one of his classmates, asks her if she will join him over a cup of coffee. In response to his inquiry the woman responds with a flat, "No." That "no" is undoubtedly a "response," but it is more difficult to determine where the response began and where it ended. As she listened to the man's question, she apparently experienced some kind of emotional reaction. Her emotional reaction was then somehow translated into a verbal response. But the response does not even end there. Presumably neither she, nor he, would immediately return to a state of nonresponding. In all likelihood some sort of uncomfortable disengagement process would ensue. Even after they had gotten away from one another the chain of behaviors would not end. They both would probably think about the encounter for some time. The situation obviously involves a chain, or series, of complex actions and reactions.

We must now try to handle this enormously complicated situation with our S–R conception of behavior. We must do two things in order to isolate a distinct response from this "behavior chain." First, we acknowledge the fact that behavior is *continuous*. We are always doing something; we never stop behaving. We may be more or less active, but we are always behaving. For example, we behave even when we are asleep: we breathe, we produce antibodies, we jump at the tiny suspicious sound of a window being rattled, but we remain undisturbed when a truck goes by. Many of us keep track of time, so that we awaken more or less at the time we wish to awaken.

Second, having acknowledged that behavior never ceases, we may define a response as any IDENTIFIABLE SEGMENT OF THIS CONTINUOUS BEHAVIOR PROCESS. As Logan (1970) puts it, "A response is any glandular secretion, muscular action, or other objectively identifiable aspect of the behavior of an organism [p. 25]." The key here is that the segment must be *objectively identifiable*. Scientists must be able to agree that a given segment of behavior has occurred. If they cannot agree that a given segment has, or has not, occurred then they have gotten nowhere. For example, psychologists probably would not agree that our female friend had rejected the male. They could agree that she had responded with a *verbal* rejection, but they might not agree as to whether she meant it or not. Further observations would have to be made before agreement could be reached.

In summary, we accept the notion that behavior is not discrete. It is a continuing process from which we select segments to study. They may be short segments (e.g., pronouncing the letter "T"; eyeblinks) or long segments (e.g., success in college; the development of political attitudes). We then attempt to devise methods of measurement that will ensure that we can all agree our chosen behavior segment has, or has not, occurred. The psychology of learning is the study of how these behavior segments become more and more likely to occur in the presence of particular stimuli.

THE SEARCH FOR NONCONTIGUOUS LEARNING

Remote Associations in Serial Learning

Ebbinghaus's Doctrine of Remote Associations

To return to the main thread of this chapter, we now begin our search for learning that occurs in the absence of S–R contiguity. If we can convince ourselves we have some clear examples of noncontiguous learning, then we may want to reconsider the contiguity principle.

The first of several areas which we will review has to do with the Ebbinghaus (1885) doctrine of remote associations. Hermann Ebbinghaus (1850–1909) is often remembered as one of the pioneers in the field of learning. He proposed what has come to be known as the doctrine of remote associations. The doctrine has to do with the nature of serial learning. As you know, subjects in a serial learning task are required to remember a sequence of verbal units in a given order. Ebbinghaus argued that, as we learn a serial list, we are establishing associations between adjacent items in the list. If we visualize a serial list as A–B–C–D–E–F–G–H–I–J–K–L–M, where *each letter stands for a given word or syllable within the list*, then item B serves as a stimulus for item C *and* as a response for item A. Each item in the list has a double function. It serves as a response for the previous unit, and as a stimulus for the next item.

It is at this point that the doctrine of remote associations comes in. It is a two-part doctrine. The first canon states that, in addition to the adjacent associations just described, *remote* associations are formed among *all* of the items in the list. Item B is not only associated with items A and C but with all the other items in the list as well, both in a forward and a backward direction. Item H is not only associated with items G and I but all other items in the list as well. Each item in the list is connected to, or associated with, every other item in the list. Figure 5.2 contains some of these hypothesized remote associations. The second rule, or law, states that the greater the degree of remoteness the weaker the strength of the remote association. The further apart the items are in the list the weaker the remote association binding them. In Figure 5.2 items B and K are remotely associated, but the strength of that remote association is weaker than the remote association between (say) B and D.

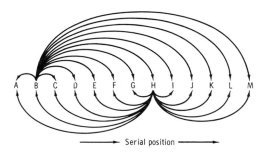

Serial position

Figure 5.2. Hypothetical remote associations between the second item (B) and all other items in the list, and between the eighth item (H) and all other items in the list.

Relevance to the Contiguity Issue

If remote associations truly exist, then learning can occur in the absence of S–R contiguity. Items that are separated in a serial list by several intervening items do not occur together in time. For example, if each item is presented for 3 seconds then items occurring near the end of the list will not occur until some time after the first items have been removed.

Ebbinghaus's Evidence for Remote Associations

If we can find good evidence for the existence of remote associations then we may have to reconsider the contiguity principle. Ebbinghaus used what has come to be known as the *derived-lists method*. In this kind of experiment the subjects first learn a given serial list such as A–B–C–D–E–F–G–H–I–J–K–L–M–N–O–P. (Each letter stands for a verbal unit such as a word or a nonsense syllable. The letters index the *position* each unit holds within the sequence.) Subjects then learn a second list which is composed of the same first-list units, which have been rearranged in a specific manner. One derived list might be the same units rearranged in the order A–C–E–G–I–K–M–O–B–D–F–H–J–L–N–P. A second derived list might be A–D–G–J–M–P–B–E–H–K–N–C–F–I–L–O. If remote associations are weaker as the degree of remoteness increases, the first derived list should be easier to learn than the second derived list, because, in the first derived list adjacent items (e.g., E and G) are items that were separated by *one* intervening item in the first list (E–F–G). In the second derived list, adjacent items (e.g., G–J) are items that were separated by *two* items in the original list (G–H–I–J). Thus, the remote association that the subject could use in learning the first derived list (E–F–G) would be *stronger* than the remote association he could use in learning the second derived list (G–H–I–J), and there would be more positive transfer from the original list to the first derived list.

Ebbinghaus's hypothesis was confirmed. He found greater savings in learning lists like the first derived list than in learning lists such as the second derived list. His results seemed to support the notion that the remote association does exist and, in turn, that learning may occur in the absence of S–R contiguity.

Empirical Challenges to the Doctrine of Remote Associations

It was not until after the first half of this century that Ebbinghaus's experiments on remote associations were seriously challenged. The long delay—well over half a century—certainly marks the degree to which Ebbinghaus was ahead of his time.

In any case, the doctrine of remote associations has been severely damaged. Although some investigators (Bugelski, 1965; Dallett, 1965b) have tried to keep an open mind, the weight of the accumulating evidence goes against the doctrine. A series of papers (Slamecka, 1964, 1965; Young, 1968; Young, Hakes, & Hick, 1965) has revealed serious deficiencies in the original Ebbinghaus methodology. This is not to disparage Ebbinghaus's work. After all, it took us over 70 years just to recognize something was wrong with what he did. The major criticisms that have been leveled at his research are detailed in Table 5.1.

When the problems outlined in Table 5.1, and other subtle shortcomings, are corrected it is difficult to obtain support for the doctrine of remote associations. *Using naive groups of subjects, serial anticipation rather than whole-list presentation methods, statistical analyses, and controls for the use of perceived patterns* positive results often fail to appear in derived-list studies (Hakes, James, & Young, 1964; Slamecka, 1964).

TABLE 5.1

Criticisms of the Original Ebbinghaus Remote Association Experiments

---

1. Ebbinghaus used himself as a subject. Obviously, this is not good. He knew the purpose of the experiments and may have unintentionally affected their outcomes. Furthermore his performance many have been heavily affected by his extensive experience with the materials and procedure of experimental work.

2. He used what is called the whole-list presentation technique. Ebbinghaus did not have memory drums that present single items in a timed fashion. He merely sat down with the entire list in full view on a sheet of paper and practiced it from top to bottom. By accidentally moving his eyes about the paper he may have inadvertently brought items from one end of the list into a contiguous relationship with items from some other section of the list. These accidentally, but contiguously, established associations would then be taken as remote, or noncontiguous, associations.

3. He did not analyze his data statistically because there were no appropriate statistical techniques available at the time. What appeared to be a lawful relationship in his data may have been due to chance.

4. The subject in a derived-list experiment may use his perception of the *pattern* of the items to master the derived list. For instance, a subject learning the first derived list described above might be able to say, "The first item is correct. Skip the next item. The third item is correct. Skip the fourth item," etc. Using this technique he could easily master the derived list, but he would be doing it without the aid of remote associations. By merely running through the *entire* original list, and leaving out every other item, he could achieve a perfect score on the derived list. Derived lists involving greater degrees of remoteness might be expected to be more difficult to learn because the pattern would be more difficult to perceive.

In summary, for many decades Ebbinghaus's data appeared to challenge the contiguity principle. More recent experimentation has revealed that the remote association effect may well be an artifact. We must look elsewhere if we are to discover our elusive instance of noncontiguous learning.

For a fuller discussion of remote associations, including different methods of study and alternative theoretical interpretations, the reader is referred to Kausler (1974) and Millward (1971).

Subjective Organization and the Contiguity Principle

Tulving (1962, 1964, 1966) introduced the concept of subjective organization (SO) to the field of learning. In the simplest kind of SO experiment, a randomly arranged list of unrelated words is presented, one word at a time, to the subjects. The subjects then attempt to recall as many of the words as they can, *in any order* they wish. The list is then presented to the subjects again, but this time in a *new random order*. The subjects again attempt to recall the words. The experiment involves a series of these successive presentation and recall phases. Tulving noticed that the subjects began to recall certain items next to one another, or sequentially, even though the items were scattered throughout the random presentation orders. The number of pairs the subjects began to recall sequentially increased as the experiment progressed. Each subject began to develop his own unique sets of items which he consistently recalled together. It seemed that each subject somehow organized the materials "inside his head." This subjective organization was presumed to be reflected in the increasing tendency to recall randomly presented materials in a given order. The SO experiment does not really allow us to know *why* certain subjects recall certain items together. It merely lets us know the *degree* to which such organization is occurring. There have been a number of methods devised to measure the SO phenomenon (Bousfield & Bousfield, 1966; Bousfield, Puff, & Cowen, 1964; Pellegrino, 1971). Basically they all attempt to assess the growing tendency to recall together items that are not presented together. Structure emerges in the form of two or more items being recalled together consistently.

We shall return to a more detailed consideration of SO in a later chapter. For now, our interest lies in its relevance to the contiguity issue. The fact that items are consistently recalled together in the absence of temporal contiguity during the input phase suggests that we may have found an instance of noncontiguous learning. Two items do not occur together in time during the presentation phase, yet they are consistently recalled together. Some kind of association has developed between them. Where is the temporal S–R contiguity?

There are at least two possible answers to this question. The first is somewhat speculative. It may well be that the subject merely brings items together "in his own mind." That is, even though the items are never presented together externally, there is nothing to prevent the subject from carrying *traces* of the items over long periods of time. Such an argument is certainly reasonable, but there are few hard data to support it. It may well be a correct hypothesis, but we would not want to accept it without some objective demonstration of its validity.

There is another analysis that suggests that S–R contiguity occurs in SO experiments, which has to do with the output, or recall, phase of the experiment (Wallace, 1970). In many SO experiments, the subject is asked to write down all the words he can remember on a sheet of paper. In addition he is typically given several minutes to attempt recall on each trial. Suppose the subject randomly recalls "Barn" and "Fiction" together on the very first trial. Let us assume there is no association between them at this time. There they are, right in front of him. He has several minutes to run back and forth over the list. He knows he is going to have to try to recall the list again. He rapidly rehearses the items he has already recalled, hoping to preserve them for the next trail. By looking at "Barn" and "Fiction" together he is, in effect, experiencing S–R contiguity. They occur together in time after all. We can see how SO might build up over trials. Two items randomly recalled together on the first recall trial would be rehearsed as a pair. The resultant association between them would lead to a greater likelihood that they would be recalled together on future trials, and so on.

Wallace (1970) presents data which support this output rehearsal hypothesis. He found that amount of SO decreased when he set up experiments such that rehearsal during the output phase was reduced. For instance, SO decreased when the duration of each recall period was reduced. He found that SO decreased when he substituted oral recall for written recall. In oral recall S–R contiguity is much more fleeting and less stable than in written recall. He found SO decreased when the subject was required to write down successively recalled items in noncontiguous positions on the recall sheet. The scattered positions of successively recalled items presumably reduced the probability that they would be rehearsed in a contiguous manner. Others have demonstrated that recall phases are generally important in free recall (Bregman & Wiener, 1970; Lachman & Laughery, 1968).

In summary, what appeared to be noncontiguous learning may be the result of either "mentally" established contiguity, or S–R contiguity established during the recall phase of the experiments. Subjective organization experiments do not, after all, provide us with a clear instance of noncontiguous learning.

Paired-Associate Learning and the Contiguity Issue

In paired-associate (PA) experiments temporal S–R contiguity is the rule rather than the exception. The experimenter generally ensures that the response will occur in the presence of the stimulus. Each time through the list the stimulus term is normally presented alone for 2 seconds. The stimulus and the response terms are then presented together for 2 seconds. Hence PA research is not an ideal place to look for learning in the absence of S–R contiguity.

However, there have been a few studies in which the *time* between the PA stimulus and the PA response has been varied. In these studies, the stimulus is first presented alone. Then there ensues an empty time interval, which is varied in length. Finally the response term is presented alone. The question is whether learning will occur when the stimulus and the response are separated in time. In a very early study, Froeberg (1918) varied the interval from 0 to 5 seconds and obtained rather unclear results. More recently, Guthrie (1933) and Martin and Schultz (1963) employed intervals ranging from 2 to 6 seconds. Interestingly, both studies revealed *better* learning with *longer* intervals. These results would seem to be in conflict with the contiguity principle. The greater the separation of the S and the R in time the better the learning. The reason for this seeming contradiction soon became apparent. Martin (1966) attempted the same type of experiment, but with one major modification. He had subjects count backward by threes during the intervals. Under these conditions the effect reported by Martin and Schultz (1963) could not be replicated. In other words, the increase in learning with increases in the interval in the earlier experiments must have had something to do with what the subjects did during that interval. In the earlier experiments, subjects were left free to rehearse and/or to carry the stimulus trace forward in time and their performance increased as the interval increased. On the other hand, in Martin's (1966) experiment the subjects were prevented from rehearsing and/or carrying the stimulus trace forward, and their performance did not increase as the interval increased. Counting backward by threes presumably distracted the subjects from the task at hand, and prevented them from utilizing the time in rehearsal or maintaining a stimulus trace. So you may better understand the impact of this distraction technique, try counting backward by threes. Start with the number 378. The task clearly occupies one's mind, doesn't it?

The ideal experiment investigating S–R contiguity in the PA situation would involve, not only temporal separation of the stimulus and the response, but also control of the subject's activities during the interval. Nodine (1969) has run an experiment with these qualities in mind. Subjects learned PA lists with intervals ranging from 0 to 6 seconds. In addition, Nodine varied the interval activities of the subjects. In some conditions subjects named numbers in an attempt to *minimize* rehearsal and the carrying forward of the stimulus. In other conditions subjects were asked to pronounce the stimulus over and over again during the interval, thereby *maximizing* mediated S–R contiguity. In a final set of conditions the subjects were free to do as they wished during unfilled intervals. Nodine's analyses suggest that *both* S–R contiguity and rehearsal within the interval are important. The two factors appear to operate against one another. On the one hand, as the interval increases there is a *decrease* in the tendency for an association to be formed between the stimulus and the response. This is the contiguity principle in action. On the other hand, if the subject is not prevented from rehearsing and/or carrying the stimulus trace forward, then there is an *increase* in the tendency for an association to be formed as the interval increases. In other words, if the interval is increased, and the subject is free to rehearse, then he will use this extra time to rehearse, and learn the pair.

In summary, these studies suggest that unless the stimulus is closely followed by the response, or unless the subject can carry the stimulus trace forward in time, there is little chance that learning will occur. Once again the contiguity principle is upheld.

The CS–UCS Interval and Contiguity

In Chapter Two (see Figure 2.3, p. 29) we stated that a CS–UCS interval of about .5 second is the best one to use in obtaining classical conditioning. Longer and shorter intervals result in poorer conditioning. Generally speaking, these facts tend to support the contiguity principle: For learning to occur a response (the UCR elicited by the UCS) must occur at the same time, or very soon after, the stimulus (the CS). But if there are any exceptions to this rule then we may be able to think about them in terms of noncontiguous learning.

Revusky (1968) ran an interesting bait-shyness experiment in which a sweet solution (the CS) was ingested at a given time. *Seven hours later* the rats were X irradiated and became ill (the UCS → UCR sequence). Despite this incredibly long CS–UCS interval an aversion for the sweet flavor developed. Many investigators have obtained similar results (Garcia, Ervin & Koelling, 1966; Smith & Roll, 1967).

This result does seem to come closer than the other types of experimentation we have discussed to demonstrating noncontiguous learning. But some have argued persuasively that learning over long CS–UCS intervals does *not* represent noncontiguous learning. In presenting their argument they evoke the idea of *trace* conditioning. Some kind of lingering trace of the CS (sweet flavor) might bridge the long CS–UCS interval.

There are two types of traces that might be operating here. First, we might consider actual *physical* traces of the stimulus, such as chemicals lingering in the mouth or other parts of the system. Although such *physical* traces might bridge the time gap, Garcia, McGowan, and Green (1972) have argued against such a possibility. They report that extremely transient tastes are as effective in ensuring conditioning as stronger, more lingering tastes. If a physical trace had mediated the learning we would have expected the more durable physical traces to be more effective, but they were not.

A more likely trace interpretation is based upon the mechanisms of memory. That is, the *memory* of the CS, or the neurological remainder, of the physical stimulus, is much more likely to mediate the time gap than is an actual physical trace of the stimulus. Although some investigators (Garcia, McGowan, & Green, 1972) feel that mediators cannot account for the full effect, these kinds of potential "mental" mediators have not been eliminated from the methodology of these experiments.

The question is still unresolved. No one is quite sure what to make of the effect. It does resemble noncontiguous learning, and yet potential mediators have not been eliminated from the experimental designs. Hence no firm conclusions can be drawn (see also Smith and Balagura, 1969).

Another way to look at this issue is to consider learning over long CS–UCS intervals as a *special case* of learning, which has its roots deep in the demands of the evolutionary process. As Seligman (1970) puts it, "Selective advantage should accrue, moreover, to those rats whose associative apparatus could bridge a very long CS–UCS interval and who could ignore contiguous, as well as interpolated, exteroceptive CSs in the case of taste and nausea [p. 409]." Seligman (1970) is arguing that learning over long CS–UCS intervals is an instance of extreme preparedness. It may well be that some animals are neurally wired to associate certain survival-related events, over long time intervals, while more ordinary learning must occur under conditions of S–R contiguity. But it is only a possibility, and must be considered as such at the present time.

CONCLUSIONS

Noncontiguous learning has not been demonstrated conclusively. Experimental situations that might be taken as providing evidence for noncontiguous learning often possess methodological faults. In addition, S–R contiguity may occur through the involvement of some sort of stimulus trace. Contiguity of the *physical* stimulus and the response is not necessary. A "mental" trace of the stimulus will do very well. The most reasonable conclusion to draw at the present time is that S–R contiguity is extremely important, if not actually necessary, for the establishment of S–R associations. Whether learning can occur in the absence of S–R contiguity remains to be seen.

SUMMARY

1. One of the oldest and most widely held assumptions in the field of learning is that temporal contiguity of the stimulus and the response is necessary for learning to occur.

2. Some psychologists feel S–R contiguity is sufficient for learning to occur, whereas others think it is necessary, but not sufficient. Although an acceptance of the contiguity principle is inherent in most existing theories of learning the validity of the principle has not been well documented.

3. One reason for the lack of documentation is that it is difficult to study S–R contiguity. Any interval established between the stimulus and the response may be bridged by a trace of the stimulus brought forward in time by the subject.

4. As background for the contiguity issue the S–R language adopted in this text was discussed.

5. The strength of an S–R association is revealed by the likelihood of a particular response occurring in the presence of a particular stimulus situation. The strength of an association may also be independently indexed by alternative factors, such as number of reinforcements, etc.

6. A stimulus may be defined as any detectable energy change. Offset and onset of such things as lights, sounds, odors, and tastes may serve as stimuli. Relationships may serve as stimuli. Responses may serve as stimuli. Some energy changes are more effective as stimuli than others, particularly across species. An energy change must be attended to before it can function as an effective stimulus.

7. The total stimulus situation surrounding an organism, and not just the stimulus manipulated by the experimenter, is important. This is demonstrated by the fact that if a person masters a particular task in a given room then his ability to perform that task may be reduced if he is shifted to another room. The state of consciousness in which a subject learns a given task also provides important cues in the learning process. Performance of that particular task may be reduced if the subject is in some alternative state.

8. The notion of a stimulus trace refers to the fact that the continuation of a stimulus is not dependent upon continued stimulation of sensory receptors. Once an external stimulus has activated sensory receptors the message is "taken in to" the organism and maintained therein. Afterimages represent stimulus traces of an essentially sensory nature. Memories represent traces of a more complicated, "cognitive" nature.

9. A response may be defined as any objectively identifiable segment of the continuous behavior process.

10. We challenged the validity of the contiguity principle by searching for an instance of noncontiguous learning. The first possibility in-

volved Ebbinghaus's doctrine of remote associations. The doctrine states that remote associations are established among *all* the items in a serial list. The greater the degree of remoteness the weaker the remote association. These remote associations are presumed to be formed in the absence of S–R contiguity. Thus, if they truly exist, S–R contiguity is unnecessary in learning. For many years, it appeared Ebbinghaus had effectively demonstrated their existence using his derived-lists method. Recent experimentation has revealed serious flaws in Ebbinghaus's methodology. When these flaws are corrected this particular challenge to the contiguity principle collapses.

11. In subjective organization experiments, the subject is presented a list of randomly arranged words and asked to recall them in any order he wishes. The list is then presented again, but in a new random order. The subject again tries to recall them, and so on. Subjective organization refers to the fact that, as the experiment progresses, the subject begins to recall the words in the same order, even though they are presented in a new random order on each trial. Items separated in time during presentation begin to appear together in recall. This would seem to suggest noncontiguous learning. But additional research has revealed that the subject may either (*1*) bring the elements together "in his own mind," or (*2*) rehearse them contiguously during the recall phase when he is typically asked to write the words on a single sheet of paper. Thus, another challenge collapses.

12. Studies in the area of paired-associate learning also support the contiguity principle. If the time between the stimulus and response items is increased, *and* the subject is prevented from rehearsing or carrying a trace of the stimulus forward in time, then learning decreases rapidly.

13. Research reported in an earlier chapter indicated that the best CS–UCS interval in classical conditioning is a very brief .5 second and this supports the contiguity principle. Yet bait-shyness studies reveal that conditioning may occur with CS–UCS intervals of several hours. Rats that have been X irradiated several hours after ingesting distinctly flavored solutions will still form an aversion for that flavor. Some feel this demonstrates noncontiguous learning. Others evoke the trace conditioning notion to explain away the challenge. At present, it must be admitted that the possibility of stimulus traces being carried forward in these experiments has not been effectively eliminated.

14. While the bait-shyness effect is provocative, noncontiguous learning has not been demonstrated clearly and conclusively. The constant possibility of confounding through the action of stimulus traces has, so far, defeated our quest for learning in the absence of S–R contiguity.

The Role of Practice in Learning

6

INTRODUCTION

What is the role of practice, or rehearsal, in the learning process? Does practice increase learning and, if so, how? To put it in terms of our S–R language, what happens to the strength of the association as we increase the frequency with which the response occurs in the presence of the stimulus? Intuitively, the answer seems simple: The more we practice the more we learn. The more we study, or rehearse, materials for an exam the better we know them—up to a point, of course. Once we have mastered the materials, further practice will lead to little additional gain. The more an athlete practices his particular specialty the better he will be at it. Our intuitive sense of the world argues that the relationship between practice and learning is a positive one, with continued practice leading to continued gains until the task is mastered.

Psychological research and thinking has suggested that the relationship between learning and practice may not be so simple. There is, in fact, a heated controversy concerning the role of practice in the learning process. Some psychologists argue that our intuitive sense is correct, and that learning is a gradual process, like stage lights coming up slowly in a theater. Other psychologists have argued that learning occurs in an all-or-none fashion, like a kitchen light being snapped on abruptly. According to the all-or-none position learning occurs completely in one trial, or it does not occur at all.

At first glance the all-or-none interpretation does not seem to make sense. The psychology of learning is shot through with data that suggest that performance gains are gradual, or incremental, and not abrupt. The data from classical conditioning, instrumental conditioning, discrimination learning, free-recall learning, and just about any other type learning situation suggest that increases are gradual, building sorts of events. There are few dramatic rises from zero performance to complete performance in one trial. How does the all-or-none position explain these kinds of data? For now, think of it this way. When you sit down to study for the examination in this class it will appear that your mastery of the material is gradual. Your overall grasp of the content of the class will increase slowly through the agonizing hours. And yet, even though it appears your grasp of the material is slowly strengthening, any given bit of learning may occur in an all-or-none fashion. You may, all of a sudden, hook up, or associate Garcia's name with bait-shyness. You might, in an all-or-none fashion, connect the label "backward conditioning" with the notion of the UCS coming before the CS. Similarly, a golfer's game might gradually improve over the years, but this improvement might be the result of lots of little bits of learning which occur in an all-or-none fashion. One day the golfer might abruptly learn to keep his head down. The next week he might abruptly learn to follow through properly, and so on. The appearance of gradual improvement might be the summed result of many little, discrete bits of learning that occur in an all-or-none fashion.

It is an interesting question, and we shall pursue it, both theoretically and empirically, in this chapter. Our discussion will take the following form. First, we shall discuss the nature of learning curves. Second, we shall consider the alternative theoretical interpretations already outlined. Third, we shall consider some of the tests of these alternative theories in the interest of determining which of the two is the better conception of the role of practice in learning. Fourth, we shall discuss some additional areas of research which relate to the role of practice in learning.

LEARNING CURVES

In Chapter Three we pointed out that the relationship between performance and practice is typically summarized by a negative accelerated learning curve (see Figure 3.4). That is, as practice progresses, performance increases rapidly at first and then levels off. This negatively accelerated curve is a widespread phenomenon appearing in many diverse areas of investigation. But it is not the only curve which appears in our research. Even though the negatively accelerated curve is very characteristic we do not want to fall into the trap of thinking of it as "the" learning curve which represents some irrefutable mathematical law of nature.

Learning Curves Are Not Learning Curves

Learning curves are not really learning curves at all. They are performance curves. That is, they are the result of how much the organism has learned *and* how motivated he is. If you will recall, performance refers to the activation of learning through the involvement of motivation. In a sense we may say, Performance = Learning $\times$ Motivation. To infer the amount of learning that has occurred we must be able to measure performance *and* estimate the organism's level of motivation.

For example, one student might know the answer to a question posed by his instructor, but might not be motivated to speak up in class. A second student might know only half the answer, but might be highly motivated to answer in class. Thus the performance of the second student might be higher than that of the first student even though the second student had not learned as much.

Similarly, if we observe one rat rapidly running down a straight alley to food, and a second rat walking along in the same apparatus we cannot immediately conclude that the first rat has learned more than the second rat. It may just be more motivated. We can see how errors could be made in estimating amount of learning. If we are not aware that the first rat is hungrier than the second we might incorrectly conclude that the first rat had learned more. There are experimental designs that help us decide whether performance differences are due to learned or motivational factors. These designs will be discussed in the section concerned with amount of reinforcement.

Performance Measures

Given that we infer amount of learning from some index of performance, what measures of performance are available? How do we measure performance of a rat running down a straight alley for food? We could do it any number of ways. We could measure its running speed—the faster it runs the more we assume it has learned. We could measure the latency of its response, that is, we could measure how long it remains in the start box before it starts off down the alley. The quicker it leaves the box, or the shorter the latency, the more learning we would infer. We could use resistance to extinction by removing food from the situation. The longer the rat persists in running down the alley to an empty goal box the more learning we would want to infer.

If we consider something like paired-associate learning we run into a number of different performance measures. For example, amount of paired-associate learning is often estimated by counting the number of correct responses the subject produces in a given number of trials. Trials to criterion is also used as a performance measure in paired-associate learning. The experimenter counts the number of times the subject must go through the list before he reaches some predetermined criterion such as once, or perhaps twice, through the list without an error. The availability of all these performance measures creates problems. We will now examine a few of them.

Reliability of the Measure

Suppose a psychologist wishes to study the effects of smoking marijuana upon driving an automobile. He has his subject puff away, and then observes his ability to drive through a carefully constructed driving course. He finds, relative to some appropriate control, that the subject shows superior driving ability. The experimenter is tempted to conclude that smoking marijuana enhances driving ability, but before he does so, he must ask himself several questions. One of these has to do with the reliability of his performance measure. The measure must yield similar results on different occasions. If the experimenter ran the same subject through the same test on several different occasions he should obtain similar results. If he does then he is using a reliable measure. If he does not then his measure is unreliable, and his conclusions are invalid.

Measuring Learning at all Levels

The top half of Figure 6.1 contains some hypothetical data produced by two rats in a straight runway situation. In each case the rats were fed upon reaching the goal box at the end of the runway. Rat 1 was given 30 trials and then taken out of the testing situation. At that time, it was running at a constant speed. Its performance had leveled off. After 30 trials Rat 2 was running at the same constant speed as was Rat 1. But, instead of being removed from the situation, Rat 2 was given an additional 10 trials. During these additional trials (trials 31–40) Rat 2 showed no improvement whatsoever. Thus, after 40 trials, Rat 2 was performing at the same level Rat 1 had reached after 30 trials. The question is this: How much have the two rats learned? If we use running speed as an index of how much was learned then we conclude that the two rats had learned the same amount, and that Rat 2 had learned nothing during Trials 31–40.

There is a problem with this conclusion. A rat can run just so fast. Once it has reached its top speed, it can go no faster, *but it might still be learning*. Rat 2 may be learning during Trials 31–40, but the increase in learning would not show up in running speed because a ceiling had been reached. If we assume that some learning might occur during Trials 31–40, it would be a mistake to use running speed as our performance measure, as it would not reflect learning at all levels, especially the higher levels.

One way to resolve this issue would be to utilize some other, more appropriate, performance measure such as resistance to extinction. If we removed food from the situation, and allowed Rat 1 and Rat 2 to extinguish, we might find that Rat 2 would run for no food longer and faster than Rat 1 (see the bottom half of Figure 6.1). We would then conclude that Rat 2 actually had learned more than Rat 1, even though the difference did not appear when we used running speed as our measure.

The point is that whenever we choose a performance measure we must assure ourselves that it will accurately reflect learning at all levels,

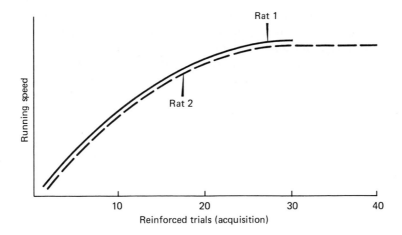

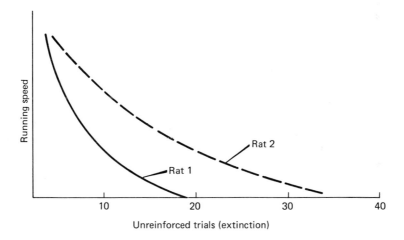

Figure 6.1. Hypothetical acquisition and extinction curves for two rats given different numbers of acquisition trials.

or at least at those levels likely to be involved in our study. If we do not then we may be led to incorrect conclusions.

Averaging Data

Group versus Individual Data

A learning curve is a visual representation of performance over a series of trials, or time intervals. Typically, trials are placed on the abscissa and the units in which the behavior is measured are placed along the ordinate. Given such a system it would be helpful if we could plot a *single* individual's performance across trials, and then make some sense of it, but most of the time, we cannot. Individuals are variable in their behavior, and follow strange, unique courses through the learning process, so we are often forced to average the scores from several individuals to obtain a clear picture of the stable and consistent trends underlying the variable individual behaviors.

For example, the top four panels in Figure 6.2 contain hypothetical

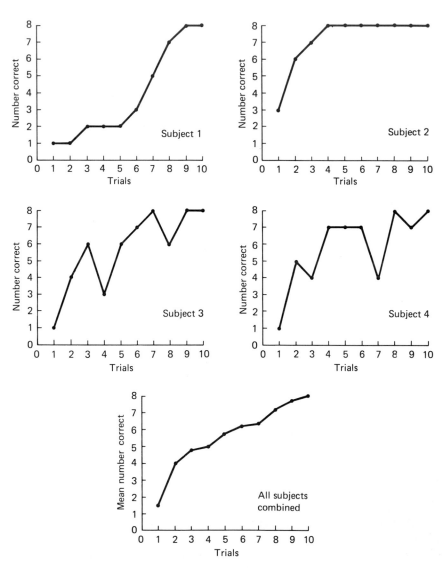

Figure 6.2. Some hypothetical paired-associate data.

data from four different subjects as they learned a simple paired-associate list. As you can see their progress through the trials is extremely variable. Subject 1 begins slowly and finishes with a bang. Subject 2 begins rapidly and then levels off. Subjects 3 and 4 provide equally unique records. If we were left with these four unique records we would not know what to say about how the learning of the list progressed. So we combine the four records in an attempt to obtain a clearer picture. The averages of the scores of the four individuals on each trial are depicted at the bottom of Figure 6.2. Here we see something that begins to approximate the familiar negatively accelerated learning curve. This trend, or function, was obscured by the variability of the individual records. The assumption we must make is that if we could control all the unknown factors that yield high individual variability, then each individual curve would approximate the average curve. We are, in a sense, assuming that the averaged data reveal the "real" learning curve. Without averaging we might miss these stable trends or relationships. We would not see the forest for the trees.

Types of Averaging

There are a number of ways to average data and each method has its advantages and disadvantages. The experimenter chooses the one that best suits his needs and purposes. We have just discussed one of the most popular methods, wherein curves are smoothed by combining the scores from a number of individuals on each trial. In another method, scores obtained from a single individual over a series of runs through the task are combined. In still another technique, scores from adjacent trials are combined. For example, one might plot average performance in successive blocks of five trials, rather than performance on each trial. This technique loses detail, but it does make it easier to see general trends by eliminating minor peculiarities in the data.

CUMULATIVE RESPONSE CURVES are quite popular. They are curves in which the units of behavior, or scores, are allowed to *accumulate* over trials, or periods of observation. For example, Figure 6.3 contains data obtained from a pigeon pecking a key for food over a series of 4-minute intervals. The left half of Figure 6.3 contains a cumulative record of the responses. The same data are presented in the right half of the figure, but in this case the average numbers of responses per time interval are plotted against successive time intervals.

At any given point on the cumulative curve we may read the total number of responses made from the beginning of the experiment. If the bird stops pecking, the cumulative record levels off and remains horizontal until the bird begins pecking again. It can never go down. When the bird begins to respond again the curve goes up as we add on new re-

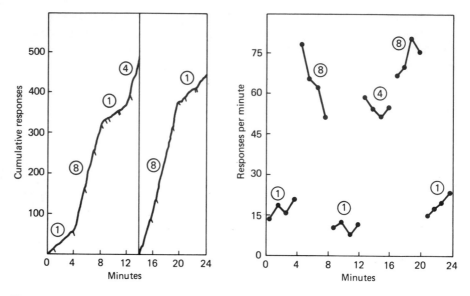

Figure 6.3. Comparison of two procedures for presenting results. The panel on the left contains a segment of a record obtained from a cumulative recorder. The paper is fed through the recorder at a constant speed; each response moves the pen a fixed distance across the paper. Thus, the rate of response is shown by the *slope* of the curve. The pen automatically resets to the baseline at some preselected point (in this case, after 500 responses). The same responses were also indicated on electro-mechanical counters, and those counts are plotted in the panel on the right. The results show the effects of training a pigeon with different amounts of food per rein-forcement. The bird was occasionally reinforced (on the average, once per minute) for pecking an illuminated key. The color of the key indicated which reinforcement condition was in effect. Reinforcements consisted of delivery of either 1, 4, or 8 hemp seeds. The reinforcement condition changed every four minutes. Occurrences of rein-forcements are shown by slight oblique marks on the record. Among the advantages of the cumulative record are instant information concerning the progress of the experi-ment, and an indication of the sequential changes in the behavior. The plot of re-sponses trial-by-trial (or minute-by-minute in this case) allows the dependent variable to be read with greater ease: in the first minute of this experiment, for example, it is clear from the right panel that the average response rate was approximately 14 pecks per minute, but it would be difficult to determine this from the cumulative record. In practice, both cumulative recorders and digital counters are usually used since each form of recording has its own advantages. (Adapted from Kling, J. W. Learning: An introductory survey. In J. W. Kling and L. A. Riggs (Eds.), *Woodworth and Schlos-berg's experimental psychology.* New York: Holt, Rinehart and Winston, 1971. Fig. 14:7, p. 610.)

sponses. The advantage of the cumulative curve is that we can quickly and easily observe changes in the bird's rate of responding. The steeper the slope of the curve the faster it is responding. The flatter the slope the slower it is responding.

The noncumulative method employed in the right side of Figure 6.3 also has its advantages. For example, we may quickly determine how many responses the bird produced during any given time interval. It is not so easy to obtain this information from the cumulative curve. Many experimenters try to use both methods of plotting their data, for each yields quick and convenient information about the subject's performance.

These methods, and others (see, for example, Melton, 1936; Munn, 1950; Vincent, 1912), are all available to the psychologist. Unfortunately, psychologists as a whole have never been able to decide which method is best. Some psychologists have, in fact, gone so far as to say group curves are next to worthless in attempting to understand individual behavior (Sidman, 1952). Perhaps the best we can do at present is to be extremely careful in interpreting averaged data, and to be aware of the differences among the alternative methods. We should be cautious about putting too much weight on one method, and should attempt to look at our data from several different angles.

Learning Curves and the All-or-None Hypothesis

Suppose, for the sake of argument, that the all-or-none interpretation of learning is correct. That is, learning is accomplished completely in one trial. The top two-thirds of Figure 6.4 contain hypothetical scores from four individuals, all of whom mastered a given task in an all-or-none fashion. As you can see, each individual rose from zero performance to 100% performance in one trial. There is nothing gradual about their performance gains. Notice that the individuals vary in terms of the trial in which all learning took place. Some completed their learning in early trials, whereas others did not do so until later trials. But, in each case, it is clear that, when learning did occur, it occurred in an all-or-none fashion.

Now, if we apply the standard averaging technique wherein the scores from *all individuals* on a given trial are averaged, we end up with the curve in the lower left-hand corner of Figure 6.4—a gradually increasing curve. By utilizing this averaging technique, we have completely misrepresented the nature of the learning. If we were to publish this curve based upon averaged scores, we would completely mislead our readers. The gradual rise would misrepresent what actually happened. It would be an artifact of our averaging technique.

BACKWARD LEARNING CURVES (Hayes, 1953) can be useful in a situation of this sort. In backward learning curves, the anchor point is not the beginning of practice, it is the end of practice, or the trial in which 100% performance was attained. The lower right-hand corner of Figure 6.4 contains such a backward curve. Trials *preceding* 100% performance

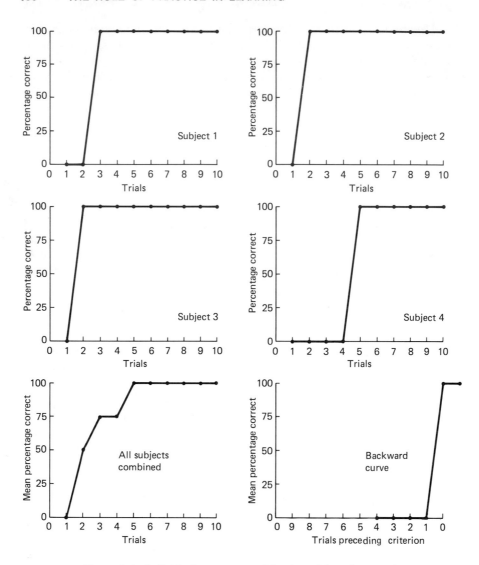

Figure 6.4 Individual, average, and backward learning curves.

(or any other chosen criterion) are placed along the abscissa. The general procedure is to average the group's scores on the last trial, then on the next to the last trial, or the trial before 100% performance was attained, and so on. In this way, a picture of the dramatic rise in performance is preserved. The backward learning curve will not tell us what was happening on any *specific* trial (say, the fifth trial from the start of practice), but it will preserve the course of acquisition once it has begun, which, in this case, is what we are really interested in recording.

Learning curves are designed to present data in a clear, simple fashion, and, to an extent, they do just that. But no single learning curve can tell the whole story. A given curve merely represents one vantage point from which we may view our results. We must always keep in mind that alternative methods of plotting scores might shift our attention to alternative aspects of our data, and lead us to alternative conclusions. Learning curves can be helpful, but they can also be dangerously misleading. With this cautionary note in mind we now turn to a consideration of the two opposing theories of the role of practice in learning.

HULL'S SYSTEM: A THEORY OF GRADUAL GROWTH

There are two reasons why we want to discuss Clark L. Hull's (1884–1952) theory. First, the theory has been extremely influential in the field of psychology. Although few psychologists accept the theory in its entirety, it has had a significant impact upon the field of learning. Clearly Hull was one of the most influential figures in the field during the 1940s and 1950s. Although his system now receives less attention than it once did, it remains a monumental effort, and its final impact upon the field cannot yet be estimated. Hull's analyses, and modes of thinking, are so ingrained in the field that it is difficult to discern what is, and what is not, the result of this man's thought and experimentation. The second reason for discussing Hull's system is that it provides a good example of the incremental approach to the role of practice in learning. Hull believed that LEARNING INCREASES GRADUALLY AS A RESULT OF REINFORCED PRACTICE. Hence we can both catch a glimpse of an enormously influential theory from the recent past, and at the same time pursue our quest for an understanding of the role of practice in learning.

Hull's Basic Approach

Hull was a behaviorist. Behaviorists are not particularly interested in what "goes on in the mind," or in the content of consciousness. Internal events, such as thoughts, ideas, and images, are, for the behaviorist, unmeasurable and, therefore, to be avoided in a science of psychology. What Hull was interested in was in making predictions about behavior based upon *observable, measurable* qualities of the real world. Measurement and quantification of observables were the cornerstone of his approach.

His system represented one of the last of the "master theories." Although many of the postulates within the system were developed from animal data, the system was designed to account for the behavior of all species in all situations. In other words, he wished to encompass all of behavior in one grand system. The titles of his books reveal this hope:

Principles of Behavior (1943), *Essentials of Behavior* (1951), *A Behavior System* (1952).

His attempts to encompass all behavior in a single system were not entirely satisfactory. It was just more than anyone could hope to do. Modern psychologists limit themselves to "microtheories." Few would tackle what Hull attempted. Today, psychologists choose one specific task (e.g., serial learning), or one small aspect of behavior (e.g., recognition memory), and attempt to build a model of that limited bit of behavior.

A Distilled Picture of Hull's Theory

Hull's work was complicated, mathematical, and constantly changing. He died soon after the completion of his last book, and in no way did he ever consider his system to be finished. For the purposes of this text we shall attempt to boil the system down, and to avoid becoming entangled in its immense complexity. The full system in all its elaborate, detailed splendor may be found in his books. A good, detailed summary is presented by Hilgard and Bower (1975).

Let us take a quick look at the system. Once we strip away the great detail, the basic concerns underlying the theory are sound. (Keep in mind that this is an extremely simplified version of the theory.) Hull developed an equation for behavior which may be expressed as:

$$\text{Response Probability} = D \times H \times K \times V - I$$

The equation implies that the probability of a response occurring is a function of the interaction of at least five major variables. The elaboration of the system is complicated, but the underlying ideas are not. If you give it a moment's thought you will probably be able to identify most, if not all, of Hull's major variables. Imagine a rat faced with a lever in a Skinner box. Imagine a child in the kitchen faced with a refrigerator. The question is this: What factors will determine whether or not the rat presses the lever, and whether or not the child opens the refrigerator door? In both these situations the reward for making the response in question (pressing the lever or opening the door) is food. So the hungrier each is, the more motivated each will be to perform the required behavior. The first of Hull's variables, *D*, or DRIVE, is designed to encompass the influence of how motivated the subject is to perform. Drive level is measured in terms of time of deprivation and/or amount of noxious stimulation. The more deprived the animal, or the more noxiously stimulated the animal, the greater his drive state and, hence, the greater the tendency to act in an attempt to reduce that drive state. Drive instigates action and action seeks to reduce drive. The theory is a survival system. Hull went through several steps in his thinking about drive but, for our purposes, we may think of it as a motivational construct tied to, or measured in terms of, time of deprivation and/or amount of noxious stimulation.

Another factor that might contribute to the rat's, or the child's, tendency to respond is how many times they have responded in the past and been reinforced for doing so. Experience in a given situation clearly affects the probability of a response occurring. That is what H, or HABIT, is all about in Hull's system. Habit reflects how much the organism has already learned. If the child has opened the refrigerator door in the past, and been reinforced for doing so, then he will be more likely to open it in the future. Hull measured H in terms of the number of reinforced responses. The more times the rat presses the bar and is reinforced the greater the habit strength.

Two points should be made here. First, reinforcement in Hull's system is produced by a rapid diminution of D. A response is reinforced if it is quickly followed by a reduction in drive. For Hull, learning, or an increase in H, is the *result* of a response being followed by drive reduction. The rat learns to press the bar because he is reinforced for doing so. If he is not fed, and D is not reduced, learning will not occur. Hull's drive reduction interpretation of reinforcement is not the only way to think of reinforcement, as we shall see later, but it has been an influential conception. The second point we wish to make is that D activates H; D and H multiply yielding a response probability. This conception corresponds to our earlier distinction between learning and performance. Performance (response probability) refers to the activation of learning (H) through the involvement of motivation (D).

To return to the thread of the discussion, we should ask what else might determine behavior, and what is in the refrigerator seems likely to have some bearing. A chocolate cake might induce the child to respond, whereas something less palatable might be less likely to stimulate a response. Hull acknowledged the importance of these kinds of factors with his K construct. Hull's K, or INCENTIVE MOTIVATION, is measured in terms of the *quantity* of the goal (the more the better) and in terms of the *quality* of the goal (cake might be better than turnips). The greater K is, the greater is the probability of the response occurring; K is a kind of "pull" factor. The child is pulled toward the cake. Drive, or D, on the other hand, is a "push" factor. The child is driven toward the refrigerator by his hunger.

The clarity of the stimulus situation might also help to determine the behavior of our organisms. If the rat can barely see the lever, it will be less likely to respond to it. If the lever is bright, distinct, and intense then the rat will be more likely to respond to it. It seems this was what Hull was trying to account for when he postulated V, or STIMULUS INTENSITY DYNAMISM. Hull's V refers to the fact that the probability of a response increases as the intensity of the stimulus increases. In other words, we are more likely to respond to intense stimuli than to less intense ones.

If you will notice, the four of Hull's variables we have discussed so far all contribute positively to the probabilty of a response occurring. If any one of them is zero then response probability is zero. The fifth, and last, variable subtracts from response probability. Hull calls this last factor I, or INHIBITION. In a very rough sense I is a fatigue factor. It is measured in terms of the amount of work involved in making a response, and in terms of the number of times the response has been made. The harder it is for the child to open the refrigerator door, and the more times he has done it in a row, the less likely he is to do it again.

Thus there is nothing esoteric about Hull's model. It is based upon a series of intuitively obvious assumptions about what might contribute to behavior. It is a survival model in which *contiguity, practice,* and *reinforcement* are all important. Learning occurs when a response is quickly followed by a drop in drive level. Learning occurs in a gradual, incremental fashion, and not in an all-or-none manner.

One of the tasks Hull set for himself was to work out the relationships between each of the intervening variables (D, H, K, V, I) and their observable measures. For example, D must first increase and then decrease as time of deprivation increases. There must eventually be a decline in D as time of deprivation, and the resulting states of weakness and eventual starvation, increase.

Although we will not consider this relationship for every one of the five variables, we might take a look at one more: the relationship between H and number of reinforcements. Hull theorizes that H increases at first and then levels off as the number of reinforced responses increases—the function is *negatively accelerated*. What he is saying is that there is a limit to learning. Hull believed H increased in a gradual, incremental fashion, rapidly at first and then more slowly until a limit was reached. Hull could have proposed that H increases indefinitely as the number of reinforced responses increases, but his data indicated to him that H has a limit, and that is the position he took.

Another interesting aspect of Hull's conception of H is that learning is permanent. Once reinforced practice ceases, H does not dissipate or fade away, it remains constant forever. Such a conception suggests that once we learn something it is "in storage forever," even though we may not always be able to retrieve it. Studies using hypnosis, and other prompting techniques, suggest that there are, in fact, many viable memories within our storage systems that are not normally retrievable. Yet, the fact that childhood memories may be stimulated under hypnosis does not prove that *all* of our experiences are permanently stored, it merely indicates that *some* memories normally beyond our ability to retrieve may be brought out under special prompting conditions. The question, though fascinating, is unresolved.

We will return to Hull's system now and then, as it has influenced many subareas in the field of learning. For now, we should keep firmly in mind the fact that it is an INCREMENTAL THEORY IN WHICH LEARNING IS ASSUMED TO INCREASE IN A GRADUAL FASHION AS REINFORCED PRACTICE PROGRESSES. Although we have spent some time examining various elements of the theory, you should keep in mind that our principal focus in this chapter is upon the role of practice in learning, and that Hull's system is one in which learning is assumed to increase gradually as reinforced practice increases (up to a point, of course). To the student interested in the developments in the Hullian tradition, the works of Miller (1959), Mowrer (1960), and Spence (1956, 1960) are all relevant.

ALL-OR-NONE THEORY

Guthrie's Approach

We now turn to a consideration of the all-or-none approach. Although there have been many variations of the basic all-or-none position (see Millward, 1971) we shall limit our discussion to two of the more influential systems. First, Guthrie's original interpretation of learning laid the groundwork and formed the foundation for later, more formal, expressions of the all-or-none position. Second, Estes' stimulus-sampling model represents one of these more recent mathematical statements of Guthrie's earlier ideas.

The very simplicity of Guthrie's theory is intriguing. It can be summed up in one sentence. "A combination of stimuli which has accompanied a movement will on its recurrence tend to be followed by that movement." (Guthrie, 1935, 1952). If a response occurs in the presence of a stimulus, learning will be complete and automatic. No further practice is necessary, and no reinforcement is necessary.

On the surface, Guthrie's statement seems contrary to the real world. It implies that learning occurs completely in one pairing of the stimulus and the response. Yet we know that in most situations (e.g., a rat pressing a bar for food), the strength of a response seems to grow gradually as practice continues. To resolve this apparent contradiction, Guthrie distinguishes between *acts* and *movements*. Acts are the complex responses we observe and study. Riding a bicycle, discovering a concept, and typing a letter are acts. Each of these total acts is made up of *many different movements*. For example, a movement in bicycle riding might be pushing down with the left foot, or grasping with the right hand. Each individual movement is learned in one trial, although the mastery of the total set of movements may require many trials. To master the total complex act, many different responses must be connected to many different stimulus configurations. THE GRADUAL IMPROVEMENT WITH PRACTICE WHICH WE OBSERVE IS THE RESULT OF A GROWING NUMBER OF LEARNED MOVEMENTS, EACH OF WHICH IS ACQUIRED IN ALL-OR-NONE FASHION.

Estes' Stimulus-Sampling Model

Estes (1959) attempted to translate Guthrie's basic notions into a more formal, mathematical mode of expression. The sketch of the model presented here is a simplified one. Students interested in the many versions and elaborations of statistical learning theory are referred to Atkinson, Bower, and Crothers (1965), Atkinson and Estes (1963), Estes and Suppes (1959), Hilgard and Bower (1975), and Millward (1971).

We may restate Guthrie's original proposition in the following form:

(*1*) If R_1 occurs in the presence of S_1, then R_1 will be connected to S_1 completely and automatically.

(*2*) If a different response (R_2) occurs in the presence of S_1 then R_2 will be completely and automatically connected to S_1, and R_1 will be completely and automatically disconnected from S_1. In other words, a stimulus can only be connected to one response at a time and it will be connected to the most recently occurring response.

(*3*) The probability of a response occurring equals the proportion of stimuli to which it is connected.

Let us try to clarify these statements. The critical point to notice is that the probability of a response occurring equals the proportion of the stimuli to which it is connected. This implies that any given situation in which a response may occur probably consists of many stimuli, each of which may or may not be connected to the response. Imagine the *total* set of stimuli that may impinge upon an animal in the learning situation (say, in a bar press paradigm). Not just the set of stimuli that are actually impinging upon him at any given moment, but the total set containing all the different stimuli that might possibly impinge upon him at different times. These stimuli include all the sights, sounds, smells, odors, and tastes, etc., which may act upon the animal. No one really knows how many there are, nor, for that matter, exactly what they are. This total set of stimuli, which must exist but cannot be measured, is represented at the left of Figure 6.5. Imagine further that some of these many stimuli are already connected to the bar press. Next imagine a subset of stimuli that actually act upon the animal at a given moment. This subset represents a sample drawn from the larger total set. That is, at any given moment, the animal is facing in a particular direction, it is hearing certain sounds, smelling certain odors, etc. The animal cannot experience the total set at any given moment, but does experience a subset of the total set.

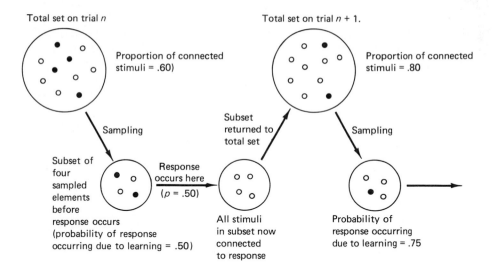

Figure 6.5. The stimulus sampling model. ○ = Stimulus connected to response; ● = Stimulus not connected to response.

    Figure 6.5 contains a very stylized example of the way in which learning progresses in the stimulus-sampling model. Focus upon the first subset of four stimuli drawn from the total set. Two of these stimuli have already been connected to the response and two have not. At this point in time the probability of a response occurring *due to learning* is .50. (The italics are important here for the response may actually occur with a much higher probability. For instance, in classical conditioning the occurrence of the response is assured on every trial by the presence of the UCS. Thus the .50 probability refers to the probability of the response occurring *due to learning* and does not encompass the fact that the UCS evokes the response on each trial.) If the response does occur then the two previously unconnected stimuli become completely con- nected. The four stimuli, now all connected to the response, are returned to the total set. The proportion of conditioned elements in the total set has now increased to .80. On the next trial a second subset is sampled. Because all stimuli are equally likely to be sampled, the proportion of connected stimuli in this second subset is likely to be higher than in the preceding subset. Thus the probability of the response occurring *due to learning* is higher the second time around (.75 in Figure 6.5), and so on. On each successive trial a subset of stimuli is sampled from the total set. If the response occurs, then all the unconnected elements of the subset are connected to the response, and the entire subset is returned to the total set. There is a gradual growth in the proportion of connected stimuli on successive trials. The model, although it considers learning to be an all-or-none event, predicts the incremental result we obtain in the real world. In fact, it predicts a negatively accelerated performance curve as the proportion of connections that can be established on successive trials must eventually decrease as the supply of unconnected stimuli is gradually exhausted.

Having presented the basic Guthrie–Estes position let us spend a little time thinking about the implications of this sort of approach. The stimulus-sampling position can account for the negatively accelerated performance curve. Now let us see how it fares with respect to other common learning phenomena.

Guthrie's Interpretation of Reinforcement

We know from the laboratory that if we reinforce a bar press with food, the probability of that response will increase. It is a fact that reinforcement strengthens behavior. Yet Guthrie states that reinforcement is unnecessary for learning to occur, and he accounts for this apparent contradiction in the following manner. Imagine that a hungry rat has just pressed a lever. Automatically the response is connected to the existing stimulus situation, which consists of the total visual, tactile, auditory, olfactory, and gustatory array. Now if, at this point in time, the rat happens to make another, different response (presumably through the introduction of additional stimuli already connected to that new response) in the presence of our given array (e.g., turning away) then the turning away response will be completely connected to that particular stimulus configuration, and the bar press will become completely disconnected. Guthrie says that the unlearning of the bar press response can be prevented by giving the animal a reinforcement. By presenting food immediately after the bar press has occurred we alter the stimulus situation. We are removing some of the stimuli to which the bar press is connected. The animal sees, smells, and perhaps hears the delivery of the reinforcement. This stimulus complex is quite different from the one impinging upon the animal as he pressed the bar. If another response (e.g., turning away) occurs now it will be connected to the new stimulus array, but not to the stimuli removed by the presentation of the reinforcement. These removed stimuli, the ones connected to the bar press, are still associated with the bar press. They do not become disconnected from the bar press and connected to the turning away response because they were not present when the turning away response occurred. The bar press has been protected. For Guthrie, reinforcement is effective because it removes stimuli and thereby protects associations between stimuli and responses.

This interpretation of reinforcement ties in directly with Guthrie's analysis of the extinction phenomenon. For Guthrie extinction is nothing more than new learning. If we remove the reinforcement from the lever-pressing situation the lever-pressing response will not be protected or preserved. The stimulus situation will not be changed following the lever press. Hence any additional responses made by the animal will become connected to that stimulus situation and will replace the lever press.

A Challenge to Guthrie's Interpretation of Reinforcement

If Guthrie's interpretation of reinforcement is correct, it follows that *anything* that changes the stimulus situation immediately after a response should protect learning. The *Star-Spangled Banner* should work. Seward (1942) ran an interesting experiment which bears upon this issue. In a lever-pressing situation, Seward removed the rats from the box after each response, rather than giving them food. According to Guthrie's position, this should serve to change the stimulus situation even more than the presentation of food. Removal from the box should thus lead to greater improvement than food reinforcement. Seward's results did not confirm Guthrie's position. Rats reinforced with food displayed many more responses than did rats removed from the box. This kind of finding tends to cast serious doubts upon Guthrie's interpretation of reinforcement.

However, the argument does not end yet. One way to circumvent Seward's results is to argue that certain stimuli are more important than others. Removal from the box may change a greater number of stimuli, but it may also change fewer of the most important ones (e.g., those associated with hunger). If we assume the connections between the bar press and hunger stimuli are particularly important in maintaining the behavior, then the presentation of food will change more of these critical stimuli (thereby protecting learning) than will removal from the box. Hence we would expect food reinforcement to lead to more responses than removal from the box.

It is the very vagueness of Guthrie's theory which leads to much of this sort of confusion. The theory has led to a good deal of thinking concerning the nature of learning but, when compared to something like Hullian theory, it has stimulated little rigorous experimentation. We turn now to one type of experimentation which it has stimulated.

Experimental Tests of the Alternative Theories

There have been a number of attempts to pit the all-or-none and incremental positions against one another. Although we will not be able to discuss them all (e.g., Voeks, 1954), two of the more prominent attempts should be mentioned.

In an effort to support Guthrie's position Rock (1957) conducted a paired-associate experiment containing two conditions. In the Non-drop-out condition subjects merely learned a 12-item paired-associate list. Study and test trials were alternated. In the Drop-out condition subjects also learned a 12-item paired-associate list. But in this condition items that were not recalled correctly on the very first recall test were dropped out, or removed, from the list and replaced by new items. All subjects, both Drop-out and Non-drop-out, performed their task until all 12 items were recalled correctly in one recall test. The Non-drop-out subjects began and ended with the same list. The Drop-out lists were altered by the process of dropping out and replacing items that were not recalled correctly on the very first recall test.

If learning occurs in an incremental fashion, then the Non-drop-out subjects should have learned their list more quickly than the Drop-out subjects. Even though an item was not recalled correctly on any given trial, some learning should have been accruing. The subthreshold learning should transfer to, or facilitate, performance on the next recall trial. On the other hand, if Guthrie is correct, and learning occurs in an all-or-none fashion, then the two groups should not have differed in terms of the ease with which they mastered their lists. Rock's results seemed to support Guthrie's position. The mean numbers of trials to criterion was 4.75 for both conditions. Rock concluded that repetition, or practice, prior to the establishment of the connection added nothing to the strength of the association.

Rock's experiment has been thoroughly discredited (Postman, 1962a; Taylor & Irion, 1964; Williams, 1961). Briefly, dropping out items removes difficult items from the list. If an item comes along that the subject cannot master in one trial, the experimenter, in effect, says, "Don't bother about that one. We'll put in another one for you and hope it's easier. If it isn't we'll give you still another, and another, until we find a very easy one." Thus the final lists mastered by the Drop-out subjects were so simple that all the items could be mastered in one trial. Clearly the Drop-out subjects had a distinct advantage over the Non-drop-out subjects who were required to learn a given list regardless of how difficult it was.

This artifact may be negated by (1) using the final lists which evolved in the Drop-out condition as the lists that the Non-drop-out subjects have to learn, or (2) by ensuring that all items, including replacements, are of equal difficulty (this is accomplished by pretesting all items to be used in the experiment). Interestingly, Postman (1962a) corrected the artifact and found support for the incremental position. That is, without the item difficulty artifact operating, Non-drop-out performance was superior to Drop-out performance. What began as an attempt to support the all-or-none position backfired and ended up supporting the opposing viewpoint.

There have been some other, equally interesting attempts to support Guthrie. Estes (1960) ran a study which has often been labeled the RTT experiment (reinforcement, test, test). In this three-stage study, subjects are first given a single exposure to a paired-associate list. This is called the reinforcement phase. The stimuli are then exposed one at a time, without responses, and the subject is asked to recall the correct response. Following the completion of Test 1 subjects are again tested in exactly the same manner (Test 2). The stimuli are again exposed one at a time, without responses.

If the all-or-none position is correct, then *all* of the items that were correct on Test 1 should be recalled correctly on Test 2. Similarly, all items that were not recalled on Test 1 should not be recalled on Test 2. According to Estes the incremental position would be that *some* strength will be built up for *all* items during the reinforcement phase. On Test 1 some of these items will be recalled correctly, not because they are stronger than the others, but because they temporarily oscillate above threshold. This oscillation effect is similar to what we experience when we can remember something one moment, but cannot quite seem to get it out the next. On Test 2 different items may oscillate above threshold. Items recalled correctly on Test 1 may or may not be recalled correctly on Test 2. Items not recalled correctly on Test 1 may well be recalled correctly on Test 2. The pattern of Estes's results seems to support Guthrie. That is, items correct on Test 1 were extremely likely to be recalled on Test 2. Items incorrect on Test 1 were almost never recalled correctly on Test 2.

Unfortunately, other investigators have raised problems and reached different conclusions using this type of design (e.g., Battig, 1968; Jones, 1962). Underwood and Keppel (1962) point out that if we assume that the increments established for items recalled correctly on Test 1 are *larger* than the increments established for items not recalled correctly on Test 1, then Estes's results will be predicted by the incremental position. In addition, Underwood and Keppel showed that items never recalled correctly in this type of design will, in subsequent tests, be easier to learn than entirely new items. This suggests that there was some strengthening of the associations during initial training even though the strength was not enough to allow the items to be recalled.

What, After All, Is One Trial?

The conclusion we can reach after all this is that conclusive evidence for the all-or-none position is lacking. We can see why the controversy remains: It is difficult to imagine an experiment that will clearly judge the two theories. No one has been successful yet. One of the problems inherent in many of these comparative experiments has to do with the nature of "the trial." What is one trial? Is it one presentation of the stimulus and the response by the experimenter? Is it one subvocal rehearsal by the subject? Is it one, but only one, firing of some complex, unknown sequence of neural activities? These questions are seldom addressed in all-or-none research. For example, in both the Rock and the Estes experiments there is the implicit assumption that one presentation of the materials represents, or corresponds to, a single occurrence of the response in the presence of the stimulus. And yet, if we look a little closer, it seems these experiments must involve multiple repetitions or rehearsals. If we present a stimulus and a response to a subject for 2 seconds, more than likely he rehearses the pair as many times, and in as many ways, as he can before the next pair appears. Humans are certainly capable of several such mental rehearsals in 2 seconds. Hence, neither the Rock nor the Estes experiments control for number of rehearsals. They do not restrict the subject to a single rehearsal.

Two-Step Models

All-or-none models do sometimes generate accurate predictions (e.g., Bower, 1961, 1962; Kintsch, 1964; Suppes & Ginsberg, 1962), there can be no doubt about that. But the applicability of the all-or-none models has been limited (Hilgard & Bower, 1975). One possible response to the fact that all-or-none models are not perfect is to discard them and seek alternative ways of thinking about learning. Another alternative is to modify the all-or-none approach. The development of two-step models represents such an alternative (Bower & Theios, 1964; Estes & DaPolito, 1967). According to this position, learning does not leap from 0 to 100% in a single bound. Instead, it occurs in two steps as illustrated in Figure 6.6. In the simplest two-step model, response probability is presumed to remain at 0 until it jumps, in an all-or-none fashion to, say, .50. It remains at .50 until it completes the move, again in an all-or-none

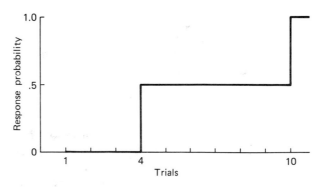

Figure 6.6. Example of an individual learning function for a two-step model.

fashion, to 1.0. The two-step model involves three states; complete lack of learning, some intermediate level of learning, and complete learning. The exact nature of each of these states and, for that matter, the numbers of states and steps are all open to question at the present time.

The two-step model represents a compromise between the all-or-none and the incremental positions. We can see that the three conceptions of learning represent different points along a single continuum. At one end of the continuum we have the notion that learning is accomplished completely in one step. At the other end, learning is conceived of as a process involving a large number of tiny little increments. Between these two positions we have all sorts of possibilities involving any number of states and steps.

It seems the controversy may be a matter of degree rather than kind. Everyone would agree learning moves forward. The confusion comes when we try to decide how many steps and stages are involved in that movement. In the final analysis, it may not be a question of whether the incremental or the all-or-none position is correct. The nature of the relationship between practice and learning may depend upon the learning situation. In some cases, particularly very simple ones, learning may well progress in a fashion best described as an all-or-none process. In other, perhaps more complicated situations, learning might best be described as an incremental process. The controversy began in the 1930s (Krechevsky, 1932), and it continues today in such diverse areas as partial reinforcement (Koteskey, 1972; Koteskey & Hendrix, 1971) and discrimination learning (Biederman, 1970; Wolford & Bower, 1969). The most reasonable position to assume at present is that neither conception is totally adequate, nor totally without value.

PATTERNS OF PRACTICE

The all-or-none versus incremental learning controversy may thus be laid to rest, at least temporarily. Although the theoretical distinctions remain clear, attempts to resolve the issue experimentally have not been particularly elucidating. Presumably the issue is not dead, for psychology has a way of revisiting unresolved issues when new developments in the technology of experimentation warrant such a return. We simply have to wait until someone develops a better way of examining the issue.

The study of practice in learning forges ahead in other areas. The role of practice is so basic to the understanding of learning, so inherent in so many areas of endeavor, that it would be impossible to describe all of those areas here. We shall return to the role of practice many times. For now, mention of a few selected areas should suffice.

The emphasis today is not so much upon whether or not practice helps learning but upon how LEARNING VARIES AS THE CONDITIONS OF

PRACTICE VARY. There are an enormous number of ways in which practice may vary. For example, suppose we wish to master a foreign language vocabulary list. We could rehearse the list rapidly or very slowly, in a constant or varied order, with the TV on or off, in the presence of others or alone, silently or aloud. We could reward ourselves for learning each item or for mastering the entire list. We could punish ourselves for missing an item, and so on. We could attempt to practice the list all at once or take it in segments. The possibilities seem unlimited.

For coverage of some of these topics the interested reader is referred to Cole and Kanak (1972), Hopkins, Boylan, and Lincoln (1972), Hopkins and Epling (1971), Postman, Burns, and Hasher (1970), Postman and Goggin (1966), Mandler and Dean (1969), McGeoch (1931), Seagoe (1936), Tragash and Newman (1967), and Wallace (1969). For our purposes, the following sections deal with some selected issues related to patterns of practice.

The Total Time Law

The total time law refers to the idea that the amount of learning that will occur in a given time interval is constant, regardless of how that time is spent in rehearsing. In other words, if we study a list of 10 words for 1 minute we will learn the same amount, regardless of how we spend the study time. It should not make much difference whether we go over the list six times, spending 1 second on each item each time through the list, or go through the list only once spending 6 massed seconds on each item. Bugelski (1962) presented evidence that supports the total time law. He found that the total time required to learn a given list was unaffected by the rate at which the items were presented within that total time. Since Bugelski's early work, many investigations have supported and elaborated upon the total time law (Baumeister & Kistler, 1974; Cooper & Pantle, 1967; Zacks, 1969). It is an interesting idea because it suggests that, so long as we are working, the patterns of our rehearsal are unimportant.

Massed versus Distributed Practice:
A Challenge to the Total Time Law

The study of massed practice (MP) versus distributed practice (DP) has a long history. As we shall see, it bears directly upon the total time law. For the moment, let us review the MP–DP area. In its simplest form, the MP–DP controversy is this: If our practice trials are spaced, or separated in time, will learning be more or less efficient than if we bunch our practice trials together? If we have 6 hours to study for three exams should we give each topic 2 consecutive hours, or should we give each topic eight 15-minute segments separated by intervals during which we study one of the alternative topics? The most common hypothesis has been that DP will be superior to MP. Early experimental data bearing upon this issue were extremely complicated, and often contradictory (see Archer, 1954; Jung & Bailey, 1966; Kimble, 1949; Underwood, 1961). But more recent investigations have begun to yield consistent MP–DP effects. Melton (1970) points out that these new and significant MP–DP effects began to appear as new verbal tasks were developed. For example DP have proved to be superior to MP in "continuous paired-associate learning" (Calfee, 1968; Landauer, 1969; Peterson, Wampler, Kirkpatrick, & Saltzman, 1963; Young, 1966). In this type of task the subject is given a list of paired items of indefinite length. Within the list, a given pair may be presented twice and then tested by providing the stimulus alone. The number of items that intervene between the two presentations of the critical item may be varied by the experimenter. Thus the first and second presentations of a given pair might be separated by five, or ten, intervening items (distributed practice) or they might be presented back-to-back (massed practice). The most common finding is that, up to a certain point, distributed practice yields better recall than massed practice. The effect is limited by certain constraints, but it is reliable and does seem to be quite consistent when compared to the earlier efforts.

Significant MP–DP effects have also appeared in free-recall learning situations (Madigan, 1969; Underwood, 1970; Waugh, 1970). If you will recall, items in this type of experiment are presented in a random order and the subject is asked to recall them in any order. Although there have been exceptions (Waugh, 1967), the general finding is that recall of items presented twice is better if the two presentations are separated by one or more intervening items. Again DP seems to be superior to MP.

Melton's Lag Effect

Melton (1970) has labeled these free-recall effects the lag effect. As can be seen in Figure 6.7 the effect refers to the fact that the probability of recalling a repeated item in free recall is positively related to the number of intervening items. The further apart the two presentations of the repeated item the better the recall of that item.

Although there have been other interpretations of the lag effect (e.g., Greeno, 1970), one of the more popular ones has to do with the subject's ability to code the item in a context of other items (D'Agostino & DeRemer, 1973; Elmes, Greener, & Wilkinson, 1972; Gartman & Johnson, 1972). If the two presentations of the critical item are separated by other items then each presentation of the critical item occurs in a

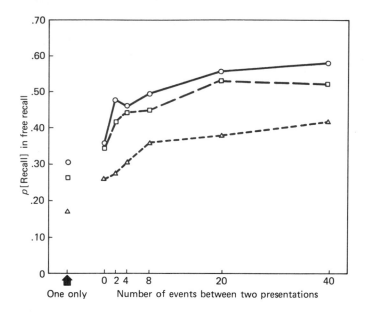

Figure 6.7. Probability of recall of words that occur once or twice, with varying numbers of other words occurring between the two presentations of a given word. Presentation rates: ◯ = 4.3 seconds; ☐ = 2.3 seconds; △ = 1.3 seconds. (Adapted from Melton, A. W. The situation with respect to the spacing of repetitions and memory. *Journal of Verbal Learning and Verbal Behavior,* 1970, *9,* 596–606. Fig. 1, p. 602.)

unique verbal context, and is surrounded by a variety of different items. The subject can associate the critical item with these different contexts, thereby enriching his coding of the critical item. Massed presentations, on the other hand, represent a reduction in the richness and variety of the context in which the critical item is to be learned. Both presentations occur in the same context.

Relevance of the MP–DP Effect for the Total Time Law

It is fairly obvious at this point that the discovery of significant MP–DP effects goes against the total time law. The total time law would argue against any differences between MP and DP. So long as the total study times remain constant, spacing or massing practice should make no difference. The data just outlined directly contradict this prediction. The patterns of practice do affect learning. The total time law, which has been widely accepted, appears to be more limited than previously believed.

Students often ask if the MP–DP effect means that we should distribute our practice, say, when we study for exams. It is probably too early to be definite about this sort of thing. Although DP has been shown to be superior to MP, one must remember that these effects have been obtained with very limited kinds of tasks in very limited experimental situations. Whether the effects can be generalized to situations outside the laboratory remains to be seen.

CONCLUSION

The role of practice has been of critical importance in the study of learning. Early efforts were directed toward a resolution of the all-or-none versus incremental learning controversy. Experimental solutions to this knotty problem are still lacking.

Additional research has indicated that variations in the pattern and type of practice strongly affect amount of learning. Learning varies with the *nature* of practice as well as the *amount* of practice. Such developments as the apparent failure of the total time law and the discovery of significant MP–DP effects clearly indicate that, even if the incremental position is correct, a simple incremental interpretation will not suffice. The growth of learning has been shown to be strongly affected by the quality as well as the quantity of practice.

SUMMARY

1. The negatively accelerated learning curve is common, but it is not the only curve that appears in our research.

2. So-called LEARNING CURVES are not learning curves at all. They are performance curves, and their form is determined by both learning and motivation.

3. We try to infer amount of learning from a wide range of performance measures including such factors as running speed, response latency, resistance to extinction, number of correct responses, and trials to criterion.

4. When choosing a performance measure we must be sure it is: (*a*) reliable and (*b*) that it reflects learning at all levels.

5. Individual performance data are often so variable we are forced to average scores to obtain a clear picture of the stable trends underlying variable individual behaviors.

6. Depending upon our purposes we may smooth our curves by combining scores from a number of individuals on each trial, by combining scores from adjacent trials, or by combining scores obtained from a single

individual run through the task several times. CUMULATIVE LEARNING CURVES and BACKWARD LEARNING CURVES also represent popular ways of displaying data.

7. Although learning curves present data in a clear, simple fashion no one curve can tell the whole story. A given curve merely represents one vantage point from which we may view our data. Examples of the ways in which averaging techniques may distort our data are discussed.

8. The INCREMENTAL and ALL-OR-NONE CONCEPTIONS of learning are considered. Hull's incremental system was designed to explain all behaviors of all species. Although the theory has been extremely influential, few psychologists have been willing to accept the specificity with which Hull wished to quantify the conditions of behavior.

9. Stripped of its detail Hull's system assumes behavior to be a function of at least five major variables. DRIVE, a motivational factor, is measured in terms of time of deprivation and/or extent of noxious stimulation. HABIT refers to how much the organism has learned about a particular situation through reinforced responding. INCENTIVE MOTIVATION is measured in terms of the quantity and quality of the reward. As STIMULUS INTENSITY increases the probability of the response increases. INHIBITION, which detracts from the tendency to respond, is measured in terms of how much work is involved in making the response and how many times the animal has made the response.

10. Reinforcement in Hull's system refers to the rapid diminution of drive. HABIT is a negatively accelerated function of the number of reinforced responses.

11. The ALL-OR-NONE position is illustrated by Guthrie's theory and Estes' stimulus sampling model. Guthrie's theory may be summed up by saying, "A combination of stimuli which has accompanied a movement will on its recurrence tend to be followed by that movement." Acts, or the total behaviors we observe and study, are made up of many movements. The gradual improvement in an act is the result of an increase in the number of these small movements which are each learned in an all-or-none fashion.

12. Estes' STIMULUS SAMPLING model represents an attempt to translate Guthrie's basic notions into a more formal, mathematical form. According to Estes response probability equals the proportion of stimuli to which it is connected. "Learning" refers to the gradual growth in the proportion of stimuli connected to the response over successive trials.

13. For Guthrie, reinforcement is effective because it removes stimuli and thereby protects associations between stimuli and responses. Extinction merely refers to new learning.

14. Several investigators, including Rock and Estes, have unsuccessfully attempted to find conclusive experimental support for the all-or-none position. These experiments do not control for numbers of rehearsals.

15. Two-stage models represent a compromise between all-or-none and incremental models.

16. Much current research centers not so much on whether or not practice helps learning but upon how learning varies as the conditions of practice vary.

17. The TOTAL TIME LAW states that the amount of learning which will occur in a given time interval is constant, regardless of how that time is spent rehearsing.

18. The fact that distributed, or spaced, practice has been shown to yield better learning than massed practice (at least in continuous paired-associate, and free-recall learning) suggests that the total time law may be more limited than previously believed.

19. Melton's LAG EFFECT refers to the finding that the probability of recall of a repeated item in free recall is positively related to the number of intervening items.

Reinforcement

OPERATIONAL AND THEORETICAL DEFINITIONS

On an operational level, there is very little disagreement about the nature of reinforcers. Reinforcers are defined in terms of their effects. Any stimulus is a reinforcer if it increases the strength of a response. If you will recall, we distinguished between positive and negative reinforcers in Chapter Two. A positive reinforcer is anything that will, when presented to the animal, increase the probability of the response occurring (e.g., food, sex). Negative reinforcers are anything that will, when taken away from the animal, increase the probability of the response (e.g., shock). Reinforcers, both positive and negative, increase response probability.

That seems to be the limit of common agreement. At this point, opinions concerning the nature of reinforcement begin to diverge. As soon as we begin to ask *why* reinforcers reinforce we lose any semblance of unanimity. For example, we have already seen that Hull (1943) thought of reinforcement in terms of the rapid diminution of drive level, whereas Guthrie (1952) conceived of the effects of reinforcers in terms of changed stimulus arrays. At an even earlier date, Thorndike (1913) defined reinforcement and punishment in terms of satisfying and annoying states of affairs. According to Thorndike, S–R connections are strengthened if the occurrence of the response is followed by a satisfying state of affairs, and weakened if followed by an annoying state of affairs. In an attempt to avoid circularity in his definitions, Thorndike independently defined a satisfying state of affairs as one that the animal does nothing to avoid, and often attempts to maximize. An annoying state of affairs is one that the animal attempts to terminate. As a final example of the diverse kinds of thinking that have developed around the concept of reinforcement we might note Skinner's position. Skinner (1953) apparently wants to limit the debate by focusing upon the operational definition just outlined. He does not seem interested in the *why* question, and does not want to theorize. Skinner is willing to restrict his attention to *how* behavior changes, and to *how* it can be modified. This limited objective, or goal, may be obtained without going into detail concerning the underlying nature of reinforcement. He, in effect, argues that so long as we can identify reinforcers, and know how to apply them, we need not worry too much about why they reinforce behavior.

With these brief examples we can begin to see the extent of the controversy surrounding the theoretical nature of reinforcement. We shall return to these traditional theories, and to the newer varieties, in a later section. For now, let us focus our attention upon some empirical questions that do not require the adoption of one or the other of these various theoretical positions. We shall hold off on the theoretical controversy and attempt to outline some of the more important *parameters* of reinforcement.

PARAMETERS OF REINFORCEMENT

Imagine a hungry rat in a Skinner box. Imagine a student in a college course. Each creature can be induced to acquire more or less complicated responses through the application of certain reinforcers. The rat will work for food, whereas grades and/or praise and satisfaction will be sufficient to reinforce the student. There are many attributes, or characteristics, of these kinds of reinforcing situations that can be varied. One of the most obvious factors is the AMOUNT OF REWARD presented immediately following the occurrence of a response. The rat might receive one, two, three, or more food pellets following a correct response. The student might be heartily praised for a correct response, or he might receive nothing more than a curt nod from the instructor. It is not unreasonable to suspect that these kinds of variations would be important in learning. A second major factor has to do with the time between the occurrence of the response and the receipt of the reward, or the DELAY OF REINFORCEMENT. The rat might receive his reinforcement immediately after making the response, or he might be forced to wait 10 seconds, 20 seconds, or even longer, before receiving his reward. Similarly, the student might be praised immediately during class, or the teacher might wait until after class to deliver the praise. Although these are crude examples, we can begin to see the potential importance of the delay of reinforcement factor. Finally, we may reinforce every response our subject makes, but we need not. We can *partially* reinforce the subject, or reinforce something less than every response. For example, we might want to set up a SCHEDULE OF REINFORCEMENT, wherein we only reinforce every second, or third, or fourth, or nth response, leaving the remainder of the responses unreinforced. Intuitively one would expect learning to be strongly affected by manipulations involving the schedule of reinforcement.

These three factors (*amount, delay,* and *schedules* of reinforcement) have emerged as critical parameters of reinforcement. We shall deal with each of them individually.

Schedules of Reinforcement

Continuous reinforcement (CRF) refers to situations in which every response is reinforced. As we have noted, we need not reinforce every response our laboratory subject makes. We are free to present reinforcements in any pattern we wish. We may reinforce any portion of the occurring responses. Continuous reinforcement is probably the exception rather than the rule in the real world. When a kitten is learning to pounce on moving objects it is far from completely successful in its early attempts. As a youngster learns to play basketball he misses more baskets than he makes. And yet these behaviors are learned. Continuous reinforcement is not necessary for learning to occur (even though it is often used in the laboratory). The study of schedules of reinforcement is concerned with the impact of these patterns of partial reinforcement upon the acquisition of behaviors and represents the formalized investigation of everyday patterns of reinforcement and their effects upon behavior.

Potential variations in schedules of reinforcement are almost unlimited. We shall mention but a few of the more basic varieties. The student interested in pursuing schedules of reinforcement is referred to Ferster and Skinner (1957), Honig (1966), Karen (1974), Williams (1973) and *The Journal of the Experimental Analysis of Behavior.*

Fixed-Interval Schedule

In a fixed-interval (FI) schedule the animal is reinforced for the first response which occurs after the end of a given time interval. For example, in an FI 3 schedule the animal is reinforced for the first response he makes after 3 minutes have elapsed since his last reinforced response. He must then wait another 3 minutes before he can obtain another reinforcement. He is free to respond during the 3 minute intervals but he will not be reinforced for these responses. The very first response following the end of the interval is the only one that is reinforced.

An FI schedule of reinforcement leads to a very specific kind of responding. The animal develops a response strategy to fit the reinforcement schedule. A reasonable strategy for an FI schedule would be to pause after the receipt of the reinforcement, as there is no need to respond continuously, and then, as the end of the interval approaches, respond more and more frequently. This is exactly the kind of responding we observe in laboratory animals. Long pauses follow reinforcements. The rate of responding accelerates as the end of the interval approaches. As can be seen in Figure 7.1 a characteristic "scalloping" effect is observed in the cumulative records of FI schedules.

In a very rough way, students' studying behavior sometimes follows this pattern. Suppose a given class has a midterm and a final exam. These exams represent reinforcing events (positive or negative, depending upon how you look at them). Many students do very little studying as the semester begins. As the midterm approaches studying behavior picks up until, just before the exam, it reaches a high rate. After the exam it drops to zero and remains there only to accelerate again as the final approaches. Obviously, not all students study in this manner, and, obviously, not all materials are handled in this fashion (for example, students may be less likely to "scallop" their reading assignments than they are the memorization of lecture notes). But there is an interesting, and quite striking, correspondence between the effects of FI schedules and the effects of our traditional examination patterns.

It might be argued that "mail-checking behavior" also resembles behavior under the control of an FI schedule. If we know the mailman arrives promptly at noon we do not begin to look for him at 8 A.M. As noon approaches we begin to look, listen, and check the mailbox. After the delivery arrives there is very little chance we will check again until the next day.

As a final example, Weisberg and Waldrop (1972) have presented

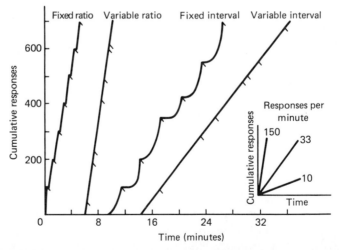

Figure 7.1. Stylized cumulative response records obtained under four common schedules of reinforcement. Slash marks in the records indicate presentations of reinforcements. (Adapted from *Operant Learning: Procedures for Changing Behavior* by J. L. Williams. Copyright © 1973 by Wadsworth Publishing Company, Inc. Reprinted by permission of the publisher, Brooks/Cole Publishing Company, Monterey, California.)

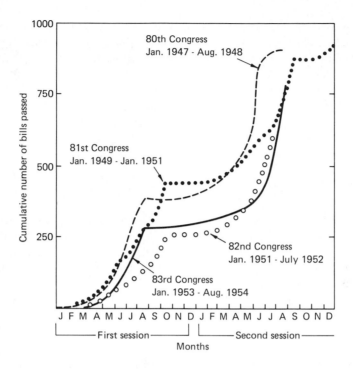

Figure 7.2. Fixed interval work habits of Congress. (Adapted from Weisberg, P., & Waldrop, P. B. Fixed-interval work habits of Congress. *Journal of Applied Behavior Analysis,* 1972, *5,* 43–97. Fig. 1, p. 94).

an amusing analysis of the bill-passing behavior of the U.S. Congress. As can be seen in Figure 7.2 Congress passes very few bills during the first few months of a given session. As the time for adjournment approaches the rate of bill passage accelerates—just like a rat in a Skinner box, scalloping and all. Actually, the similarity between the two situations may be more fanciful than real, for we know very little about the pressures upon Congress that produce this pattern of behavior. As Lundin (1974) suggests, the scalloping could be due to the increasing demands of various lobbies, special interest groups and powerful constituents.

The Variable-Interval Schedule

In a variable-interval (VI) schedule the animal is again forced to wait for a time before it can obtain a reinforcement, but the time interval is variable in this schedule. After the animal has responded and been reinforced it might have to wait for 5 minutes before being able to receive a reward. Then it might have to wait for 3 minutes, and then 30 seconds, and so on. A VI 2 schedule would be one in which the *average* time interval between reinforcement is 2 minutes.

It seems steady responding is the most efficient in this case (see Figure 7.1). As the subject is unable to judge the length of the time intervals he cannot pause as he does in the FI situation. He must constantly "check in" with a steady stream of responses. As one would expect, the response rate will be high if a short average interval is employed and lower if a longer average interval is utilized.

Some types of still fishermen might well operate under a VI schedule. They drop their lines in and wait. They do not know when the fish will bite, if at all, but they check their lines regularly and steadily.

The Fixed-Ratio Schedule

In a fixed-ratio (FR) schedule (e.g., Hobson, 1975), the animal must make a certain number of responses before it is rewarded. In an FR 10 schedule the pigeon must peck the key 10 times before being reinforced. This schedule yields extremely high rates of responding (see Figure 7.1). The animal responds rapidly until it receives its reinforcement. Interestingly, the FR schedule often produces a mild postreinforcement pause. It is not nearly so pronounced as the scalloping effect obtained with FI schedules, but it is a definite characteristic of the FR schedule. The higher the ratio, the longer the postreinforcement pause.

Men and women doing piecework in factories find themselves required to process large numbers of units for a certain amount of pay—the more they process the greater their pay. They are working under an FR schedule. In the old "sweat shop" days, unscrupulous employers would require a certain number of units for a certain amount of pay. Once that level of responding was obtained they would raise the ratio, forcing the worker to produce more and more for the same amount of pay. It is easy to understand why organized labor has often opposed piecework.

Extremely high fixed ratios can be established by gradually increasing the number of responses required for a reward; it cannot be done all in one step. Findley and Brady (1965) describe an experiment in which 120,000 responses were required before a chimpanzee received food. Of course, this is an extreme example, and most situations, both inside and outside the laboratory, involve much smaller ratios.

The Variable-Ratio Schedule

In the variable-ratio (VR) schedule the number of responses required of the subject varies. A rat may first be required to press a lever 10 times for a reward. Then 3 responses may be required, then 7, then 4, and so on. In a VR 20 schedule, the *average* number of required responses is 20. This schedule also produces extremely high rates of responding. The principal difference between this schedule and the FR schedule is the absence of the postreinforcement pause in the VR situation. Variable ratio responding is strong and steady.

The most striking examples of VR scheduling outside the laboratory come from the world of gambling. When the little old school teacher stands in front of a slot machine in Las Vegas punching in nickels for hours on end she is in the grip of a VR schedule. The machine is programmed to pay off after irregular numbers of responses. Some machines pay off quite frequently, especially in casinos where the customer's quick return is desired. Jackpots obtained all over the casino are announced over a loudspeaker in order to create the impression of a more favorable ratio. Slot machines located in spots where the customer is unlikely to return (e.g., airports, bus terminals) are probably programmed to pay off only rarely.

Every year the Girl Scouts come round with their boxes of cookies. Every year, damp, eager little Cub Scouts show up at the door with tickets to the annual Scout-o-rama. These children may be under the spell of a VR schedule. They must ring door bells to sell, but they do not know how many they will have to ring before they make a sale. Sitting at home waiting for the end of an interval will not make sales either. They have to make variable numbers of responses to sell. What makes it worse is that they know every other member of their organization is out there doing the same thing, raising the ratio minute by minute.

Multiple Schedules

Multiple schedules consist of two or more simple schedules presented one after the other. In addition, distinctive cues, such as colored lights, are associated with, or presented during, each of the simple phases. For example, suppose a pigeon is pecking a key for food under a *mult* FI 3 VR 10 schedule. What this means is that he is first trained under an FI schedule. Some cue, such as a red light, is present while the bird is undergoing training. When the schedule is shifted to VR 10, the red light is replaced by, say, a green light. Each time the schedule is changed the cue is changed.

As one might expect, the animal shifts its pattern of responding as the schedule shifts. But it is not a simple situation. The animal's responding under any given schedule is often affected by the nature of the preceding schedule. Multiple schedules involve complicated interaction effects. Although beyond the scope of this text, the nature of these complex interactions have recently come under rather intense investigation (e.g., Green & Rachlin, 1975; Keller, 1974; Nevin, 1974a,b; Richards, 1974).

The *mixed schedule* is a variation of the multiple schedule in which no external cues (e.g., colors) are associated with the schedules. The shift from one schedule to another can only be detected from the changed patterns of reinforcement. As expected, this often reduces the ease or efficiency with which the animal shifts from one form of responding to the next.

Chained Schedules

In chained schedules (e.g., Davidson, 1974; Miller, 1975) two or more successive schedules *must* be completed before a reinforcement can be obtained. For example in an FI 5 FR 10 chained schedule the animal must first respond after 5 minutes have elapsed and must then give 10 responses regardless of their timing before it will be reinforced.

In chained schedules external stimuli (e.g., colors) are associated with each successive phase in the chain. *Tandem schedules* (e.g., Weisman & Davis, 1975) are the same as chained schedules except that there are no such changes in external stimuli when the successive phases are completed. Thus, in tandem schedules, the animal is not provided with information concerning the completion of successive phases.

Autoshaping

To this point, we have noted that there are many different types of schedules, each producing its own characteristic pattern of behavior. Ferster and Skinner (1957) list at least 16 different varieties and document the patterns of behavior which will be obtained with each one.

There is an interesting variation on the theme of schedules of reinforcement which may turn out to be extremely important. Autoshaping (Brown & Jenkins, 1968; Gamzu & Schwam, 1974; Jenkins & Moore, 1973; Wasserman & Molina, 1975) refers to what happens when reinforcement is presented regardless of whether or not the animal responds. In a typical autoshaping experiment, the illumination of a key is always followed by food delivery. Thus a hungry pigeon need not respond at all in this situation. All it has to do is wait until the key lights up and then eat the food, which always follows the light. And yet it has been observed that the pigeon does peck the key. The key-pecking response develops even though it is not necessary for the receipt of a reward.

This effect, although quite controversial (see Wessells, 1974), calls into question the very nature of what is normally called instrumental conditioning. What it suggests is that there is a strong element of classical conditioning in the typical instrumental conditioning situation. It also suggests that, to some extent, responses such as the key peck develop independent of any reinforcing event. The UCS is the food. The food (UCS) automatically elicits a pecking response (the UCR). The UCS (food) is paired with a CS (the light). After a series of such pairings the CS (light) comes to elicit a CR (pecking in response to the light), which resembles the UCR (pecking in response to the food).

This all goes back to the problem we outlined in an earlier chapter. The distinction between classical and instrumental conditioning is difficult to maintain. The autoshaping effect suggests that classical conditioning is so intertwined with even the simplest instrumental conditioning situation that it is impossible to conclude that we ever have a pure case of classical or instrumental conditioning.

Automaintenance

Automaintenance (Gamzu & Schwam, 1974; Williams & Williams, 1969) is an even more unusual effect involving an unusual schedule of reinforcement. Williams and Williams (1969) set up their experiment such that the illumination of a key was always followed by food. But if the pigeon pecked the key, the light went out and food was not presented. In other words the response resulted in nonreinforcement. *Not* responding to the lit key insured the receipt of food. They found that some of the birds would peck away at the light despite the fact that such responses guaranteed nonreinforcement.

Hursh, Navarick, and Fantino (1974) have taken some steps to clear up this mystery. They note that every time the animal pecks the lit key, the light goes out. They suggest that it may be light offset which is reinforcing the pecking response. It has long been known that light offset and onset can be reinforcing (see Kish, 1955). Accordingly they set up their apparatus such that pecking the lit key removed the possibility of food reinforcement but did not terminate the light. Under these conditions the automaintenance effect disappeared, suggesting that it is, after all, light offset that maintains this mysterious response.

Schedule of Reinforcement and Human Behavior

Acquisition: Humans and Animals

Most of the schedules and data we have discussed have been developed using "lower" animals. It may legitimately be asked if the same kinds of effects will always be obtained with humans. The answer varies depending upon the psychologist with whom you converse and upon the task involved. The position taken in this text is that there is quite good, though not perfect, correspondence between the patterns obtained with animals and humans. For example, Yukl, Wexley, and Seymore (1972) reinforced the scoring of IBM answer cards with either continuous reinforcement or aVR 2 schedule. The pattern of their results tended to agree with the data obtained in animal experiments. Using mentally deficient children, candy as reinforcement, and a variety of schedules, Orlando and Bijou (1960) found the behaviors generated by their selected schedules were quite similar to those obtained with experimental animals. Verplanck (1956) presents data suggesting that normal college students act very much like experimental animals when subjected to various scheduling manipulations. In a more recent study, Davidson and Grayson Osborne (1974) conclude that children's behaviors under FR and FI schedules are similar to those obtained with animals. Karen (1974) presents an interesting analysis of chaining behavior in humans which resembles that observed in animals. Thus there is substantial evidence for the notion that we are learning something about humans when we manipuate schedules of reinforcement with animals.

Of course, as one might expect, there are exceptions to this tidy correspondence between animal and human behavior. For example, in investigating human choice behavior, Schmitt (1974) has been led to suggest that humans and animals differ quite markedly in terms of their responses to variations in rate of reinforcement.

Extinction: The "Partial Reinforcement Effect"

So far we have been speaking of the relationship between schedules of reinforcement and the acquisition process. We will now look at how extinction is related to schedules of reinforcement. One of the most widely noted phenomena in the field of learning is the fact that resistance to extinction following partial reinforcement is greater than resistance to extinction following continuous reinforcement (Lewis, 1960). All four of the simple schedules (VI, FI, VR, FR) produce greater resistance to extinction than does continuous reinforcement (CRF). Although we will not deal with these points in detail it should be noted that (1) each of the four simple schedules produces its own characteristic pattern of responding during extinction (see Williams, 1973), and (2) there have been attempts to theorize about the partial reinforcement effect (e.g., Mowrer & Jones, 1945). What we are primarily concerned with here is the fact that all partial schedules yield greater resistance to extinction than does CRF. The question we wish to ask is this: Does the partial reinforcement effect appear with humans as well as with experimental animals? The answer is that the available results are inconclusive. On the positive side, we have reports that resistance to extinction is greater following partial reinforcement when the subjects are children and the responses are such things as pressing down the nose of a clown and placing rubber balls in holes (Bijou, 1957a,b). Furthermore Brackbill (1958) found learned smiling responses in infants to be more resistant to extinction following partial reinforcement.

On the other hand there have been some failures to obtain the partial reinforcement effect in human situations. For example, Keppel, Zavortink, and Shiff (1967) attempted to demonstrate the effect in a paired-associate situation. Subjects first learned a paired-associate list under varying schedules of reinforcement. A reinforcement was defined in terms of response confirmation. It was assumed that the subject would be reinforced if he were informed that his response was correct. Correct responses that were not confirmed as correct were assumed to be unreinforced. The authors then attempted to extinguish the lists. Contrary to their expectations partially reinforced lists were no more resistant to extinction than continuously reinforced lists. Although this may be taken as a failure to find the partial reinforcement effect in a human conditioning situation one should exercise caution in adopting such an interpretation. This failure might be due to procedural and methodological shortcomings rather than to any real difference between animals and humans. For example, Silverstein (1967) has been successful in obtaining the partial reinforcement effect in a similar paired-associate situation.

In summary, it may be argued that the similarities between human and animal responses to schedule manipulations outweigh the differences. Failures to find similar effects may be due to methodological differences between animal and human experiments. Some failures may be due to our inability to define and adequately control reinforcements in human situations. When we deprive a rat of food for 12 hours we can be fairly sure he will be operating in the service of that need. But if we deprived a normal, devilish college sophomore of food for 12 hours we could not be sure what he would be thinking and doing. We could not be sure his main interest would be in obtaining food. It is not unreasonable to assume that at least one of our subjects would be more interested in proving he *didn't* need food than in obtaining food. He might reinforce himself each time he did not take food. Self-reinforcement is a viable concept in the study of human reinforcement (see Marston, 1969; Speidel, 1974).

In view of this complex unpredictability on the part of the human it is not surprising that our animal and human data do not always look alike. Failures to find similarities between animal and human behavior may not be due to any basic differences in the underlying mechanisms of learning. They may be due to our ignorance of the multiple interests and purposes of the complex human.

Delay of Reinforcement

The investigation of delay of reinforcement began decades ago (e.g., Skinner, 1938; Wolfe, 1934) and continues into the present (e.g., Culbertson, 1970; Keesey, 1964; Richards, 1974). If the time between a response and the subsequent delivery of the reinforcement is increased, then learning tends to be inhibited. If a rat is forced to wait for his reward after

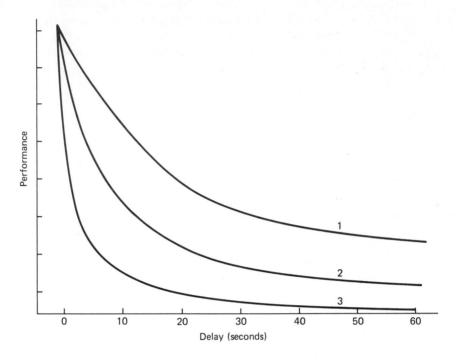

Figure 7.3. Some hypothetical delay of reinforcement gradients.

each lever press it will learn the response much less quickly than if it were reinforced immediately after each response. If a child is rewarded immediately for picking up his toys he will be more likely to learn than if he is forced to wait until the end of the week for his reward. If the reward is delayed too long, learning may not occur at all. The relationship between delay of reinforcement and learning tends to assume a character-istic form. Figure 7.3 contains several stylized DELAY OF REINFORCEMENT GRADIENTS. Two things should be noted about these gradients. First, per-formance drops off rapidly as the delay increases. Second, even though it does drop off *some* performance gains do occur even under conditions of delayed reinforcement. Most of the experimental work has involved delays from several seconds to several minutes. Under some conditions delays of a few seconds can eliminate learning, whereas, under other conditions, long delays have little effect upon performance. Let us turn to a consideration of why these differential effects appear.

Delay of Reinforcement and the Role of Secondary Reinforcers

Over the years, a little story has developed concerning delay of rein-forcement effects. In a very early experiment Watson (1917) trained rats to dig down through sawdust to reach a cup containing food. Half the animals were permitted to consume the reward immediately. The other half were required to wait for 30 seconds before eating the food. Surprisingly, Watson found no differences between the two groups in terms of their digging performances. Delaying the reinforcement for 30 seconds did not hinder learning in the slightest. One obvious reason why this occurred has to do with the fact that the delayed animals waited in the vicinity of the food cup. They could smell the food and see the cup, which they associated with food. In other words, the presentation of the cues which the animal *associated* with food (smell, sight) probably reinforced the digging response *immediately*.

These cues (smell, sight of cup), which the animal associated with the primary reinforcer (food), are called *secondary reinforcers*. A secondary reinforcer is a neutral stimulus which, through constant association with primary reinforcers, acquires reinforcing properties itself. For example, money is a secondary reinforcer. Green rectangles of paper are, in and of themselves, of little value to us. And yet many of us will work madly to obtain them. The green paper has acquired reinforcing properties because it has been associated with, or paired with, more primary reinforcers (food, warmth, drink, sleep, sex, comfort, etc.)

We will consider secondary reinforcers in detail in a later section. For now it is sufficient to understand that secondary reinforcers have been heavily implicated in delay of reinforcement effects. Over the years, a hypothesis concerning delays and secondary reinforcers has developed: Immediate reinforcement is necessary for learning to occur. If an experiment demonstrates performance increases when primary reinforcers are delayed then that performance increase must be due to the immediate, and not delayed, delivery of secondary reinforcers.

This is an interesting hypothesis, and, to test it, we could eliminate potential secondary reinforcers from our delay experiments. Performance under conditions of delay then should be reduced. With successive eliminations of additional secondary reinforcers we should note a continuing drop in our gradient, such as the shift from gradient 1 to 2 to 3 in Figure 7.3. It is just such an experimental strategy that has developed in the literature. A well-known group of studies (e.g., Grice, 1948; Perkins, 1947; Perin, 1943) was concerned with the removal of contaminating secondary reinforcers in delay of reinforcement experiments. An example of their strategy will suffice. Wolfe (1934) trained rats to choose one arm (left or right) in a T maze. Once the rats were released from the start box, they were allowed to proceed to the choice point and to turn and move in the direction of the goal box. But before reaching the goal box the animals were held in a delay chamber for varying amounts of time. As the interval ended they were released and allowed to proceed to the end of the arm. Wolfe found that rats could be delayed as long as 20 minutes and still learn the response. Perkins (1947) called attention to a very important aspect of this situation. When the rat turns in the correct direction it is always held in a very distinct goal box. It might not seem so distinct to us, but to a rat confined within the box it must surely be a distinctive environment. It might contain a smudge here, or a unique crack there, or perhaps slight variations in the paint. It is this distinctive delay box which is always followed by reward. Hence the distinctive goal box must become a secondary reinforcer. Every time the animal chooses the correct arm and is held in the distinctive delay box he is reinforced immediately by the presence of that delay box. If he chooses the incorrect arm he is confined in another distinctive delay box (different smudges, smell, etc.). This delay chamber is never associated with reward. Hence it does not become a secondary reinforcer.

To remove the distinctive delay box as a source of secondary reinforcement Perkins (1947) merely switched delay boxes on successive trials. Thus neither delay box was consistently associated with either reward or absence of reward. Under these conditions the gradient fell. Less learning was observed under conditions of delay when the secondary reinforcer was removed.

Additional sources of secondary reinforcement (e.g., proprioceptive cues, or "feelings," associated with making a left or a right turn) were eliminated in subsequent experiments. As each successive source of secondary reinforcement was removed the gradient fell an additional step. Hence for many (e.g., Spence, 1947) it has been assumed that learning might not occur at all in the absence of some kind of immediate reinforcement. According to this position either primary or secondary reinforcement must occur immediately after the occurrence of the response. And yet the issue has yet to be resolved to everyone's satisfaction. More recent experimentation has suggested that some learning may, after all, occur in the absence of any immediate reinforcement (Lett, 1973; Revusky, 1917; Revusky & Garcia, 1970; Rozin & Kalat, 1971). These results have been obtained in both aversive conditioning and T maze situations.

Thus it is really too early to tell where this story will end. The most reasonable position to take is that secondary reinforcers are often involved in delay of reinforcement experiments, and that their removal does reduce learning under conditions of delayed primary reinforcement. On the other hand there may well be situations (e.g., bait-shyness) in which learning can occur when reinforcement is truly delayed.

Humans and the Delay of Reinforcement Effect

Given that the situation is confusing with respect to animal studies what can we possibly hope to say about human learning and delay of reinforcement? One thing that can be said with some certainty is that if secondary reinforcers are involved in animal experiments they are enormously involved in human delay situations. Humans are capable of performing very well under conditions of extreme delay. Presumably many of the readers of this text are plowing on without the hope of anything remotely resembling a primary reward in the foreseeable future. And yet they keep after it, slogging away, presumably being maintained by the presence of all sorts of secondary reinforcers (e.g., congratulating themselves upon having beaten down one more chapter). Any sort of long-range human learning endeavor (e.g., pursuit of career goals) is probably maintained through the involvement of secondary reinforcers.

Experimental work supports the notion that reinforcement delays (e.g., delaying feedback on performance) are not particularly effective in reducing human learning (Bilodeau, 1966; Brackbill, Adams, & Reaney, 1967). Most studies show humans capable of learning despite long delays.

What it may come down to is that humans are generally better able to bridge time gaps than animals. For example, language allows the human to reinforce himself upon the completion of any given response even though the primary reward may be delayed. We can think ahead, see the relationship between our current action and our ultimate goal, and thereby reinforce ourselves "ahead of time."

Amount of Reinforcement

What is the relationship between *amount* of reinforcement and performance level? Will a rat's running speed vary as a function of the amount of food he is given at the end of the runway? Will a child do better in school if he receives more praise from the teacher? These are the kinds of questions which prompt a consideration of the relationship between amount of reward and performance.

The answers we have been able to obtain in the laboratory are not as clear cut as we would like them to be. Studying the effects of variations in amount of reward has been difficult through the years. In a very general, oversimplified way, we may suggest that performance increases as amount of reward increases. The greater the amount of reward, the better the performance. Beyond a certain point, further increases in the magnitude of the goal may fail to result in further increases in performance.

Two early and widely quoted studies relating performance to amount of reward were done by Crespi (1942) and Zeaman (1949). Zeaman had rats run down a 3-foot runway to a goal box. Different groups of rats received different amounts of cheese (.05, .2, .4, .6, .8, 1.6, or 2.4

grams) once they reached the goal box. Zeaman found that the latency of the running response (time required to leave the start box) decreased as the magnitude of the reward increased. These and similar studies led to the general notion that performance increases as the amount of reward increases. But, as psychologists continued their examination of the amount of reward variable, they began to realize that it is quite a complicated problem, that there are at least three distinct components to the amount of reward situation.

First, one must consider the *mass or volume of the reinforcer* (e.g., grams of food ingested or volume of water consumed). Second, the *amount of consuming activity* the animal engages in may be important (e.g., number of licks, pecks, or swallows). Third, one must consider the *quality* as well as the quantity of the reward (e.g., sweet versus neutral flavors). Two or more of these factors are often confounded in a given experimental situation. For example, if we merely vary the number of pieces of corn we give to pigeons we have confounded volume of food with amount of consuming activity (one peck per kernel).

Much of the work in this area has been designed to tease out the independent effects of these various components. For example, one way to separate the consuming component from the ingested volume component is to surgically sever the animal's esophagus in the neck area. In this way liquids may be introduced directly into the animal's stomach, thereby eliminating the potentially confounding effects of consuming activities. Similarly, liquids may be consumed only to emerge from the fistula (sham feeding), thereby allowing the measurement of the effects of consuming activity independent of the effects of ingested volume (Mook, 1963). Another way to study the independent effects of consuming behavior is to divide a given amount of reward into varying numbers of parts. Thus consuming activity (e.g., number of pecks or licks) may vary even though the total volume of ingested material is constant (Hulse, 1960; Hall & Kling, 1960). The quality versus quantity issue may be examined by simultaneously varying the volume of the reward (e.g., small, medium, large) and the quality of the reward (e.g., citric, basic, saccharin) (Collier, 1962; Hutt, 1954). There have even been some attempts to explore the complicated effects of variations in quantity and quality of reward in human subjects (e.g., Weiner, 1966).

In general, it may be said that all three components (quantity, quality, and consuming activity) appear to contribute to the reinforcing effect in a positive fashion. At present it is impossible to determine which of the three is the most influential, although one guess would be that the quality is most important, followed by quantity and consuming activity, in that order. The student interested in a detailed discussion of these effects is referred to Kling & Schrier (1971).

Reinforcement Contrast

An interesting phenomenon has developed within the context of the study of amount of reward effects. Suppose you have a summer job picking fruit. You are paid 25¢ for each basket you fill. For three weeks, you work furiously. Then the boss informs you that the pay rate has been reduced to 12.5¢ a basket. More than likely your performance will go down. The reinforcement contrast effect refers to the fact that it may drop *below* the level you would have been performing at if you had received 12.5¢ right from the beginning. This is a negative contrast effect, and it reflects your depression. Temporarily you do not even pick at the rate you would have maintained had you received the lower pay rate all along. A positive contrast effect might be demonstrated if your pay rate were suddenly shifted upward, say, to 37.5¢ a basket. You would be elated, and your performance might temporarily jump *beyond* the level it would have been at had you received 37.5¢ all along (Fig. 7.4).

These effects have been demonstrated in the laboratory. They were originally observed and described by Crespi (1942) and Zeaman (1949). Zeaman trained rats to move down runways for either small or large rewards. The amounts were then suddenly shifted. His data appeared to reveal both positive and negative contrast effects. More recently, Collier

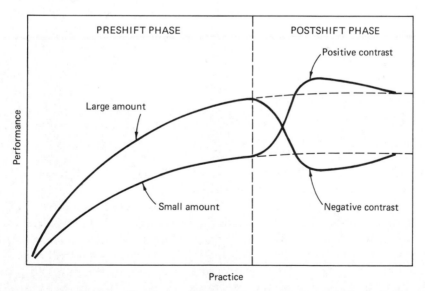

Figure 7.4. Idealized positive and negative reinforcement contrast effects. During the preshift phase one group receives a large amount of reinforcement while the other receives a small amount. The amounts given to the two groups are then reversed during the postshift phase, yielding the contrast effects.

and Marx (1959) first reinforced rats with one of three concentrations of sucrose solution. All three groups were then trained to lever press for the middle concentration. Rats initially reinforced with the lower concentration and shifted to the middle concentration produced higher response rates than did the rats trained throughout on the middle concentration (positive contrast). Rats initially trained on the high concentration and shifted to the middle concentration displayed lever pressing rates *below* those displayed by the rats trained on the middle concentration throughout (negative contrast).

Although the negative reinforcement contrast effect stands as a viable concept in the field (Peters & McHose, 1974), there have been questions about the validity of the positive contrast effect. Beginning with Spence (1956), and continuing into more recent years (Dunham, 1968; Dunham & Kilps, 1969; Hulse, 1973), a number of investigators have failed to obtain a positive effect and/or have discredited apparent positive effects. For example, Hulse (1973) first rewarded rats using a random arrangement of 1 and 10 pellets. Half the rats then learned to lever press for 1 pellet while the remaining half learned the same response for 10 pellets. When rats learned to lever press for 1 pellet following the mixed condition they learned more slowly than if they had received initial learning with just 1 pellet. But, in contrast to earlier reports, the corresponding positive effect was not obtained. That is, rats shifted to 10 pellets did not exceed the performance level they would have attained had they been trained on 10 pellets throughout. Whether this, and similar failures to find the positive contrast effect, is due to a true lack of the effect or to methodological difficulties remains to be seen.

SECONDARY REINFORCEMENT

As we have noted, a secondary reinforcer is a neutral stimulus that has, through repeated associations with a primary reinforcer, acquired reinforcing properties. If a neutral or nonreinforcing stimulus is repeatedly paired with a primary reward it will tend to take on reinforcing qualities. In a typical animal experiment rats might first be trained to run down a straight alley to a black goal box containing food. Once the running response is well established, the animals would be removed from the alley and placed in a T maze. One arm of the T maze would be black, whereas the other would be white. No food would ever be presented in the T maze. The rat would be allowed to run from the start box and to choose one of the two arms. In this situation rats typically learn to choose the black arm even though food is never presented. Through association with the food the black color became a secondary reinforcer, and it reinforces the turning response in the T maze.

Psychologists have devised a number of different procedures for detecting the existence and strength of secondary reinforcers. The method just described is called a *choice test*. The animal is allowed to choose between the secondary reinforcer and some neutral stimulus configuration (Saltzman, 1949). In a typical *extinction test* (Bugelski, 1938; Skinner, 1938), the animal may first be trained to obtain food by bar pressing. Each time the bar is pressed the releasing mechanism yields a distinctive clicking sound. This sound becomes a secondary reinforcer. Following initial training extinction is carried out under two conditions. In one, the mechanism is adjusted such that the bar press yields the clicking sound but no food. In the other condition a bar press produces neither the click nor the food. In this situation, resistance to extinction tends to be greater when the bar press produces the click, demonstrating that the click does, in fact, maintain the response.

Parameters of Secondary Reinforcement

Amount of Primary Reinforcement

It seems intuitively possible that a neutral stimulus will become a stronger secondary reinforcer if it is paired with a larger amount of primary reward. A $5 bill is of greater value than a $1 bill, presumbly because it is associated with more food, comfort, excitement, and so on. The experimental data indicate that if a subject learns to associate one particular stimulus with a large amount of reward and another distinct stimulus with a smaller amount then the stimulus associated with the larger amount will become a stronger secondary reinforcer (D'Amato, 1955; Reynolds, Pavlik, & Goldstein, 1964). This finding supports our intuitive notion.

On the other hand, if several groups of subjects associate a *single* neutral stimulus with a *single* amount of reward, and are not allowed to associate *different* amounts of reward with *different* stimuli, then the relationship is somewhat more tenuous. Although Butter and Thomas (1958) found a significant effect in this type of single stimulus situation, others (Reynolds, Pavlik, & Goldstein, 1964; Hopkins, 1955) have observed little or no relationship between amount of primary reward and strength of secondary reinforcer. It is as though you would not work any harder for a $5 bill than someone else would for a $1 bill if all you had ever experienced was the purchasing power of a $5 bill and all he had experienced was the purchasing power of a $1 bill. But if you suddenly discovered one another, and compared the amounts of goods you could obtain with your respective bills, or secondary reinforcers, then you would both be willing to work harder for the $5 bill. It is only when comparison is allowed that the $5 bill becomes a stronger secondary reinforcer than the $1 bill.

Number of Pairings with the Primary Reinforcer

It also seems reasonable to assume that the strength of a secondary reinforcer will increase as the number of times it is paired with the primary reinforcer increases. The available data (e.g., Bersh, 1951; Fantino & Hernstein, 1968; Miles, 1956) suggest that such is the case, although the effect seems to be less than overwhelming. There is only a slight increase in the strength of a secondary reinforcer as the number of pairings with the primary reinforcer increases.

Time of Deprivation and Strength of
Secondary Reinforcers

A number of investigators have been concerned with the relationship between time of deprivation, or drive level, and the strength of secondary reinforcers. Interestingly, the conclusion we can draw from the results of a sizable amount of experimentation has been that this variable is not particularly important in determining the strength of a secondary reinforcer. It seems to affect the overall activity level of the animal but not necessarily the strength of a secondary reinforcer. For example, in one type of experiment, rats are deprived of food for varying amounts of time. The animals are then trained under these varying drive levels. That is, they are given pairings of a neutral stimulus and a primary reward under varying degrees of, say, hunger. That is the training phase. During the test phase, two things change. First, all animals are tested under the same drive level. Second, only the secondary reinforcer is presented. During these kinds of tests, the performances of the two groups do not differ, even though they were trained under different drive levels. Several studies have shown this to be true (e.g., Brown, 1956; Hall, 1951). The animal's drive level at the time of training has very little impact upon its performance during the testing phase. Secondary reinforcers acquired under conditioning of high drive are no stronger than secondary reinforcers acquired under conditions of low drive.

Schedules of Reinforcement and
Secondary Reinforcement

Finally, the influences of schedules of reinforcement upon the strength and durability of secondary reinforcers have been, and are being, examined. The details of the experiments and their results are beyond the scope of this text. In general, investigators have been concerned with (*1*) the effects of the partial presentation of the primary reward during the initial establishment of secondary reinforcers, and (2) the effects of partial presentation of the secondary reinforcer during tests of its effectiveness. The tentative conclusion that emerges from these kinds of investigations is that intermittency tends to *increase* the durability of secondary reinforcers (Kelleher, 1966; Marr & Zeiler, 1974; Stubbs, 1971; Wike, 1966; Zimmerman, 1957).

Some Theoretical Considerations

Secondary Reinforcement and Classical Conditioning

Many psychologists feel that secondary reinforcers are established through a process of classical conditioning. If a neutral stimulus is repeatedly paired with primary reward(s) then the animal's reaction to the primary reward becomes classically conditioned to the neutral stimulus.

This mechanism may not be all there is to the establishment of secondary reinforcers; there are other theories. And yet the classical conditioning interpretation does receive some support in the literature. Bersh (1951) gave rats a pellet of food 0, .5, 2, 4, or 10 seconds after the onset of a light (see Figure 7.5). Following this phase, all rats bar pressed for the light alone. Bersh found that the strength of the secondary reinforcer was strongest when the CS–UCS interval (time between light and pellet) was approximately half a second. Longer and shorter intervals

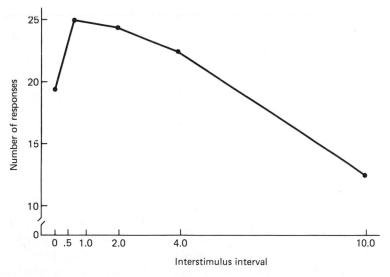

Figure 7.5. Secondary reinforcer strength as a function of the CS–UCS interval. (Adapted from Bersh, P. J. The influence of two variables upon the establishment of a secondary reinforcer for operant responses. *Journal of Experimental Psychology,* 1951, *41,* 62–73. Fig. 1, p. 66. Copyright 1951 by the American Psychological Association. Reprinted by permission.)

resulted in weaker secondary reinforcers. The superiority of the .5-second interval corresponds with the known superiority of the .5-second CS–UCS interval in general classical conditioning situations (see Figure 2.3).

Secondary Reinforcers as Carriers of Information

Egger and Miller (1962, 1963) came up with the interesting notion that the mere pairing of a neutral stimulus with a primary reward is not sufficient for the neutral stimulus to become a powerful secondary reinforcer. To become powerful the neutral stimulus must convey information about the forthcoming appearance of the primary reinforcer. If the neutral stimulus provides the animal with no additional information about the upcoming primary reward then it will be a less effective secondary reinforcer. This hypothesis is an extension of an earlier hypothesis, sometimes called the discrimination hypothesis (Schoenfeld, Antonitis, & Bersh, 1950; Marx & Knarr, 1963).

In one condition of their 1962 experiment Egger and Miller presented two neutral stimuli (e.g., light and tone) prior to the presentation of food. One of the stimuli (say, the light) was switched on first. One-half second later the tone began. Both stimuli would then remain on for 1.5 seconds, at which time the food was presented. In this situation the light informed the animal that food was forthcoming. The subsequent beginning of the tone, .5 second later, provided the animal with little or no new information (it already knew the food was coming). In agreement with their hypothesis, the light became a much stronger secondary reinforcer than the tone.

This line of reasoning does not deny that the mere pairing of a neutral stimulus with a primary reward will be sufficient for the establishment of a secondary reinforcer. Mere pairing probably is sufficient (Ayres, 1966; Seligman, 1966). But it does suggest that a neutral stimulus will become a more *powerful* secondary reinforcer if it carries nonredundant information about the upcoming occurrence of a primary reward.

Do Secondary Reinforcers Have
Motivating Properties?

In addition to their reinforcing properties secondary reinforcers may have motivating properties. For example, a $5 bill may not only be a reward. It may also activate us, motivate us, or urge us toward action. If you were walking calmly along the street, and suddenly spied a $5 bill on the sidewalk, your behavior would probably change rapidly, taking on an extremely motivated quality: The sight of the bill would urge you to action. Although this issue is an old one (e.g., Dinsmoor, 1950), Williams (1970) has provided some more recent evidence which supports the notion that secondary reinforcers motivate as well as reinforce. Rats were trained to run down an alley for food. Presentation of the food was accompanied by a tone (the secondary reinforcer). During testing, all animals were confined in the start box for 20 seconds. During this delay interval the tone was either not sounded or sounded for an interval of .5, 5 or 15 seconds. The tone was terminated by the opening of the door. Williams found that the longer the animals were subjected to the tone in the start box the faster they left the box once the door was open. The tone seemed to have energized or motivated the animals.

Secondary Reinforcers as Undetected Primary Reinforcers

A sneaking suspicion that creeps into secondary reinforcement experiments is that some supposedly neutral stimuli may actually be primary reinforcers, and hence not neutral at all. An enormous body of literature documents the fact that humans and other animals will respond to, and seek out, novel and changing stimuli. For example, animals will easily respond for nothing more than a change in illumination (McCall, 1966). Human infants, as young as 3 months, can be trained to make a variety of responses when rewarded with various visual and auditory stimuli (Sisqueland, 1970). Such "neutral" stimuli as light and sound onset and offset, changed visual patterns, novel odors, and the opportunity to explore visually the surrounding environment can be shown to have reinforcing properties (Berlyne, 1969; Butler, 1965; Fowler, 1965). Many secondary reinforcement experiments employ these kinds of "neutral" stimuli. Adequate controls are needed to ensure that they are, in fact, neutral and not reinforcing in and of themselves. In choosing neutral stimuli, experimenters must be aware of this type of possible confounding.

Secondary Reinforcement and Humans

It almost goes without saying that secondary reinforcers operate in the human realm. In the case of the human, secondary reinforcers may be very concrete or quite abstract. On a very physical level *tokens* may serve as secondary reinforcers (O'Leary & Drabman, 1971). For example, Everett, Hayward, and Meyers (1974) gave tokens to people who rode buses on a university campus. These tokens could later be turned in for such things as ice cream, beer, pizza, coffee, cigarettes, and so on. The authors noted a dramatic rise in "ridership" as a result of the delivery of token reinforcements. In addition, many experiments suggest that performance in school systems may be improved through the application of tokens which may later be turned in for more primary rewards (e.g., Dalton, Rubino, & Hislop, 1973). On a less physical level Skinner

(1953) has suggested that social reinforcers such as attention, approval, affection, and submission of others may actually be secondary reinforcers. For example, such verbal gestures as "fine," "good," "excellent," and so on, may represent secondary reinforcers. In addition, confirmation of correct responding, or positive feedback, may be a source of secondary reinforcement (Fitts & Posner, 1967).

We shall return to the role of secondary reinforcers, both physical and social, in a later section. Although secondary reinforcers are not completely understood, there is little question that they are extremely relevant in a consideration of human action.

THEORIES OF REINFORCEMENT

So far we have been concerned with observable reinforcement effects resulting from the manipulation of a number of critical independent variables. We now turn to a consideration of some of the analytical thinking psychologists have done with respect to the reinforcement issue. Why do reinforcers reinforce? What are the mechanisms underlying reinforcement effects? What are some of the major theoretical interpretations of reinforcement? We shall review a few of the more important conceptions, drawing upon a taxonomy suggested by Tapp (1969).

Drive-Reduction Theory

Drive-reduction theory, as exemplified by Hull's system, has already been introduced. According to this approach, reinforcement is equivalent to drive reduction. An animal is in a high drive state if it is experiencing some homeostatic imbalance, some internal physiological need, or some type of strong unpleasant stimulation. If the animal makes a response that reduces the noxious stimulation caused by these sorts of events, then that response is strengthened. Reinforcement refers to the diminution of noxious drive stimuli. Animals will acquire responses which have been instrumental in reducing drive stimuli.

The drive-reduction conception of reinforcement is perhaps the most convincing of them all. Its strongest opponents cannot deny its explanatory powers. But this does not mean that the theory is without faults. Few psychologists are willing to accept it as a comprehensive system encompassing all types of reinforcing events. It is difficult to believe that all reinforcement involves the reduction of noxious stimuli. There are just too many types of reinforcing events that do not fit into this sort of conception. For example, Sheffield (1966), and others, have demonstrated that the ingestion of saccharin is reinforcing. This situation does not appear to involve a reduction in noxious stimulation; it seems more a case of the presentation of pleasant stimulation. Additional examples of these maverick behaviors will be discussed in what follows.

Too Many Drives?

The drive-reduction conception appears to be adequate when one considers learning related to basic biological drives such as hunger, thirst, and sex. When deprived of food, liquid, or sex the animal experiences a state of tension. Responses that reduce these tension states are learned. If the basic biological drives were all we had to consider then the drive-reduction conception would seem to be a comprehensive theory. The difficulty lies in the fact that the past 20 years have seen an explosion of research concerned with rewards that do not reduce any known, or apparent, tissue need. Hundreds of studies have shown that humans and other animals will seek novel, changing, and complex stimuli, and that the receipt of these kinds of stimuli will be reinforcing. For example, Butler (1953) has shown that monkeys will learn visual discriminations for nothing more than the opportunity to look about a typical laboratory for a few moments. What noxious biological drive state is reduced by looking about a laboratory? Opponents of the drive conception claim that all sorts of curiosity and exploratory behaviors cannot be related to any *known* drive state.

The drive-reduction theoreticians respond bravely by postulating *new* drives to account for these sensory seeking behaviors. For example, Montgomery (1955) and others have spoken of an exploratory drive which parallels the more basic drives. That is, deprivation (denial of the opportunity to explore) should increase the exploratory drive. Subsequent opportunities to explore should do two things. First, responses that were instrumental in bringing about the opportunity to explore should be reinforced. Second, continued exploration should reduce the drive level, and thereby result in an eventual, temporary cessation of the exploratory behavior itself. The exploratory drive is not the only drive invented to fit the facts. Fowler (1965) and others have proposed a boredom drive to account for certain sensory seeking behaviors. Harlow (1953) has postulated a manipulation drive. An activity drive has been suggested by several authors (see Cofer & Apply, 1964). Houston and Mednick (1963) speak of a need for novelty in human subjects. These are but some of the new drives proposed; the list grows longer.

It is too early to determine whether the postulation of these drives is justifiable. Strong criticism has been directed toward the business of inventing new drives to account for new reinforcers. First, many psychologists have doubted that such drives can be independently demonstrated. To prove that such drives exist they must be shown to have the characteristics of more basic biological drives. Deprivation must lead to greater activity. Responses that result in exposure to the appropriate stimuli must be reinforced. Continued exposure to the stimuli must lead to a temporary cessation of the activity. Fortunately, at least for the drive-reductionists, such demonstrations do exist in the literature (Eisenberger, 1972; Fowler, 1965). These demonstrations have not convinced everyone, but the deprivation, reinforcement, and satiation effects do appear to parallel those obtained with more basic biological drives.

A second criticism has to do with the necessity of inventing a new drive every time a new stimulus is found to be reinforcing. For example, Olds and Milner (1954) have demonstrated that animals will work to receive electric shock in certain portions of their brains. To account for this sort of thing the drive-reductionists may well have to postulate a "brain-stimulation drive," which is reduced by electrical shock. The critics of the drive-reduction position feel there must be a simpler way to account for these diverse behaviors. To fit them all into the drive-reduction mold requires, for some, too much bending and tailoring. They feel the drive-reductionists are stretching their point. The drive-reduction notion might account for a good deal of behavior but, why must it account for *all* reinforcing events? Perhaps there are other reinforcement mechanisms which may supplement, and not necessarily replace, the drive-reduction conception.

The issue becomes further complicated when one considers human needs and motives such as achievement motivation (Entwisle, 1972) and power motivation (Veroff & Veroff, 1972). These urges do not readily lend themselves to a simple drive-reduction interpretation.

Optimal-Arousal-Level Theories

One alternative to the drive-reduction approach may be labeled the optimal-arousal-level conception. A number of psychologists (e.g., Berlyne, 1969; Fiske & Maddi, 1961; Routtenberg, 1968) have noted that reinforcement does not always seem to involve a *reduction* in stimulation, as implied by the drive-reduction position. It would appear that *increases* in tension, or arousal, or stimulation sometimes seem to be reinforcing. Accordingly, optimal-arousal-level theoreticians argue that there is some *preferred level* of arousal that the animal seeks to maintain. If arousal becomes too great, then any response that reduces arousal will be reinforced. If we are hungry then responses that are instrumental in reducing the hunger will be reinforced. If we are at a noisy party, and have had enough, then escape from that party will be a reinforcing event. On the other hand, if arousal falls *below* a certain level then any response which *increases* the arousal level will be reinforced. If we have been sitting about our apartment for days with nothing to do, we will probably engage in behavior that will increase our level of arousal or stimulation. Any movement toward the optimal level, whether an increase or decrease, will be reinforcing.

This type of theory is appealing because it fits the fact that animals sometimes seek to increase, and sometimes seek to decrease, stimulation. Its principal shortcoming lies in the fact that it is difficult to quantify, or define, exactly what is meant by arousal. Although Routtenberg (1968) does attempt to correlate arousal with certain brain functions, the concept is, in general, poorly defined. The arousal concept seems similar to the drive concept. Each refers to a state of tension. The principal difference between the two is that drive-reductionism argues that the animal strives to attain a zero drive level while the optimal-level theory argues that the animal attempts to maintain some preferred level greater than zero.

Stimulus Theories

The drive-reduction and arousal-level theories emphasize some internal state that the animal attempts to change or maintain. There are a number of theories that differ from these two in that they focus upon the impact of external stimuli rather than upon the internal state of the organism. There are several different varieties. Some of them are quite distinct, whereas others overlap with each other and/or with the conceptions just outlined. None of them is accepted by all, or even a majority, of psychologists.

Guthrie–Estes

The Guthrie–Estes type theory has already been introduced. If you will recall, the presentation of a reinforcing stimulus (such as food) merely changes the existing stimulus situation. This, in turn, protects learning that has already occurred.

Stimulus-Change Theories

McCall (1966) has argued that changes in level of stimulation will be reinforcing. Up to a point, the greater the change the greater the reinforcing effect. McCall (1966) has been able to demonstrate that rats will work to obtain changes in level of illumination. The emphasis here is upon a change in *quantity* rather than in *quality*. Although perhaps somewhat limited the theory does have heuristic value. It is easy for us to imagine ourselves acting in a manner that will bring about stimulus change. With further refinement and experimentation, this type of theory could become an important addition to the growing family of reinforcement theories.

Preferred-Level Theories

In contrast to McCall's theory, Lockhard (1966) suggests that the animal seeks a PREFERRED LEVEL of stimulation rather than a SIMPLE CHANGE in stimulation. Any change that is in the direction of the preferred level will be reinforcing. Any change that is away from the preferred level will be punishing. The similarity between this theory and the optimal-arousal-level theories is obvious. The primary difference between them is that one focuses upon internal states, whereas the other attends to external stimulation.

Stimulus Quality Theories

While the stimulus-change and the preferred-level theories focus upon the *amount* of stimulation Pfaffmann (1969), Young (1966), and others, have directed their attention toward the *quality* of the stimulus. In general, their theories are concerned with the fact that certain stimuli (e.g., sweet ones) are genetically preferred. The presentation of these stimuli is assumed to be reinforcing in some predetermined fashion, regardless of the arousal state of the animal. Thus an animal will work for a saccharin solution, even though the solution has no nutritional value. The animal merely likes the flavor, and will work for it.

Response Theories

Response theories of reinforcement emphasize the fact that most reinforcing events involve some associated consummatory response (e.g., chewing, manipulating, drinking, swallowing, copulating). The making of the response itself may be an important part of the reinforcing event. The emphasis in these theories is upon the rewarding properties of consummatory responses. For example, we all like to chew food, and to swallow it. These acts can be reinforcing. Consummatory theories do not focus upon that which is consumed, or upon any tension reducing events. While consummatory theories have taken several forms (e.g., Glickman & Schiff, 1967; Sheffield, 1966) one of the more interesting variations is that proposed by Premack (1965). According to Premack one response may be used to reinforce another. Given two responses, one of which is more likely to occur than the other, the more likely one can reinforce the occurrence of the less likely one. For example, Premack (1959) found that if a child would rather eat candy than play a game then it is possible to increase the child's game playing by reinforcing it with candy eating. Similarly, if a child prefers to play a game then his candy eating behavior may be increased by reinforcing it with game playing. Parents often hear their children saying things like, "I'll play checkers with you if you'll play cards with me." (What appears to be a marvelous example of cooperation may then, of course, be scuttled by the impossible question, Which game is to be played first?)

Premack's theory is an interesting one, and it supports the contention that the making of a response can be reinforcing. Of course, as is true of all these theories, it has not escaped criticism (see Eisenberger, Karpman, & Trattner, 1967).

Conclusion

We have no lack of theories concerning the nature of reinforcement. At present, none is really any more valid than the others. Each seems to encompass some of the data but not all of it. More than likely we will eventually discover that each has something to contribute to the overall picture of reinforcement. Perhaps psychologists will be able to bring about a synthesis of these varying positions. Changes in drive and arousal states, the pull of certain types of stimuli, and the occurrence of consummatory responses probably all contribute to the overall effect which we term reinforcement.

Theorizing on a behavioral level is an ongoing process (e.g., Bindra, 1974; Klinger, 1975; Solomon & Corbit, 1974; Timberlake & Allison, 1974). In addition, the relationships between events within the brain and external reinforcing events are now under intensive study. Psychologists, in what promises to be an exciting endeavor, are beginning to probe the chemical and electrical nature of reinforcement (see Valenstein, 1973). We will discuss research relating to the physiological basis of reinforcement in Chapter Fourteen. Without doubt, it will be some time before we fully understand reinforcement. We are fairly dexterous in manipulating behavior through the use of reinforcement but we have a long way to go before we understand why that manipulation occurs.

SUMMARY

1. Beyond simple operational notations there is very little agreement among psychologists concerning the nature of reinforcers. For example, Hull conceived of reinforcement in terms of drive reduction, Guthrie thought of it in terms of stimulus change, and Thorndike defined reinforcement and punishment in terms of satisfying and annoying states of affairs. Beyond the theoretical controversy it is clear that the important parameters of reinforcement include *schedules*, *amount*, and *delay* of reinforcement.

2. CONTINUOUS REINFORCEMENT (CRF) refers to situations in which every response is reinforced.

3. In a FIXED-INTERVAL schedule the animal is reinforced for the first response which occurs after the end of a given time interval. Long

pauses that follow reinforcement in the FI schedule produce a characteristic "scalloping" effect in cumulative response records.

4. In VARIABLE-INTERVAL (VI) schedules, the animal is forced to wait for varying amounts of time before he can receive reinforcement. The VI schedule produces steady responding. The longer the average interval the slower the responding.

5. In the FIXED-RATIO (FR) schedule, the animal must make a certain number of responses before he is rewarded. The FR schedule yields high rates of responding and a mild post-reinforcement pause. The higher the ratio the longer the post-reinforcement pause.

6. In the VARIABLE-RATIO (VR) schedule, the number of required responses varies. This schedule also produces high response rates, but normally does not yield post-reinforcement pauses.

7. MULTIPLE SCHEDULES consist of two or more simple schedules presented one after the other. Distinctive cues are associated with each simple phase. Performance on any given phase may be affected by previous phases. In MIXED SCHEDULES, a variation of the multiple pattern, the distinctive cues are not present.

8. In CHAINED SCHEDULES two or more successive simple schedules must be *completed* before a reinforcement can be obtained. Distinctive cues are associated with each simple phase. TANDEM SCHEDULES are like chained schedules except that the distinctive cues are not present.

9. AUTOSHAPING refers to the fact that animals will sometimes develop a response to a cue even though that cue is *always* followed by reinforcement. Autoshaping suggests that classical conditioning is intertwined with what is normally called instrumental conditioning.

10. AUTOMAINTENANCE refers to the finding that animals will sometimes develop a response to a cue even if the occurrence of such a response ensures the *absence* of a reinforcement that would have been received had the animal not responded. Automaintenance is a controversial, and perhaps false, effect.

11. Humans respond to many schedule manipulations in roughly the same manner as do the "lower" animals.

12. The PARTIAL REINFORCEMENT EFFECT refers to the fact that resistance to extinction following partial reinforcement is greater than resistance to extinction following CRF. The partial reinforcement effect is not always easy to demonstrate with humans.

13. Failures to find similarities between scheduled animal and human behaviors may be due to methodological differences between animal and human experiments rather than to any important differences in underlying learning mechanisms. The differences between animal and human learning abilities may be more quantitative than qualitative.

14. If a reward is *delayed* following the occurrence of a response

then performance drops off. If the reward is delayed too long, then learning will not occur at all. And yet sometimes long delays appear not to hinder learning in the slightest. Successful learning under these conditions has been attributed to the presence of undetected secondary reinforcers immediately following the response. (A secondary reinforcer is any neutral stimulus which, through repeated pairings with a primary reward, has acquired reinforcing properties of its own.)

15. If confounding secondary reinforcers are removed from delay of reinforcement experiments then learning under conditions of delayed primary reinforcement drops off dramatically. Some psychologists feel that learning cannot occur at all unless some type of reinforcement (primary or secondary) is immediate.

16. Delays in the receipt of primary reinforcement are not particularly effective in reducing human performance. Humans are better able to bridge the time gaps than are animals.

17. Performance tends to increase as the *amount* of reinforcement is increased, up to a point.

18. Three components of amount of reward have been identified. They include the volume or mass of the reward, the amount of consuming activity, and the quality of the reward. All three have been found to be important in determining reinforcement effects.

19. NEGATIVE REINFORCEMENT CONTRAST refers to the fact that if an animal has been working for a high level of reward, and is suddenly shifted to a lower level, then his performance will temporarily drop below the level it would have been maintaining had it experienced only the lower level all along. Although the negative reinforcement contrast effect is fairly well established, the corresponding POSITIVE REINFORCEMENT CONTRAST effect has been difficult to obtain.

20. The existence and strength of secondary reinforcers are detected by various means including choice tests and extinction tests.

21. SECONDARY REINFORCERS can become stronger if they are paired with larger amounts of primary reward. This effect only appears when the animal is allowed to associate different amounts of reward with different stimuli.

22. The strength of a secondary reinforcer increases slightly as the number of times it is paired with the primary reward is increased.

23. Time of deprivation, or drive level, seems to be relatively unimportant in determining the strength of secondary reinforcers.

24. Schedules of reinforcement appear to have a significant impact upon the strength of secondary reinforcers. In general, intermittency leads to an increase in the durability of secondary reinforcers.

25. Secondary reinforcers may be established through a process of classical conditioning.

26. To become powerful secondary reinforcers stimuli may have to carry nonredundant information about the forthcoming occurrence of the primary reward.

27. Some so-called secondary reinforcers may be nothing more than undetected primary reinforcers, in that some so-called neutral stimuli may satisfy the animal's requirements for novel, changing and complex stimulation.

28. Human performance is strongly affected by secondary reinforcers.

29. Returning to the theoretical controversy we find that drive-reduction theory has difficulty encompassing certain sensory seeking behaviors such as exploration. Many psychologists are unwilling to believe that all reinforcing events involve the reduction of noxious stimulation. They also object to the endless invention of new drives to account for newly discovered reinforcing stimuli. The drive-reduction theory is a good one, but it may not be comprehensive.

30. Alternative theories include the optimal-arousal-level conceptions, in which it is assumed that the animal seeks to maintain some preferred level of arousal. If arousal becomes too great then any response that reduces arousal will be reinforced. If arousal falls below a certain level then responses that increase arousal will be reinforced. It is very difficult to measure, or to define exactly what is meant by, arousal.

31. There are several stimulus theories of reinforcement. The Estes–Guthrie theory was discussed earlier. The stimulus-change theories argue that changes in level of stimulation are reinforcing. The preferred-level theories argue that any change away from a preferred level of stimulation will be punishing while any change toward the preferred level will be reinforcing.

32. Stimulus-quality theories contend that certain stimuli (e.g., sweet ones) are innately preferred. Their presentation will be reinforcing. The emphasis here is upon quality rather than quantity.

33. Response theories of reinforcement argue that consummatory responses are reinforcing. Making a response (e.g., chewing and swallowing) is presumed to be reinforcing regardless of what is consumed, or what tension states are reduced. Premack's variation on this theme argues that if one of two responses is more likely to occur then the occurrence of the less likely one may be increased by reinforcing it with the opportunity to perform the more likely one.

34. None of these theories is, at present, any more valid than the others. Each probably has something to contribute to the overall picture of reinforcement.

35. Although behavioral and physiological theorizing is an ongoing process it is unlikely we will obtain a full understanding of reinforcement in the near future.

3

TRANSFER

We now turn to a consideration of the second of our three phases, or aspects, of the learning situation. As we have seen, *acquisition, transfer* and *retention* are all inextricably bound up with one another. And yet, in an attempt to understand the overall learning process, we may focus upon any one of these three facets of the total learning situation. In this section we will direct our attention toward *transfer,* or the effects of prior learning upon subsequent learning. Retention will be taken up in Section Four.

It is almost unnecessary to point out the tremendous importance of transfer in our daily lives. We never truly learn anything in a vacuum. Each time we are faced with a new learning task, our past experiences and acquired skills are brought to bear upon the demands of the new task. No matter how unique or novel the new learning task, it is hard to imagine that we could master it without being influenced by our past learning experiences. For example, the mere fact that we have acquired language guarantees that many new learning situations will be, in effect, transfer tasks. To the extent that the new learning task involves language, we will be involved in a transfer situation. Our past experience with language will probably affect, either positively or negatively, any new verbal learning task we face.

Our intent in this section is to present an introduction to those areas of learning psychology which emphasize, or focus upon, the effects of prior learning upon subsequent performance. In Chapter Eight we consider the complimentary processes of generalization and discrimination. Generalization refers to the fact that, if a response is connected to one particular stimulus, then the subsequent presentation of similar stimuli will tend to elicit that same response. Generalization is a type of transfer effect in that training with one particular stimulus value affects future performance. Discrimination is, in a sense, the opposite side of the same coin. It refers to the process wherein generalization is reduced through a process of differential reinforcement. The range of stimuli that will elicit a particular response is reduced. The issues and facts relating to generalization and discrimination will be discussed in terms of both animal and human action.

In Chapter Nine we will consider transfer of training. In transfer of training studies, subjects typically learn two successive verbal tasks, which may vary in terms of their similarity to one another. Under some circumstances, second-list learning is facilitated by prior learning. Under other circumstances, it is hindered. Both empirically determined and theoretically envisioned principles of transfer will be outlined.

In addition an attempt will be made to point out the ways in which generalization and transfer of training are intimately related to one another. Both involve the impact of prior learning upon subsequent performance.

Generalization and Discrimination

GENERALIZATION

If you will recall, stimulus generalization refers to the fact that if a response is learned to one particular stimulus then similar stimuli will tend to elicit that response. The greater the similarity the greater the tendency. For example, babies may say "dada" to any approaching man, even though they have only been reinforced for saying "dada" in the presence of their fathers. The more the stranger looks like the father the more likely the baby is to say, "dada." Racial prejudice represents another example of stimulus generalization. Emotional or evaluative responses that have been connected to one, or perhaps a few, individuals will generalize to other people who are perceived as being similar. Thus, we hear things like, "They're all alike. You can't trust any of them," and, "I think they are such wonderful people. So industrious." Regardless of the accuracy of the perception, individuals who are perceived as similar evoke the same responses.

On a more experimental level we may note the widely quoted results obtained by Guttman and Kalish (1956). They trained pigeons to peck an illuminated key of a certain color. Following training the birds were presented with a random sequence of colored keys that varied in terms of their similarity to the original training stimulus. Each group produced what is known as a *stimulus generalization gradient*. That is, the greatest numbers of responses occurred during the presentation of the *original* training stimuli. As the various *test* stimuli became less similar to the original stimulus the numbers of evoked responses decreased. The birds, originally trained at different points along the color continuum, produced relatively symmetrical generalization gradients around their particular training stimulus value. Figure 8.1 contains some idealized gradients that might be obtained in this sort of experiment.

It is clear that the ability to generalize can be either adaptive or maladaptive. For example, it would be inconvenient, to say the least, if we failed to recognize strangers as humans. On the other hand, it would

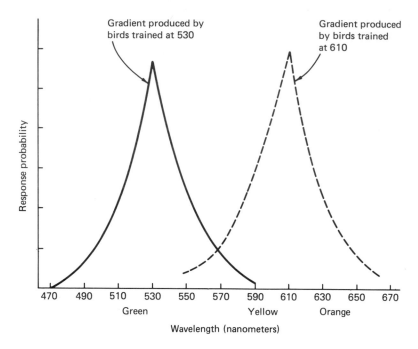

Figure 8.1. Idealized stimulus generalization gradients which might be obtained from groups of birds trained at different points along a wavelength continuum.

not be particularly adaptive if we generalized too much (e.g., if we "recognized" approaching animals as humans).

Variables Affecting Stimulus Generalization

As is true of many of our learning phenomena, there are many variables that affect the shape and form of the stimulus generalization gradient. We shall discuss only a few of them.

Extended Training

What will happen to stimulus generalization as reinforced responding to the training stimulus is increased? For example, what will happen to the baby's tendency to say "dada" to strangers as the number of times he is reinforced for saying "dada" to his father is increased? On an intuitive level we might expect an initial increase in stimulus generalization. When first receiving reinforcement for saying "dada" the father might not be all that distinct to the baby. Hence, we might find an initial failure to distinguish between the father and strangers. But as training continues the baby gains experience. The father becomes more distinct to the baby. After considerable training the baby might be much less likely to confuse strangers with his father. Generalization might decrease.

The experimental data give some support to this increase–decrease hypothesis. The initial increase in generalization seems to be fairly well established. The subsequent decrease appears sometimes (Hovland, 1937; Razran, 1949), but not all the time (Margolius, 1955). Thus evidence substantiating the increase–decrease hypothesis is encouraging, but not completely convincing. The interested student is referred to Kimble's (1961) analysis of the complexity of this issue.

Stimulus Generalization and Partial Reinforcement

Suppose, when referring to his father as "dada," our baby is some-times rewarded ("Gooood baby!") and sometimes not (silence). What effect might this partial reinforcement have upon the extent to which the response will generalize to other men? An intuitive answer is not so obvious in this case. The experimental data suggest that generalization will be *more* extensive following partial reinforcement (Humphreys, 1939; Wickens, Schroder, & Snide, 1954).

Stimulus Generalization and Motivation

Do you think a response acquired under conditions of high drive will result in more or less generalization than a response acquired under a low level of drive? The experimental results appear to be consistent. Increased drive level appears to increase stimulus generalization both in animals (Jenkins, Pascal, & Walker, 1958) and in humans (Bersh, Notterman, & Schoenfeld, 1956).

Brain Stimulation and Generalization

Several studies have shown that the bait-shyness effect will generalize (Balagura, Brophy, & Devenport, 1972; Smith & Balagura, 1969). These investigators first poisoned animals with nonlethal doses of lithium chlo-ride (LiCl), which creates an aversion for LiCl. They then tested for generalization by presenting similar substances (e.g., sodium chloride, NaCl). It was found that the aversive reaction would be evoked by related substances, or stimuli.

Balagura, Ralph, and Gold (1972) and Ralph and Balagura (1974) took the investigation a step further by introducing brain stimulation immediately following the ingestion of the LiCl. They found that brain stimulation introduced *after* LiCl ingestion, and *before* the testing with NaCl, did two things. First, it left untouched the aversion for the LiCl.

Second, it created a distinct drop in the aversion for NaCl. That is, the generalization gradient became significantly steeper with the introduction of postingestion brain stimulation even though the response to the original training stimulus (LiCl) remained unchanged. This effect is not well understood, but it does exemplify the growing trend within psychology to explore behavioral phenomena on a physiological level.

You should be aware that we have discussed only a few of the variables which have been investigated in connection with generalization effects. Although we will not discuss them, others include amount of reward, number of extinction trials, time between training and testing, individual differences, stimulus intensities, punishment, and the effects of changing more than one aspect of the stimulus. The interested student is referred to Mostofsky (1965).

The Role of Experience in Generalization

Suppose our baby is the kind that is kept at home most of the time. He sees very few strangers. The only man he knows is his father, and he calls him "dada." He has had no experience with a dimension of men. Suppose we now expose the baby to a variety of strange men. What kind of generalization will occur? Will he generalize more or less than a baby who has been exposed to many different men all along? There have been two general positions concerning this issue. Lashley and Wade (1946), on the one hand, argue that the inexperienced baby will respond equally to all men. The stimulus generalization gradient will be flat. They argue that the stimulus dimension (e.g., a dimension of men varying in similarity to one another) does not "exist" for the baby until he has had experience with it. Until the baby has had a chance to distinguish among, or compare men, all men will be equivalent. All men, including the father, will be perceived as the same and will be responded to identically. On the other hand, Hull (1943) and Spence (1937) would argue that the baby will be less likely to respond to less similar men even though he has never had the opportunity to experience various points along the dimension. They would argue that the gradient generated by our inexperienced baby would be steep, and not flat.

There is some evidence which supports the Lashley–Wade position. Peterson, N. (1962) raised ducks in yellow light (589 nm). They never had the opportunity to distinguish one wavelength from another. A control group was raised in normal light. Both groups were then trained to peck a key illuminated by the 589 nm light. Stimulus generalization was then tested by illuminating the key with eight different wavelengths ranging from 490 to 650 nm. Figure 8.2 contains the results of the experiment. The ducks raised in yellow light generalized perfectly, or failed to discriminate among the various test stimuli. The controls, on the other

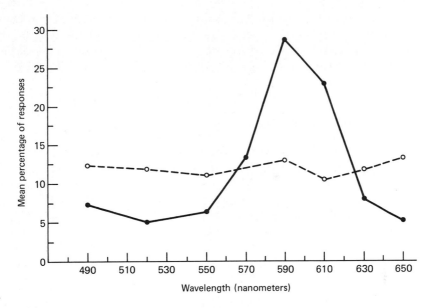

Figure 8.2. Generalization gradients obtained from birds raised in monochromatic environment (dotted line) and from birds raised in normal light (solid line). (Adapted from Peterson, N. Effect of monochromatic rearing on the control of responding by wavelength. *Science,* 1962, *136,* 774–775, Fig. 2, p. 774. Copyright 1962 by the American Association for the Advancement of Science.)

hand, sharply curtailed their responses as the similarity between the training and the test stimuli decreased. This result supports the Lashley–Wade notion that experience with the stimulus dimension is important in producing generalization decrements. Ganz and Riesen (1962) have obtained similar results with infant monkeys raised in total darkness.

Walk and Walters (1973) raised one group of rats in the dark (for up to 60 days) and a control group in normal light. The visually deprived rats showed definite deficiencies in the ability to discriminate depths. They tended to respond to cliffs of varying depths (4, 6 and 8 inches) as though they were not really there. That is, they tended to tumble over the cliff more often than rats raised in normal light.

Unfortunately, there are also data that indicate that steep rather than flat gradients may be obtained in the absence of any prior exposure to the many points along the stimulus dimension (Jenkins & Harrison, 1960; Thomas, Mariner, & Sherry, 1969). These investigators have shown that, under certain rather specific conditions, steep gradients may be obtained when the animal has experienced but a single value along a stimulus dimension (see also Tracy, 1970).

The conclusion we can draw is that prior experience with many points along the dimension may not be absolutely *essential* for the appearance of a steep rather than a flat gradient, but it *helps*. Our stay-at-home baby might be less likely to call strangers "dada" than his real father, but in all likelihood, the tendency to restrict his response to his father would be even stronger had he had prior experience with a variety of strangers.

Primary and Secondary Generalization

Hull (1943) describes primary generalization as that involving some innate or predetermined stimulus dimension. Secondary generalization refers to generalization in which the dimension of similarity is acquired, or learned. For instance, the words "house" and "home" are similar, but that similarity is not innate. It is learned. Generalization across these two stimuli would be considered secondary generalization.

Semantic Generalization

The semantic generalization effect may be used to illustrate the concept of secondary generalization. In a semantic generalization study, a response is conditioned to one verbal unit, such as a word. The subject is then presented with additional words, which vary in terms of their similarity to the original training word. The greater the similarity the greater the tendency for the test word to elicit the response. For example, Lacey and his associates (Lacey & Smith, 1954; Lacey, Smith, & Green, 1955) ran a series of studies in which subjects free-associated to long lists of words. The lists contained, among others, several words pertaining to rural life (e.g., cow, corn, plow, tractor). One of these words was selected by the experimenter as the training word. After each presentation of this critical training word the subject was shocked, and his heart rate monitored. The results indicated that the mere presentation of a word that had been previously followed by a shock would yield an increase in heart rate. In addition, and more to our point, the heart rate response was elicited by the other related rural words. If the presentation of "plow" was followed by a shock, then the presentation of "corn" would produce an increase in heart rate even though "corn" had never been followed by a shock. This demonstrates generalization along a dimension of learned meaning similarity. Parenthetically, it also demonstrates the complexity of generalization effects in human activity.

Acquired Equivalence of Cues

Another pertinent area of research involves the acquired equivalence of cues. In a typical experiment (Jeffrey, 1953) children were taught to move a lever in one direction when a white stimulus was presented, and in another direction when a black stimulus was presented. Half the subjects were then taught to call a gray stimulus "white," whereas the other half learned to label the same gray stimulus "black." All subjects were then presented a random sequence of white, black, and gray stimuli, and were required to move the lever in response to each stimulus. When the gray stimulus was presented to children who had learned to call it "white" they moved the lever in the direction appropriate for white. Similarly, children who had learned to call the gray stimulus "black" moved the lever in the direction appropriate for black. Through learning, gray and white (or gray and black) had been "made similar." Through stimulus generalization the lever responses originally connected to the white (or black) were elicited by the gray stimulus.

Semantic generalization and the acquired equivalence of cues phenomena are quite closely related. One difference between the two is that in semantic generalization studies the learned similarity between the stimuli is usually established before the subject enters the test situation. In the acquired equivalence paradigm the learned equivalence is actually established within the experimental situation.

DISCRIMINATION

Generalization and discrimination may well be opposite sides of the same coin. They may bear an inverse relationship to one another. A decrease in stimulus generalization refers to a decrease in the tendency to give the same response to similar stimuli. An increase in discrimination refers to the same thing—the tendency to restrict responses to one stimulus value chosen from a set of similar stimuli. Discrimination refers to a breakdown in the tendency to generalize. The two processes are, in a sense, complimentary. An increase in one represents a decrease in the other. It is difficult, if not impossible, to untangle the two processes. Although their exact relationship has never been defined to everyone's satisfaction, some experimental work supports the idea that they are closely related (Thomas & Mitchell, 1962; Ganz, 1962).

Sometimes the environment demands, or reinforces, generalization. For example, to function successfully, and to maximize reinforcement, one must be able to generalize along such dimensions as red lights. On the other hand, the world sometimes rewards discrimination rather than generalization. For example, the successful wine taster is not one who says, "Hey, all this stuff tastes the same." He is the one who can make finer and finer discriminations among very similar stimuli. (Amateur wine tasters often unknowingly discriminate among labels and colors rather than actual taste differences. Blindfold your local wine expert and you may well find he has trouble distinguishing one wine from another.)

The successful animal is one who can, depending upon the demands of the environment, both generalize and discriminate. He must be able to distinguish between those occasions which require generalization and those which demand discrimination. Too much of either process will lead to less than maximum reinforcement.

The mechanism whereby generalization is reduced, or discrimination is increased, involves the reinforcement of responses made to one particular stimulus, and the nonreinforcement of responses made to similar stimuli. This is what we mean by differential reinforcement. For example, the baby comes to distinguish his father from other men through a process of differential reinforcement. His initial tendency to generalize, or to say "dada" to all men, is reduced by reinforcing "dada" in response to the father and not reinforcing it when it occurs in response to other men.

Simultaneous versus Successive Presentation Methods

Two of the more common methods used in the investigation of discrimination learning have been labeled the simultaneous and the successive presentation techniques. In the simultaneous method two stimuli are presented together. A pigeon might be presented with two different illuminated keys. A response to one (the positive stimulus) would be reinforced. A response to the other (the negative stimulus) would not be reinforced. With repeated differential reinforcement the pigeon will come to restrict his pecking response to the positive stimulus. As an additional example, imagine that our baby lives with his parents and an uncle. Much of his discrimination training would probably be simultaneous in that the positive stimulus (father) and the negative stimulus (uncle) would appear simultaneously.

The successive presentation method involves the sequential presentation of the positive and negative stimuli. The two stimuli are presented one at a time in some random order. The animal is free to respond or not respond to each stimulus as it appears. This would be comparable to a situation in which the baby saw either his father or his uncle, but never both at the same time.

Theories of Discrimination Learning

Let us consider two opposing views of the nature of discrimination learning. Theorizing in this field is extensive and complicated, and you should keep in mind that our discussion is an introductory one. Further detailed information concerning discrimination theory can be found in Riley (1968), Blough and Lipsitt (1971), and Blough (1975).

The Algebraic Summation Interpretation

Hull (1943) and Spence (1936, 1937) developed what has come to be known as the absolute, or the algebraic summation interpretation of discrimination learning. Imagine a dimension of circle size (see Figure 8.3). Choose from this dimension two particular circle sizes. Call one the positive stimulus and the other the negative stimulus. Present these two circles, and *only* these two, to a pigeon. Reinforce the pigeon when it pecks the positive stimulus. Do nothing when it pecks the negative stimulus. According to Hull and Spence, each time the pigeon responds to the positive stimulus, and is reinforced for doing so, there results an increase in the tendency to respond to that stimulus (see the upward arrow in Figure 8.3). Each time the pigeon pecks the negative stimulus, and is not reinforced for doing so, there is an increase in the tendency *not* to respond to that particular stimulus value (see the downward arrow). The excitatory or positive tendency to respond to the reinforced stimulus generalizes (see the positive gradient in Figure 8.3) along the stimulus dimension. Similarly a negative or inhibitory gradient is established (see the negative gradient). These two gradients, the positive and the negative, sum algebraically. The resulting net gradient in Figure 8.3 is the result of the algebraic interaction of the positive and negative gradients. The probability of a response occurring at any point along the dimension is determined by the strength of the competing positive and negative tendencies at that point. For example, consider stimulus X in Figure 8.3. At this point, the generalized strength of the inhibitory tendency is considerable. But it is not as great as the generalized excita-

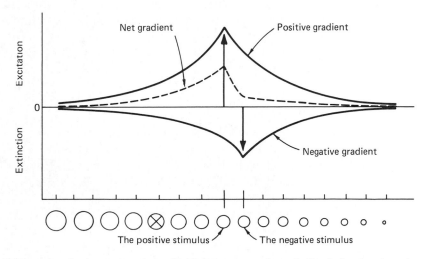

Figure 8.3. An example of the Hullian interpretation of discrimination learning.

tory tendency. Hence, if we present circle X to our pigeon, it will probably peck it. The positive tendency outweighs the value of the inhibitory tendency at that point. The net gradient summarizes the resolution of the opposing positive and negative tendencies pulling upon the animal.

It is an interesting model, and it leads to many testable hypotheses. For example, what will happen to the probability of the response to the positive stimulus as we increase the number of unreinforced responses the animal makes to the negative stimulus? What will happen to our baby's tendency to say "dada" to his father as we increase the number of times he says "dada" to his uncle and is not reinforced for doing so? On an intuitive basis we might suspect that such training might sharpen the baby's perception of the differences between his father and his uncle, and lead to a stronger tendency to respond to the father. But notice carefully what the Hullian model suggests. If we increase the number of unreinforced responses to the negative stimulus, the negative gradient increases. This increase detracts from the tendency to respond to the positive stimulus. Through repeated nonreinforced responding to the uncle we would expect the baby's tendency to say "dada" to his father to decrease rather than increase. This curious, and somewhat unexpected result has received support in the laboratory (e.g., Gynther, 1957).

This effect is but one of many predictions generated by the model. You might try to think of a few yourself. For example, what should happen to the tendency to respond to the positive stimulus as the *difference* between the positive and the negative stimuli is increased?

The Relational Theory

There is an opposing view concerning the nature of discrimination learning. According to this position, the animal, in forming a discrimination, learns a relation between the positive and negative stimuli. When discriminating between our two circle sizes the pigeon may well be attending to the fact that one stimulus is larger than the other. In a sense he may be learning that "bigness is goodness." The emphasis here is upon the cognitive, somewhat fuzzy, concept of relationship learning rather than upon the summation of independently established positive and negative gradients. The relational position emphasizes a comparison process, and suggests that the animal's response to the stimuli is based upon a perceived relation between them. Although somewhat ambiguous, the relational theory may well yield predictions that differ from those generated by the Hullian scheme.

The first differential prediction has to do with a comparison of the simultaneous and the successive methods just outlined. If the relational position is correct we might expect the simultaneous method would produce better discrimination learning than the successive method, simply because the relationship between the two stimuli might be more easily perceived if they are presented together. If presented together, the perception of the relation would not be dependent upon a "memory" of one of the stimuli, as would be the case in the successive presentation method. Unfortunately, the experimental data contain all possible results with respect to this question. Neither method seems to be superior under all conditions (see Blough & Lipsitt, 1971; Kimble, 1961). Thus, although the theory seems to generate a distinctive hypothesis, nature and our experiments have not been particularly cooperative in yielding a definitive answer to the question.

Transposition

The transposition effect is another phenomenon that bears upon the relational versus absolute issue. Suppose an animal has been trained to discriminate between a dark stimulus (the positive stimulus) and a light stimulus (the negative stimulus). Now suppose we remove the light stimulus from the situation and pair the dark positive stimulus with a new, heretofore unseen, *darker* stimulus. The animal's choice is now between the old positive stimulus, which has been consistently reinforced, and the new darker stimulus, which has never even been seen before. Common sense would argue that the animal would continue to respond to the old positive stimulus. But the relational position would argue that if the animal, in fact, has learned the relation between the light (negative) and the dark (positive) stimuli, and responds on the basis of that relation, then it should respond to the new darker stimulus rather than the old positive stimulus when given a choice between these two. It has learned that, "darkness is goodness." This is exactly what happens. The animal responds to the new darker stimulus rather than the old positive one. This transposition effect has been observed with all sorts of animals under many different conditions (see Reese, 1968; Riley, 1968).

The transposition effect seems to support the relational position. It suggests that the animal is responding upon the basis of a perceived relationship rather than discrete stimulus–response connections. And yet Spence (1937), in a classic analysis, argues that simple S–R relationships can, after all, account for transposition effects.

According to his model (see Figure 8.4) a positive excitatory gradient is built up around the positive stimulus (value 256). A negative gradient (dotted gradient) is built up in connection with the negative stimulus (value 160). The probability of responding to any point along the stimulus dimension depends upon the *difference between the positive and negative gradients*. If you will spend a moment with this model, you will realize that it predicts transposition effects very nicely. For example, suppose the old positive stimulus (256) was paired with a new test stimu-

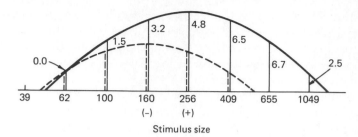

Figure 8.4. Spence's analysis of transposition. During training, responses to stimulus 256 are reinforced while responses to stimulus 160 are extinguished. (Adapted from Spence, W. K. The differential response in animals to stimuli varying within a single dimension, *Psychological Review, 1937, 44,* 430–444. Fig. 1. Copyright 1937 by the American Psychological Association. Reprinted by permission.)

lus (say, of value 655). According to the model, the probability of responding to stimulus 655 would be greater than the probability of responding to the old positive stimulus (256). This would be a transposition effect, and it is predicted upon the basis of discrete S–R connections without any reference to the learning of relationships.

The model generates many interesting hypotheses. For example, we may ask what will happen to transposition as the difference between the positive and the negative stimuli is increased. Keep the positive stimulus and the test stimulus in their fixed positions in Figure 8.4. Slide the negative stimulus, and hence the negative gradient, to the left. As this is done, what will happen to the probability of responding to the test stimulus relative to the probability of responding to the positive stimulus? As the negative gradient is gradually withdrawn to the left the probability of responding to the old positive stimulus will "catch up with," and finally exceed, the probability of responding to the new test stimulus. In other words, as the negative stimulus is moved to the left, transposition should decrease and eventually disappear.

What should happen to the transposition effect as the difference between the positive stimulus and the test stimulus is increased? Keep the positive and the negative stimuli in their fixed positions in Figure 8.4. Now imagine the test stimulus to be moving away from the positive stimulus toward the right. If we begin testing close enough to the positive stimulus, transposition should first increase and then decrease.

Spence's analysis still stands as one of the more ingenious interpretations of transposition. In effect, it broke the strong grip that the relational theorists had had upon the transposition effect since the beginning of the century. This is not to say that Spence's model is perfect either. For example, it is dependent upon how one draws the hypothetical gradients. If one wishes, one may redraw the gradients such that transposition is *not* predicted. In addition, there are certain facts, beyond the scope of this text, which his model does not seem to explain (see Honig, 1965). There have also been some fairly recent attempts to revive the relational interpretation (Zeiler, 1967).

At present, neither model is accepted by a majority of psychologists. As has been true with other models we have examined, both the absolute and the relational theories seem to account for some of the data, but neither seems to encompass them all. Having spent some time considering major theories of discrimination we now turn to a consideration of some additional issues relating to the discrimination process.

Behavioral Contrast

The behavioral contrast effect is an interesting one. It was investigated by Reynolds (1961a,b) and others some time ago, and is still undergoing rather extensive investigation (e.g., Keller, 1974; Redford & Perkins, 1974). The work done by Reynolds provides a good example of the effect. Pigeons were trained to peck a key. Sometimes the key was red and sometimes green. At first the color made no difference, for the pigeon was reinforced regardless of the color of the key. In this phase of the experiment the pigeon pecked the two colors equally frequently. Then, in the second phase of the study, the red stimulus became the positive, or reinforced, stimulus while the green cue became the negative, or unreinforced, stimulus. As one might expect, the response rate to the green key dropped. Responses to this key went unreinforced, and hence they extinguished. But what about the rate of response to the red key? Remember, a response to this key was treated identically in the two phases—it was always reinforced. The shift from the first to the second phase did not involve a change with respect to the red key. Despite this constant treatment the rate of response to the red stimulus went *up* during the second phase. This is the contrast effect.

How might one explain this effect? Why did the pigeon *increase* its response to the red key even though the size and frequency of the reinforcements stayed the same? Let us first look at what the Hull–Spence model would say about the issue. It seems their model would predict a decrease in the rate of response to the red key rather than in increase. With the shift to phase two a negative or inhibitory tendency would be assumed to build up in association with the unreinforced green key. This negative tendency should generalize and detract from the positive tendency to respond to the red key. Thus this aspect of the Hull–Spence model does not seem to account for the behavioral contrast effect.

What other ways are there to think about the contrast effect? Williams (1973) and others suggest that *frustration* may be involved. They argue that the animal experiences frustration when it pecks the green key and receives no reinforcement in phase two. (We really have no idea of the nature of the pigeon's subjective experience. We call it frustration for convenience. We assume it's something like what we experience when we put a dime in the coffee machine and coffee, but no cup, is returned.) Call it what you like, it is assumed to act as a drive or motivating agent. Frustration activates and motivates the pigeon such that it increases its behavior in the presence of the red stimulus.

It is clear that the behavioral contrast effect does occur. No doubt about that. *Why* it occurs is another question. No one is quite sure why. The following discussion lends some support to the frustration hypothesis.

Errorless Discrimination Learning

Terrace (1961, 1963a,b) devised a method for discrimination learning in which the animal never actually responds to the negative stimulus. In simple terms, Terrace first establishes a strong response to the positive stimulus alone and then very gradually, very slowly, introduces the negative stimulus into the situation. He brings the negative stimulus in so slowly, in such small steps, that the pigeon never responds to it. For example, pigeons may be trained to discriminate a red key from a green key (negative stimulus) without ever making an unreinforced response to the green key. First, the pigeon is trained to peck the red key alone. Then, during the presentation of the illuminated red key, the light in the key is momentarily turned off. During these brief dark intervals the pigeons typically draw away from the key. The dark intervals may gradually be lengthened without the pigeon responding. Then a very dim green light is presented instead of the totally dark key. The pigeon still does not respond to it, even though it is pecking resourcefully at the key when it is red. Very gradually the intensity and the length of the green light may be increased. Eventually the key may be green half the time and red half the time. Birds trained in this manner will produce few, if any, responses to the green stimulus. The full blown discrimination is formed without errors. (It should be kept in mind that, although the effect has been obtained many times, it is difficult to establish. Terrace, in fact, describes some situations in which it seems impossible to establish errorless discrimination learning.)

The frustration interpretation of the behavioral contrast effect and errorless discrimination learning are interconnected. If an animal forms a discrimination without ever experiencing the "disappointment" which follows an unreinforced response then the animal will not experience frustration. If an animal is trained under the errorless method, it never makes unreinforced responses to the negative stimulus. If it never experiences nonreinforcement, then it is never frustrated. Thus, if we look for the behavioral contrast effect in an errorless-trained pigeon we should not expect to find it. If the errorless trained pigeon does not experience frustration, then there will be no frustration to motivate it, or to goad it into responding more frequently to the positive stimulus. Terrace (1964) has obtained just this result. He compared contrast effects obtained with errorless-trained birds and normally trained birds. A greater contrast effect appeared under normal (frustrating) conditions. This lends some support to the frustration interpretation of the behavioral contrast effect. On the other hand there have been some more recent failures to find this effect (Rilling & Caplan, 1975).

Insoluble Discrimination Problems

So far we have been speaking of discrimination problems that the animal can solve. Through experience he can maximize reinforcement by responding to one particular stimulus and not responding to another. What happens to his behavior if the problem is too difficult, or even impossible for the animal to solve? For instance, there is a point beyond which we cannot detect differences between the brightness of two lights. What happens to our behavior if we are forced to respond in such an impossible situation, receiving reward for correct responses and perhaps punishment for incorrect ones?

There are two experimental techniques for observing behavior in insoluble discrimination situations. In the first method, the animal can perceive the differences between the two stimuli but reward is randomly associated with them (Maier, Glazer, & Klee, 1940; Maier & Klee, 1945). The animal can never be sure which stimulus to respond to. For example, Maier and his associates used a Lashley jumping stand which, if you will recall, requires the animal to leap across an open space and through one of two little doors. Typically, one door is white and the other black. In a normal, soluble discrimination situation one color (e.g., black) will be the correct choice whereas the other (white) will be incorrect. If the animal jumps toward the black door it opens and he flies through to safety. If it jumps at the white door it remains closed, the animal bumps into it, and drops down into a net. As you know, the typical procedure would be to switch the color cues from left to right to ensure that the animal learns a color rather than a position discrimination. In this soluble situation the animal easily learns the discrimination, and comes to restrict its responses to the black stimulus.

Things are not so simple in the insoluble situation. In this condition the experimenter may reinforce the animal (allow safe passage through the door) half the time, regardless of whether the animal jumps to black, to white, to the right, or to the left. There is no way the animal can solve the problem. The animal tries, but it is impossible to obtain reinforcement all the time. Maier found that rats will develop some very peculiar behaviors in this situation. Typically they begin to respond to one side or the other. One rat might jump to the left no matter what the color. Another might fixate on the right-hand door. (You might ask why the rat jumps at all. Simple. The experimenter applies shock until the rat leaps.) Maier describes this fixated jumping as "perseverative responding." We might ask, "So what? As long as there is no way to solve the problem why not jump to one side? Jumping to one side results in as much reinforcement as switching from side to side." Well, the interesting aspect of the situation develops when we suddenly make the problem soluble. That is, we begin reinforcing every response to the black and punishing every response to the white. A naive rat would learn this discrimination quickly. But a frustrated rat does not readjust its behavior even though the cues necessary for such a readjustment are there. This fixated behavior will persist through hundreds of trials. In addition, the animal begins to develop some additional, peculiar characteristics: It loses muscle tone; it may become flaccid and unresponsive. Maier (1949) draws a parallel between this condition and that of the typical catatonic schizophrenic human. A catatonic schizophrenic is a schizophrenic who will adopt fairly rigid bodily positions (e.g., raised arms or bent back, etc.) and will hold them for long periods of time. Maier (1949) suggests that the frustrating conditions which underlie the schizophrenic condition might possibly be similar to those which produce flaccidity in the rat.

Of course, insoluble discrimination problems need not have such extreme consequences. Imagine this situation. An individual is involved, in a romantic fashion, with another individual. Half the time being with the other person seems fine. Half the time it seems more trouble than it's worth. Similarly, being alone seems satisfying some of the time and unpleasant some of the time. The situation is depressing and confusing. It is difficult to know what to do to maximize a sense of well being. One reaction to this situation is to become passive, and to "take it as it comes." One may become, in a sense, fixated or unable to act. Whether research with rats and jumping stands will really shed any light upon this sort of human conflict situation remains to be seen. But the parallel is an interesting one.

The second paradigm which involves insoluble discrimination problems has been labeled the "experimental neurosis" situation. In the Maier situation just described, reinforcement is randomly associated with distinct stimuli. In the experimental neurosis paradigm, reinforcement is consistently associated with one of two stimuli but the stimuli become so similar the animal cannot tell them apart. For example, Brown (1942) trained rats to distinguish between lights of two degrees of brightness. An approach to the bright one, or a retreat from the dimmer one, was reinforced with food. Incorrect responses were punished with shock. After the discrimination was established Brown began to make the two stimuli more and more similar. It became increasingly difficult for the animals to distinguish between the two stimuli. The animals became excited: they trembled, defecated, urinated, and leaped about. Some animals even displayed convulsive behavior. Pavlov (1927) demonstrated similar sorts of behaviors using dogs and salivary responses. The dogs were forced to discriminate between a circle and an ellipse. The ellipse was then made progressively more like the circle. As the two stimuli became very similar the dogs began to salivate at the sight of the apparatus. They whined, barked and tried to leap free of the restraining apparatus. These so-called "neurotic" behaviors persisted beyond the confines of the experimental situation.

The parallel between these experimental effects and human experiences is pretty straightforward. For example, if overly ambitious parents push a child in his school work, they may exceed his abilities. Behavior problems may result, and the child may become disruptive and unhappy. If he is pressed to respond differentially to stimuli that are beyond his ability to discriminate, or seem to him to be the same thing, then he may break down. For example, if parents consistently demand that a normal 7-year-old distinguish between such words as "laziness" and "idleness," they may be exceeding his capacities, and they may force the child into a state of agitation and discomfort.

Fortunately, attempts are made to use the knowledge we have gained from animal experiments in a constructive rather than a destructive manner. We shall discuss some of these attempts in a later section concerned with applied learning theory.

THE PHYSIOLOGY OF DISCRIMINATION

Before turning to a consideration of discrimination processes in human verbal learning, mention should be made of the fact that the investigation of discrimination learning has not been limited to the behavioral level. To the contrary, recent efforts have been, and are being made, to explore the physiological correlates of discrimination learning. These investigations attempt to understand how observable discrimination behaviors are related to underlying physiological events.

The intricacies of this approach are well beyond the scope of this text, but an example of the kind of effort that is being made should illustrate the move toward the physiological analysis of behavioral phenomena. One hypothesis that has been forwarded is that different structures of the brain are associated with different types of discrimination learning. In other words, there may not be one "discrimination learning" center, or function, that encompasses all types of discrimination learning. This hypothesis has been supported by work done by Buerger and Gross (1974) and Gross (1973). They have found that certain structures (e.g., the inferotemporal cortex and related structures) play an important role in visual discrimination learning, but not in other types of discrimination learning, such as that involving the auditory system. Removal of the above-mentioned structures causes poor visual discrimination learning, but does not appear to affect learning in other modalities. The functioning of these structures seems to be specific to visual discrimination learning (at least in monkeys). Whether some common brain function underlying both visual and auditory discrimination learning will be discovered remains to be seen. At least on the level described by Buerger and Gross there does seem to be a difference between the brain functions associated with the various types of discrimination learning. The near future should see an increase in investigations of this sort, which attempt to examine the physical basis of observable discrimination behaviors.

DISCRIMINATION PROCESSES IN HUMAN VERBAL LEARNING

Grant (1964) has concluded that, "a valid psychology of human learning is vastly more complicated than a valid psychology of animal learning, because vastly more numerous, more diversified, and more complicated processes are involved [p. 28]."

There are, of course, two ways to read such a statement. On the one hand we might conclude that animal and human learning processes are qualitatively different and that all the information we have accumulated in studying animal learning is irrelevant, and of little use in attempting to understand human learning. On the other hand, we may choose to believe that the basic components, or elements, of the animal and human learning processes are essentially similar (e.g., reinforcement, discrimination, and generalization). Most, although perhaps not all, of the principal differences between animal and human learning activities may have to do with matters of degree rather than kind. Humans do more of everything and we do it in more complicated, diversified, and interrelated ways. Our learning apparatus may be bigger, better, faster, and more efficient. But it may be composed of the same basic stuff that is found throughout the animal kingdom. That we are somehow set apart from, or qualitatively different from, the rest of the animal kingdom remains to be seen.

It may be our egocentricity and/or our lack of information, rather than reality, which leads us to suspect that we are somehow fundamentally different from the "lower" animals. For example, it has often been suggested that proof of our superiority lies in the fact that we possess language while the lower animals do not. And yet recent research (e.g., Premack, 1971) suggests that animals such as the chimpanzee may, after all, be capable of acquiring language. The reason they have not is not that they cannot but that we have always thought of language acquisition in terms of vocalization or vocalizing. Although controversial (see Brown, 1973), Premack appears to have demonstrated that chimpanzees can acquire a rudimentary form of language utilizing movements rather than sounds. They can use symbols. They just do not have the vocal apparatus necessary for speech. If not required to express their language vocally, and if movements are substituted for sounds, then the chimpanzee appears to do quite well.

The point here is that we may not be all that different from animals when it comes to learning. The information we have gained through a study of animal discrimination should have some bearing upon our understanding of human verbal learning. We may reasonably expect many of the processes and principles to apply.

Since our primary concern is with the human, rather than rats or pigeons, we should spend a little time considering the role of discrimination processes in human verbal learning tasks. We do not intend to suggest that all research concerning human discrimination learning has to do with verbal tasks. Quite to the contrary, the investigation of the human's ability to discriminate along nonverbal dimensions is an ongoing, viable process (e.g., Hébert, Bullock, Levitt, Woodward, & McGuirk, 1974; Thomas, Svinicki, & Vogt, 1973; Hansen, Tomie, Thomas, & Thomas, 1974). These and other investigators have been concerned with the human's ability to discriminate points along such dimensions as weight, brightness, size, area and so on. And yet the pervasiveness of verbal activities within our lives demands that we give some special attention to verbal discrimination activities. For the purposes of this text we must be selective. The number of investigations relating to discrimination in verbal activities is enormous. For example, some recent efforts have revealed that pictures are more easily discriminated than verbal labels of those pictures (Levin, Ghatala, & Wilder, 1974; Rowe, 1972; Wilder & Levin, 1973). This finding raises all sorts of interesting questions. Why, for instance, are pictures more easily discriminated than verbal labels? One suggestion has been that the pictures are more likely to be coded both verbally and visually, and that dualistically coded materials are more easily retained. Be that as it may, it should be apparent that this somewhat minor problem could engage our attention for some time. The same is true for many other types of research. Hence, we must select. Rather than becoming enmeshed in a long series of investigations, we shall try to present an overview of the importance of discrimination processes in human learning. The discussion will take the following form. First, we shall consider the "stage analysis" of verbal learning. Basically this analysis suggests that the association of two verbal units is, after all, quite a complicated event consisting of many (at least three) subprocesses. Some of these subprocesses, or components of the overall learning event, parallel the classical discrimination paradigms we have already outlined.

Second, having taken a look at the overall complexity of the verbal learning situation we shall focus upon one selected area of research which has been labeled VERBAL DISCRIMINATION LEARNING or VD for short. A brief review of this area should serve as an example of the way in which traditional thinking about discrimination has been extended to the realm of human verbal activities.

The Stage Analysis

The stage analysis of verbal learning should provide us with an example of the complexity, but not necessarily the uniqueness, of the human verbal learning process. We approach the stage analysis from the position that the overall verbal learning event is something that is difficult, if not impossible, for the "lower" organisms to accomplish. But we assume that the subprocesses within the overall verbal event converge with those which are within the capacity of the "lower" organisms.

Response Learning

The stage analysis assumes that verbal S–R learning involves at least three distinct components (i.e., response learning, stimulus learning, and associative learning). Underwood and his associates (Underwood, Runquist, & Schulz, 1959; Underwood & Schulz, 1960) took the first step toward the full-blown stage analysis when they distinguished between response learning and associative learning. Associative learning refers to those processes whereby the subject associates a response with a stimulus. Underwood and his colleagues suggested that, in addition to associative learning, subjects are typically required to engage in response learning. That is, in order to hook up a response with a stimulus they must learn that response.

What do we mean by learning a response? There are two types of response learning which are assumed by the stage analysis. The first, termed RESPONSE INTEGRATION, must occur when the subject is not familiar with the responses. Suppose a subject is attempting to learn a paired-associate list composed of digits as stimuli and nonsense syllables, such as QZK, KZQ, and ZKQ, as responses. In order to hook up the responses with the appropriate stimuli, the subject must learn the responses. The trigram QZK is not something he already "knows," or has already integrated. It takes time and effort to learn these kinds of responses. Obviously, if the responses were units such as "cat," "book," and "road" then response integration would not be required. It would have been accomplished before the experiment began. As one would expect, paired-associate learning is accomplished more quickly when already integrated responses are utilized.

We can see how this process of response integration involves discrimination learning. When the subject is first exposed to the paired-associate list all those similar response items are rather confusing. The subject must distinguish, or discriminate, one from another as he goes about learning them and hooking them up with the stimuli. Presumably this subprocess is, in and of itself, complicated. But it is clear that it must involve a process of discriminating among verbal units that are to be learned and used as responses.

The second response-learning process, which may be termed LIST DIFFERENTIATION, has to do with distinguishing the set of actual response units from all other possible response units. If the subject thinks of an incorrect response unit he must be able to recognize it as incorrect. Suppose the actual response units are words such as "cat," "book," and "road." These units do not have to undergo the response integration process. They are already integrated. But the subject must be able to limit his overt responses to this set of words, and to refrain from bringing in incorrect items. The list differentiation process must also involve a discrimination process. The subject must be able to distinguish between items that are members of the set of responses and items that are not.

Stimulus Learning

A second subprocess which occurs within the overall verbal S–R learning event has to do with the fact that the subject must discriminate one stimulus from another in order to associate the appropriate responses. This is another instance of discrimination learning that is an integral part of the overall learning event. For example, if the stimuli in a paired-associate task are QZKX, QKXZ, XQZK, KZXQ, and so on, the subject obviously has a problem. At first glance, these stimuli are confusing. In order to hook responses to these stimuli, the subject must sort them out, and distinguish one stimulus from another in some reliable manner.

One interesting process which relates to stimulus learning is that of STIMULUS SELECTION. Look at the four stimulus items just mentioned. The clever subject would probably not try to distinguish, and order, and memorize all four letters in each stimulus unit. He could simplify his learning task by attending to only the last letter in each stimulus. He could remember that a particular response item "goes with the stimulus ending in Q," and so on. Thus, without any loss in efficiency, he can effectively ignore the first three letters in each stimulus. Underwood, Ham, and Ekstrand (1962) distinguished between the NOMINAL and the FUNCTIONAL STIMULI. Nominal stimuli are those which the experimenter presents to the subject (e.g., the entire four-letter unit). The functional stimulus is that which the subject actually attends to, and utilizes as a stimulus (e.g., in our example, the last letter). The functional and the nominal stimuli may be the same thing, but they need not be. If there are extraneous components of the stimulus, which the subject does not need in distinguishing one stimulus from another, then he may ignore them.

Associative Learning: S–R and R–S

Once the subject has the responses learned, and has the stimuli discriminated, he can go about hooking up the responses with the appropriate stimuli. This is called the associative learning phase. (We do *not* intend to imply that these three processes occur in some unchanging, prescribed order. They may very well overlap in time.) This associative phase is also enormously complicated. It might sometimes occur through a process of rote rehearsal. In other instances it might occur through more complicated verbal and visual mnemonic processes.

One interesting question that has arisen in connection with the study of the associative phase has to do with R–S, or backward, learning. The question is this: When we learn to give a particular response to a particular stimulus (S–R learning), are we also acquiring the ability to produce the stimulus unit when presented the response unit (R–S learning)? For example, suppose we learn to say "horn" each time we are presented the stimulus unit "page" in a paired-associate learning situation. If the experimenter suddenly changes the task and presents "horn," will we be able to say "page?" If we learn to translate Spanish to English, will we be equally able to translate English to Spanish?

This issue is still pretty much up in the air. Although early studies (see Ekstrand, 1966) suggested that R–S learning might be weaker than S–R learning, Asch and Ebenholtz (1962) proposed the PRINCIPLE OF ASSOCIATIVE SYMMETRY. According to this principle, R–S learning is equal to S–R learning. One of the methodological problems inherent in attempts to test this hypothesis is the fact that when a subject learns to give a response (say XZK) to a stimulus (say QVY) he sometimes does not attend to the entire nominal stimulus. As we know, he might select one letter (say Q) from among the three, and ignore the rest. As a result, when presented the response item (XZK) and asked for the nominal stimulus term, his R–S performance *seems* poor because he cannot recall the entire stimulus. But he *can* recall the functional stimulus, or that part of the nominal stimulus to which he actually attended (i.e., Q). The argument here is that the failure to recall the entire nominal stimulus term is not due to the inferiority of R–S learning but rather to the subject's understandable tendency to attend to no more of the stimulus than is absolutely essential during learning. Like the rest of us, subjects operate according to the LAW OF LEAST EFFORT. Thus it has been suggested that if we can equate stimulus and response learning, or ensure that stimulus and response items are *equally available*, then R–S performance should be equal to S–R performance. One way to ensure that stimulus units are available is to use units such as digits, which cannot be broken down by the subject. Another is to give the subject pretraining on the stimulus units to ensure that they are totally learned. Still another is to test the subject for the functional rather than the nominal stimuli. Unfortunately, the data are somewhat contradictory. The controversy goes on, with some studies supporting symmetry (Houston, 1964a; Kanak & Neuner, 1970; Wollen, 1970) and others offering less than clear support for the symmetry hypothesis (Nelson, Rowe, Engel, Wheeler & Garland, 1970; Newman & Campbell, 1971). The interested reader is referred to Kausler (1974) for a detailed review of this problem.

Summary of the Stage Analysis

Our purpose has been twofold. First, a discussion of the stage analysis should indicate the ways in which discrimination processes are intricately involved in the several phases of the verbal learning event. It is impossible to consider verbal learning without acknowledging the involvement of discrimination. Second, a discussion of the stage analysis characterizes the complexity of human verbal learning. Associating a simple response with a simple stimulus turns out to be a multiprocess event. Recent years have seen many studies concerned with the separation and measurement of these various subprocesses. The stimulus, response, and associative learning phases have formed the basis for a number of verbal learning models (e.g., Martin, 1968; McGuire, 1961).

And yet the student may legitimately ask, "Why all this fuss over paired-associate learning? Who cares? Have we lost track of our ultimate goals? Have we become so emersed in attempting to understand one insignificant little laboratory task that we have, in effect, substituted the means for the end?" It seems the danger is there. We may well be overly concerned with paired-associate learning and a number of other laboratory tasks. And yet exercises such as the stage analysis may serve to underline the elements that are important in *all* verbal learning situations, including those in the "real world." Although couched in paired-associate terms the elements of the stage analysis may prove to be important in varied and diverse types of verbal learning. In addition, the stage analysis brings us an acute, if not perfect, awareness of the difficulties we face when trying to understand ourselves.

Verbal Discrimination Learning

The verbal discrimination (VD) paradigm (Ekstrand, Wallace, & Underwood, 1966; Underwood, Jesse, & Ekstrand, 1964) represents a direct extension of the discrimination paradigm into the field of verbal learning. In a typical VD experiment the subject is presented with a long series of pairs of verbal items (e.g., words). One member of each pair has been arbitrarily designated as the "correct" item by the experimenter. The subject's task is to identify the correct items. He does not have to recall the items, nor does he have to associate them with any other item. His sole task is to identify which of the two items within each pair is the "correct" item. He guesses at first, and if he is correct, the experimenter so informs him; he is also made aware of his errors. At first, not knowing which of the two items is correct, the subject will respond to them somewhat randomly. As trials progress, and the subject is "reinforced" through response confirmation, he comes to restrict his choice to the correct items. It seems quite similar to the pigeon pecking colored lights for food.

On the other hand, one difference between the VD procedure and typical animal discrimination techniques is that the human is faced with the task of forming multiple, and almost simultaneous, discriminations. The pigeon is faced with but two stimuli. The human is presented with a long list of pairs, each of which contains a correct and an incorrect stimulus. If presented with a single pair, the human would solve the problem in one trial. In order to study the gradual formation of a discrimination in humans, the task must be made more difficult than that used with animals. The human task is rendered more difficult by adding additional pairs of stimuli.

This does not necessarily mean that the human solves his discrimination problems in a manner fundamentally different from that of the pigeon. It may merely mean that the human is far superior at forming the same sorts of discriminations.

Verbal discrimination research is ongoing (e.g., Mueller, Kausler, Yadrick, & Pavur, 1975; Newman, Suggs, & Averitt, 1974), and has been examined in transfer situations (e.g., Pasko & Zechmeister, 1974) as well as single list situations. It has also been investigated in connection with such diverse topics and variables as concept attainment (Schwartz, 1974) and rate of pair presentation (Mueller & Flanagan, 1972).

Frequency Theory

Aside from parametric investigations, much of the work done with VD has centered around the "frequency theory" interpretation of VD effects (Underwood, Jesse, & Ekstrand, 1964). According to frequency theory the discrimination between right and wrong items is made upon the basis of the relative frequencies of the members of each pair. Basic to this theory is the idea that items acquire FREQUENCY UNITS each time the subject responds to them. The more frequency units an item has acquired the more likely the subject is to label that item as the correct one. Ekstrand, Wallace, and Underwood (1966) have clarified what is meant by frequency units. There are a number of different types of responses which can add frequency units to an item. First, *perceiving* an item is one type of response that is presumed to add frequency units to that item. Since the subject probably perceives both the right and the wrong items on each trial, it is presumed that this type of response adds frequency units to both right and wrong items. Second, *pronouncing* an item adds frequency units. Each time the subject 'says the correct item an additional frequency unit is added to that item. The third, and perhaps most important type of response which adds frequency units, is the *rehearsal* response. These responses presumably occur during the feedback interval when the correct item is clearly identified for the subject. The subject rehearses the correct item at this point, adding frequency units. He therefore increases the probability of identifying that item as the correct item in the future. Presumably the right item will be rehearsed much more than the wrong item. Hence a differential number of frequency units begins to build up in connection with the right and wrong items.

Although couched in brand new terms this theory sounds somewhat familiar. Each time the subject responds to the correct stimulus there is an increase in the tendency to respond to that stimulus in the future. This sounds a bit like the excitatory, or positive, tendency outlined in the Hull–Spence model. Kausler (1974), in fact, has expressed the uneasy feeling that, once the new language is stripped away, the frequency theory may be nothing more than a restatement of traditional S–R theory.

There are several aspects of the frequency theory which seem to be closely related to the Hull–Spence interpretation. For example, suppose the correct items within two pairs in a given experiment are related to one another. Suppose "house" is the correct item in one pair and "home" is the correct item in another pair. Frequency theory assumes that responses to "home" will add frequency units to "house" (it is assumed that "home" always implicitly elicits "house"). Thus, the pair containing "house" should be easier to learn, or solve, than it would have been had the word "home" not been the correct item in another pair. This prediction sounds a bit like something that would be predicted by the Hull-Spence notion of a *generalized* excitatory tendency. If you will recall, what they suggested was that if a response is built up to one stimulus then similar stimuli will tend to elicit that same response. If a response tendency is built up to "home" then that positive tendency will generalize to similar stimuli (e.g., "house"). It sounds as if both theories yield the same prediction.

Although the parallel between frequency theory and the traditional Hull–Spence theory of discrimination learning has not been traced in any great detail, we are suggesting that there may be important points of contact between the two approaches. Of course, there are bound to be some predictions that do differ. For example, frequency theory predicts that the more the subject responds to the wrong stimulus the more likely he will be to respond to it in the future. In contrast, the Hull–Spence theory predicts that the tendency to respond to the negative stimulus will decrease as the number of responses to that stimulus increases.

It should be noted that the overall track record of the frequency interpretation of VD has been spotty. Without going into detail, some experiments seem to support certain deductions (Cole & Kanak, 1972; Hopkins, Boylan, & Lincoln, 1972; Palermo & Ullrich, 1968; McCarthy, 1973) whereas other predictions have received little or no support (Howell, 1973; Kanak, Cole, & Eckert, 1972).

In summary, VD learning, as an experimental paradigm, represents an extension of the traditional discrimination paradigm into the field of verbal learning. Frequency theory as an interpretation of VD learning may well represent a restatement of at least some aspects of the earlier Hull–Spence theory. The extent of the correspondence between the two theories has yet to be determined.

RESPONSE DIFFERENTIATION

Before we close this chapter mention should be made of RESPONSE DIFFERENTIATION. Discrimination, as we have seen, refers to the situation wherein the subject limits a given response to one of many similar stimuli. Response differentiation, on the other hand, refers to the situation where the subject comes to give one of several similar responses to a specific stimulus situation. For example, when first reinforced for pecking a key a pigeon's pecking behavior may be somewhat varied and haphazard: It pecks here and there; some pecks are weak whereas others are strong. As training progresses the responses become more consistent. The pecking behavior is shaped to the point where it maximizes reinforcement. The pigeon differentiates between more and less successful responses, and restricts itself to those which are maximally efficient. When a baby first begins to speak his words are poorly framed. His parents praise him when his responses are accurate and withhold reinforcement when they are not. The baby's responses gradually become differentiated. Poorly vocalized instances drop out. The probability of clearly enunciated sounds, or those which will most likely result in reinforcement, increases.

Verbal Conditioning

By and large, more experimental work has been done with discrimination than with response differentiation. But there are some available examples of response differentiation in the literature. The concept of shaping, wherein the experimenter gradually induces the subject to emit a particular response by reinforcing successive approximations to that response, has already been discussed. VERBAL CONDITIONING represents another area of research that encompasses the concept of response differentiation. In a typical verbal conditioning experiment (Greenspoon, 1955), the subject is asked to say words as they come to mind. As the subject responds, the experimenter murmers "mm-hmm" (or some other subtle form of reinforcement) each time the subject says a plural word. Control subjects do not receive this form of social reinforcement. Greenspoon (1955) found evidence for an increase in the rate of plural word production in the experimental group. In other words, the subject was able to differentiate between responses that were effective in producing a reinforcement (plural) and those that were not effective (singular). Other varieties of verbal conditioning (e.g., Taffel, 1955) have required the subject to make up sentences using one of six pronouns. The experimenter reinforced the choice of one arbitrarily designated pronoun, and did not respond when one of the remaining pronouns was used. Taffel found that the use of the reinforced pronoun increased during the experiment.

The controversy that has swirled about the verbal-conditioning effect has to do with the subject's awareness of what is going on in the experiment. Some authors (Spielberger, 1965) suggest that subjects who exhibit the verbal conditioning effect are usually aware of the conditions of the experiment. They know, or have discovered, that the experimenter is reinforcing a particular kind of response. These authors also suggest that subjects who are unaware of the reinforcement contingency usually fail to condition. On the other hand, other investigators appear to have demonstrated verbal conditioning in the absence of awareness (e.g., Kennedy, 1971). Rosenfeld and Baer (1969) ran an experiment in which the experimenter was really the subject and the subject was really the experimenter. One individual was informed that he was to be an experimenter. During an interview with a subject he was to reinforce the subject's chin rubbing response by nodding his head each time it occurred. In reality, this experimenter was the subject and the subject was the experimenter. The presumed subject (the true experimenter) was in league with Rosenfeld and Baer. During the interview the true experimenter was actually trying to condition the true subject. Each time the true subject said "yeah" the true experimenter reinforced him by rubbing his chin. The results indicated that the true subject increased the rate at which he said "yeah" even though he thought he was the experimenter and in control of the situation. The true subject apparently had no idea he was being conditioned, and yet his response rate went up.

With this classic example of devious psychological experimentation we come to the end of this chapter. We have discussed stimulus generalization, discrimination, and the related process of response differentiation. In the next chapter we shall move on to another related topic: transfer of training. In the coming chapter we shall concentrate upon the impact that a given instance of learning may have upon subsequent instances of learning. The overlap between transfer effects and the effects described in the present chapter should become apparent as we trace through positive and negative transfer phenomena.

SUMMARY

1. GENERALIZATION refers to the fact that if a given response is connected to a particular stimulus then similar stimuli will tend to elicit that same response. The greater the similarity the greater the generalization.

2. There is some evidence that suggests that generalization will first increase and then decrease as the number of reinforced responses to the training stimulus is increased.

3. Generalization tends to be greater following partial reinforcement than after continuous reinforcement.

4. Increased drive level appears to increase stimulus generalization.

5. Certain types of brain stimulation, introduced after the training phase but before the test phase, may result in a decrease in generalization even though the strength of the response to the original training stimulus remains unchanged.

6. Prior experience with the stimulus dimension tends to result in steeper generalization gradients.

7. Primary generalization involves some innate stimulus dimension. Secondary generalization involves acquired, or learned, stimulus dimensions.

8. In SEMANTIC GENERALIZATION a response is first connected to a given word. It is then found that similar words tend to elicit that same response.

9. In the ACQUIRED EQUIVALENCE of cues paradigm two distinct stimuli are paired together. A response is connected to one of the two. It is then found that the remaining stimulus will tend to elicit that same response.

10. DISCRIMINATION refers to an increase in the tendency to restrict a response to one stimulus value(s) along a stimulus dimension. It is brought about by differential reinforcement. Stimulus generalization and discrimination may well be opposite sides of the same coin. An increase in one represents a decrease in the other.

11. In the SIMULTANEOUS PRESENTATION technique both the positive and the negative stimuli are presented together. The SUCCESSIVE PRESENTATION technique involves the sequential presentation of the positive and negative stimuli.

12. According to the HULL–SPENCE THEORY of discrimination learning each reinforced response to the positive stimulus increases a tendency to respond to that stimulus. This tendency generalizes. Each unreinforced response to the negative stimulus increases a tendency not to respond to that stimulus. This negative tendency also generalizes. The net probability of responding to any point along the dimension is reflected by the algebraic sum of the values of the generalized positive and negative tendencies at that point.

13. The RELATIONAL INTERPRETATION argues that, in solving a discrimination problem, the subject is learning a relation between the stimuli, and that he responds on the basis of that perceived relationship.

14. TRANSPOSITION refers to the fact that if a subject learns to discriminate between, say, a large positive stimulus and a smaller negative stimulus, and is then presented the large positive stimulus and a still larger new test stimulus, he will tend to respond to that new stimulus rather than to the old positive one.

15. The relational theoreticians argued that the transposition effect proved that subjects learn a relation between the positive and negative stimuli. But Spence was able to predict the same transposition effect using the Hull–Spence model.

16. There have been recent efforts to explore discrimination learning on a physiological level.

17. If a pigeon is first reinforced for pecking either of two keys and then one key is made the positive stimulus (reinforcement is continued) while the other key becomes the negative stimulus (reinforcement is discontinued) then the response to the positive stimulus increases even though its treatment is constant across the two phases of the experiment. This is called BEHAVIORAL CONTRAST. It may be due to a motivating frustration factor.

18. In ERRORLESS DISCRIMINATION LEARNING a firm response to the positive stimulus alone is established. The negative stimulus is then introduced into the situation so gradually that the animal never responds to it.

19. In INSOLUBLE DISCRIMINATION SITUATIONS the stimuli are made so similar, or the reinforcement is presented so randomly, that the subject cannot solve the problem. Behavior disturbances, which have been likened to human neurotic and psychotic behaviors, have been observed in animals in these situations.

20. We may reasonably expect that human verbal discrimination processes are related to discriminations formed by "lower" animals. The fact that chimpanzees can acquire the rudiments of language suggests that we are not qualitatively different from the rest of the animal kingdom in terms of our learning mechanisms.

21. The STAGE ANALYSIS of verbal learning suggests that a simple S–R association involves at least three distinct subprocesses, or stages,

including stimulus learning, response learning and associative learning. Each stage appears to involve discrimination processes.

22. STIMULUS SELECTION refers to the process wherein the subject may attend to some component or aspect of a given stimulus rather than focusing upon the entire stimulus. The NOMINAL stimulus is that presented by the experimenter. The FUNCTIONAL stimulus is whatever the subject actually uses in learning.

23. When we learn to give a response unit to a stimulus unit we are also acquiring the ability to produce the stimulus unit when presented the response unit. FORWARD and BACKWARD LEARNING may be symmetrical in terms of strength.

24. In VERBAL DISCRIMINATION LEARNING (VD) the subject is presented long series of pairs of items over and over again. His task is to identify which member of each pair is the "correct" item (as arbitrarily chosen by the experimenter). This paradigm represents a direct extension of the discrimination paradigm into the field of verbal training.

25. The FREQUENCY THEORY interpretation of VD learning argues that the discrimination between "right" and "wrong" items is made on the basis of the relative frequencies of the members of each pair. The more frequency units an item has acquired the more likely it is to be labeled as the correct item. Perceiving responses, pronouncing responses and rehearsal responses all add frequency units to an item.

26. The frequency theory of VD learning may represent a restatement of the older Hull–Spence model.

27. RESPONSE DIFFERENTIATION refers to the process wherein the subject refines his response down to the point where it yields reinforcement with a minimum of effort.

28. VERBAL CONDITIONING represents an example of response differentiation. The subject is asked to say words as they come to mind. The experimenter may increase the occurrence of certain types of words (e.g., plural nouns) by reinforcing such words with a murmured, "mm-hmm."

29. A controversy exists as to whether or not such verbal conditioning can occur when the subject is unaware of the reinforcement and its relationship to the critical response class.

Transfer of Training: The Impact of One Task upon Another

9

The more skills and knowledge we acquire the more our new learning will be affected by these past experiences. The effects of prior learning upon present learning may be either positive or negative. For example, bad study habits acquired during high school may have a negative influence upon attempts to establish better study habits in the college setting. Our attempts to master tennis may be affected by our prior experience with such related activities as badminton and ping-pong. Learning one romance language might facilitate the acquisition of subsequent languages. Learning to drive a car certainly aids in learning to drive a truck. Learning to respond fearfully in one social setting might hinder our attempts to adjust comfortably in a new set of social circumstances.

It is clear that we rarely, if ever, learn anything entirely new. No matter how novel the new learning situation appears past experiences and habits will be brought into play. In this sense, transfer seems to be part and parcel of the entire learning process. We have already noted that even the simplest acquisition process involves transfer effects. But when we *focus* upon the impact of prior learning we say we are primarily interested in transfer effects.

In studying transfer of training we attempt to bring under control the conditions of prior training. In this way we hope to be able to identify the mechanisms of transfer. It is obvious that our experimental manipulations represent a very small segment of human transfer experiences. Learning successive paired-associate lists in a laboratory is a far cry from the more global kinds of transfer effects we might hope to understand in the world outside the laboratory. And yet the hope is that, through carefully controlled experimentation, we may identify some of the principles and generalizations that will eventually help us to understand the more complicated, relevant examples of everyday transfer.

An enormous body of literature has grown up around the concept of transfer of training. The basic transfer experiment involves two stages. The subject first learns one task (quite often a paired-associate list) and then attempts to master a second somewhat similar task. Within this simple, convenient framework, any number of variables may be manipulated. Historically, the most important variable has been that of the SIMILARITY BETWEEN THE SUCCESSIVE TASKS. We would like to be able to state the relationship between transfer and interlist similarity in a simple fashion. For example, it would be satisfying if we could comfortably state that positive transfer increases as the similarity between the two tasks increases. But we cannot. The relationship has proven to be much more involved than that.

One of the primary concerns of this chapter will be to outline the complex relationship between similarity and transfer. In addition, we want to clarify the close relationship between generalization, as discussed in the preceding chapter, and the concept of transfer of training. The two are closely tied to one another. Finally, we will discuss some of the theoretical issues concerning the mechanisms of transfer of training.

TRANSFER DESIGNS:
SPECIFIC AND NONSPECIFIC TRANSFER

Suppose we are interested in the effects of learning one paired-associate list upon the subsequent learning of a second list. Furthermore, suppose that the two lists comprise what is commonly known as the A–B, A–C paradigm. What this means is that the *stimuli* in the two successive lists (the A units) are identical, but the *responses* in the two successive lists (the B and C units) are different. One item from the first list might be "valiant–rotten," whereas the corresponding pair in the second list might be "valiant–complex." The subject is required to associate "rotten" with "valiant" in the first list and then to associate "complex" with the same stimulus term during second-list learning. We want to know if A–C learning will be helped or hindered by the A–B experience. On an intuitive basis we might suspect that the A–B learning would interfere with, or compete with, or disrupt the subject's attempts to connect C to A. Each time the subject tries to come up with "complex" during A–C learning he is hampered by the fact that "rotten," so recently acquired, continues to pop into his mind. Intuitive notions aside, we have to find a way to measure the impact of A–B learning upon A–C learning. We need a control group that learns the A–C but not the A–B list. This pattern is designated as Design I in Table 9.1. We may compare the ease with which the experimental and control groups master the A–C list. Typically, the experimental groups have a more difficult time of it in this particular situation, confirming our intuitive suspicion that the A–B, A–C paradigm is a highly negative transfer paradigm or a paradigm in which the learning of the second task is hindered by the learning of the first task. It is difficult to connect Cs to As after Bs have already been associated with As.

It is at this juncture that the first of many complications arises.

TABLE 9.1

Transfer Designs

	First Task	Second Task
Design I		
Experimental condition	A–B	A–C
Control condition	none	A–C
Design II		
Experimental condition	A–B	A–C
Control condition	B–D	A–C

There are at least two transfer factors which contribute to the experimental subject's ability to master the A–C list. The first, as we have noted, has to do with the fact that the B responses probably compete with the C responses during A–C learning. This influence is termed SPECIFIC TRANSFER. It refers to the impact of *specific* first-list associations upon attempts to establish *specific* second-list associations. In this particular paradigm the specific transfer effect is a negative, or disruptive, one. (In other situations, as we shall see, specific transfer effects may be positive.) But there is another type of transfer factor that contributes to the experimental subject's ability to acquire the A–C list. It is referred to as NONSPECIFIC TRANSFER and is, in this particular paradigm, a positive influence. What is it about this design that would give the experimental subjects an *advantage* over the control subjects in learning the A–C list? What about such factors as *learning to learn* and *warm up?* At the beginning of A–C learning the experimental subject has an advantage over the control subject in that he has already learned one paired-associate list, whereas the control subject has not. The experimental subject has undoubtedly already learned something about how to master a paired-associate list. He already knows what to look for, what strategies to use, and how to hook up items in efficient ways. In addition the experimental subject is already "warmed up" at the beginning of A–C learning, and will not be as distracted as the control subject. He has already established sensory, postural, and attitudinal sets to learn paired-associate lists. He is ready, whereas the control subject must settle in. Warm up and learning to learn represent important nonspecific transfer factors (Postman, 1969, 1971; Postman & Schwartz, 1964; Thune, 1951). They are independent of the specific contents of the two lists.

Learning to learn may be distinguished from warm up in terms of its temporal persistence. Warm up effects are presumed to be transitory. Once practice ceases the advantage gained by having "warmed up" dissipates rapidly. The effects of learning to learn are, on the other hand, assumed to be more permanent. Once a subject has developed efficient strategies and methods for mastering a particular type of learning task, regardless of the specific content of the task, these strategies and methods may be maintained, or remembered, over time.

To return to our consideration of the A–B, A–C paradigm, it is clear that two transfer influences operate in the experimental condition. One is negative specific transfer associated with competition between the A–B and A–C associations. The other is positive nonspecific transfer identified with warm up and learning to learn. Overall transfer in Design I will be determined by both types of transfer.

But suppose we are *only* interested in specific transfer. We want to estimate specific transfer accurately. We want our estimate to be free of nonspecific transfer effects. If we were to use Design I we would underestimate the amount of negative specific transfer. The negative specific transfer effect would be partially mitigated by the advantage the experimental group gains over the control group through positive nonspecific transfer. Hence, we need an alternative design in which the control subjects are given an *equal* opportunity to warm up and learn to learn. Design II in Table 9.1 represents such a design. In this design the control group first learns a list that is *entirely unrelated* to the A–C list. Hence the control condition in this design is free from any specific transfer. But it does involve nonspecific transfer. The control subjects are allowed the opportunity to warm up and learn to learn. In Design II the control and experimental conditions are equated in terms of nonspecific transfer. They differ only in terms of specific transfer. Thus any difference in the ease with which the experimental and control subjects learn the A–C list must be due to specific transfer alone. The design is free from contamination by unwanted nonspecific factors.

SPECIFIC TRANSFER: SIMILARITY EFFECTS

Having outlined the manner in which psychologists isolate specific from nonspecific transfer we now turn to a more detailed consideration of some of the more important specific transfer phenomena. The A–B, A–C paradigm just discussed is only one of many possible transfer patterns. For example, we may construct successive lists such that they conform to an A–B, A–B′ pattern. In this paradigm the stimuli in successive lists are identical, whereas the responses are similar (B′ is a unit that is similar or related to B). A pair from the first list might be "valiant–scared," whereas the corresponding A–B′ pair would be "valiant–frightened." If the similarity between the first-list and second-list responses is strong enough, this paradigm tends to yield positive transfer.

TABLE 9.2

Sample Items Representing Five Basic Two-List Transfer Paradigms

First List	Second, or Transfer, List				
(A–B)	C–D	A–C	A–B′	C–B	A–B$_r$
LOH–tranquil	GOZ–royal	LOH–royal	LOH–calm	GOZ–tranquil	LOH–afraid
TUN–afraid	WIF–barren	TUN–barren	TUN–fearful	WIF–afraid	TUN–complete
BAV–insane	DEX–spoken	BAV–spoken	BAV–crazy	DEX–insane	BAV–tranquil
JAX–complete	PEC–double	JAX–double	JAX–total	PEC–complete	JAX–insane

When attempting to connect "frightened" to "valiant" the stimulus term "valiant" might cue off the already learned "scared" response which, in term, might stimulate "frightened."

We may also construct an A–B, A′–B paradigm in which the responses in the successive lists are identical and the stimuli are similar. This also tends to be a positive transfer paradigm. Then there is the A–B, C–B paradigm in which the responses are identical and the stimuli are unrelated. The more patterns we devise and test, the more confusing the situation becomes, the more difficult it becomes to keep them all straight in one's mind (Table 9.2).

Osgood's Transfer Surface

Fortunately, Osgood (1949) has developed a mnemonic device which summarizes the transfer effects expected in many paradigms. The device is neither perfect nor comprehensive. But it is convenient, and it does provide us with a simple method for keeping the welter of transfer paradigms and similarity relationships somewhat organized in our minds. Figure 9.1 contains a partially modified version of the original Osgood surface. Consider the flat two-dimensional plane depicted in the left side of Figure 9.1. Degrees of similarity between first-list and second-list stimuli, ranging from identity to neutrality (unrelated), are arranged along the width of the plane. Degrees of response similarity, ranging from identity to neutrality, are spread along the length of the plane. (Actually, the Osgood surface extended the response dimension to include opposed and antagonistic responses but neither extension has proven to be of much value.) The plane contains points that represent all possible combinations of stimulus and response similarity. The location of a few of the more important paradigms are indicated on the plane. For example, the A–B, C–B paradigm is located in the upper left corner where response similarity is

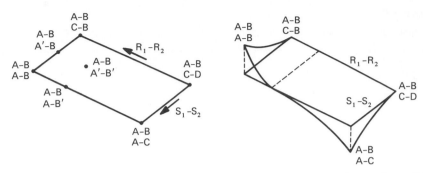

Figure 9.1.   A modified version of the Osgood transfer and retroaction surface. (After Osgood, C. E. The similarity paradox in human learning: A resolution. *Psychological Review,* 1949, *56,* 132–143. Fig. 5, p. 140. Copyright 1949 by the American Psychological Association. Reprinted by permission.)

at a maximum (identity) and stimulus similarity is minimal. The A–B, A–B paradigm (identical lists) is located in the near left corner, and so on.

Now, having located all possible combinations of stimulus and response similarity on a flat plane we may ask the next question: How much and what kind of transfer (positive or negative) do we expect in each of these paradigms? To answer this question we turn to the right side of Figure 9.1. Here we find a flexed surface that is superimposed upon, and that cuts through our flat plane at the dotted line. This surface will indicate the kind of transfer we expect in any given paradigm. Notice that the surface is above the plane at its left end and below the plane at its right end. The vertical dimension represents the direction and amount of expected transfer. If the surface is *above* the plane we expect *positive* transfer in those paradigms lying under the surface. If the surface is *below* the plane we expect *negative* transfer.

Suppose we wish to predict transfer in the A–B, A–C paradigm. First, we locate the A–B, A–C paradigm on the plane. Second, we draw a line, perpendicular to the plane, from the plane to the surface. The *direction* of the line represents the *direction* of the expected transfer. A line drawn upward represents positive transfer. A line drawn downward represents negative transfer. The *length* of the line represents *amount* of transfer. The longer the line the stronger the transfer effect. Thus we expect a large amount of negative transfer in the A–B, A–C paradigm. We must draw a long line downward to reach the surface from the plane at point A–B, A–C. Try predicting transfer in the A–B, A′–B paradigm. First locate the paradigm on the plane. Then draw a line from the plane to the surface at that point. The surface predicts moderate positive transfer in this paradigm.

It is an interesting and important model. Once one grasps it, it serves as a convenient summary device. What it says in words is this: When responses are identical and stimulus similarity increases then transfer will increase from zero to maximum positive (this is the function represented by the left edge of the surface). When responses are unrelated and stimulus similarity increases then transfer will increase from zero to maximum negative (the right edge of the surface). When stimuli are unrelated and response similarity increases transfer remains at zero (the back edge). When stimuli are identical and response similarity increases transfer shifts from maximum negative to maximum positive (the front edge of the surface).

The overall surface has received experimental support. Dallett (1962) chose 12 points on the surface representing three degrees of response similarity and four degrees of stimulus similarity. He constructed lists corresponding to these 12 paradigms and tested for transfer. His results support the overall shape and nature of the hypothetical surface.

The Role of Meaningfulness:
Some Problems for the Transfer Surface

Despite a good deal of experimental support, serious objections to the surface have been raised. The most important of them has to do with the impact of meaningfulness upon transfer. It would be fair to say that, with a few exceptions, the Osgood surface does a good job of summarizing the transfer effects obtained with highly meaningful, or familiar, materials such as words. But it is not very accurate at all when materials of a low level of meaningfulness, such as unfamiliar nonsense syllables, are utilized. For example, the surface predicts zero transfer in the A–B, C–B paradigm. But when the response items in this paradigm are nonsense items then substantial *positive* transfer appears (Dean & Kausler, 1964; Jung, 1963; Merikle, 1968). As a further example we may note that the prediction of high negative transfer in the A–B, A–C paradigm is confirmed when highly meaningful materials are used. But when materials of a low level of meaningfulness are employed this negative effect tends to disappear (Jung, 1963; Richardson & Brown, 1966).

Thus our use of the Osgood surface must be tempered by an awareness of its limitations. It seems most suited as a summary statement of the transfer effects expected when highly meaningful materials are employed (the principal exception to this generalization is the fact that with highly meaningful materials the A–B, C–B paradigm seems to yield slightly negative rather than the predicted zero transfer). It does not accurately predict the amounts of transfer that will be obtained under conditions of low meaningfulness. The reasons for the enormous impact of meaningfulness upon transfer will be discussed in an upcoming section.

Additional Surfaces

S_1–R_2, S_2–R_1 Surfaces

The Osgood surface is truly limited in still another important sense. It is restricted to a consideration of the effects of similarity between first-list and second-list stimuli (S_1–S_2) and similarity between responses (R_1–R_2). But these are not the only loci of similarity within a two-list sequence. One may also consider the similarity between first-list stimuli and second-list responses (S_1–R_2) and the similarity between first-list responses and second-list stimuli (S_2–R_1). We can conceive of all possible combinations of S_1–R_2 and S_2–R_1 similarity just as we did in the case of Osgood's similarity loci. We can explore transfer in paradigms such as A–B, B–A; A–B, B'–A; and A–B, C–A. Without going into any detail it should be sufficient to point out that these loci of similarity have been considered, and that a transfer surface has been developed which summarizes many of the transfer effects expected in the S_1–R_2 and S_2–R_1 paradigms (Houston, 1964b, 1966b; Thompson, 1966).

The A–B, A–B_r Paradigm and the Re-paired Surface

The A–B, A–B_r paradigm is a maverick paradigm. It has created quite a stir in the field of transfer. In this paradigm subjects first learn an A–B list. The second list is composed of the *same* stimulus and response materials. But they are re-paired in the second list (see Table 9.2). For example, suppose two pairs from the first list are "profane–bitter" and "severe–ready." These materials would be re-paired in the second list yielding "profane–ready" and "severe–bitter." It is fairly obvious that the second, or A–B_r, list would be a bit confusing. In fact, when the response materials are words, this paradigm produces massive amounts of negative transfer. Negative transfer in the A–B, A–B_r situation often exceeds that obtained in the A–B, A–C paradigm (Postman, 1962b; Kausler & Kanoti, 1963).

The A–B, A–B_r paradigm is not to be found on the Osgood surface. It represents a type of transfer that is beyond the scope of that particular summary device. In addition, the re-pairing concept is not limited to the A–B, A–B_r paradigm. Other paradigms may be re-paired as well. For example, we may re-pair the A–B, A–B' paradigm creating an A–B, A–B'_r paradigm. In this situation two pairs from the first list might be "complex–brave" and "bitter–ready." The corresponding items in the A–B'_r list would then be "complex–prepared" and "bitter–valiant." Needless to say, this tends to be a negative transfer situation too, particularly when the materials are highly meaningful. Many of the Osgood paradigms may be subjected to the re-pairing procedure. We may develop and test such patterns as A–B, A′–B$_r$ and A–B, A′–B$_r'$, among others. Dallett (1965b) has developed a transfer surface which summarizes the transfer effects expected in all the re-paired Osgood paradigms.

In general, when highly meaningful materials are used all the re-paired paradigms tend to produce negative transfer. But special note should be made of the fact that transfer obtained in the re-paired paradigms is also strongly affected by the meaningfulness of the materials. With low meaningfulness the negative transfer effects appear to be reduced. Some investigators have, in fact, obtained *positive* transfer in the A–B, A–B$_r$ paradigm when responses of a low level of meaningfulness are employed (Mandler & Heinemann, 1956; Merikle, 1968).

THE STAGE ANALYSIS OF TRANSFER OF TRAINING

In the last chapter, we discussed the stage analysis of verbal learning. According to this analysis the learning of a simple verbal association involves at least three stages, or subprocesses. These include stimulus, response, and associative learning. In addition, we noted that R–S, or backward, learning also occurs during forward, or S–R, learning. If these stages affect the learning of a single list they will, of course, also affect the learning of a second, or transfer, list. The strengths of the various processes established during first-list learning will determine transfer, or will affect the ease of second-list learning. A prediction of overall transfer must involve a consideration of the separate effects of each of these subprocesses. Second-list learning is multiply determined. It is affected by each of the first-list learning stages. A few examples should clarify the nature of the stage analysis of transfer. The reader should realize that these examples are selected from among many.

The Importance of Response Learning in Transfer

Consider the A–B, A–B$_r$ paradigm. We have already noted that this paradigm yields heavy negative transfer when words are used, and some positive transfer when nonsense materials are employed. We now wish to find out why this is so. The control condition in this situation may be indexed as C–D, A–B (unrelated lists). The important point to note here is that the control subject is first faced with the B responses during second-list learning. He is not exposed to the B responses during first-list learning. He must learn the B responses before he can hook them up with the correct A stimuli. If the B units are familiar words, then the problem of response learning is reduced; he already has them learned. But if the B responses are nonsense materials he must do a lot of response learning before he can hook them up. Now switch your attention to the experimental, or A–B, A–B$_r$, subjects. Note that when they are faced with the second, or A–B$_r$, list they have *already* been exposed to the B units as responses in the first list. If the B units are familiar words this fact does not make much difference. Familiar B units such as words have already been learned by both experimental and control subjects before they come into the experimental situation. But what if the B units are low-meaningfulness nonsense materials such as XLQZ and XCGQ? In this case the experimental subject has an advantage over the control subject. He has had the opportunity to learn these nonsense materials during first-list learning so that, by the time the second list rolls around, he already has them learned and is ready to move on to the hook up stage. He has an advantage over the control subject who is first faced with the B units during second-list learning. While the control subject is struggling to do *two* things during second-list learning (learn responses *and* hook them up) the experimental subject has but one task; to hook up the already learned B units with the correct stimuli. The advantage the experimental subjects gain by having learned the responses during the first-list phase partially offsets or mitigates the trouble they have learning the second list (which is due to the confusion over re-paired materials). Thus it can be seen that it is response learning that accounts for the reduction in negative transfer observed in the A–B, A–B$_r$ paradigm when nonsense materials are employed.

Parenthetically, it should be noted that response learning is also important in other paradigms. For example, the same analysis may be applied to the A–B, C–B paradigm, wherein positive transfer is also obtained when materials of a low level of meaningfulness are employed.

The Importance of Stimulus Learning in Transfer

To make a prediction about overall transfer we must weigh the influences of these various subprocesses. Some contribute positively and some negatively. The overall effect will, in a sense, be represented by the sum of the various positive and negative influences (Martin, 1965). We have just considered the importance of response learning in transfer. We now turn to a consideration of the importance of stimulus learning in transfer. Again, remember this is but one selected example of the importance of stimulus learning.

Consider the A–B, A–C experimental condition as compared to the appropriate B–D, A–C control. We have already noted that substantial negative transfer in this paradigm may be decreased if the meaningfulness of the stimuli is decreased (Richardson & Brown, 1966). Why? At the beginning of A–C learning the experimental subject has already had the opportunity to learn or differentiate the stimuli (A units) during A–B learning. The control subjects have not had this opportunity. They are faced with the A units for the first time at the beginning of A–C learning. With highly meaningful stimuli the experimental subject would have no real advantage over the control subject; both control and experimental subjects would have little or no trouble differentiating highly meaningful stimuli. But if the materials are nonsense materials then the stimulus learning, or differentiation, phase is more difficult, and the experimental subjects should have an advantage over the controls. The experimental subjects have completed the stimulus learning task by the time A–C learning begins, whereas the control subjects have not. This advantage, which appears with nonsense materials, mitigates the negative transfer effect in the A–B, A–C paradigm.

The Encoding Variability Hypothesis

There is another way in which the reduction in negative transfer in the A–B, A–C paradigm with decreasing degrees of stimulus meaningfulness might be explained. Martin (1968, 1972) has proposed an encoding variability hypothesis which may be extended to the present situation. If a subject is faced with a highly meaningful stimulus, such as a word, he will probably connect the first-list response to that *entire* word. He will not break the stimulus word down into component parts. He will think of the word as a unit, or a whole, and use it as such. Then, when faced with the second-list task of associating a new response with that same stimulus, he suffers from considerable interference. The stimulus word continues to elicit the competing first-list response. But if the first-list stimulus is low in meaningfulness (e.g., XZLK) he may connect the first-list response (B) to *part* of the stimulus (e.g., X–B) and the second-list response (C) to *another part* of that stimulus (e.g., K–C). With stimuli of low meaningfulness, he is able to avoid much of the interference and confusion by connecting the different responses to distinct and different components of the overall stimulus.

It should be pointed out that the encoding variability hypothesis is not limited to the A–B, A–C paradigm. It is a general hypothesis which states that *the availability of alternative encoding possibilities should reduce interference effects*. The hypothesis has received considerable attention and support in the literature (Goggin & Martin, 1970; Houston, 1967; Merryman & Merryman, 1971; Pagel, 1973; Weaver, 1969).

The Importance of R-S Learning In Transfer

As a final example of the role of subprocesses in the overall transfer process we may take note of the A–B, C–B paradigm. We find some negative transfer in this situation when highly meaningful materials are used

(Twedt & Underwood, 1959). (It should be noted again that this is one result that the Osgood surface does not predict.) Why is this negative transfer obtained? There is no apparent negative influence due to forward associations. Stimulus learning should not contribute negatively. If anything, response learning should contribute positively. The culprits must be backward associations. Consider the fact that while the subject is learning A–B he is also learning B–A. It is felt that this backward B–A association causes some interference when the subject attempts to learn the second, or C–B, list. During second-list learning, when the subject sees C he may well think of B, the correct response. But, because of the previously established backward B–A association, he may think, "Wait a minute. B goes with A. I'm confused." Consequently, he may reject B as the correct second-list response, thereby contributing to the observed negative transfer effect.

It should be apparent by now that overall transfer effects are the result of many interacting subprocesses, or learning stages. Forward and backward learning, response learning, and stimulus learning all contribute to overall transfer phenomena. In some situations these stages counteract one another. In others they supplement one another. Table 9.3 contains some of the positive and negative influences expected in several of the more important transfer patterns. A "0" entry implies that that particular stage contributes in neither a positive nor a negative fashion to that particular paradigm. A "+" entry implies that that process can contribute positively to second-list learning, and a "−" entry implies a possible negative contribution. The *strengths* of these positive and negative contributions are, as we have seen, often dependent upon the meaningfulness of the materials. A complete treatment of these interactions is beyond the scope of this text. The interested reader is referred to Kausler (1974), Martin (1972), and Postman (1971).

TABLE 9.3

Component Analysis of Selected Transfer Paradigms

	Paradigm			
Component	A–B C–D	A–B A–C	A–B C–B	A–B A–B$_r$
Response learning	0	0	+	+*
Stimulus learning	0	+*	0	+
Forward associations	0	−	0	−
Backward associations	0	0	−*	−

* Entries marked with an asterisk are discussed in text.

GENERALIZATION AND TRANSFER OF TRAINING

We have repeatedly noted that transfer and generalization are related in that they are both concerned with the effects of prior learning upon subsequent performance. Despite the fact that the two fields have developed somewhat independently (e.g., different variables, designs, methods, vocabularies, and investigators) psychologists have taken note of the basic correspondence between the two phenomena.

Consider stimulus generalization. We train a response to a given stimulus. We then present similar stimuli and observe whether or not the response occurs. The A–B, A'–B transfer paradigms, wherein stimulus similarity is varied, seem to be related to stimulus generalization. We connect B to A and then present a similar stimulus (A'). The more similar A' is to A the more likely A' is to elicit B. We may label this effect either stimulus generalization or positive transfer. Variations in interlist stimulus similarity correspond to variations in the similarity between the training and the test stimuli in a typical stimulus generalization study. An awareness of this basic continuity formed the basis for Gibson's (1940) classic analysis of verbal transfer effects in terms of the principles of stimulus generalization.

But a consideration of stimulus generalization is not enough to account for all our observed transfer of training phenomena. For example, what about the A–B, A–B' paradigm? This does not seem to involve stimulus generalization, but it does involve another type of generalization which we may term RESPONSE GENERALIZATION. It was left to Osgood (1946, 1949, 1953) to mesh, or integrate, the concepts of both stimulus and response generalization in his analysis of transfer effects. Very simply, response generalization refers to the fact that if a given response is connected to a given stimulus then that stimulus will also tend to elicit similar responses. The less similar the response the less likely it will be to occur. For example, if a girl's name is "Melodie" then there will be a tendency for people to call her "Melanie," but not much of a tendency to call her "Joan." If we connect the word "house" to a given stimulus in the laboratory then that stimulus will, in one way or another, also tend to elicit "home." To return to the thread of the analysis, the A–B, A–B' transfer paradigms seem to involve varying degrees of response similarity. If we connect "house" to a given stimulus, and then require the subject to associate "home" with the same stimulus, we will observe a positive transfer effect brought about by response generalization.

Osgood's surface represents an integrated estimation of the effects of both stimulus and response generalization in transfer of training paradigms. It is largely through his efforts that the concepts of stimulus and response generalization were extended into the field of verbal learning, and contributed to the theoretical analysis of transfer of training effects.

The student should not be misled by the fact that generalization and transfer of training are often treated as separate topics within the field of psychology. [Their intimate relationship is discussed in more detail by Postman (1971).]

MEDIATION PARADIGMS AND TRANSFER OF TRAINING

When a subject learns an A–B, A–B′ sequence we are tempted to assume that the experiment involves two associative, or hook up, stages; A–B and A–B′. But might there not be an undetected third hook up step involved in this experiment? We have already suggested that when the subject learns A–B′ the A stimulus may elicit the recently acquired B unit which, in turn, elicits the B′ unit. But why does B elicit B′? Where did that connection, or association, come from? Presumably it was established before the subject ever came into the experimental situation. But it does represent a distinct instance of learning. The elusive third associative step in the so-called two-step transfer paradigm is accomplished pre-experimentally. Cast in terms of these ideas our two-step transfer paradigm (A–B, A–B′) becomes a THREE-STEP MEDIATION PARADIGM (B–B′, A–B, A–B′), where the first step is accomplished preexperimentally and the last two stages are established within the laboratory. When the subject learns the A–B′ list, it is assumed that A leads to B which, in turn, leads to B′. A number of psychologists have investigated transfer of training within this mediational framework.

Three-Stage Paradigms

In a major investigation, Horton and Kjeldergaard (1961) devised and tested a number of three-stage paradigms. These paradigms form three distinct groups. First, paradigms such as the A–B, B–C, A–C paradigm are labeled CHAINING PARADIGMS. In this situation (and in all other three-stage paradigms) the subject masters three successive lists conforming to the prescribed pattern. The ease with which the subject masters the final list is compared to the performance of an appropriate control group. If the prior learning of the first two lists facilitates the learning of the third list then we say mediation has occurred. The A–B, B–C, A–C paradigm produces such facilitation. If you will focus upon the third, or A–C, stage, you will observe that when the subject sees the A unit he may well think of the B unit (due to stage-one, or A–B learning); B may, in turn, lead to C (due to stage-two, or B–C, learning). A *chain* of associations is involved (i.e., A leads to B leads to C). It is easier to learn A–C after having learned A–B, B–C. The learning of the first two stages facilitates, or mediates, third-stage learning.

Some of the chaining models involve backward, or R–S, associations. For example, in the B–A, C–B, A–C paradigm third-stage, or A–C learning, can only be facilitated by backward associations. In the third stage, A might lead to B, but only if a backward association between B and A was established during first-stage B–A learning. Similarly, B might then lead to C, but only if a backward association was established during second-stage C–B learning. As one might expect, Horton and Kjeldergaard predicted that mediation effects will be greater when the chains of associations involve forward rather than backward bonds.

The second group of paradigms devised by Horton and Kjeldergaard are called the STIMULUS EQUIVALENCE PARADIGMS. For example, in an A–B, C–B, A–C paradigm, it is assumed that A and C "become equivalent" in that B is associated with both of them. Thus A–C learning is expected to be facilitated.

The third and final group of Horton and Kjeldergaard paradigms are called the RESPONSE EQUIVALENCE PARADIGMS. In the B–A, B–C, A–C pattern A and C are assumed to become equivalent because they are both elicited by, or connected to, the same stimulus (B). It is a little like saying "child" and "youngster" are equivalent responses because we have associated them both with the same stimulus (actual children). The B–A, B–C, A–C paradigm is also expected to yield a positive mediating effect.

Parenthetically, it should be noted that an experimenter may establish all stages within the laboratory (i.e., have the subject learn three successive lists). On the other hand, one or more of the stages may be assumed to have occurred before the experimental session. By assuming various stages (through the use of various measures of verbal relatedness) the experimenter may cut down on the number of actual lists the subject must master in the laboratory.

Tests of the paradigms developed by Horton and Kjeldergaard have yielded a distinctive pattern of results. Generally speaking, most of the paradigms yield significant facilitation effects. This seems to occur when all lists are learned in the laboratory (Horton & Kjeldergaard, 1961) and when some of the associations are assumed to have occurred outside the laboratory (Cramer, 1967). On the other hand, reports of reliable differences *among* the various paradigms have been noticeably lacking. The only exception is the A–B, B–C, A–C paradigm which seems to yield more facilitation than all the rest (Horton & Hartman, 1963; Shanmugam & Miron, 1966).

Four-Stage Paradigms

Jenkins (1963) developed a series of four-stage mediation paradigms. For example, in the A–B, B–C, C–D, A–D paradigm fourth-stage, or A–D, learning is presumed to be facilitated by the fact that A leads to B, which leads to C, which leads to D. Although Jenkins himself found no significant mediation effects in any of his paradigms, others have found some evidence for four-stage mediation (Grover, Horton, & Cunningham, 1967). In general, however, the four-stage paradigms have proven to be fairly ineffective in producing facilitation.

In summary, three-stage and four-stage paradigms really represent attempts to understand the complicated events that underlie the more traditional two-stage transfer paradigms. When a subject learns an A–B, A–B' sequence the traditional investigator of transfer essentially ignores the third stage, or that which accounts for the relationship between B and B'. The mediation investigator attempts to make this assumed B–B' stage explicit, and to manipulate it in a controlled fashion. The fact that mediation research has produced spotty results does not detract from its importance. It merely suggests that our techniques and procedures are not yet refined to the point where we can bring under control the mediational events that underlie transfer effects observed in situations involving two lists.

SUMMARY

1. The study of transfer of training focuses upon the positive and negative effects of prior training upon subsequent training.

2. Although much of the transfer research has been cast in a two-list paired-associate mold, the hope is that the principles and mechanisms discovered with this limited task will help us understand transfer effects that occur outside the laboratory.

3. Two general classes of transfer events are referred to as SPECIFIC and NONSPECIFIC TRANSFER. Specific transfer refers to the impact of specific first-list associations upon attempts to establish specific second-list associations. Nonspecific transfer refers to transfer due to such factors as LEARNING TO LEARN and WARM UP. These factors are independent of the specific contents of the lists. Warm up effects are presumed to be transitory, whereas learning to learn phenomena are more permanent. Transfer designs have been developed that separate specific from nonspecific transfer.

4. The similarity between successive lists has proven to be one of the more powerful transfer variables. The relationship between transfer and interlist similarity is not a simple one.

5. Osgood has developed a TRANSFER SURFACE that summarizes the direction and amount of transfer expected in transfer situations, which vary in terms of stimulus and response similarity.

6. The surface predicts that when responses are identical and stimulus similarity increases then transfer will increase from zero to maximum

positive. When responses are unrelated and stimulus similarity increases then transfer will shift from zero to maximum negative. When stimuli are unrelated and response similarity increases then transfer remains at zero. When stimuli are identical and response similarity increases then transfer will shift from maximum negative to maximum positive.

7. With a few exceptions the surface summarizes transfer effects obtained with highly meaningful, or familiar, materials. But when materials of a low level of meaningfulness are employed the surface is not accurate.

8. Osgood's surface is further limited in that it only considers the similarity between first-list and second-list stimuli and the similarity between first-list and second-list responses. Additional surfaces have been developed that summarize transfer effects expected when the loci of similarity are between the first-list stimuli and the second-list responses (S_1–R_2) and between the second-list stimuli and the first-list responses (S_2–R_1).

9. In addition, a surface has been developed that summarizes transfer effects expected in RE-PAIRED PARADIGMS (such as the A–B, A–B$_r$ pattern). The paradigms found on these additional surfaces are also heavily affected by the meaningfulness of the materials.

10. The stage analysis of transfer emphasizes the fact that transfer is not a single, simple process. The various stages of first-list learning (S, R, S–R, R–S) all affect the ease with which second-list associations are acquired. Selected examples of the roles of response learning, stimulus learning, and backward learning are discussed in connection with the A–B, A–B$_r$; A–B, A–C; and A–B, C–B paradigms, respectively.

11. The encoding variability hypothesis states that nominal stimuli may vary in terms of the number of alternative ways in which they may be utilized as stimuli. For example, a nominal stimulus may possess a number of components, each of which may be chosen by the subject to serve as the functional stimulus. Interference effects in transfer situations should be reduced as the availability of such alternative coding possibilities increases.

12. The relationship between transfer of training and generalization is a close one. Transfer of training paradigms involves both stimulus and response generalization. For example, the A–B, A′–B paradigm involves interlist stimulus generalization, whereas the A–B, A–B′ paradigm involves response generalization.

13. TWO-STAGE TRANSFER PARADIGMS involve an implicit third stage. For example, in the A–B, A–B′ paradigm an implicit B–B′ stage is assumed. Three- and four-stage mediation paradigms attempt to bring this, and other implicit stages, under experimental control.

14. In THREE-STAGE PARADIGMS, the subject typically masters three paired-associate lists, which conform to some predetermined pattern, such

as the A–B, B–C, A–C chaining pattern. Third-stage learning is facilitated, presumably through the action of a chain of associations established during the first two stages (i.e., A leads to B, which leads to C).

15. Eight different three-stage paradigms have been developed, including the CHAINING, the STIMULUS EQUIVALENCE, and the RESPONSE EQUIVALENCE varieties. Most of these yield significant mediation effects. The A–B, B–C, A–C paradigm appears to produce more facilitation than all the others, which do not differ from one another.

16. FOUR-STAGE MEDIATION PARADIGMS (e.g., A–B, B–C, C–D, A–D) have been developed, but they tend to yield few significant mediation effects.

4

RETENTION

In this section, we will focus upon retention processes. Once again it should be remembered that it is impossible to separate completely *acquisition, transfer,* and *retention.* A concern for one of these three is a matter of emphasis rather than of clear and distinct differences among them. In this section we concentrate on what happens to memory traces after learning has been accomplished. Toward the end of the section we shall attempt to underscore important points of contact between the study of human and animal memory.

The field of memory and retention is enormous, and in a text such as this we must be selective. Sometimes the field is organized around different memory tasks: Some authors consider, in a sequential fashion, theory and data associated with such tasks as paired-associate learning, serial learning, free recall, and recognition learning. Each of these tasks is then subdivided (e.g., we may consider free recall in which the items are presented for either a single trial or for multiple trials). The organization assumed in this text is a bit different. We will focus upon alternative theoretical positions and issues rather than upon tasks per se. We will draw data from the various task situations when

it is relevant to a particular theoretical issue.

In Chapter Ten we shall discuss the first of two major theoretical approaches to the understanding of memory. The basic assumption behind interference theory is that retention losses may be traced to the interfering effects of previous and/or subsequent learning. For example, if we learn a phone number such as 872–6314 we will have little trouble remembering it over time. On the other hand if, after processing this number, we go on to learn 843–1762, 782–6413, 287–1463, and 378–2614, we may then have trouble recalling the original number. In other words, the subsequent learning somehow interfered with our ability to recall the original number. In Chapter Ten we will discuss basic interference phenomena and the two-factor theory of interference, which is presumed to account for these data.

In Chapter Eleven, we will discuss the information-processing approach to memory. This is a relatively new approach that draws heavily upon information measurement concepts and the language of digital computers. The individual is seen as an information-processing system. Memory is thought of in terms of the encoding, storage, and retrieval of information. In contrast to the single theory associated with the interference approach, many information-processing models of memory are available. We shall discuss several of them. In addition, we shall try to outline points of contact between the information-processing approach and the interference approach.

In Chapter Twelve we begin by noting that psychologists have distinguished among many different types of memory. We ask whether or not these distinctions are valid, and whether or not distinct models will be necessary for the proposed types of memory. Four widely discussed distinctions are considered (i.e., short-term versus long-term memory, recall versus recognition, different models for different types of information, and animal versus human memory). By drawing upon available experimental data we attempt to assess the validity of these various distinctions.

In Chapter Thirteen we will consider the role of organization in memory. Organization in memory refers not so much to a particular model, as to an orientation toward the study of memory. The basic assumption behind organization research is that we remember materials by relating them to one another, by building "mental structures," and by ordering materials in many different ways. In a sense, the organizational approach represents a return to an awareness of the complexity of mental events. New methods of assessing organization have stimulated this return to some very interesting problems. In Chapter Thirteen we will discuss several lines of research (e.g., clustering in recall, subjective organization, encoding, mnemonics, and imagery) and attempt to relate them to issues of general concern in the field of memory.

Interference: Data and Theory

10

PROACTIVE AND RETROACTIVE INHIBITION: THE FACTS

Proactive Inhibition

Suppose you are invited to learn an ordinary ten-item paired-associate list. After mastering the list completely you are dismissed with instructions to return at the same time the next day. When you return, the experimenter presents the stimuli one at a time with instructions to recall the correct responses. You find you can only remember eight of the ten responses. You want to know what happened to the other two items and why they were forgotten. One possibility is that the associations somehow decayed, or grew fainter, with the passage of time. This possibility has intuitive appeal, since it does seem that our memories fade with disconcerting regularity. The decay notion suggests that forgetting is a simple, inexorable function of the passage of time, as though our memories grow weaker as they grow older.

The decay notion corresponds to our everyday conception of what retention is all about. But there is a powerful alternative interpretation of forgetting. It may best be introduced by extending the experiment described above. Suppose, on Day 2, after you have recalled the list you learned on Day 1, the experimenter gives you *another* paired-associate list to learn. After you master this second list he dismisses you with instructions to return the next day. On Day 3, you attempt to retrieve the second list. You then learn a third list, and so on. Let us say you learn 20 somewhat similar paired-associate lists on 20 successive days. On each day you are required to recall only the list you learned the previous day. In other words, the retention interval for any given list is 24 hours. The question is this: How much of the twentieth list will you be able to recall 24 hours after it is learned?

Some students suggest that recall of that final list will be almost perfect. You have, after all, had all sorts of practice in learning and recalling paired-associate lists. But that is not what happens at all. Recall of that final list is extremely poor. In fact, you probably will not be able to recall more than two or three of the items you learned just 24 hours ago. You have forgotten, or are unable to produce, 80% of the correct responses. That is a large effect and we will want to find out what causes it. Obviously, it must have something to do with all those prior lists you learned. The language usually used here suggests that the first 19 lists somehow interfere with, or compete with, attempts to recall the twentieth list. The materials from all those other lists keep popping into your mind as you try to recall the twentieth list. The old materials block the correct responses, or confuse you when you try to recall them.

This effect is called PROACTIVE INHIBITION. It refers to a disruption in our ability to retrieve a given set of materials due to the interfering effects of previously learned materials. The more previous lists we have learned the greater the retention loss. Figure 10.1 clearly indicates that recall of a given list over 24 hours declines as a function of the number of prior lists learned in the same experiment (Underwood, 1957).

Table 10.1 contains the basic experimental design used to demonstrate proactive inhibition (PI). The critical comparison is between the experimental and control recall of Task 2. If the experimental subjects display poorer Task 2 recall, then we say PI has occurred. The recall of a given list (Task 2) has been disrupted by prior learning (Task 1).

Proactive inhibition is not a theory or an explanation. It is a fact, and an important one. It refers to the fact that an enormous amount of forgetting can be attributed to the interfering effects of prior learning.

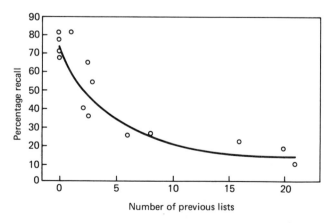

Figure 10.1. Proactive inhibition as a function of the number of previously learned lists. Each point represents the results of a different experimental study. (Adapted from Underwood, B. J. Interference and forgetting. *Psychological Review,* 1957, *64,* 49–60. Fig. 3, p. 53. Copyright 1957 by the American Psychological Association. Reprinted by permission.)

TABLE 10.1

Proactive Inhibition Experimental Design

Group	Task 1	Task 2	Task 3
Experimental	Learns A	Learns B	Retention of Task B
Control	—	Learns B	Retention of Task B

The more we learn, or store, the more susceptible we are to this type of interference. The more organic chemistry we commit to memory the greater the probability of confusion. The more names and faces a professor attempts to match in his lecture section the greater the chances are that he will have difficulty remembering additional name–face pairings. This is *not* to say that adding to our storage necessarily, or invariably, leads to poorer retrieval of newly acquired materials. To the contrary, it is possible to overcome potential PI effects by ordering and choosing our materials such that they do not fall into an interfering pattern. In addition, we may build upon, or structure, our knowledge such that we actually find PROACTIVE FACILITATION, or improved retention, rather than PI. And yet PI has to be considered a major factor in many observed retention losses. Prior learning constitutes a powerful source of interference.

Retroactive Inhibition

There is another type of interference called RETROACTIVE INHIBITION (RI). Retroactive inhibition refers to interference due to *subsequent* learning. The basic RI design is depicted in Table 10.2. The experimental subject learns two successive tasks. Then, at the end of some retention interval (typically ranging from zero seconds to several weeks) the subject's ability to retrieve the Task 1 materials is tested. If his retention is poorer than that of the controls we say that RI has been demonstrated. If a 10-year-old learns all the baseball statistics connected with the National League and then proceeds to do the same with

TABLE 10.2

Retroactive Inhibition Experimental Design

Group	Task 1	Task 2	Task 3
Experimental	Learns A	Learns B	Retention of Task A
Control	Learns A	—	Retention of Task A

the American League statistics then his ability to recall the National League statistics may well be less than if he had not acquired the American League materials.

(Note that Table 10.2 suggests that the controls rest, or do nothing, while the experimental subjects learn the second task. Control subjects are not actually allowed to rest during this interval of time. If they were they would spend the time rehearsing Task 1, which would give them an advantage over the experimental subjects. During this interval control subjects typically engage in some unrelated filler task, which is designed to prevent them from rehearsing Task 1. These filler tasks include such things as working perceptual–motor puzzles, counting backward, solving simple mathematical problems, and crossing out designated digits on sheets of endless digits.)

Retroactive inhibition effects are large. That is, a great percentage of our responses may be made unavailable through the manipulation of subsequent learning. No matter what one's theoretical orientation, undeniable RI effects must be considered.

In summary, it seems our ability to remember a given set of materials is strongly affected by both prior and subsequent learning. The very act of learning itself constitutes an ironic source of forgetting. Learning can, under various circumstances, reduce our ability to remember what we have already learned, and has the potential to disrupt our ability to remember what we will learn in the future. In one way or another, instances of learning are not independent of one another. The process of storing knowledge may, under certain circumstances, disrupt the retention of additional bits of information. The exact nature of these disruptive processes will be the subject of the upcoming section concerning interference theory.

Decay versus Interference

As we have noted, decay, or the notion that memory traces fade with the passage of time, seems intuitively appealing. And yet the decay hypothesis has proven to be relatively unfruitful. It has not led to many testable hypotheses. The reason for this may have to do with the fact that it may well be impossible to eliminate all sources of interference from a given experimental situation. For example, suppose we wish to demonstrate that the memory traces of a learned list decay with time. Accordingly, we have our subject learn a list and then test for retention after a designated interval. To ensure that any loss we observe is due to decay, and not RI, we must ensure that the subject learns *nothing* during the retention interval. If he learns anything at all then the loss could be due to RI. It is difficult to "turn a subject off" during a time interval. We could put him to sleep, but such a procedure does not eliminate the possibility that some kind of learning activity will occur while the subject is dropping off to sleep, while he is actively dreaming, or while he is awakening. [Interestingly, studies involving such sleep procedures seem to support an interference, rather than a decay, interpretation of forgetting (Ekstrand, 1967).] And even if we were sure the subject learned nothing at all during the retention interval we still could not attribute a retention loss to decay, because of possible PI effects. All the subject's preexperimental experiences constitute potential sources of proactive interference. (We have to assume he has learned *something* before he enters the experimental situation.) In short, the definitive decay experiment is, so far as we know, impossible. To run a good decay experiment we would have to round up subjects before they had learned any potentially interfering material at all. Then, after they learned the critical materials, we would have to "turn them off" immediately and completely until the time of the retention test. So far, no one has been able to establish such a pattern, although attempts to demonstrate decay continue (Reitman, 1974).

This is not to say that decay does not operate or contribute to observed retention losses. Interference theoreticians are very aware that some portion of our retention losses may be due to decay. They are merely pointing out that it is presently impossible to isolate the decay effect, or to separate it from interference effects. It is like a constant added to all our interference effects. But we *can* create, predict, and observe enormous variations in retention due to obvious interference factors (e.g., by varying the amount, or type, of interfering activity). Hence much more emphasis has been placed upon interference effects simply because (*1*) they are extensive and (*2*) we can relate them to changes in our independent variables.

Variables Affecting PI and RI

What are some of these variables that are so important in determining interference effects? It is clear that a great number of variables may be manipulated within the framework of the designs contained in Tables 10.1 and 10.2. The literature is filled with studies involving parametric work in RI and PI situations. The most important variables have been INTERTASK SIMILARITY, DEGREES OF LEARNING, AND TEMPORAL FACTORS.

We will not attempt to summarize the enormous body of available parametric research. Instead we will briefly note the nature of each of these important variables. In the next section, when we consider theory, we will have occasion to examine some of them in greater detail, but only when their impact is pertinent to some theoretical issue or question.

Intertask Similarity

In the last chapter, we discussed variations in stimulus and response similarity in two-list transfer situations. Osgood's (1949) transfer surface summarized the various transfer paradigms. Exactly the same similarity variations can be investigated in three-step RI and PI situations. For example, we may devise an RI paradigm corresponding to the A–B, A–C pattern. The subject learns two successive lists (possessing identical stimuli and unrelated responses). He is then tested for retention of the first or A–B list. Similarly, we might want to investigate an A–B, A–B′ PI situation in which the subject is tested for retention of the *second* list (A–B′) after he has learned two lists that possess identical stimuli and similar responses. We can vary the similarity of the stimuli and/or the responses in any manner we wish. We can then test for either first-list retention (RI) or second-list retention (PI).

The close relationship between transfer paradigms and RI and PI designs should now be apparent. In transfer paradigms we focus upon, or test, *second-list learning* while in RI and PI paradigms we focus upon, or test, *retention of the materials* over time. The PI and RI paradigms add a third step (the retention test) to the two-step transfer paradigms. Thus, transfer is involved in every PI and RI design. It is just that in PI and RI designs, we do not focus upon second-list *learning*. Rather, we are interested in what happens to the strengths of the materials after learning has been completed. For example, in an A–B, A–C transfer paradigm, we look at the subject's performance while he is learning the second list. In an A–B, A–C PI paradigm we test for A–C strength, not while the subject is first learning A–C, but after learning has been completed and some retention interval has elapsed.

We can devise PI and RI paradigms that correspond to every point on the Osgood surface. For example, we can develop RI and PI paradigms that correspond to the A–B, C–D; A–B, C–B; and A–B, A′–B paradigms. Osgood (1949) developed his surface with the idea that it would predict retroactive inhibition effects as well as transfer effects. It is, in fact, called the transfer and retroaction surface. Thus the A–B, A–C paradigm is expected to yield both high negative transfer and strong retroactive inhibition (which it does). Similarly the A–B, A′–C paradigm is expected to yield moderate negative transfer and moderate retroactive inhibition, and so on.

The surface's predictions with respect to RI have received some limited support (Bugelski & Cadwallader, 1956; Gibson, 1941; Hamilton, 1943; Kanungo, 1967). But, as is true of the surface's transfer prediction, the RI predictions have proven to be less than perfect. The student should thus look upon the surface, not as a perfect predictor, but as a convenient mnemonic device. When one becomes lost in the maze of RI and PI paradigms the Osgood surface provides a handy mechanism for sorting them all out, and for perceiving their relationships to one another. The intricate details of the relationships between intertask similarity and RI and PI are beyond the scope of this text (for that matter, they may presently be beyond the grasp of psychology). Clearly, intertask similarity is a powerful variable. The Osgood surface can do little more than give us a very rough idea of the expected RI–similarity effects (see Postman, 1971).

Degrees of Learning

It is easy to see why degrees of learning might be considered an important variable in interference paradigms. For example, we might reasonably expect RI to decrease as the degree of first-list learning increases. The stronger the first list the more resistant it might be to any kind of interference generated by the second list. Similarly, we might expect RI to increase, at least up to a point, as second-list learning increases. The stronger the second list the more it might interfere with retention of the first list. Degrees of first-list and second-list learning should also be important and powerful variables in PI situations. Degrees of learning have, in fact, been extensively investigated in PI and RI situations. Without going into detail, and despite many conflicting reports, it seems that at least some of our intuitive expectations have been confirmed (Atwater, 1953; Postman & Riley, 1959; Slamecka, 1961; Underwood & Ekstrand, 1966).

Temporal Factors

Because the effects of temporal arrangements are particularly critical in interference theory, we will delay a detailed consideration of these factors until the upcoming theory section. For now, it is sufficient to point out that in a three-step paradigm there are three major time intervals that can be varied. We can vary the time between the learning of the first and second lists. We can vary the time between the learning of the second list and the retention test. And we can vary the time between the learning of the first list and the retention test. All of these time intervals have proven to be important in producing interference effects. For example, proactive inhibition has been shown to increase as the time between second-list learning and the retention test is increased (e.g., Slamecka, 1961). Similarly, retroactive inhibition appears to decrease as the retention interval is increased (Postman, Stark, & Frazer, 1968).

These and other studies involving temporal manipulations will be more closely scrutinized in upcoming sections.

One of the immediate and obvious problems here is that we cannot vary these intervals in a completely independent fashion. For example, if we hold the time between the first list and the retention test constant, while varying the time between the first and second lists, then we find that we are also varying the time between the second list and the retention test. Such procedural difficulties have never been entirely overcome.

The Generality of Interference Effects

Before we move to a consideration of interference theory, one final point should be made. Interference effects may be quite general and operate in the world outside the laboratory. Even though most of the research seems to be cast in paired-associate, serial, and free recall situations, we should keep in mind that interference effects are pervasive, and not limited to these somewhat artificial tasks.

For example, interference effects may be observed with what psychologists call connected discourse (e.g., Slamecka, 1960, 1961), or such things as meaningful sentences and paragraphs. Interference effects may also be obtained using two languages (López, Hicks, & Young, 1974). That is, if one task is in one language and the second task is in a different language interference effects may be observed. Finally, deficits in animal memory may arise from interference factors (Campbell & Spear, 1972; Spear, 1973). The traditional emphasis upon human research in the area of memory does not necessarily imply that human and animal memory systems are qualitatively different.

So far we have been speaking of nothing more than the facts. Retroactive and proactive inhibition do occur, and they are powerful. They are strongly affected by such factors as intertask similarity, degrees of learning, and temporal variations. We now turn to the problem of trying to explain these facts. Why do PI and RI occur at all? What factors or mechanisms contribute to their particular forms? How much do we know, and how much do we not know, about the processes that underlie and cause these undeniably powerful interference effects? We will be stepping into the world of theory.

THE TWO-FACTOR THEORY OF FORGETTING

An Overview of the Original Formulation

To this point we have been discussing facts. We now turn to the theoretical analysis of these facts. What are the mechanisms and principles that account for these powerful, reliable memory effects?

For many years the TWO-FACTOR THEORY OF FORGETTING (Melton & Irwin, 1940) stood as the uncontested framework within which psychologists attempted to understand forgetting. Although the two-factor formulation has come into sharp conflict with more recent conceptions of memory, it still stands as one of the major explanatory developments within the field. In this chapter, we will outline the basic elements of the system, and will comment upon some of the recent challenges that have been directed toward the theoretical bastion known as the two-factor theory of forgetting.

The original formulation of the theory proposes that a given retention loss, or interference effect, may be determined by at least two important factors. These two factors have come to be known as COMPETITION and UNLEARNING. Let us first consider competition. Suppose we have just learned an A–B, A–C sequence. We then attempt to recall the B responses when the A stimuli are presented. We find we cannot recall all the correct B responses. Some portion of this retention loss may be due to RESPONSE COMPETITION AT THE TIME OF RECALL. When A is presented during the recall phase, and we are asked for B, our ability to produce B will sometimes be blocked by C. We mistakenly recall C instead of B. Incompatible responses have been connected to the same response. The recall of one temporarily blocks recall of the other. The incompatible responses compete with one another, cause confusion, and lead to errors in recall. We will elaborate upon the concept of response competition shortly. For now, realize that if we attempt to recall the first-list responses, unwanted recall of the second-list responses may disrupt first-list recall (this would be an RI effect). Similarly, if we attempt to recall the second-list responses, unwanted recall of the first-list items may interfere with recall (this is a PI effect).

The second of the two interference factors is commonly known as UNLEARNING. Perhaps not the best choice of labels, but it will have to do. The idea behind the concept of unlearning is that the acquisition of new materials (e.g., the A–C list) can bring about losses of the old materials (e.g., the A–B list). As the subject learns the A–C list, there is a concomitant loss in the strength of the first-list associations. During the learning of the A–C list, the A–B materials are somehow unlearned, weakened, extinguished, or made less available. First-list associations are extinguished during second-list learning. Exactly how this unlearning or extinction occurs will be the topic of an upcoming section.

For now, several points should be kept in mind. First, either or both of these factors (unlearning and competition) may contribute to an observed interference effect. Second, competition is presumed to be operating *at the time of recall* whereas unlearning operates *during second-list learning*. The two factors have their impact at different points within the experimental sequence. Confusion or competition occurs during the recall phase when the subject's retrieval of one response is blocked by his presumed recall of the other response. Unlearning, on the other hand, occurs at an earlier point—during second-list learning. The A–B list is somehow undergoing extinction, not at the time of recall, but during second-list, or A–C learning. The third and final point we wish to make here is that response competition is presumed to contribute to both PI and RI whereas unlearning contributes to RI alone. Let us first take up the notion that competition contributes to both RI and PI. Unwanted recall of the second-list may compete with recall of the first list (RI). Similarly, unwanted recall of the first list can compete with attempts to recall the second list (PI). Now let us turn to the notion that unlearning contributes to RI but *not* PI. As we have noted, unlearning refers to the fact that first-list associations are somehow made unavailable, or extinguished, during second-list learning. Hence, first-list retention is clearly affected by unlearning (RI). But second-list, or A-C, materials do not undergo unlearning or extinction in our experiment. Hence, losses in second-list retention, or PI, is often presumed to be *totally* determined by competition at the time of recall, whereas RI is presumed to be determined by *both* competition and unlearning.

The Separation of Competition and Unlearning

In view of the fact that both unlearning and competition may affect retention, how might we go about separating the effects of these two factors in an experimental fashion? For years no one knew quite how to do it. For example, RI experiments would be run in which the subject would be given the usual 2 seconds to recall each of the B responses following A–B and A–C learning. A–B losses would be observed, but no one knew whether they were due to competition at the time of recall or to unlearning or both. Attempts were finally made to eliminate the effects of competition from these experiments. When this was done whatever retention loss was left could be safely attributed to the unlearning factor. Competition effects were eliminated in a very simple manner. The subject was asked to recall both the B and C responses and was given *unlimited time* to do so. The idea was that if the subject was not pressed for time, and was free to spend as much time as he wished in searching for, and sorting out, the B and C responses, then the competition effect would be minimized. The obvious assumption here is that competition effects are dependent upon time pressure. If we remove the requirement of recalling the critical item within a few seconds then the confusion, blocking, and momentary competition between B and C responses is eliminated. This line of reasoning led to the development of what is commonly called the MMFR (or modified, modified free-recall) test (Barnes & Underwood, 1959). In this type of recall test, the subject is not pressed for time at all and is asked to recall the B *and* C responses in any order they come to mind. When this unpaced recall task is used any remaining retention losses may be attributed to the unlearning factor alone and are presumed to be free from the effects of the momentary competition factor.

PI and MMFR

As we have seen, classical two-factor theory states that PI is determined completely by response competition at the time of recall. It has also been commonly assumed that the MMFR task effectively eliminates the effects of competition. Hence it follows that *no* PI should appear when the MMFR task is employed. After learning an A–B, A–C sequence, a subject should have no trouble recalling the C responses if he is given plenty of time to do so, and is not subjected to the confusion produced by paced or limited recall time. This seems to be a reasonable prediction. Unfortunately, PI effects *have* been consistently observed with the MMFR task (Ceraso & Henderson, 1965; Postman, Stark, & Fraser, 1968). It might be that the MMFR task does not effectively eliminate competition effects after all. Or PI might be due to something beyond the competition factor. Whatever the final outcome, this contradiction, or unpredicted result, typifies the kind of problems facing the ongoing development and refinement of the emerging two-factor theory. The interested reader is referred to Postman, Stark, and Burns (1974) for a recent conception of the nature of PI.

Unlearning as Extinction

Is human forgetting anything like animal "forgetting?" If we know something about the ways in which animals "forget" do we know anything about the mechanisms of human forgetting? Does human "unlearning" resemble an extinction-like process? We have already discussed the phenomenon of experimental extinction, a phenomenon that has its origins in the animal literature. Animals "forget," or lose responses, through a process of extinction. The rat, after learning to press a lever for food, will stop the pressing response if food, or reinforcement, no longer follows the occurrence of that response. If the animal does not undergo this active unreinforced responding then the response will be maintained for long periods of time. Thus, for the rat to stop its response, it must undergo an active process wherein the previously reinforced response occurs repeatedly without reinforcement.

Do humans lose such things as verbal responses in a similar manner? Do we forget because we undergo extinction? On an intuitive level it does not seem likely. When we forget someone's name, or the title of a book, or a section of a text it does not *seem* as though we have undergone extinction. Where and when did we make the response and suffer a state of nonreinforcement?

Interestingly, although the mechanism is not obvious, some human forgetting has been thought of as analogous to experimental extinction (Keppel, 1968; Postman, 1971; Postman & Underwood, 1973). Specifically, the unlearning factor just outlined has been conceived of as an instance of experimental extinction. The analogy is as follows: Consider the A–B, A–C situation. During A–C learning, the subject sometimes mistakenly responds with B rather than C. The subject has just learned the A–B list and it is "on his mind." These errors may be either overt or covert. Each time the B response occurs as an error it is not reinforced. (The memory drum, or the experimenter, does not confirm the B response as correct.) *The occurrence of the B response during A–C learning constitutes an instance of unreinforced responding, or experimental extinction of the A–B association.* The greater the number of overt or covert B responses occurring during A–C learning the greater the extinction or unlearning of the A–B associations. This is an interesting idea. It suggests that human forgetting of verbal materials may occur in a manner analogous to the basic process of experimental extinction. It represents an important point of contact between the animal and human literature, and suggests that at least some animal and human forgetting may be comparable.

Spontaneous Recovery and Human Forgetting

If the unlearning factor is truly analogous to experimental extinction then human forgetting should display the important properties of the extinction phenomenon. Spontaneous recovery is a case in point. If you will recall, a response which has been extinguished will, with rest, recover some of its strength. For example, suppose a rat's bar-pressing response has been completely extinguished and the animal has been removed from the Skinner box for, say, 24 hours. We find that when the animal is returned to the box after the rest interval the response has spontaneously recovered some of its strength.

If the analogy between unlearning and extinction is to be maintained then a similar sort of recovery phenomenon must occur with verbal materials. If an A–B list is extinguished during A–C learning then, as time passes, the A–B list must show some recovery. The unlearning or extinction must be at least partially reversible. Although the results have not been completely consistent, such a recovery phenomenon has been demonstrated (Forrester, 1970; Martin & Mackay, 1970; Shulman & Martin, 1970). It is not an easy effect to obtain, but the fact that it has been observed lends some support to the extinction interpretation of unlearning.

Additional Tests of the Extinction Hypothesis

Another major effort to substantiate the extinction interpretation of unlearning has involved the idea that greater extinction, or more RI, should occur if the number of B responses occurring as errors during A–C learning is increased. In other words, as the number of unreinforced B responses increases then extinction of the A–B associations should increase. Experimenters have attempted to vary the number of B responses occurring as errors during A–C learning in several ways (e.g., Goggin, 1967; Keppel & Rauch, 1966). In one attempt, Postman, Keppel, and Stark (1965) argued that a substantial number of these unreinforced errors should occur when the B and C responses in the successive lists are drawn from the same class of materials (e.g., using different letters as B *and* C units, or using different adjectives as B *and* C units). On the other hand, they proposed that few such errors should occur when the B and C materials are drawn from different classes (e.g., letters as B units and adjectives as C units). In the condition involving a change in class of materials the subjects would hardly confuse letters and adjectives and would thus give few Bs as errors during A–C learning. Proceeding from this analysis these authors predicted more unlearning, or greater RI, when the class of the responses remained unchanged. Their hypothesis was confirmed, supporting the idea that unlearning is an extinction-like process (see also Friedman & Reynolds, 1967).

Not all studies have supported the extinction interpretation of unlearning (e.g., Keppel & Rauch, 1966). But the failure to find totally consistent support for the extinction interpretation does not necessarily deny the validity of the formulation. It may merely highlight the enormous complexity of the human mental apparatus. The uneven results may reflect our inability to control the conditions of human learning and forgetting in a completely adequate manner. The extinction interpretation of the unlearning phenomenon currently stands as a viable hypothesis.

Competition: Specific versus Generalized

In our introductory discussion of response competition, we referred to the notion that retrieval of one response will sometimes be blocked by the unwanted recall of the remaining response. This effect is referred to as SPECIFIC RESPONSE COMPETITION. The recall of one specific response blocks the recall of another specific response. But there is another type of competition that leads to disruption of the retention process. It is referred to as RESPONSE-SET INTERFERENCE, and has been elaborated by Postman, Stark, and Fraser (1968). (The ideas behind the response-set interference hypothesis were originally put forward by Newton and

Wickens in 1956.) The response-set interference analysis goes like this: While a subject is learning a first list, he restricts his responses to those which are appropriate to that list. He inhibits the occurrence of incorrect responses, or responses that do not belong to the set of correct first-list responses. Then, when the subject is shifted over to a second list, he shifts over to the set of correct second-list responses. He inhibits the occurrence of the entire set of first-list responses. He concentrates or focuses upon the set of correct second-list responses. But the subject cannot shift from one set of responses to another instantaneously. As Postman and Underwood (1973) put it, the tendency to give responses from a given list is possessed of a certain amount of inertia. There will be a strong tendency for the subject to continue to give responses from the most recently learned list. It takes a while for the subject to shake off this tendency, or to change his orientation. Hence, after the subject has completed second-list learning the tendency to give second-list responses persists for awhile.

Now suppose we ask the subject for the first-list responses immediately following the completion of second-list learning. Presumably, the subject will be plagued by the persisting tendency to give responses from the most recently learned list (the second list). These second-list responses will compete with, and block, retrieval of the first-list responses. Thus at least part of the subject's inability to come up with the first-list responses in an RI situation may be attributed to response-set interference.

There have been many attempts to test the response-set interference hypothesis. The formulation has led to a good number of testable hypotheses, and has received considerable support in the literature. The interested reader is referred to Cofer, Failie, and Horton (1971), Lehr, Frank, and Mattison (1972), and Postman and Stark (1969).

One point should be kept firmly in mind. The notion of response-set interference is not intended to *replace* the other interference mechanisms (i.e., unlearning and specific response competition). It is intended to *supplement* them. In any given situation *any* of these interference mechanisms may contribute to overall retention losses. It is the task of the proponents of the two-factor position to clearly delineate when, and to what extent, each of these potential sources of interference determine overall forgetting.

The two-factor theory is undergoing almost constant revision and refinement. Despite what its detractors say it does have explanatory power, and it has generated an enormous amount of research. This is not to say that the theory is without faults. It is not entirely comprehensive, nor can it adequately account for all known interference effects (e.g., PI obtained with the MMFR test). We will begin our exploration of alternative conceptions of memory by examining some of the recent challenges to the classical two-factor interpretation of interference effects.

Then, in successive chapters, we will discuss alternative models of memory and their adequacy in relation to the two-factor position.

A CHALLENGE TO UNLEARNING:
THE INDEPENDENT RETRIEVAL PHENOMENON

According to classical two-factor theory, A–B associations are unlearned during A–C learning. Martin (1971) and a number of other investigators have suggested that there is evidence that denies this unlearning principle. They reason that if learning A–C entails unlearning of A–B, then the recall of B should be less likely when C is recalled than when C is not recalled. In other words, the recall of B and C should be dependent upon one another. As the strength of A–C is built up, the strength of A–B should decrease. Thus if we test for the recall of both responses the subject should be less likely to recall B when C is recalled. The probabilities of recalling B and C should be inversely related.

A number of investigators have obtained results that appear to contradict this expected inverse relationship between B and C recall (Greeno, James, & DaPolito, 1971; Martin, 1971; Wichawut & Martin, 1971; Martin & Greeno, 1972). In general, they found that B and C recall are independent of one another. That is, the recall of B is just as likely given that C is recalled as it is given that C is not recalled. This effect has been labeled the INDEPENDENT RETRIEVAL PHENOMENON. Martin (1971) suggests that it deflates the concept of unlearning because the unlearning principle requires, or implies, an inverse relationship between B and C recall. Martin suggests that we must look elsewhere for an explanation of RI effects.

We shall examine Martin's alternative interpretation of RI in a moment. But first it should be noted that the validity and relevance of the independent retrieval phenomenon is not universally accepted (see Hintzman, 1972). Postman and Underwood (1973) have attacked the very logic put forward by Martin (1971). They suggest that Martin is wrong in assuming that the unlearning principle demands an inverse relationship between B and C recall. They argue that it is not the actual acquiring of the C response that is critical in the unlearning of the B response. As we have seen, it is the *occurrence of B as an unreinforced response during A–C learning* that is the critical factor in the unlearning of the A–B association. Second-list, or A–C, learning merely provides the *opportunity* for the B response to occur as an error. There is nothing in two-factor theory that states that it is the learning of the A–C association that actually causes the A–B loss or that A–B associations must be unlearned before A–C associations may be learned. Thus two-factor theory, according to Postman and Underwood (1973), does not demand an inverse relationship between C and B recall.

INTERFERENCE AND ENCODING VARIABILITY

In any case, whether or not the independent retrieval phenomenon actually invalidates the unlearning principle, Martin (1971) has proposed an alternative interpretation of interference effects. His formulation is intended to replace, and not merely supplement, the classical two-factor interpretation. It is based upon his concept of stimulus encoding variability. If you will recall, a given stimulus is conceived of as possessing many different attributes or components. During A–B learning the B response is not connected to the entire A stimulus, but rather to some selected portion of the overall stimulus. Then, during A–C learning, the C response is not connected to this same set of attributes. It is connected to a different, or at least partially different, set of stimulus attributes. Thus C and B are connected to different *functional* stimuli even though the *nominal* stimulus is identical in A–B and A–C learning. For example, if the A stimulus is ZQKO, then the B response might be connected to Z, whereas C might be connected to Q. Granting that this is true, how does RI occur and why does the subject have trouble recalling the B responses when presented the total A stimulus after A–B and A–C have been learned? According to Martin, it happens because of a *persisting tendency to sample, or select, or attend to those stimulus attributes utilized during A–C learning.* Following A–C learning the subject continues to "pay attention to" those stimulus attributes that he has *most recently* used in hooking up the C responses. Hence, because of his continuing attention to these most recently utilized attributes, the C response is cued off rather than the B response.

Let us consider a very simplified example. Suppose a subject is required to connect "dog" to "norlop" during A–B learning. Imagine that this subject once owned a dog named "Norton." Hence he might easily master this particular item by associating "dog" with "nor" and might ignore the remaining letters in the nominal stimulus ("lop"). Now, during A–C learning the subject might be required to connect "eye" to the stimulus "norlop." The letters "op" might remind the subject of "optical." Thus he might find it convenient and simple to associate "eye" with "op" and ignore the remaining letters ("norl"). Thus "dog" is connected to "nor" and "eye" is connected to "op." Then, during the retention test following A–C learning, the subject is asked to recall "dog" given "norlop" as a cue. Martin (1971) argues that the subject will continue to attend to, or sample, the stimulus attributes most recently utilized. The subject will focus upon, or sample, "op." "Op" leads to "eye" rather than "dog." Hence we have a disruption in the subject's ability to recall the first-list response, or an RI effect.

Martin (1971) does not mean to limit his notion of stimulus encoding variability to the use of some selected subset of letters drawn from the total stimulus. He feels that the subject may sample many different attributes of a stimulus (e.g., the sound of it, the shape, the color, the letters, or the associations and images it cues).

Martin's explanation of interference sounds a bit like the Postman, Stark, and Fraser (1968) notion of response-set interference. In both analyses the subject cannot recall the first list because he is still bound up with the second list. The involvement with the second list persists after second-list learning, and in some sense, blocks out recall of the first list. The two analyses do differ in terms of their emphasis. On the one hand, Martin focuses upon a persisting tendency to attend to the set of stimulus attributes utilized during second-list learning. On the other hand, Postman, Stark, and Fraser (1968) emphasize a persisting tendency to give second-list responses. Martin focuses upon STIMULUS PERSISTENCE, whereas Postman focuses upon RESPONSE PERSISTENCE. It would seem reasonable to suspect that both might be right. The tendency to continue giving recent responses *and* to continue attending to recently utilized stimuli might both contribute to RI. Martin's analysis might best be taken as a supplement to, rather than as a replacement for, the more traditional interference mechanisms.

Martin's stimulus encoding variability hypothesis has received considerable attention in the literature (e.g., Ellis, 1973; Goggin & Martin, 1970; Martin, 1972; Mueller, Gautt, & Evans, 1974; Williams & Underwood, 1970). Although some studies seem to support Martin's ideas, others do not. The final impact of this formulation remains to be seen.

In summary, the investigation of interference effects is an ongoing process. Few would deny that interference effects (e.g., PI, RI, and spontaneous recovery) are real. But heavy disagreement does descend upon us when we consider the theoretical implications of these basic findings. The two-factor theory is undergoing constant scrutiny and development (e.g., Hanley & Scheirer, 1975; Houston, 1971; McCrystal, 1970; McGovern, 1964; Postman, Stark, & Burns, 1974; Warren, 1974; Winograd, 1968). In addition, Martin (1971) and others (Greeno, James, & DaPolito, 1971; Slamecka 1969) have suggested alternative interpretations of interference effects. These alternative systems do not yet appear to be replacing the two-factor theory. In fact, these challenges may serve to revitalize and stimulate thinking about the original two-factor formulation [e.g., see Postman, Stark, and Burns (1974)].

In the next chapter we will turn to a consideration of some of the new, developing models of memory which draw heavily upon an information processing conception of human learning and memory. Then, in the subsequent chapter, we shall compare the two-factor theory and the information processing models.

SUMMARY

1. The two major interference effects in memory are proactive inhibition and retroactive inhibition.

2. PROACTIVE INHIBITION (PI) refers to losses in our ability to remember a given set of materials that may be attributed to the interfering effects of *previously* learned materials.

3. RETROACTIVE INHIBITION (RI) refers to memory losses that may be attributed to the interfering effects of *subsequently* learned materials.

4. The DECAY HYPOTHESIS, or the notion that memory traces somehow fade with the passage of time, has been proposed as an alternative to the interference mechanisms. The decay hypothesis has proven to be relatively unfruitful, for it is currently impossible to eliminate all sources of interference within a memory experiment.

5. INTERTASK SIMILARITY has been recognized as important in determining RI and PI effects. Osgood's transfer and retroaction surface gives us a rough idea of the kinds of RI effects expected under conditions of varying intertask similarity.

6. Degrees of first-list and second-list learning, and temporal arrangements have also been recognized as important determinants of RI and PI effects.

7. Interference effects are not limited to arbitrary tasks such as paired-associate learning. For example, they appear with connected discourse, with varying languages and when animals are employed as subjects.

8. The classical TWO-FACTOR THEORY OF FORGETTING proposes that interference effects are determined by COMPETITION at the time of recall and by the UNLEARNING of first-list associations which occurs during second-list learning.

9. Specific competition is presumed to contribute to both RI and PI, whereas unlearning affects RI but not PI.

10. Unlearning effects are presumed to be separated from competition effects through the use of unpaced retention tests. If a subject is given as much time as he wishes to attempt retrieval then his performance will not be affected by competition. This type of unpaced retention test has been labeled MMFR.

11. If the MMFR task eliminates competition, and PI is determined completely by competition, then no PI should appear when the MMFR test is used. This straightforward prediction has not been confirmed. Proactive inhibition does occur with MMFR. This could mean that the theory needs revision, or that MMFR does not eliminate competition.

12. Unlearning has been thought of as an extinction-like process. During A–C learning the subject sometimes makes B responses, either overtly or covertly. These B responses, which are occurring as errors

during A–C learning, are unreinforced (unconfirmed), and are thus thought to be analogous to responses undergoing experimental extinction. This formulation provides a point of contact between human verbal learning and the basic animal literature, wherein the concept of experimental extinction developed.

13. If the extinction interpretation of unlearning is correct, then unlearned first-list associations should recover some of their strength with rest. In support of this interpretation spontaneous recovery of first-list associations has been demonstrated.

14. Similarly, if the number of unreinforced (unconfirmed) B responses occurring as errors during A–C learning is increased then unlearning, or extinction, of the A–B associations should increase. This deduction has also received considerable (although not completely consistent) support.

15. There are two types of response competition. SPECIFIC RESPONSE COMPETITION refers to the recall of one specific response blocking the recall of another specific response. RESPONSE-SET INTERFERENCE, on the other hand, refers to the blocking of one set of responses (e.g., the entire set of first list responses) by the tendency to continue to give responses from the most recently learned list (e.g., the second list).

16. Response-set interference is intended as a supplement to, rather than as a replacement for, the other interference mechanisms (i.e., specific competition and unlearning).

17. The INDEPENDENT RETRIEVAL PHENOMENON refers to the fact that recall of B is just as likely given that C is recalled as it is given that C is not recalled. It has been suggested that this phenomenon invalidates the unlearning principle. A controversy swirls around the logic of this attack upon the two-factor theory.

18. In any case, alternative interpretations of interference effects have been proposed. For example, the encoding variability interpretation suggests that subjects connect B and C to different attributes of A in an A–B, A–C situation. Then, when tested for B given A as a cue, the subject displays an RI effect because of a tendency to continue to select, or attend to, those attributes of A which were attended to during the most recent learning task (A–C).

19. The ENCODING VARIABILITY interpretation and the response-set interference hypothesis seem similar in that they both suggest that RI is due to a persisting involvement with the second task. The former emphasizes a persisting tendency to attend to certain stimulus attributes whereas the latter emphasizes a persisting tendency to give second-list responses. Both tendencies probably contribute to overall RI effects. One interpretation need not invalidate the other.

20. The existence of interference effects is undisputed. But the theoretical interpretation of these effects is, at present, highly controversial.

The Information-Processing
Approach to Memory

11

INTRODUCTON

We now turn to the alternative approach to the understanding of memory. Prior to the 1960s, the two-factor theory of interference pretty much dominated the field of forgetting and retention. With its foundations in Hullian-type S–R psychology, and its emphasis upon such basic experimental phenomena as extinction and spontaneous recovery, it stood as the major, relatively uncontested, conception of forgetting. But the last 15 years have seen a spectacular explosion in thinking and theorizing about human memory processes. In contrast to the early years, we now have many models of memory, with more appearing all the time. Many of them may be subsumed by the rubric of INFORMATION-PROCESSING MODELS OF MEMORY. In general, these new models conceive of the human as an information-processing system. Their concern has been the flow of information through the human, beginning with the registration of incoming information by the sense organs, through the encoding and storage of this information, to the eventual retrieval and utilization of the information. According to this way of thinking, memory involves, in a very basic sense, the encoding, storage, and retrieval of information.

These models were stimulated by the development of information measurement concepts (Shannon, 1948), the investigation of speech recognition (Cherry, 1953), and the development by Broadbent (1958) of a model of selective perception. The concepts of communication theory and digital computers quickly infiltrated the field of memory, leading to a proliferation of memory models. For the most part, these models do not define "information" in its strict, technical sense. In a very general way, most psychological models of memory refer to "information" as that which reduces uncertainty. The answer to a question, or the response to a given stimulus, reduces uncertainty, hence, it provides information. The specific, technical definition of information need not concern us in this text (see Abramson, 1963).

New ways of thinking about memory were stimulated by the advent of the computer age. Whereas, prior to the 1960s, theorizing about memory was pretty much restricted to talking about stimuli, responses, and associations between them, the language of computers has become commonplace. Mathematical models and computer-simulation models are on the upsurge. Psychologists have begun to try to describe memory in terms of mathematics, and have begun to conceptualize human memory in terms of elements such as flow charts, outputs, control programs, buffers, instructions, execution, processing, and storage.

The number of memory models currently available is quite astounding (e.g., Craik & Lockhart, 1972; Feigenbaum, 1970; Murdock & Wells, 1974; Patterson, Meltzer, & Mandler, 1971; Rundus, 1973; Shiffrin, 1970a,b; Wickelgren, 1969). Some of the available models are intended to be very general, others are quite specific. They vary in terms of the degree to which they can be characterized as "mathematical" models. Some are assumed to deal with many different types of information, whereas others are designed to deal with a limited range of materials. They vary in terms of the numbers of assumptions they make. Some are simple, others are complicated. It is impossible to review more than a few of them in this text. The interested reader is encouraged to turn to Murdock's (1974) outstanding review of many of these models. Hilgard and Bower (1975) also provide a helpful discussion.

By selecting a few representative examples, we may be able to characterize the so-called information-processing approach. Because many of the models draw upon computer-based concepts, the models we will review strongly represent this tendency. When attempting to select representative examples from this fine array of models one is forced to admit that there is a certain blindness, or hit-and-miss quality about the choice process. There are many models available, and most of them are new. Many of them are vague, and they are often untested. We cannot be sure which ones will stand the test of time and which ones will fade from view. Although many of them appear to account for a good portion of the available experimental data, none of them has emerged as "the" model.

The discussion in this chapter will take the following form: First, we will review several information-processing models. Second, we will focus upon the current distinctions made among encoding, storage, and retrieval. Third, we shall ask whether the new information-processing approach is antithetical to the older S–R associationistic approach, which underlies the two-factor theory of interference.

THE WAUGH–NORMAN MODEL: PRIMARY AND SECONDARY MEMORY

Let us begin with a relatively simple information-processing model. The model proposed by Waugh and Norman (1965) is contained in Figure 11.1. It represents a relatively early attempt to distinguish between two types of memory, and to couch a description of these two stores in terms of information-processing language.

According to Waugh and Norman (1965) every item (stimulus) that is perceived enters PRIMARY MEMORY (PM). Once in PM, an item will be lost, or forgotten, unless it is rehearsed. Rehearsal can be overt or covert, intentional or unintentional, conscious or unconscious. If an item is rehearsed, it remains in PM, and may enter SECONDARY MEMORY (SM). Secondary memory is considered to be a more permanent store. Once in SM an item need not be rehearsed to be maintained. Waugh and Norman were trying to capture the following kind of event or experi- ence. Suppose you are presented with a series of digits (say, 87391063). If you read off this series, and then *prevent* yourself from saying it over and over again, you will forget it quite quickly (probably within a minute). On the other hand, if you rehearse it, either silently or aloud, you can maintain it; you will not forget it and you will be able to pro- nounce it on demand. If you rehearse it long enough it will enter SM. In contrast to items in PM, items in SM are not lost when they are not rehearsed. If we rehearse the example sequence of digits enough times it will become a relatively permanent memory or enter our SM. We will be able to retrieve it even after it has left consciousness.

The capacity of PM is limited. That is, there is a limit to the number of items we can hold in our PM. If we are given a string of dozens of digits we probably will not be able to hold them all in our working memory. On the other hand, most people can handle 5, 6, 7, 8, or 9

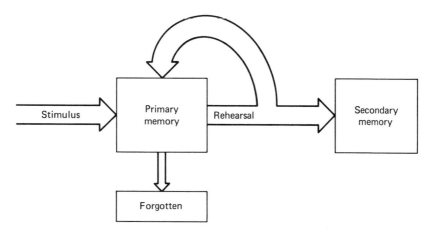

Figure 11.1. The Waugh–Norman Memory Model. (After Waugh, N. C., & Norman, D. A. Primary Memory. *Psychological Review,* 1965, *72,* 89–104. Fig. 2, p. 93. Copyright 1965 by the American Psychological Association. Reprinted by permission.)

items without too much difficulty. The *exact* capacity of primary memory is unknown (Glanzer & Razel, 1974).

New items will "bump out" old ones. Suppose we have been presented a series of eight words and we are having a little trouble rehearsing them without forgetting any of them. Now the experimenter presents additional words. According to Waugh and Norman something has to go. If we are to take in the new words then we must drop, or lose, a corresponding number of old items we have been holding in PM. Old items will be lost as we try to accommodate the new ones. We cannot handle an unlimited number of items in our PM.

An event in PM has not left consciousness. Primary memory is part of the psychological present. On the other hand, an item recalled from SM has been absent from consciousness. Secondary memory represents the psychological past. According to Waugh and Norman (1965), PM contains a relatively accurate record of recently perceived events. Materials stored in SM may be distorted and full of gaps.

Obviously, this type of model is far from complete. Many questions are left unanswered. For example, how much rehearsal is required for different types of materials to pass from PM to SM? Can some information pass directly through PM into SM without being rehearsed at all (e.g., "traumatic events")? How are materials brought back from SM to PM? Waugh and Norman (1965) never intended their model to be complete and perfect. They presented it as a beginning, and as an approach to the understanding of human memory. It is more a way of thinking about memory than a detailed statement of all the processes involved in memory.

One aspect of the Waugh and Norman (1965) model deserves special attention because it is characteristic of many of the current information-processing models. The authors postulate two memory stores, one for materials retained for short periods of time and one for materials to be retained for longer periods of time. The dichotomy between SHORT-TERM STORE (STS) and LONG-TERM STORE (LTS), or PM and SM, has become one of the focal differences between the information-processing approach and the older two-factor theory of interference. If you will recall, interference theory makes no mention of any distinction between short-term store and long-term store. There is only one memory system. Materials may be learned to different degrees, thereby becoming more or less resistant to interference, but memory over short periods of time is not conceived of as fundamentally different from memory operating over longer periods of time.

We will consider the proposed dichotomy between LTS and STS in detail in Chapter Twelve. For now, we might ask ourselves what it means on an intuitive level. What it suggests is that the principles and mechanisms that govern the retention of materials for short periods of time are somehow fundamentally different from those that govern the retention of materials for longer periods of time. Can we, on an intuitive level, sense the operation of these different memory stores? Does it seem we remember materials for short periods of time in a manner distinct from the way in which we remember them for longer periods of time? Is there a distinct break between STS and LTS, or does it seem memory is continuous, with more rehearsal merely leading to more and more firmly entrenched traces of whatever it is we are trying to remember?

Of course, our *intuitive* answers to these questions really mean very little. But it is interesting to "introspect" with regard to the proposed distinction. Obviously, the validity of the distinction will finally rest, not on our intuitive feelings, but upon the results of a concerted experimental attack upon the problem. The nature of the ongoing experimental efforts to resolve the issue, one way or the other, will be described in upcoming sections. To say the least, the distinction between short-term and long-term memory is controversial.

THE ATKINSON–SHIFFRIN BUFFER MODEL

The Waugh–Norman model serves as a simple introduction to the realm of model building. It possesses the basic dichotomy between LTS and STS, which is inherent in so many current models. But the model developed by Atkinson and Shiffrin (1965, 1968, 1971) provides a more full-blown example of the information-processing trend.

The Sensory Register

A brief glance at the flow chart in Figure 11.2 will reveal certain characteristics that appear to be similar to those of the Waugh and Norman (1965) model. For example, the buffer model contains a box labeled "short-term store" and a box labeled "long-term store." A detailed description of these two memory systems is upcoming. For now, notice that the buffer model introduces a new store, a third box, called the "sensory register." This third component of the overall memory system precedes STS. The buffer model thus expands the number of stores from two to three.

There seems to be good reason for postulating this new memory store. The principle characteristic of the sensory register is that information stored within it decays in a *very* brief period of time. The exact length of this decay interval is not known. It generally has been estimated at about .5 second, although some investigators have proposed slightly longer or shorter estimates. In contrast to STS, where information is often thought to be lost within, say, 5, 10, or perhaps 15 seconds, unrehearsed information in the sensory register is never thought to persist much longer than .5 second.

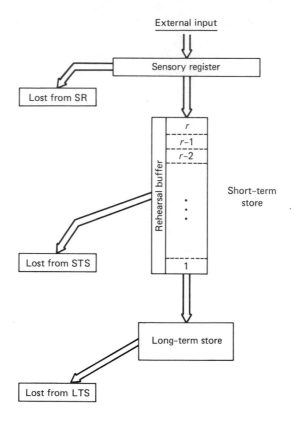

Figure 11.2. A version of the Atkinson–Shiffrin Memory Model. (After Atkinson, R. C., & Shiffrin, R. M. The control of short-term memory. *Scientific American,* August, 1971, 82–90. Fig. on p. 82. Copyright © 1971 by Scientific American, Inc. All rights reserved.)

What evidence is there for the existence of this newly proposed structure or system? The original evidence for the sensory register came from investigations of visual memory (Averbach & Coriell, 1961; Sperling, 1960, 1963). Although different investigators used varying techniques the work done by Sperling (1960) is representative. Sperling used a tachistoscope which is a piece of equipment which will present visual stimuli for very brief periods of time. Sperling presented rectangular arrangements of letters such as,

T D R

J R N

F Z R

These arrays were flashed before the subject for 50 milliseconds ($\frac{1}{20}$ of a second). The subject was then asked to report what he had seen.

Without any special instructions subjects are able to report no more than four or five letters correctly. Now comes the interesting part. By using a prearranged signal, which was presented immediately after presentation of the letter array, Sperling asked subjects to recall a *specific* row. A high-pitched tone meant that the subject was to recall the top row. Low and intermediate tones indicated to the subject that he was to recall the bottom or middle rows, respectively. The surprising result was that the subject could recall any given row with 100% accuracy. This finding suggests that there is a very rapidly decaying "visual image," or "after-image," or "visual sensation," which persists beyond the termination of the actual stimulus. It is as though the subject "sees" the entire array of letters for a moment after the actual physical stimulus has been terminated. It is there for him to read off. But this "afterimage" is not there for long. When asked to report the top row, the subject can do so without error. He merely refers to the "visual image," or whatever you wish to call it, and reads off the correct letters. But while he is reading off the top row, or encoding the top row, the other rows are decaying rapidly. By the time he has finished reading off the top row the lower rows have faded to the point where he can no longer report them. The Sperling test procedure forces the subject to attend to some portion of the total array. While he is attending to this selected portion the entire array is decaying, rendering a report of the remaining items impossible.

This is a rather interesting result. It suggests that incoming visual information is present as a rapidly decaying "visual image." If encoded, or read off from this visual sensation, the information moves into STS. If it is not attended to almost immediately it will be lost. Thus, in the buffer model, it seems to be ATTENTION that moves information from the sensory register into STS.

What about stimuli that the subject hears rather than sees, is there an *auditory* sensory register? While much of the research has involved memory for visual stimuli there have been some attempts to extend the analysis to other modalities. For example, Massaro (1970, 1972) has presented evidence for what he calls a "central auditory image," or a rapidly decaying trace of auditory stimuli (see also Neisser, 1967).

In summary, although the sensory register has not received the attention given to the STS, it does seem its inclusion by Atkinson and Shiffrin (1968) is warranted by the facts. Detailed information concerning the exact nature of the sensory register, and the transfer of information from the sensory register to STS, is presently not available.

The Short-Term Store

Focus upon the STS in Figure 11.2. This component is somewhat similar to the concept of primary memory proposed by Waugh and Norman (1965). At the same time, it represents an elaboration upon a theme. Notice that the rehearsal buffer is *part* of the STS. This buffer is composed of a certain number of slots, or bins. These are locations within which item information is stored. The number of these slots is definitely limited (that is, the buffer is composed of r slots). In addition, the bins are ordered. There is a definite sequence to them. The order is conveyed by the notation $r, r - 1, r - 2, \ldots, 1$. Slot r holds the newest information in the buffer, while slot 1 holds the oldest, or the item information that has been in the buffer for the longest period of time.

Because there is a fixed number of slots in the buffer the inclusion of a new bit of information can only be achieved through the displacement of an old one (given that all the slots are full). New items are assumed to come in at the top, or to fill the r slot. Which item will be lost when a new item enters slot r? In a very general sense, we may say that the older an item the more likely it is to be displaced by the inclusion of a new item. Obviously this statement is an oversimplification. Atkinson and his colleagues were well aware that the displacement of an item is a complicated event (see Phillips, Shiffrin, & Atkinson, 1967).

Without going into any great detail we can grasp the complexity of item displacement by imagining a child picking up pebbles on the beach. His hand will hold just so many stones. Each time he picks up a new one he must, if he wishes to keep it, drop one of the old ones. Which one will he drop? Just imagine what goes into this "simple" decision. It is true there may be a tendency to drop the stone that has been held the longest. On the other hand the child will probably consider which pebbles he likes the most, and which ones he has examined closely. In an analogous manner, the process of dropping items from STS is probably multiply determined.

Be that as it may, the system does postulate an additional mechanism concerning the displacement effect. Once an item is displaced from, say, a slot near the bottom of the column of slots what happens to the information in the remaining slots? According to the theory, all items older than the displaced item hold their place. They stay in the same slots. All items newer than the displaced item move down one slot. Obviously this postulation complicates matters, for it requires that older and newer items be given separate consideration.

As is true of the Waugh and Norman (1965) model, items in STS may be maintained through rehearsal. If items are not rehearsed they will be lost from STS (Anderson & Craik, 1974). Thus there may well be two ways in which items are lost from STS. First, old items may be displaced by new, incoming items. Second, items may be lost if they are not rehearsed.

Item rehearsal does something in addition to maintaining information in STS. Namely, rehearsal of information held in STS may contribute to its transfer to LTS. Notice we say that rehearsal *may* contribute to transfer. It does not *necessarily* lead to transfer to LTM (Jacoby & Bartz, 1972). Items may be rehearsed in STS without being transferred to LTS. But for items to be transferred from STS to LTS they must be rehearsed (Atkinson & Shiffrin, 1971).

In general, then, the longer an item has been maintained in STS by rehearsal the more *likely* it is to be transferred to LTS. The longer we hold information (for example, the sequence BXGBJKL) in STS by rehearsing it the more likely it is to become part of our "permanent" memory.

An item can be in both STS and LTS at the same time. For example, think of your mother's name. When you think of it, it will be in both STS and LTS. An item can be in LTS but not STS. For example, all of the things we "know" but are not now thinking of are in LTS but not STS. An item may be in STS but not LTS. For example, "NELZIPRELLY" is now in your STS. But it probably will not enter your LTS unless, for some peculiar reason, you rehearse it several times.

We will return to a consideration of STS in the next chapter. At that time, we will consider the validity of the construct. We will ask whether or not it is even necessary to distinguish between STS and LTS and we will trace some of the experimental data that bear upon this issue. It should also be noted that our characterization of the buffer model has been very simplified. The interested reader is directed to Atkinson, Brelsford, and Shiffrin (1967) for a full exposition of the model.

Long-Term Store

Long-term storage or memory over long periods of time, has not received the attention given to STS in the information-processing tradition. In contrast, a good deal of the thinking and experimentation done in connection with interference theory has been concerned with long-term memory. Theoreticians within the information-processing framework have focused upon short-term memory. Hence relative to the STS concept the notion of LTS is often not well developed in information-processing models. The information-processing approach has involved not only a new language, but a shift away from the long-term retention of lists of items toward short-term retention of individual items.

In the Atkinson and Shiffrin buffer model information is presumed to enter LTS from STS through the process of rehearsal. Once information is in LTS it is no longer rehearsed (unless it is brought back to STS). Information is often assumed to be lost from LTS through the combined effects of both decay and interference. Presumably the decay rate is much slower than that of STS. Although information is often thought to decay from STS in a matter of seconds, estimates of the LTS decay rate range up to years. Once in LTS information is presumed to be stored quite permanently. (We might add that the *exact* values of the decay rates associated with the sensory register, STS and LTS are not particularly important at this point in our investigations. In fact, we are not even sure decay necessarily operates in all of these stores.)

Let us consider the proposition that LTS is affected by interference factors. Presumably when information-processing theoreticians speak of interference effects in LTS many, although not all of them, are referring to such factors as proactive and retroactive inhibition and the associated concepts of unlearning and response competition. Thus the information-processing models often acknowledge and attempt to incorporate the interference mechanisms outlined in the last chapter. There is a tendency to locate these interference effects in LTS and to leave STS and the sensory register relatively free of them. In fact, one of the most controversial distinctions between STS and LTS has been based upon the notion that information in STS is not subject to interference effects. Many psychologists have raised questions concerning the validity of this distinction. We shall consider the problem in the next chapter.

In any case, the Atkinson and Shiffrin buffer model proposes that information is transferred from the sensory register to STS through a process of attention. The short-term store has a limited capacity. Information is transferred from STS to LTS through a process of rehearsal. Information decays from the sensory register in a fraction of a second. Unless they are rehearsed, materials may be lost from STS in a matter of seconds. Information may also be lost from STS through a process of displacement. Information stored in LTS is quite permanent. Information in LTS is subject to a very slow decay process, and to interference effects. Not everything that enters the sensory register reaches STS. Not everything that enters STS is transferred to LTS. But information that does make it all the way through to LTS is considered to be relatively permanent.

Control Processes and Structural Properties

Atkinson and Shiffrin (1968, 1971) distinguish between the fixed, structural properties of the memory system and control processes. The distinction is an important one. Control processes refer to the fact that the individual may go about *using* the fixed structural properties of the system in many different ways. For example, STS may have the *capacity* to hold a certain amount of information. This capacity represents a fixed, structural property of the system. But whether or not the individual *chooses* to fill STS is another matter entirely. He does not have to fill it, he can partially fill it or leave it empty. Just because someone flashes a lot of words in front of us does not mean we have to put them in our STS. We do, after all, have some choice in the matter. Entry into STS is not automatic. In addition, we can maintain information in STS, or "let it go." We can transfer information to LTS, or refrain from doing so. We can pull information back from LTS into STS, etc. The structural properties of the system set limits on what we can do. For example, we cannot hold an unlimited amount of information in STS. But within the limits of its structural properties we can "use our memory." These choices, decisions, and strategies are what Atkinson and Shiffrin call control processes.

It is simple to see that the buffer model becomes very complicated when we begin to consider control processes: We have a willful, unpredictable HUMAN BEING on our hands. We must consider all his needs, wants, wishes, and decision processes. At the same time, the introduction of control processes immediately makes the model much more appealing, and much more closely related to the world of human experience.

Atkinson and Shiffrin (1968, 1971) place considerable emphasis upon control processes, and their relation to the fixed structure of the model. They have many interesting things to say about control processes, and the reader is referred to their work for a full explanation of the control concept. For the purposes of this text we have chosen one example of the effects of human strategies upon the ways in which the fixed properties of the system are used. This example is merely representative of many investigations and should be understood in that light (see also Hinrichs & Grunke, 1975).

The study we refer to is one done by Bellezza and Walker (1974). It is an interesting study because it illustrates what Atkinson and Shiffrin mean by control processes. The study is based upon the assumption that what we do with information within the memory system depends upon what we want to do with it, or feel we need to do with it. Accordingly, one group of subjects was presented with a list of seven words and asked to recall all the words immediately following presentation. They were then presented with another list of words and asked for immediate recall of that list, and so on, until seven different lists had been presented and tested. Before any lists were presented the subjects had been told that they would receive "one point" for every word recalled correctly. In terms of the buffer model, these subjects were free to rehearse in such a manner as to maintain each list in STS. There was no need to try to transfer the information to LTS, for they believed they would only be given an immediate recall test. There was no need to store the information permanently for storage in STS would be more than adequate to maintain the material through the immediate retention test. Unfortunately, these subjects were "fooled" by the experimenter. Following presentation and testing of all seven lists the experimenter asked the subjects to try to recall all of the words from all seven lists in one final retention test. The subjects were told they would be given "ten points" for each correct item on this final recall test. Obviously, these subjects were not ready for this development. They had not tried to transfer information from STS to LTS in preparation for this final test. They did very well on the immediate tests but very poorly on the final test. The assumption here is that by the time the final test arrived materials had been lost from STS. In addition, they had not been put into LTS. Hence, the poor performance on the final test.

Another group of subjects was treated in exactly the same manner except that they were told, before they were exposed to any of the lists, that they would be tested for immediate retention *and* that they would be given the final recall test. Correct items in immediate recall were to receive "one point," whereas correct items in final recall would recieve "ten points." If you were placed in a similar situation, you would probably try to ensure that you would be able to remember as much as possible on that final test, because that is where the larger pay-off would be. In the language of the buffer model you would rehearse in such a way as to maximize transfer from STS to LTS. You would not especially care about what stayed in STS as long as you were sure lots of information was going into LTS. The results of this strategy are apparent in Figure 11.3. As you can see the Storage Condition (told only about the immediate tests) did well on the immediate tests and poorly on the final test. The Coding Condition (told about both immediate and final recall) did better on the final test but not so well on the immediate tests. Because of their

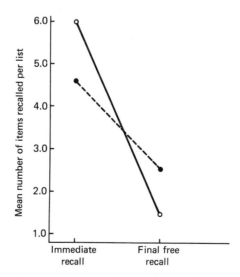

Figure 11.3. Number of words recalled per list in the storage (○) and coding (●) conditions. (Adapted from Bellezza, F. S., & Walker, R. J. Storage-coding trade-off in short-term memory. *Journal of Experimental Psychology,* 1974, *102,* 629–633. Fig. 2, p. 631. Copyright 1974 by the American Psychological Association. Reprinted by permission.)

awareness of the big, ten-point pay-off the Coding subjects utilized the fixed structural properties of the memory system such that storage in LTS was maximized. The effort these subjects put into transferring materials to LTS seems to have somehow detracted from their maintenance of information in STS. We can only speculate about the reasons for this poor performance in STS by the Coding subjects. For example, they may have merely rehearsed fewer of the presented items a greater number of times to ensure that they would be transferred to LTS.

What the study demonstrates is that, depending upon the needs of the subject, the memory system may be used in different ways to achieve different ends. It also suggests that rehearsal is not a unitary process. That is, there appear to be certain types of rehearsal that maximize storage in STS and other rehearsal strategies that maximize storage in LTS (Craik & Watkins, 1973; Jacoby, 1973; Woodward & Bjork, 1973).

Bjork's (1970, 1972) work on directed forgetting represents another good example of the operation of control processes in memory. In one situation he presented four successive paired-associates. Color background cues instructed the subjects either to forget the first two items, or to retain them for possible future testing. Bjork found that retention of the *last* two items was superior when the subjects had been informed that they need not try to maintain the first two. Bjork speculates that the "forget" cues initiate control processes which free rehearsal time for the last two items and which somehow differentiate the to-be-remembered items from the to-be-forgotten items.

We can begin to see the kind of fun psychologists can have with such a model. Propositions based upon the interaction of the structure of the system and the control processes can be tested in the laboratory and related to the world outside the laboratory. The control processes "put the human back" in the system. As is true of most available models the buffer model has been supported by some experiments (e.g., Loftus, 1971) but not by others (e.g., Murdock, 1972). The ultimate value of the buffer model remains to be seen. Whatever the final outcome, it has served as a rallying point, and a summary device, for the information-processing approach to memory.

Additional Models

As we have indicated, the models described so far represent nothing more than a very small sample of the available models. The ones we have discussed do not necessarily represent the ones that will stand the test of time. At present no one is quite sure which, if any, of the existing models will prove to be substantial and lasting.

New models are being developed all the time. For example, Broadbent (1971) has proposed an ADDRESS REGISTER MODEL which contains four "boxes," or components, rather than the three contained in the Atkinson–Shiffrin buffer model. The new component, called the address register, is placed *after* short-term store but *before* long-term store. The address register holds information *about* the items, but it does not contain the items themselves. For example, suppose we are presented with a long list of words composed of instances of several categories (e.g., a list composed of five birds, five cities, five colors, and five vegetables). According to the Broadbent model, these words (e.g., bluebird, Toledo, yellow) would be placed in, say, LTS. But the category names (e.g., birds, cities) would be placed in the address register. The information held in the address register is conceived of as being useful in the retrieval process. When called upon to produce the long list of words the subject may refer to the address register. The category names he finds there will *remind* him of what to search for in LTS. The information held in the address register assists him in retrieving information from LTS, by reminding him of action to be taken (e.g., search LTS for birds, cities, etc.).

The Broadbent model represents the latest step in quite a sequence. We began with a unitary conception of memory (interference theory). We then moved to a two-component system (Waugh–Norman). The Atkinson–Shiffrin model represented a three-component model. Finally Broadbent added a fourth component. Who knows where it will all end?

In addition to these types of models we also have what are called SAMPLING MODELS (e.g., Shiffrin, 1970a). These models maintain that LTS is comparable to an urn full of marbles. Each marble represents some stored bit of information. To retrieve a specific item a sample, or handful, of marbles is drawn from the urn. This information, or these marbles, are placed in STS. Once in STS each marble is examined, one by one. If the target marble is found the process ends with a response. If the target marble is not found the subject tries another handful. This "sample and examine" process continues until the target marble is found.

There are two ways in which we may think about the sampling process. On the one hand, once a handful of marbles is examined and found not to contain the target marble, the entire sample of marbles may be set aside before another handful is taken from the urn. This process is called sampling *without* replacement. On the other hand, sampled handfuls might be returned to the urn after they are examined. This is called sampling *with* replacement. Although psychologists have not always agreed about the replacement question, it does seem that the mind is not entirely capable of sampling without some sort of replacement (Murdock, 1974).

Obviously a simple sampling model is too simple. Some items (e.g., "well-learned ones") must have a greater probability of being sampled than others. Some marbles are more likely to be drawn up in a handful than others. In addition, the marbles within the urn are probably not just lumped all together in some random fashion. They are probably organized in many different ways. Hence a simple sampling model can only begin to explain the interlocking processes involved in the storage and retrieval of information.

The models we have discussed by no means represent the entire list. We have various computer-simulation models. These are often designated with wonderful acronyms such as FRAN for Free Recall by an Associative Network (Anderson, 1972) and HAM for Human Associative Memory (Anderson & Bower, 1973; Anderson, 1975). By now the reader should see clearly what is happening to the field of human memory. It is exploding with activity. Thinking about memory is truly opening up. New, fresh ideas are developing. The field is rapidly changing. The information-processing approach is just that—an approach. It is a new and promising way of thinking about memory. It is a way of asking questions about memory, rather than a unified theoretical framework.

THE COMPONENTS OF MEMORY: ENCODING, STORAGE AND RETRIEVAL

It has become very fashionable to speak of encoding, storage, and retrieval as the essential components of the overall memory system. The distinctions among these components have been enormously helpful in stimulating and clarifying our thinking about some very complicated mental events. At the same time the reader should be aware that these components have not been separated or, for that matter, even defined to everyone's satisfaction. Whether or not these three components truly represent distinct, independent components of the overall information-processing sequence remains to be seen. Briefly, we shall consider the definitions of the three components and then some of the techniques that have been designed to separate them.

Definition of Encoding, Storage and Retrieval

Murdock (1974) has characterized the three components about as well as anyone could. ENCODING refers to the representation of one thing by another. An external stimulus is some kind of physical energy that acts upon, or has an effect upon, the nervous system. This relatively lasting effect, which the external stimulus has upon the nervous system, is referred to as the internal code for the external object or event. The nervous system contains an encoded representation of the stimulus. STORAGE refers to the persistence of information over time. Murdock (1974) draws a parallel between the storage process and the process wherein one makes a tape recording of a musical composition and then stores the tape on a shelf. For all practical purposes, the information stored on the tape does not change over time. Human memory rarely possesses the same degree of fidelity, but it does involve the storage of information over time. RETRIEVAL, according to Murdock (1974), refers to the utilization of stored information. Stored information may be *available* (stored) but not *accessible* (easily located and utilized). For example, we may know (have stored) the names of all of the United States, but, at any given moment, we may not be able to retrieve all of them. Hence the information is available but not accessible. It is stored but we may have trouble retrieving it.

Murdock (1974) points out that although the terms encoding, storage, and retrieval have become popular in recent years, similar concepts have been discussed for decades (Melton, 1963; McGeoch & Irion, 1952).

Separation of the Three Components

Given that we have some faith in the distinctions among encoding, storage, and retrieval how do we go about separating the three? Suppose we vary an experimental variable (e.g., the amount of background noise in our experimental situation) and we observe that this variable is related to forgetting (e.g., poorer recall with greater degrees of background noise). How do we know which of our three components was affected by the background noise? Did the noise disrupt encoding, storage, retrieval, or some combination of these elements?

Storage versus Retrieval

On logical grounds the distinction between storage and retrieval is clear-cut. Information may be stored, but it may not be accessible. We all know, or have stored within us somewhere, the names of all the planets surrounding our sun. But, at any given moment, we may not be able to retrieve all of them. (Try it.) They are "in there," but, for any number of reasons, we may not be able to pull them out on demand. The information is "available" but not, at least momentarily, "accessible." The information may be stored, but before it can be produced as a response it must be found, or located, within the store. In some sense, the retrieval process involves a search through the store. Our search for the planets may take any number of forms. Some of us will begin the search nearest the sun and work outward in space. Others will search for the little planets, and then the larger ones. Others will utilize idiosyncratic characteristics of the planets (Saturn has rings, Mars is the "red planet," etc.).

There are several standard techniques for distinguishing retrieval processes from storage processes. The most popular method involves a comparison of recall and recognition (see Mandler, 1972; Tulving & Thomson, 1971). According to this approach recall involves *both* storage and retrieval processes while recognition bypasses the retrieval process. To recall something we must have it within our store *and* we must be able to retrieve it. When asked to recognize an item we do not have to search for it, it is given to us. We merely note whether it corresponds to a representation within our store. A comparison of recall and recognition of the same materials may give us an idea of the extent to which our experimental manipulation differentially affects storage and retrieval.

Another technique for separating retrieval and storage involves a comparison of cued versus noncued recall (Bahrick, 1970; Tulving & Pearlstone, 1966). In the Tulving and Pearlstone (1966) study subjects were given lists of words belonging to categories. Recall of these lists of words was better when the category names were provided (cued recall) than when they were not (noncued recall). These results suggest that there is a difference between what is accessible and what is available. Information may be stored (available) but not accessible unless it is prompted by the appropriate cues.

Acceptance or rejection of these techniques for separating storage and retrieval seems to be pretty much a matter of personal preference at the present time. Murdock (1974) suggests that our conclusions with regard to the distinction between storage and retrieval probably depend upon our theoretical orientation, or upon the assumptions that define the model of our choice.

Storage

When we focus upon storage we are concerned with what happens to stored information over time, regardless of how it was encoded or how it will be retrieved. How and why does information change during storage? Presumably losses over time are due to decay and/or interference factors. Given that we wish to study storage per se how do we go about it? The traditional method has been to vary the length of the retention interval, and to vary the type of activity that occurs during the retention interval. If the encoding and retrieval processes are held constant, and we observe a difference in retention related to variations in the length and nature of the retention interval, then these differences reflect events within the storage phase rather than within the encoding or retrieval phases. Again, the isolation of storage effects has not been accomplished to everyone's satisfaction.

Encoding

Encoding is the most difficult of the three components to study independently. At the same time, the concept of encoding currently seems to be in great favor (see Melton & Martin, 1972). Because the concept of encoding seems so essential to modern conceptions of memory, we shall consider it in detail in later sections. For now, it is sufficient to note that the separation of encoding events from storage and retrieval is particularly difficult. If we manipulate some variable (e.g., intentional versus unintentional learning), and observe a difference in retention, we are hard pressed to determine whether the effect is due to the materials having been encoded differently, to their having been retained differently over time, or to their being more or less accessible at the time of recall.

Although it is difficult to separate conclusively encoding events from storage and retrieval events several investigators have attempted to do it (e.g., Hyde, 1973; Johnston & Jenkins, 1971). The idea behind much of this work is that if one subject intentionally learns a set of materials, and another subject learns the same materials unintentionally, then differences in eventual retention may be due to differences in the ways in which the two subjects originally encoded the materials.

In summary, the distinctions among encoding, storage, and retrieval seem to be widely accepted on a theoretical level. But we have not yet progressed to the point where differences between these three components can be conclusively demonstrated on an experimental level. Perhaps the reader of this book, unencumbered by years of interfering thoughts and responses, may be able to solve this problem.

Information Processing and the S–R Approach

Most everyone in the field of learning has been faced with the "S–R associationism versus information processing" issue. There are those who strongly feel that the S–R conception of memory is outmoded, outdated, oversimplified and inadequate. They suggest that the S–R conception of human memory has seen its best days. On the other hand, there are those who strongly feel that the information-processing approach is condescending, fuzzy, and merely in vogue. They argue that the information-processing approach has contributed a sum total of nothing to the study of memory, and claim that is merely a fad that will pass. Everyone seems quite certain of their position.

This is an exaggerated characterization to be sure, and yet the conflict is there. There is the feeling that the information-processing approach and the more traditional S–R conception of memory are mutually exclusive, or antithetical. But quite the opposite may be true. As Murdock (1974) points out, the information we process may be associative. That is, there is nothing in the information-processing language which precludes the concept of S–R associations.

Associations, defined in terms of probability relationships between cues and behavior, may be the information that flows through our information processing models and diagrams. The information processed may be many related associations, or it may be a single association. Associa-

tions merely refer to probability relationships between stimuli and responses. The information-processing approach often contains new language to describe just such relationships. For example, "inputs" or
"probes" (stimuli) produce "outputs" (responses).

It seems the original flurry of attempts to choose between the two
approaches may be subsiding. Psychologists are beginning to realize the
two need not be mutually exclusive. An integration, or meshing, of the
two seems to be in the offing. The best of both ways of thinking about
memory may survive, and may lead to a better understanding of the
overall memory process. Even now, psychologists are beginning to build
models that rely heavily upon both S–R associationism and information-
processing components (e.g., Anderson & Bower, 1973; Estes, 1972.)

Perhaps one of the reasons for the conflict between S–R associationism
and the information-processing approach stems from the fact that the
two-factor theory of interference is an S–R conception that does contain
elements different from those of the information-processing models. (For
example, many information-processing models emphasize the decay concept, and postulate two or more memory stores. The two-factor theory,
on the other hand, suggests that interference rather than decay is the
essential mechanism of forgetting. In addition the two-factor position does
not acknowledge more than one type of memory.) Hence, because of
the differences between this *specific* S–R theory and the information-processing models, some psychologists have been led to believe that *all* S–R
associationism is antithetical to the information-processing approach. Such
is not the case. The two-factor theory is merely *one* example of S–R
theory. In addition, models within the information-processing framework
differ from one another, and yet they are not assumed to be antithetical
to one another. In a like manner, the two-factor theory may differ from
the information-processing models in some ways, but these differences
in no way imply a totally antithetical relationship between S–R associationism and the information-processing approach.

One final note concerning rats, men, and computers. Just as the
information-processing approach is not antithetical to the S–R conceptions
of human memory, so the information-processing approach is not antithetical to the S–R theorizing that has long been an integral part of the
animal literature. Animals process information, too. There is nothing that
precludes the development of animal information-processing models. Rats
and pigeons encode, store, and retrieve information just as we do. The
information they process may be associative just as ours may be.

SUMMARY

1. Prior to the 1960s the two-factor theory of interference dominated
the field of forgetting.

2. The last 15 years have witnessed the rapid development of the information-processing approach to the understanding of memory.

3. In contrast to earlier years we now have a large number of available memory models.

4. Many of these models emphasize the notion that the human is an information-processing system. Memory is thought to involve encoding, storage and retrieval of information.

5. According to the Waugh–Norman model perceived items enter a limited capacity PRIMARY MEMORY (PM). Rehearsal will maintain items in PM and may contribute to their transfer to a more permanent SECONDARY MEMORY (SM).

6. The introduction of new items into PM will bump out old ones.

7. An item in PM has never left consciousness. Items recalled from SM have been absent from consciousness.

8. The distinction between PM (or STS) and SM (or LTS) is characteristic of many current models. This dichotomy is in contrast to the unitary conception of memory suggested by interference theory.

9. The ATKINSON–SHIFFRIN buffer model is a three component model: SENSORY REGISTER, SHORT-TERM STORE (STS), and LONG-TERM STORE (LTS).

10. Information in the sensory register decays within a fraction of a second.

11. Information is transferred from the sensory register to STS through a process of ATTENTION.

12. Short-term store has a limited capacity.

13. Unless rehearsed, information may be lost from STS in a matter of seconds. Information may also be lost from STS through a displacement process.

14. Information is transferred from STS to LTS through rehearsal.

15. Storage in LTS is relatively permanent.

16. Information in LTS is subject to slow decay and interference.

17. CONTROL PROCESSES refer to the fact that the individual can go about using the fixed structural properties of the system in many different ways.

18. As an example of control processes, it was noted that subjects may choose between alternative methods of rehearsing. Certain types of rehearsal maximize storage in STS, whereas other rehearsal strategies maximize storage in LTS.

19. Many additional models are available. Broadbent has expanded the number of components to four. His ADDRESS REGISTER, located between STS and LTS, contains information about the items, but not the items themselves.

20. SAMPLING MODELS maintain that LTS is comparable to an urn full of marbles. To retrieve a specific item samples of marbles are drawn

from the urn. Failure to find the target marble within the sample results in resampling, probably with replacement of the previous sample.

21. The components of memory (encoding, storage, retrieval) are difficult to separate.

22. Encoding refers to the processes by which a memorial representation of physical objects and events is developed.

23. Storage refers to the persistence of information over time.

24. Retrieval refers to the search for, and utilization of, stored information.

25. A comparison of recall and recognition has often been thought to separate storage and retrieval effects. Recognition is presumed to bypass the retrieval process, whereas recall does not.

26. Storage processes may be examined by varying the length of the retention interval and the nature of the activities occurring during the interval.

27. The information-processing approach is not antithetical to traditional S–R associationism—the information we process may be associative.

28. Neither is the information processing approach antithetical to the S–R theory that has characterized the animal literature—animals may process associative information, too.

How Many Memories? 12

INTRODUCTION

In this chapter we will consider whether or not memory is a unitary process. We have already seen that there are many ways to subdivide the concept of memory. Many different types of memory systems or stores have been proposed. For example, we have seen that a distinction between short-term and long-term memory (STS versus LTS) is now in great favor. We have also noted the distinction between recall and recognition memory. The question we wish to address is this: Are these types of distinctions valid? Do they represent fundamental distinctions among various memory systems and processes? Or are they perhaps superficial distinctions which, in the long run, may well detract from our efforts to understand memory?

Memory can be divided in many ways. In this chapter we shall consider four such divisions. First, we shall consider the distinction between long-term and short-term memory. Are the principles that govern memory over short intervals truly different from those that govern longer intervals? Second, we shall question the validity of the distinction between recall and recognition memory. Third, we shall entertain the notion that we may need different theories or models to account for the retention of different *types* of information (e.g., words versus sentences or visual versus auditory information). Fourth, we shall ask if animal and human memory systems have anything in common. Will we need models of human memory that differ from those that account for animal memory? Are there fundamental parallels between animal and human memory processes?

SHORT-TERM MEMORY VERSUS LONG-TERM MEMORY

We begin by addressing the distinction between long-term memory and short-term memory. As we have already seen, it is a distinction that is characteristic of many current information-processing models of memory (Atkinson & Shiffrin, 1971; Waugh & Norman, 1965). (We will be using the terms short-term memory, STS, and primary memory as rough equivalents. Similarly, long-term memory, LTS, and secondary memory will be used interchangeably.) It has proven to be invaluable in stimulating and crystallizing our thinking about memory. But is it a valid distinction? Are the principles that govern short-term memory truly different from those that govern long-term memory? Although a final answer to this question is not yet available, we can trace several areas of research that bear upon the issue. Specifically, we shall consider four areas of relevant research in the next four sections: (*1*) interference effects in short-term memory, (*2*) acoustic versus semantic confusions in short- and long-term memory, (*3*) recency effects in serial recall, and (*4*) long-term amnesia. There are many other areas of research we might consider (see Wicklegren, 1973; Watkins, 1974), but the four we have chosen seem to be representative, and have been widely discussed.

Interference Effects in Short-Term Memory

The postulation of two (or more) memory stores obviously requires that the various stores differ from one another in important ways. If we can identify one or more ways in which the principles governing the retention of information over short intervals differ from the principles governing the retention of information over longer periods of time then we may be able to justify the distinction. If we cannot then we might as well give up the distinction as an intriguing but irrelevant idea.

Let us begin our story by going back to 1959. At that time Peterson and Peterson (1959) developed what has come to be known as the distracter technique for the study of short-term memory. It is an interesting technique. The subject is first shown a stimulus (e.g., three consonants) for a brief moment. He is then required to perform some distracter task, such as counting backward by threes for a set number of seconds (e.g., 0, 3, 9, or 18 seconds). The subject is then required to recall the original three-letter stimulus. The distracter task (counting backward by threes) is designed to keep the subject from rehearsing the stimulus during the retention interval. If the subject were not distracted in this manner he would merely repeat the stimulus item over and over again thereby ensuring perfect recall. But the distracter task prevents such rehearsal, and allows us to examine the fate of the stimulus in the absence of such rehearsal. (Try the distracter task. Count backwards by threes beginning with 576. Now try to rehearse ZQK while counting backward from 975. You may be able to sense that counting backward is quite effective in the prevention of rehearsal.)

The overall Peterson and Peterson task sounds very simple. All we have to do is remember a group of three letters for a few seconds. How have to do is remember a group of three letters for a few seconds. How could we possibly forget such a simple stimulus in such a short time? If we are presented XKZ it seems highly unlikely we would ever forget such a simple item within 18 seconds. And yet the results of these kinds of experiments are quite remarkable. Retention of a simple three-unit stimulus drops off dramatically during an 18-second retention interval. Recall of such materials has been shown to drop all the way down to 10% after 18 seconds (see Figure 12.1). That means we are not able to recall more than one out of ten trigrams presented in this fashion after 18 seconds have elapsed. A finding like that represents an enormous amount of forgetting over a very brief period of time. This type of result is very stable and has been replicated many times using different kinds of materials.

We can see how these kinds of results tie in with the notion of short-term store (STS) or primary memory. It is as though the information is lost within a few seconds because it is not rehearsed enough to maintain it within STS, or to transfer it to LTS (the distracter task prevents the requisite rehearsal).

The question arises as to what causes, or accounts for, this dramatic and unexpected loss over so short an interval. At the time the effect

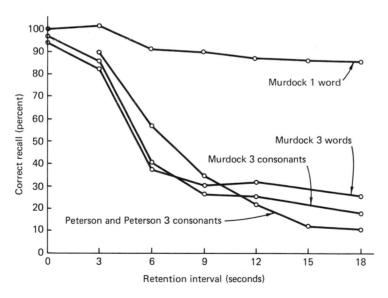

Figure 12.1. Correct recall of various types of materials as a function of the length of the retention interval filled with counting backward. Data are from Murdock (1961) and Peterson and Peterson (1959). (Adapted from Melton, A. W. Implications of short-term memory for a general theory of memory. *Journal of Verbal Learning and Verbal Behavior*, 1963, 2, 1–21. Fig. 1, p. 9.)

was first observed interference theory, with its emphasis upon PI and RI effects, was in full swing. It had been clearly demonstrated that long-term retention losses were heavily determined by PI and RI. But this new short-term memory task represented something unique and unknown. Did PI and RI operate here just as they did in long-term memory? The question was an obvious one, and one that had implications for the generality of interference theory. Could interference theory account for some or all of the enormous forgetting observed in this new procedure? At first, it seemed to some as though interference mechanisms could not account for the losses over such short intervals. It did not seem as though the loss could be an RI effect because it did not seem the subject was learning anything between the presentation of the syllable and its recall test which could cause unlearning of, or compete with, the syllable. (As we have already noted, RI effects appear to be minimal in long-term situations when the interpolated materials are drawn from a form class different from that of the to-be-remembered materials.) In addition, Peterson and Peterson (1959) and Peterson (1963) present data that suggest that recall did not decrease as the number of prior syllables which the subject learned and recalled increased. That is, they did not observe a significant PI effect. The number of prior syllables the subject learned and recalled did not seem to affect the recall of a given syllable. Hence the field was faced with a potential, and perhaps important, distinction between STS and LTS. Psychologists began to suspect that interference mechanisms operated in LTS but not in STS. The potential schism was plain for all to see. Short-term memory was perhaps free from interference effects, whereas long-term memory was heavily influenced by interference mechanisms. (The most common suggestions concerning the determining mechanisms in STS were decay and displacement.)

But the proponents of interference theory were not long in responding to this potential schism. In an excellent study, Keppel and Underwood (1962) outlined the problem and pursued a PI effect in the Peterson and Peterson (1959) situation. Using carefully controlled procedures they attempted to avoid methodological problems they identified in the original Peterson and Peterson study. In contrast to the Petersons, they found that the subject's ability to recall successive stimuli *decreased* as the number of previously learned and tested items increased (see Figure 12.2). They demonstrated that PI does, after all, operate in short-term memory. The more syllables we learn and recall the more difficult it will be for us to handle additional syllables. It was a dramatic success for the interference position, for it argues that all retention, whether long or short, is subject to PI. It argued for theoretical continuity, and against the necessity of a distinction between long-term and short-term memory.

Since the original Keppel and Underwood (1962) study PI has been found in short-term memory many times (Loess, 1964; Nowaczyk,

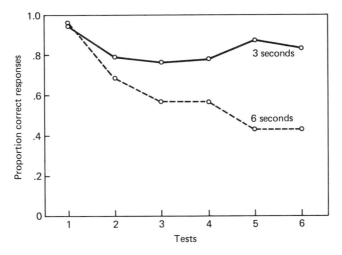

Figure 12.2. Proactive inhibition in the Peterson and Peterson situation. Proportion of correct responses as a function of the number of previous items and length of reten-tion interval. (Adapted from Keppel, G., & Underwood, B. J. Proactive inhibition in short-term retention of single items. *Journal of Verbal Learning and Verbal Behavior*, 1962, *1*, 153–161. Fig. 4, p. 158.)

Shaughnessy, & Zimmerman, 1974; Wickens, 1970). In addition, subse-quent research indicated that RI, as well as PI, operates in short-term memory situations. For reports of RI in short-term memory the interested reader is referred to Posner and Rossman (1965) and to Posner and Konick (1966).

The investigation of RI and PI in short-term memory has gone well beyond mere demonstrations of the existence of such phenomena. For example, investigators are now wondering about the *locus* of PI effects in short-term memory. At what stage in the Peterson and Peterson process does the interference effect appear? On the one hand, some investigators (Dillon, 1973; Petrusic & Dillon, 1972; Gorfein & Jacobson, 1972) suggest that PI effects in short-term memory involve coding and storage processes. On the other hand, some propose that PI in short-term memory involves retrieval rather than encoding or storage processes (Gardiner, Craik, & Birtwistle, 1972; Hawkin, Pardo & Cox, 1972; Hopkins, 1974). The issue has not been entirely resolved. But this particular line of research does illustrate the way in which the interference approach and the information processing approach are being meshed and brought together. The lan-guages of the two "schools" are coming together. In the above-mentioned studies, we have an interference mechanism (PI) being investigated within an information-processing framework (encoding, storage, and re-trieval of information). To say that PI is a function of retrieval processes (available but not accessible) may, in fact, be a restatement, or translation, of the original two-factor proposition that PI is determined by competition at the time of recall (momentary blockage). The two approaches to the study of memory are no longer alien to one another. Without doubt the near future will witness further integration of the two.

In conclusion, it can no longer be said that a distinction between short-term memory and long-term memory may be made on the basis of the notion that short-term memory is free from interference effects. Short-term memory is subject to PI and RI. If we are to find a valid basis for the distinction between short-term and long-term memory we must look elsewhere.

Acoustic versus Semantic Coding

Is there anything else that might distinguish short-term memory from long-term memory? Early research seemed to indicate that short-term memory might involve acoustic coding processes, whereas long-term memory might involve semantic coding processes (Conrad, 1964; Wicklegren, 1965). In a very general sense, what this means is that we may store information in short-term memory on the basis of the *sounds* of the items, whereas we may store information in long-term memory on the basis of the *meaning* of the material. If we wish to store information for a short period of time we may focus upon the sounds of the to-be-remembered material. For example, many of us have had the experience of having been given a phone number (824-2105, say) in a crowded, noisy room (hopefully by a creature drawn from our most erotic dreams). While frantically searching for pencil and paper we repeat the number over and over again, maintaining the sounds of the digits. We in no way attempt to deal with the material on any more complicated level. We do not try to group the digits, or to relate them to our past lives. We merely maintain the information through sound. On the other hand, if we wish to remember the same number for a long period of time we may encode it in a more complicated fashion. For example, we might relate the digits to events in our lives (8 divided by 2 is 4. 21 plus 5 is my age, etc.). In other words, we may involve meaning in our coding process.

For a time the distinction between long-term memory and short-term memory based upon semantic and acoustic coding processes seemed to be gaining wide acceptance (Adams, 1967; Baddeley & Patterson, 1971; Kintsch & Buschek, 1969). There did seem to be some experimental support for such a distinction. Many of these supporting studies were based upon the idea that if a subject is asked to recall a group of items then acoustically similar items (items that sound alike) should be confused in short-term memory but not in long-term memory. Similarly, semantically similar items (items with similar meanings) should be confused in long-term memory but not short-term memory. Studies by Baddeley (1966a,b) provide a good example of this approach. He developed lists of acoustically similar items. Items in this type of list sound alike but do not have similar meanings. He also developed lists of semantically similar items. Items in this list have similar meanings but do not sound the same (see Table 12.1). When short-term memory (immediate recall) was tested it was found that acoustic similarity produced a decrement in recall. The acoustically similar items were confused with one another. This is taken as evidence for the notion that short-term memory involves acoustic coding. In the companion long-term memory study (20 minute recall) recall was heavily affected by semantic but not acoustic similarity. This was taken as support for the idea that long-term memory somehow involves semantic rather than acoustic coding.

But the semantic–acoustic distinction between long-term and short-term memory has fallen upon hard times. Evidence began to accumulate that semantic coding may, after all, be involved in short-term memory (Shulman, 1971, 1972). Similarly, evidence for acoustic effects in long-term memory began to appear (Dale & McGlaughlin, 1971; McGlaughlin & Dale, 1971; Nelson & Rothbart, 1972).

What finally seems to be emerging is a picture of both long- and short-term memory as very flexible systems, each capable of encoding materials in a number of different ways. The demands of the task, and the desires of the subject, probably determine the exact manner in which a given set of materials will be encoded. We can probably use semantic and/or acoustic encoding for long-term retention. We can probably use semantic and/or acoustic encoding for short-term retention. Let us return to our example of the phone number in a crowded room. We *could*,

TABLE 12.1

Lists Used by Baddeley in Study of Acoustic and Semantic Similarity[a]

Acoustically Similar	Semantically Similar
MAN	Great
CAB	Large
CAN	Big
CAD	Huge
CAP	Broad
MAD	Long
MAX	Tall
MAT	Fat
CAT	Wide
MAP	High

[a] After Baddeley (1966a).

if we wished to, encode the information semantically right from the beginning. It is just that the use of acoustic coding might be easier, given the demands, distractions, and constraints of the situation.

It is an oversimplification to say that long- and short-term memory are restricted to definite, distinct modes of encoding. It may well be that short-term memory *often* involves acoustic coding and that long-term memory characteristically involves semantic coding, but neither system is as restricted as Baddeley and others originally suggested. Depending upon the demands of the task, we are capable of coding in many different ways. (For further discussion see Glassman, 1972; Jacoby & Goolkasian, 1973; Tell, 1972; and Wicklegren, 1973.)

Once again we are forced to look elsewhere for support for the distinction between short- and long-term memory.

Serial Position Effects

When we are presented with a list of items (a string of words, for example) and asked to recall them immediately in any order we wish, a very interesting pattern of results is obtained. These results are summarized by the curve in Figure 12.3. Notice that items toward the end of the list are recalled better than any of the others. This fact is called the RECENCY EFFECT. Items toward the beginning of the list are recalled more often than items in the middle, but not as well as the end items. This fact is called the PRIMACY EFFECT. Items in the middle of the list are the most difficult to recall. This pattern is quite stable

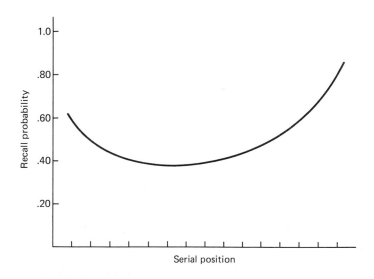

Figure 12.3. Idealized serial position curve for free recall.

and has been obtained by many investigators (e.g., Murdock, 1962; Tulving & Arbuckle, 1963).

The Primacy Effect

Let us first dispense with the primacy effect, which is of minor interest to us in attempting to distinguish short- from long-term memory. The general assumption concerning the primacy effect is that it reflects a greater amount of rehearsal given to early items in the list. Early items are recalled fairly well because they are rehearsed more than later items (see Rundus, 1971). Put yourself in the position of rehearsing a serial list. One item is exposed at a time. When the first item appears you rehearse it over and over again as many times as you can before the second item appears. When the second item does appear you probably rehearse from the beginning of the list, repeating items one and two over and over again. When item three appears you still attempt to rehearse from the beginning of the list, and so on. If this rehearsal strategy is followed, it is clear that early items will be rehearsed more than later items. Hence they are learned and recalled better than later items.

The Recency Effect

Why are the last items recalled best of all? The rehearsal strategy just outlined cannot account for the recency effect. The most common interpretation of the recency effect (see Glanzer, 1972; Murdock, 1974) involves the distinction between short- and long-term memory. During presentation, all items enter short-term memory. As additional items are presented, some of the earlier items are lost. Some items are transferred to long-term memory. Immediately after all the items in the list have been presented, the items toward the end of the list are still in short-term memory. Because they are still in short-term memory these items have an extremely high probability of being recalled in an immediate retention test. Items further back in the list are no longer in short-term memory. They have either been lost, or have been transferred to long-term memory. Hence, relative to the end items, items further back in the list have some lower probability of being recalled. The assumption is made that the recency effect is the result of the end items being *stored in short-term memory at the time of recall*. Lower recall of items further back in the list is due to some of them having been lost completely, and some of them having been moved into long-term memory.

This is an interesting explanation, but it is not without its critics. As Wickelgren (1973) points out, there is no real need to postulate two memory systems to account for the recency effect. A single memory model can account for it just as well as the two memory model. Assume for the moment that there is only one memory store. Information enters this store and is then lost over time (due to decay and/or interference). If we assume, as Wicklegren (1973) does, that this memory trace is lost *rapidly at first and then more slowly* then the recency effect can be explained by a single memory model. The critical assumption in this explanation is the notion that memory traces decay, or are lost, rapidly at first and then more slowly. It is the idea that forgetting will be most rapid immediately after learning, and that the rate of forgetting will then be reduced as time goes on. Applied to the recency effect this position would argue that end items have not yet undergone this initial, substantial loss. Items further back in the list have already suffered the initial, substantial loss in strength. In summary, the recency effect can be understood in terms of a two memory position or in terms of a single memory position involving a slowing rate of loss. The recency effect does not *prove* that short-term memory is different from long-term memory. To the contrary, the distinction between short-term and long-term memory provides but one interpretation of the recency effect.

Negative Recency

Wicklegren's interpretation of the recency effect is quite damaging to the notion that two memory stores are necessary to account for recency. Nevertheless, it is instructive to pursue the controversy a step further. The general strategy taken up by those who believe in a two memory interpretation of the recency effect has been to try to find variables that affect only one portion of the serial position curve. It is assumed that if a variable affects only the end of the curve, then that variable is affecting short-term but not long-term memory. Similarly, if a variable affects only the beginning and intermediate positions, or all positions equally, then it is assumed that that variable is affecting long-term memory and not short-term memory.

Many different variables have been found to affect part but not all of the serial position curve. Proponents of the two memory position argue that these studies support their formulation. The variables that have been investigated include mode of presentation (Watkins, 1972), interpolated activity (Glanzer & Schwartz, 1971), rehearsal instructions (Smith, Barresi, & Gross, 1971), and many others. Wicklegren (1973) provides a fine review of many of these variables.

For our purposes we shall deal with one particular variable, which has received considerable attention. Craik (1970) presented ten successive lists to his subjects. They were tested for recall immediately after the presentation of each list. This immediate recall test produced the expected kind of serial position effect, with a pronounced recency effect (see upper curve in Figure 12.4). But then Craik did something a little different.

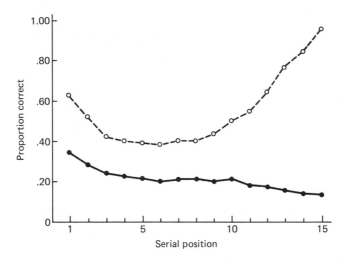

Figure 12.4. Serial position curves for immediate (○) and final (●) recall. (Adapted from Craik, F. I. M. The fate of primary memory items in free recall. *Journal of Verbal Learning and Verbal Behavior*, 1970, *9*, 143–148. Fig. 2, p. 145.)

After all ten lists had been presented and tested he asked the subjects to recall as many of the items as they could from all ten previous lists. The results of this final recall test were quite striking (see the lower curve in Figure 12.4). The recency effect disappeared. In fact, recall of the final items in the list dropped below recall of items in earlier positions. This finding has been termed the NEGATIVE RECENCY EFFECT.

The negative recency effect has received a good deal of attention (Bartlett & Tulving, 1974; Cohen, 1970; Jacoby & Bartz, 1972). Many have looked upon it as support for the distinction between long-term and short-term memory. The idea is that the end items can be recalled well in an immediate test because they are still in short-term memory. But, in the final test, the end items are not well recalled because they are no longer in short-term memory. They have either been lost or transferred to long-term memory with a relatively low probability. It is assumed that final recall of the end items drops below recall of earlier items because the end items have not been rehearsed as much as earlier items and are thus less likely to have been transferred to long-term memory.

But Wickelgren (1973) attacks this interpretation, too. He argues that the negative recency effect may also be handled by a single memory formulation. He argues that the recency effect disappears in the final recall test because the traces of the end items have undergone the kind of rapid loss, or initial decay, we described above. His explanation of the fact that end-item recall actually drops below the recall of earlier items is identical to the reasoning proposed by the two-store proponents. That is, earlier items are rehearsed more, learned better, and recalled more easily. According to Wicklegren, there is no need to postulate two memory systems.

Clinical Evidence for Two Memory Systems

Another line of potential support for the long-term–short-term distinction comes from studies of human patients who have suffered bilateral damage to, or surgical ablation of, the hippocampus. Many of the surgical treatments were undertaken in an effort to relieve severe epileptic conditions. If you are interested in the exact procedures and the nature of the damage to the brain good accounts can be found in Baddeley and Warrington (1970), Drachman and Arbit (1966), Milner (1966), Talland (1965), and Warrington and Weiskrantz (1968, 1970).

What concerns us is the peculiar effect these events, either accidental or surgical, have upon the patient's memory.

(*1*) The ability to retain new information for very short intervals of time appears to be normal.

(*2*) Memory for events that occurred before the brain damage appears to be normal.

(*3*) The patients are unable to retain any new information for long periods of time.

In other words, although old long-term memories, and the entire short-term memory system appear to be intact, the subjects display an almost complete inability to form new long-term memory traces. It seems that the patient's ability to transfer information from short-term memory to long-term memory has been destroyed. Information already in long-term memory appears to remain intact, and can be retrieved, but no new information can be entered into long-term memory. Such patients can carry on conversations (through the use of short-term memory). But they cannot remember a person they met and talked with a few minutes before (information has been lost from short-term memory without having been transferred into long-term memory). They know who they are, and what their life was like before the damage (intact old long-term memory). But they have no lasting idea of what has happened to them or the world since their brain trauma (no new long-term memory). Imagine what this condition must be like. The patients have no idea of what has happened since the trauma. In fact, they are even unaware that any time has passed at all since the trauma. For them, regardless of how long they have been there, they just came to the hospital "yesterday" (Hilgard & Bower, 1975). Nothing has happened to them (that they can recall) since they came to the hospital. The last thing they can remember is coming to the hospital, and that seems like yesterday.

This disability, although unfortunate for the individual involved, has been taken as evidence for the existence of two memory systems. Is it possible to think of these results in terms of a single memory store? Rather than argue that the brain trauma somehow destroyed the subject's ability to transfer information from a distinct short-term memory to a distinct long-term memory could we not argue that the trauma merely limits how well an item can be learned? Materials may be learned to the point where they can be remembered for a short interval of time, but they cannot be learned to the point where they will be remembered for very long. If we think of a single memory trace that can increase in strength then these results can be thought of in terms of a limit having been put on the strength that this memory trace can attain.

Who knows enough about what ablation and damage do to the brain to conclude that one or another interpretation is correct? It would seem, whatever the final outcome concerning long- versus short-term memory, that this type of evidence is difficult to accept as conclusive. There are just too many unknowns in the situation, and too many alternative explanations, to be certain we have clearly distinguished between long-term memory and short-term memory. For further clinical evidence and argument the reader is referred to Warrington and Shallice (1969) and Shallice and Warrington (1970).

Conclusion

The distinction between long-term memory and short-term memory will be with us for a long time. It is now marbled into much of our thinking about memory, but whether or not it is a valid distinction remains to be seen. We have examined four areas of study that have been proposed as providing evidence for the distinction. We have seen that none of them provides *conclusive* evidence for the distinction. We have not exhausted the relevant areas of research (Wicklegren, 1973, provides a fuller review). But the sample we have considered suggests that, at the very least, the distinction between long- and short-term memory should be approached with caution (see Bernbach, 1969, 1975; Craik & Lockhart, 1972; Melton, 1963; Murdock, 1974).

RECOGNITION VERSUS RECALL

Is recognition memory fundamentally different from recall memory? When we are asked to recognize something, such as the correct answer to a multiple-choice exam question, are we doing something fundamentally different from what we do when we try to *recall* the answer to the same question? The answers to these questions are pretty muddled at the present time. In fact, prior to 1960, very little attention was given to recognition memory per se. But the last 15 years have seen considerable growth of interest in recognition memory as distinct from recall. On an operational level, recall and recognition are clearly distinct. In a recall test we ask, "What is the item?" and in a recognition task we ask, "Is this the item?" (Underwood, 1972). We wish to find out whether or not this clear-cut operational distinction reflects any important underlying differences in the memory processes.

Before we address that question let us be sure we understand the difference between recall and recognition tasks. In a typical recall task, the subject might be presented with a list of words and then asked to recall as many of them as he can. In a recognition task the subject might be presented with the same list. But then, during the test phase, he would be presented with pairs of words. One member of the pair would be an "old" item, or one that he had already seen. The second member of each pair would be a new item, or a lure. The subject would be required to indicate which of the two items in each pair was the "old" item (Shepard, 1967). This is a typical recognition task, but there are many other varieties (see Kausler, 1974). The essence of all the recognition tasks is that the subject must be able to recognize an item as having been observed before in a certain context (e.g., in the list of presented items).

The Traditional View of Recognition Memory

Recognition is generally superior to recall (but not always, see Watkins & Tulving, 1975). Very early in the study of memory, it was discovered that we are able to recognize more than we can recall (Hollingworth, 1913; McDougall, 1904; Myers, 1914). In a typical study, subjects are presented with a list of syllables, words, pictures, or colors. They are then tested for recall and recognition. Subjects are typically able to recognize many more stimuli than they can recall. For example, sit down and try to list as many American Indian tribes or groups as you can. After a while it will seem as though you have exhausted your store of information. But you have not. You will be able to recognize many more, even though you could not recall them (for example, you may not have recalled, but may recognize, Choctow, Cree, Pueblo, Mohawk, Blackfoot, Eskimo, Yurok, Seminole, Cheyenne, Ojibwa, Chippewa, Mohegan, Seneca, Ute, Zuñi, and Arapaho).

Does this difference between recall and recognition reflect significant differences in memory processes? The traditional view has been that the difference is not particularly important. It has been assumed that the two tasks merely differ in terms of their sensitivity. Memorized items are assumed to differ in strength; the recognition test picks up, or reveals, weaker items than does the recall test. Some items seem to be strong enough to be recognized but not quite strong enough to be recalled. According to this traditional view, the difference between recognition and recall does not imply anything at all about underlying process differences. Memory is viewed as a unitary process wherein items vary in strength from weak to strong. The threshold for recognition is lower than it is for recall. Although this view is presented as a traditional view, and some psychologists feel it is outmoded, it does have its modern adherents (Tulving & Thomson, 1971).

An Empirical Challenge to the Traditional View

Suppose we present subjects with a list of 500 words. Half of the words are common (e.g., child, office, supply). Half are uncommon (e.g., ferule, julep, wattled). Then we test for recognition of these words. It has been found that UNCOMMON WORDS ARE MORE EASILY RECOGNIZED THAN COMMON WORDS. (McCormack & Swenson, 1972; Shepard, 1967). If recall and recognition involve common processes then we would expect the same sort of effect to appear when we test for recall of common and uncommon words. But just the opposite effect has appeared. COMMON WORDS APPEAR TO BE BETTER RECALLED THAN UNCOMMON WORDS (Kinsbourne & George, 1974; Murdock, 1960; Sumby, 1963). The same variable (common versus uncommon) thus has opposite effects on recall and recognition. This kind of disparity has led many investigators to suggest that recognition and recall may well involve different underlying processes (see Kintsch, 1970; Bower & Bostrom, 1968).

Differences in Retrieval?

Deciding exactly what these differences are is another matter. One common interpretation has been that recall involves retrieval processes, whereas recognition does not. In a sense, recall is seen as involving all of the processes of recognition, and then some. Recall and recognition are often seen as being different, not so much in the nature of the underlying processes, but in terms of the *number* of processes involved. In order to recognize a bit of information, the subject must have somehow encoded and stored it, but he need not search for it during the recognition test. To recall an item, on the other hand, the subject must encode, store, *and* retrieve.

Differences in Encoding and Storage?

Another possibility is that recognition and recall differ in terms of the ways in which materials are encoded and stored. For example, suppose we are going to be tested for recognition of one set of materials and for recall of another comparable set. It might be that we would go about encoding and storing these two sets of materials quite differently. For example, if we are to try to recall such items as XKLMJG we must be sure the entire item is encoded. On the other hand, if we encode the item for recognition then we might attend to some portion of the stimulus rather than to the whole thing (e.g., encode the fact that an item with L and M in the middle is an "old" item).

Various models of recognition memory have been, and are being developed. Many of them do emphasize encoding processes in recognition. Although beyond the scope of this text the reader is referred to Anderson (1973), Anderson and Bower (1972), Bower (1967), Norman and Wicklegren (1969), and Wicklegren (1970) for discussions of various recognition models, including strength theory and attribute theory.

Control Processes and Recall versus Recognition

Another way to think about the differences between recall and recognition is not in terms of fundamental differences, but in terms of variations in control processes. If you will recall, Atkinson and Shiffrin (1971) refer to the fact that we may go about using the fixed structural properties of the memory system in many different ways. Differences between recall and recognition might possibly be traced to differences in control processes rather than to fundamentally different memory systems. In attempting to memorize materials for future recall, the individual may use the fixed structural properties of the memory system in one way. In attempting to memorize for future recognition he may change his rehearsal strategy and utilize the fixed properties of the system in another way (see Griffith, 1975). [Of course the situation would become complicated if the individual were unaware of the nature of the upcoming retention test (recall or recognition). In this case the subject's strategy would be to maximize his chances of success in the light of his best guess about the nature of the upcoming test. Much of the current research concerning recall versus recognition does not give enough attention to the subject's perception of the task at hand.]

Conclusion

Recall and recognition do differ on an operational level. Certain variables do affect the two differentially. Whether or not these differences reflect fundamental differences in underlying processes remains to be seen. One possibility is that recall involves retrieval, whereas recognition does not. Another possibility is that encoding and/or storage processes differ in recall and recognition. Still another possibility is that, although the underlying memory structures are the same, the control processes utilized by the subject in recall and recognition may differ. Although beyond the scope of this text, the interested reader is referred to theoreticians who are currently arguing against a fundamental distinction between recall and recognition processes (Tulving & Thomson, 1973; Watkins & Tulving, 1975) and to those who wish to draw a qualitative distinction between the two processes (Anderson & Bower, 1974; Martin, 1975).

MEMORY FOR DIFFERENT TYPES OF INFORMATION

So far we have asked whether or not short-term memory is different from long-term memory, and whether or not recognition memory is different from recall memory. These distinctions exemplify the tendency to split or divide memory into various types. Another example of this trend is to be found in the suggestion that different *types* of information will require different memory models. Thus we might need one sort of model to account for our ability to remember words, and another model to account for our ability to remember sentences or paragraphs. We might need one model to account for the encoding, storage, and retrieval of visual information and another to account for auditory information, etc. Although the distinction between short- and long-term memory is based upon temporal factors, the present approach is based upon an acute awareness of the different types of information we are able to store. We shall consider two examples of this tendency to distinguish between memories for different types of information.

Episodic versus Semantic Memory

Tulving (1972) has distinguished between EPISODIC and SEMANTIC memory. Episodic memory is assumed to store information about temporally arranged or dated events and episodes. Personal experiences are stored in episodic memory. Semantic memory, on the other hand, refers to memory for the meaning of words, concepts, and facts, etc. Information stored in semantic memory is not temporally ordered, or related to time. Examples of the kind of information stored in episodic memory would be:

(*1*) I remember spending the early years of my life in Utica.
(*2*) I must be at school tomorrow before 8:30.
(*3*) I met a very uninteresting person on the bus yesterday.

Most laboratory experiments involve episodic memory. For example, remembering that LXG was paired with KPY *in a particular laboratory ex-*

periment would be an episodic memory. Examples of the kind of non-temporal information stored in semantic memory would be:

(*1*) $2 + 2 = 4$.
(*2*) Whales nurse their young.
(*3*) Almost everyone has a nose.

These bits of information are not temporally ordered—they are not remembered in temporal relation to other experiences. In describing the distinction, Tulving (1972) does point out that the two systems often interact with one another. On the other hand, he feels that they can function independently. He feels they may well differ from one another in terms of encoding, storage, and retrieval processes.

The distinction between episodic and semantic memory is relatively new, but it has been accepted as heuristically valuable. Whether or not it will prove to be a lasting distinction remains to be seen. There have not been very many cases in which the two types of memory have been compared experimentally. One reason for this is that the vast majority of experimental studies involve information of the episodic variety. Most experiments put the subject through an "episode," which he has to remember. Few studies have been concerned with preexperimental semantic information existing in long-term store. In any case, the distinction between episodic and semantic memory does provide us with an example of the tendency to propose different models for different types of information (see Watkins & Tulving, 1975; Light, Kimble, & Pellegrino, 1975).

Item versus Associative versus Serial Information

Murdock's (1974) influential book provides us with another example of the attention being given to the possibility that different types of information may require different models. He feels we may need at least partially independent models to account for three types of information that have been identified as important in human memory. ITEM INFORMATION refers to information that allows us to recognize objects and events, such as names, places, tastes, smells, and labels. *Associative information* refers to the concept of associations, or to the relating of two items, such as pairing names and faces or remembering the meanings of words. *Serial information* refers to information about sequences of events, such as the days of the week, spelling, and plans of attack.

Murdock contends that the processes of encoding, storage, and retrieval may differ for item, associative, and serial information. He catalogues existing models of memory in terms of their concern for these various types of information. Of course, it is too early to predict the eventual success of this sort of division process. But Murdock has clearly performed a service by perceiving that the welter of existing models does seem to break down into this three-way classification.

The distinctions among memory systems based upon the type of information to be processed may well replace the dichotomy based upon temporal factors (long-term versus short-term). At the same time we must avoid replacing one set of distinctions with another in the absence of compelling evidence. One danger inherent in the process of distinguishing among memories for different types of information is that we may not know when to stop. If we distinguish among item, associative, serial, semantic, and episodic information, should we not also distinguish other categories of information? It seems we could, if we wished, identify hundreds of different sorts of information. But we would not necessarily want to do that, for we would flounder in the resulting models.

Be that as it may, the primary question remains the same. Will the distinctions based upon information types reveal truly independent memory systems, or will they merely highlight the flexibility with which the individual may use, or control, some underlying, unitary memory system? We now turn to our last example of the ways in which memory may be divided.

ANIMAL MEMORY VERSUS HUMAN MEMORY

Let us return to a question we have asked many times. Do we need one theory, or set of theories, to account for human behavior and another to account for animal behavior? More specifically, do animals and humans forget in essentially the same manner, or are they such different kinds of creatures that we will be forced to develop distinct models for each of them?

The position taken in this text, is that, despite an enormous gap between the animal and human literatures, there are important points of contact. We shall emphasize these points of contact. The reader should be aware that this is a biased position. Many authors argue that theories of animal and human memory will have to be different (see Winograd, 1971), and that a single, unified theory of memory encompassing both animal and human behavior is highly unlikely.

We shall present the points of contact between animal and human memory by considering the two major conceptual approaches to memory (interference theory and the information-processing approach). In each case, we shall attempt to give some brief hint of the ways in which the principles and mechanisms governing human memory also seem to be relevant to a consideration of animal memory.

Until recently, memory per se did not receive a great deal of attention in the field of animal behavior. But the recent upsurge of interest in human memory has been paralleled by a similar swell of interest in animal memory. A series of papers contained in Honig and James (1971) provides a fair example of the growth of interest in animal memory.

Interference and Animal Memory

Proactive Inhibition and Retroactive Inhibition in Animals

The first question we might ask is whether or not RI and PI appear in animal situations. Do animals suffer losses in retention that may be attributed to the effects of prior learning (PI) and subsequent learning (RI)? The answer appears to be in the affirmative. Poor retention of an acquired response system in animals does appear to be related to previous and subsequent learning. As Spear (1971) puts it, interference phenomena such as PI and RI are common types of retention lapses in animals, although they are often not recognized as such. A number of studies, specifically designed to demonstrate PI and RI in animals, have been successful (Chizar & Spear, 1968; Crowder, 1967; Gleitman & Jung, 1963; Koppenaal & Jagoda, 1968; Maier, Allaway, & Gleitman, 1967). It is difficult to conclude with any certainty that PI and RI effects in animal and human designs are strictly comparable (see Revusky, 1971; Gleitman, 1971). On the other hand, the rough correspondence between animal and human experiments and results does suggest that the possibility of similar cross-species interference effects must be taken seriously.

Interference Theory and Animals

When considering interference phenomena, and the predominantly human verbal research associated with them, we must keep in mind that the origins of the theory lie in the early animal literature. We have already seen that the unlearning factor in the two-factor theory of interference has been viewed as analogous to the experimental extinction phenomenon. In addition, demonstrations of spontaneous recovery in human verbal behavior (e.g., Ceraso & Henderson, 1965) provide another point of contact between human learning and animal conditioning.

How one interprets these points of contact is another matter. Some authors (e.g., Winograd, 1971) argue that, although interference concepts have their roots in the animal laboratory, the meanings of the concepts have changed as the concepts have been applied to human situations. The labels may be the same (extinction, spontaneous recovery, etc.), but the processes to which they are applied differ in the animal and human verbal situations. On the other hand, many authors feel that there may be at least some fundamental correspondences between animal and human interference phenomena (Spear, 1971). For information concern-

ing methodological differences between animal and human studies of for
getting see Chizar and Spear (1969) and Zentall (1970).

Information Processing and Animals:
Retrograde Amnesia

We have already seen that the information-processing approach is
very popular in the field of human memory. And the investigators of
animal memory also use such terms as short-term memory, long-term
memory, encoding, storage, and retrieval. The information-processing
approach has come of age in the field of animal memory. Many of the
concepts and models developed in connection with human memory have
been paralleled by similar developments within the animal laboratory
(Estes, 1969; Kamin, 1969b; Russell, 1966).

Retrograde Amnesia: The Phenomenon

We shall consider one area of investigation that provides a prime
example of the way in which information-processing concepts have
permeated the field of animal memory. In a retrograde amnesia study,
an animal first learns a particular response (an avoidance response, for
example). After acquisition of the response, the animal is subjected to some
"amnesic agent" such as electroconvulsive shock, puromycin, or potassium
chloride. The animal then is tested for the original response. The animal's
"memory" for the recently learned behavior seems to be impaired. The
term "retrograde" applies to the fact that the amnesic effect appears
to increase as the time between the learning and the introduction of
the amnesic agent (shock) is decreased. In other words, recent memories
suffer the most. If you shock the animal immediately the learning is
less likely to become permanent than if you allow time to pass before
administering the amnesic agent.

Parenthetically, the retrograde amnesia procedures are reminiscent
of the electroconvulsive shock treatments sometimes used with human
patients, particularly those found to be deeply depressed. The general
procedure is one in which the patient is first given a muscle relaxer
(to prevent damage in the upcoming, electrically induced convulsion).
Electric current is then passed through the brain for a brief moment
by way of electrodes attached to the patient's temples. Two of the major
results of this type of treatment are (1) patients come out of their depressed state, at least temporarily, and (2) they suffer from some degree
of amnesia, with more recent memories suffering more than older memories. With repeated treatments these memory losses may become quite
permanent.

Retrograde Amnesia: Encoding, Storage or
Retrieval Effect?

Given that retrograde amnesia is a phenomenon that can easily be demonstrated with animals (see Spear, 1973) and, for that matter, with humans (Landauer, 1974; Tulving, 1969) what accounts for the effect?

Early interpretations (McGaugh, 1966; McGaugh & Dawson, 1971) emphasized the concept of CONSOLIDATION. The notion here is that the amnesic agent somehow disrupts consolidation of the memory trace. For a memory trace to become permanent, or move from short-term memory to long-term memory, it needs a little time to consolidate. Consolidation interpretations argue that factors such as electroconvulsive shock disrupt and prevent the transfer of information into permanent store. The argument is that the amnesic agents render the information unavailable on future tests.

It is clear that this sort of theorizing represents a prime example of the information-processing approach. The flow of information through the organism, from temporary to permanent storage, is presumed to be disrupted by the introduction of various amnesic agents.

This interpretation of retrograde amnesia suggests that the effect involves either encoding or storage processes, or both. The amnesic agent may block the process of encoding, or it may disrupt the storage of that information over time. (It is often unclear as to which of these processes is supposed to be involved in any given consolidation model. Encoding and storage are often left somewhat undifferentiated.) In any case, the consolidation interpretation may be cast in direct opposition to a new, developing position, which argues that retrograde amnesia involves the disruption of *retrieval* processes rather than encoding or storage processes.

Support for the retrieval interpetation goes like this. If amnesic agents disrupt encoding or storage then the amnesia should be *permanent*. If information is not encoded or is lost during storage then it will never be available. But a number of recent experiments (see Quartermain & Botwinick, 1975) have shown that retrograde amnesia is *not* permanent. Information which has been "lost" through the introduction of amnesic agents *can* be regained, or "reactivated." There are several techniques for observing the reversibility of amnesia. They include (*1*) the introduction of appropriate "reminders," or prompts, and (*2*) the observance of "spontaneous" recovery of the lost information.

The reversibility of amnesia suggests that the information is available all along (encoded and stored) but is not accessible (cannot be retrieved) until appropriate reminders, or other critical conditions, are present. In other words, electroconvulsive shock does not prevent encoding or storage of information. It merely disrupts the subject's ability to utilize or retrieve whatever information is stored. Suppose you are listening to an old time radio program. The heroine suffers a head injury in an automobile accident. She can not remember a thing. Her family and friends are upset, to say the least. She contemplates ending it all. But with the careful help and prompting of her family physician it all begins to come back. She "regains her memory," and marries Mark after all. The point here is that she never really *lost* anything. The information was still in storage, but she could not pull it out, or retrieve it, until prompted or reminded. The information was available but temporarily inaccessible.

This view, emphasizing the disruption of retrieval processes, has received considerable support in the recent literature (Miller, Ott, Berk, & Springer, 1974; Miller & Springer, 1973, 1974; Spear, 1971, 1973). At the same time, proponents of the encoding-storage position have not disappeared (McGaugh & Dawson, 1971; Gold & King, 1974). A fine, healthy controversy exists, with many interesting studies appearing in the current literature.

Whatever one's views concerning the relative merits of the two interpretations of retrograde amnesia, the point we wish to keep in mind is that the controversy swirls within an information-processing framework. The application of such concepts as encoding, storage, and retrieval in this animal situation cannot be overlooked.

In summary, theories about animal and human memory have much in common. *Many of the principles and mechanisms found in the study of human memory are also found in the animal literature. This seems to hold true for both the interference approach and for the information-processing approach.* Whether the investigations of animal memory and human memory will eventually converge or diverge remains to be seen. At present, the best that can be said is that the two fields, although somewhat isolated, do seem to be feeding into, and benefiting from, one another.

In terms of the general concern of this chapter, which is to consider the need for many different memory models, we must conclude that it is not at all clear that animal and human memory systems are fundamentally different from one another. It would be premature of us to conclude that the animal and human memory systems are inherently different. A sense of parsimony urges that we pursue the possibility that animal and human memory mechanisms may eventually be subsumed under some general, unified theory of memory. Such a theory would account for the "superiority" of human memory but it would also acknowledge basic, qualitative similarities among the "lower" and "higher" species.

CONCLUSION

Having discussed four different ways to split, or divide, memory what can we conclude? Probably the most reasonable thing to be said is that, although such distinctions should be vigorously pursued, none of them now stands clearly substantiated. It may turn out that one or more of them proves to be valid. On the other hand, caution should be applied in accepting them as they may turn out to be somewhat superficial rather than indicative of important underlying differences in memory processes.

SUMMARY

1. Memory has been divided in many different ways. These distinctions may or may not be valid. This chapter considered four proposed divisions of memory.

2. The first widely discussed distinction is between SHORT-TERM MEMORY and LONG-TERM MEMORY. Several areas of research bear upon this issue.

3. At one time it was suggested that interference effects (PI and RI) operate in long-term memory but not short-term memory. This proposal has been disproved. Both PI and RI operate in short-term memory. Recall of a given item in the Peterson and Peterson task may be influenced by the number of prior items the subject has processed (PI), and by interpolated activity (RI).

4. Research has now gone beyond mere demonstrations of PI and RI in short-term memory. For example, some investigators feel PI effects in short-term memory involve coding and storage processes, whereas others feel retrieval processes are involved.

5. Early research suggested that short-term memory might involve ACOUSTIC CODING processes, whereas long-term memory might involve SEMANTIC CODING processes. This conclusion was drawn from studies that seemed to indicate that subjects would confuse acoustically similar materials in short-term memory and confuse semantically similar materials in long-term memory.

6. But the acoustic–semantic distinction has been rejected. It now appears that short-term and long-term memory are flexible in terms of coding. Depending upon the demands of the task, and the desires of the subject, short-term and long-term memory may involve either acoustic or semantic coding, or both.

7. The RECENCY EFFECT in the free recall of a serial list refers to the fact that the items toward the end of the list will be recalled better than earlier ones.

8. This recency effect has been interpreted in terms of the two-memory position. Items toward the end of the list are presumed to be in short-term memory at the time of recall, and thus easily recalled. Earlier items are no longer in short-term memory (lost or transferred to long-term memory) and are less likely to be recalled.

9. Wicklegren argues that the recency effect may also be interpreted in terms of a single-memory position. If we assume that memory traces are lost rapidly at first and then more slowly, then there is no need to postulate two memory stores.

10. NEGATIVE RECENCY refers to the fact that recall of the end items will drop below recall of earlier items if the recall test is delayed.

11. Negative recency has also been interpreted as evidence for two memory stores. But alternative interpretations are available.

12. Patients who have suffered bilateral damage of the hippocampus have sometimes been unable to form new long-term memories. Old long-term memories remain intact. The entire short-term memory system remains intact. The loss of the ability to transfer information from short-term store to long-term store has been taken as evidence for the two memory position. But alternative interpretations are available.

13. In conclusion the distinction between short-term memory and long-term memory has not been conclusively substantiated.

14. The second major distinction of the chapter is between RECALL and RECOGNITION. In a recall task we ask, "What is the item?" In a recognition test we ask, "Is this the item?" Recognition tends to be superior to recall.

15. The traditional view holds that recognition and recall do not involve fundamentally different processes. Recognition is merely seen as a more sensitive indicator of memory traces within a single memory framework.

16. But some variables (e.g., common versus uncommon items) affect recall and recognition in opposite ways. This fact has led many to suggest that the two are truly different.

17. Some have suggested that recall involves encoding, storage, *and* retrieval, whereas recognition involves only encoding and storage.

18. Others have suggested that the encoding and storage processes may differ in recall and recognition.

19. Still another view holds that differences in recognition and recall reflect differences in CONTROL PROCESSES rather than in the fixed structural properties of the memory apparatus.

20. The third major memory division involves the suggestion that we will need different models to account for the different types of information we process.

21. EPISODIC versus SEMANTIC MEMORY refers to the idea that one model may be required for the storage of temporally ordered personal experiences (episodic) and another for nontemporal facts (semantic).

22. Murdock has split the information in a different manner. He suggests we may need distinct models to account for item, associative, and serial information.

23. The fourth and final distinction is between animal and human

memory. Some have suggested we will need different models for different species.

24. Yet, animal and human memory systems appear to have much in common. For example, PI and RI have been observed in animal situations. Extinction and spontaneous recovery have also been implicated in human as well as animal situations.

25. Furthermore, information-processing concepts and models have permeated the field of animal memory. For example, in RETROGRADE AMNESIA studies, animals first learn a particular response. Then, after the administration of some amnesic agent such as electroconvulsive shock, it is found that the response has been lost. This effect appears to be similar to the results of electroconvulsive shock treatment used with depressed human patients.

26. Retrograde amnesia has been interpreted as a disruption of the encoding and storage processes (the consolidation hypothesis).

27. But the discovery of the reversibility of retrograde amnesia has prompted many to claim that the effect involves a disruption of retrieval processes rather than encoding or storage processes.

28. It is clear that this controversy swirls within an information-processing context, and draws heavily upon concepts utilized in the study of human memory.

29. All four distinctions (long-term versus short-term, recall versus recognition, types of information, animal versus human) should be pursued. At the same time it should be remembered that none of them has been clearly and conclusively substantiated.

Organization in Memory 13

INTRODUCTION

The psychology of memory is currently awash with studies of "organization in memory," "organizational processes," and "organizational theory." The meaning of these terms varies from investigation to investigation. At present, there is no firm consensus concerning the definition of organizational processes within the overall memory process. And yet there do seem to be common elements that bind together the various uses of the term.

The purpose of this chapter will be to introduce the reader to the complexities of the "organizational" approach to memory. First, we shall consider several areas of research that clearly substantiate the existence (and the diversity) of organizational phenomena in memory. Second, we shall consider several theoretical issues, or problems, that have been stimulated by, and contribute to, the investigation of organizational phenomena.

Let us begin our discussion with an example. Consider the game children play when they are trying to fight off boredom on long road trips. The first player begins by saying, "I went to the store and bought an apple." The second player says, "I went to the store and bought an apple and a knife." The third player says, "I went to the store and bought an apple, a knife, and a shirt," and so on, until someone makes an error in recalling the building chain of items. Each player must recall all the previous items, and add one new one. How might you go about remembering the growing list of items? What strategies might you employ? One technique might involve the simple rehearsal, or repetition of the items over and over again in the correct order. But there are other possibilities. Some people find it convenient to build mental "images" with the items. Thus one player might imagine a green apple impaled on a golden knife and wrapped in a blue shirt. When recall is required the player merely summons up the picture, or image, and reads off the necessary items. These images (whatever they are) can vary tremendously. They may be simple or complex, active or passive, ordinary or unusual, etc. This process of relating items to one another in a visual image is one example of an organizational strategy. The player is doing more than rehearsing items over and over again. He is structuring the items, and relating them to one another, through the use of a mental image.

Another player might remember the same items by constructing a sentence. The words in the sentence might begin with the first letters of the to-be-remembered items. Thus, "*Another King Said* . . ." might provide a vivid means for remembering, "*Apple, Knife, Shirt* . . . ." The player relates the items to one another, or organizes the materials, by imbedding them within a sentence. Another individual might use a sentence construction technique of a different sort. This player might make up a sentence using the items themselves rather than their first letters. For example, "The old man picked up the *apple* and looked for his *knife* in his *shirt* pocket."

Each of these players is organizing, or structuring, or relating the to-be-remembered items in a different manner. The number of possible organizational schemes, or strategies, is almost unlimited. If you take a moment to think about it you can probably think of a number of different plans for remembering these items. We can categorize and group items. We can string them in series. We can relate them to one another and to information we bring into the situation. It is this vast array of mental activities that is referred to as organization in memory.

In a simple sense, organizational processes refer to whatever we do to information between input and output. We may systematize, relate, order, select, elaborate, and transform information. Mandler (1972) states that organization refers to mental structures that establish relations among items, events, and features. He mentions three types of structures: categorical, serial, and relational. It is clear why there tends to be some uncertainty and confusion concerning the exact nature of organization. A definition of organization would have to include, or encompass, an enormous number of varied mental activities. We should not be dismayed by the diversity of interests and activities that have fallen under the rubric of organization. Rather we should look upon the disorganized field of organization as an interesting, stimulating approach to the study of memory.

As we have noted, there is no clear picture of what we all mean by organization. There is no precise theory, or definition, of organization (Murdock, 1974). What the organizational approach does do is underscore the obvious fact that memory events are complicated and that organization can improve retention. An adequate conception of memory will have to go far beyond simple-minded notions of rote rehearsal. Organizational research may provide us with new insights into the workings of the mind.

In attempting to characterize the evolving organizational approach we shall discuss several areas of research that have been subsumed by the heading of organization in memory. We shall be discussing experimental demonstrations of the individual's ability to improve retention through the use of organizational processes. For a fuller review of organizational research the reader is referred to Melton and Martin (1972) and to Tulving and Donaldson (1972).

Before we turn to our review of specific areas of research we should note that an interest in organization in memory is not new. In fact, current interest in such processes really represents a *return* to areas that have long been of interest to psychologists. We are witnessing a swing of the pendulum, so to speak. As Postman (1972) and others have pointed out, one of the basic tenets of Gestalt psychology was that memory is governed by principles of organization and perceptual grouping. In the early days methods for *measuring* organizational activities were lacking. As a result the concepts of Gestalt psychology never obtained firm experimental support. Lack of adequate experimental techniques forced psychologists to lay the questions aside. But interest in the issues raised by the Gestalt psychologists never completely disappeared. The past decade has seen a renewal of interest in organization in memory. This explosion of activity was made possible by the development of some new techniques for measuring and quantifying the elusive organizational activities. Some of these new techniques, and the data they have yielded, will be discussed in the sections that follow.

WORD ASSOCIATION

Some early, relatively unsophisticated evidence for the existence of organization in memory was revealed by the development of the word-association test (Kent & Rosanoff, 1910). The test consists of 100 common words. The subject's task is to "give the first word that comes to mind" in response to each of the 100 words. It is an interesting test, and one that most individuals do not mind at all. What kinds of responses would you imagine people might give? As it turns out there are some extremely common responses to many of these words. Thus "mother" often evokes "father," and "black" elicits "white" with consistently high probabilities, etc. This is not to say that everyone gives these common responses. Some individuals come up with very unique responses, to say the least (see Table 13.1). But a great number of individuals will give the same response to many of these stimulus words. These common responses are quite likely to be elicited from different groups of subjects at different times (Fox, 1970; Jenkins & Russell, 1960). Psychologists have developed norms, or lists of the various types of responses elicited by each stimulus word (Palermo & Jenkins, 1964; Russell & Jenkins, 1954). These norms are used in all sorts of experimental situations. Mackenzie (1972) pro-

TABLE 13.1

Word-association Responses Given by 100 Subjects to Some Selected Stimulus Words[a]

Stimulus	Response Frequency	Response
Woman	59	Man
	10	Child, girl
	4	Sex
	2	Love, mother
	1	Friend, world, clean, thin, hair, old, soft, pretty, female, baby, home, lady, fold
Chair	55	Table
	15	Sit
	4	Seat, desk
	2	Legs, couch, bed
	1	Study, home, blue, soft, foot, arm, plastic, yellow, wood, rest, hard, window, floor, comfortable, professor, house
Blossom	74	Flower
	5	Apple
	4	Rose
	2	Spring, time
	1	Cut, pretty, bud, bouquet, Pasadena, sniff, smell, blooms red, tree, plant, sweet, orange

[a] Unpublished data obtained by author.

vides a review of much of the current research being done with word associations (see also Bilodeau & Howell, 1965; Entwisle, 1966).

But for our purposes, the point we wish to make is that these consistent patterns of word associations suggest that words are organized, or structured, within each of us. They are not merely lumped, or piled randomly, within us somewhere. They are related to one another in a distinct manner. In a very rough way, the word-association test reveals some of this structure.

The word-association test has been used in clinical situations. Some psychotherapists believe they can learn something about an individual by examining his responses on a word-association test. The responses may provide the therapist with insights into the patient's personality, or mental state. If, in response to "mother," the patient says "father," or "home," or "love" the therapist may be led to one set of conclusions.

On the other hand, if the patient's response to "mother" is "blood vein," or "rape," or "horror" the therapist might begin to think along different lines.

The word-association test does not provide us with a great deal of information about mental structure or organization, but it does represent an early, and ongoing, technique for tapping into existing memory structures.

CHUNKING AND REWRITING

Suppose we are presented with the following letters, one at a time: F, L, S, M, P, U, J, E. We are then asked to recall them immediately in any order. We might be able to accomplish this feat, but we would certainly be hard pressed to handle any more information. But it is possible to organize this material in such a way that our memory would hardly be taxed at all. For example, we may rearrange the letters such that they spell JUMPS and ELF. By doing this we can remember all eight letters easily, and have plenty of memory capacity left over. We could easily handle a lot more letters, especially if they could also be arranged as words. By organizing the information we have greatly expanded the capacity of our immediate memory.

The concept of the memory *chunk* was introduced by Miller (1956). Miller argues that *our immediate memory is limited by the number of chunks of information it can handle, but that the amount of information contained in each chunk may vary.* So long as the information can be expressed as a single response, then it represents one chunk. Thus JUMPS and ELF each represent one chunk, but each chunk contains several units of information (letters). In a sense, the process of increasing the size of a chunk seems to involve our ability to characterize many different units of information with fewer and fewer responses. Thus instead of having to say F, L, S, M, P, U, J, E (eight responses or eight chunks) we say JUMPS and ELF (two responses or two chunks). By transforming eight responses into two responses we are freeing ourselves to handle additional information. Immediate memory does not appear to be limited by number of physical stimuli. Instead, it is limited by the number of chunks we can handle. Miller's best guess was that we can handle seven plus or minus two chunks of information. Each chunk may vary in terms of the amount of information it contains. Thus, O is one chunk, SO is one chunk, SOP is one chunk, and STOP is one chunk. It is just as easy to remember one of these as another even though they vary in terms of number of letters. If we can increase the amount of information contained in each chunk, then we can greatly expand our memory capacity, even though it is limited to approximately seven chunks.

Here is another example of the way in which we can increase the amount of information contained in each of our seven plus or minus two chunks. Suppose we are presented the following binary digits and asked to recall the sequence: 101000100111001110. See if you can read the sequence once and then recall it correctly. Now, as it stands, that is a rather difficult task. The sequence contains 18 bits of information, and probably exceeds our memory capacity. But suppose, prior to reading off the sequence, we had learned the following: 0 means 00, 1 means 01, 2 means 10 and 3 means 11. In other words, we have given *new names* to all possible sequences of two binary digits. Having learned this new language we are now ready to tackle the original sequence. As the sequence is being presented we may recode it in terms of our new language. Thus:

Original	1 0	1 0	0 0	1 0	0 1	1 1	0 0	1 1	1 0
Recoded	2	2	0	2	1	3	0	3	2

Now, to remember the original sequence of 18 binary digits all we have to do is remember 220213032. This may *still* exceed our memory span, but it certainly represents an improvement. We have cut the number of units we must remember in half. When asked to recall the original sequence we merely recall as much of 220213032 as we can and decode it as we go along. In other words, by organizing the to-be-remembered information (through rewriting) we have vastly improved the amount of information we can retain. In this case organization clearly improves retention.

CLUSTERING IN RECALL

If you have a pencil and paper handy you might want to try the following experiment. Read the list of words contained in Table 13.2 and then immediately write down as many as you can recall *in any order you wish*. Now, having exhausted your ability to recall the items, look over your responses. Notice that you have probably grouped the items according to categories. Thus you may have recalled two or more trees together, or several animals together. Similarly, you may have recalled colors and/or cities together. This grouping phenomenon is called CLUSTERING IN RECALL. It merely refers to the fact that items drawn from various categories, and presented *randomly*, will be recalled *together*. In other words, there is not a one to one relationship between order of input and order of output. It seems we do some organizing in there somewhere.

Category Clustering

The concept of clustering has a long history. Its emergence as an important phenomenon began with the work of Bousfield (Bousfield,

TABLE 13.2

Free Recall List Used in Clustering Experiment

HEMLOCK
CARROT
PARIS
BLACK
LETTUCE
ELM
ZEBRA
PEAS
NEW YORK
RED
SEATTLE
MOOSE
BROCCOLI
WOLF
BLUE
COW
PINE
TOMATO
BROWN
SYCAMORE
MOSCOW
CROW
REDWOOD
MAPLE
SQUASH
TOLEDO
ORANGE
YELLOW
AMSTERDAM
SNAKE

1953; Bousfield & Sedgewick, 1944). In one of Bousfield's experiments subjects received a 60-item list composed of 15 instances drawn from each of four categories (animals, names, professions, vegetables). The words were read to the subjects, one at a time, in a random order. Subjects were then provided ten minutes in which to recall as many of the items as they could. Bousfield then counted the number of times items from the same category were *recalled next to one another*. This count formed the basis of his measure of clustering in recall. (Bousfield's final index of clustering is not quite so simple. For details of his measure, which accounts for *opportunity* to cluster and *chance levels* of clustering, the reader is referred to the original work.)

Given that clustering has been demonstrated, and that valid measures of clustering have been developed, what have psychologists done with this phenomenon? To begin, they have asked whether or not *total* recall of items from the list goes up as clustering goes up. In other words, is there any evidence that suggests that organizing according to categories goes hand in hand with improved retention? The answer to this question must be a qualified "yes." The relationship between clustering and overall recall has not been as strong as one might have expected. On the other hand, there have been several studies that do seem to suggest a positive relationship between clustering and recall. One procedure has been to compare overall recall of lists of categorized items with overall recall of lists of uncategorized items. Recall of the categorized lists tends to be superior. The reader is referred to Cofer (1967), Forrester and King (1971), Puff (1970), Shuell (1969), Thompson, Hamlin, and Roenker (1972), and Weist (1972) for a full exposition of this issue.

Another question asked by investigators in this area is whether or not subjects will cluster according to other types of categories. For example, will subjects cluster items that *sound* alike? The answer again seems to be a qualified "yes." The effect is a weak one. Bousfield and Wicklund (1969) and Dolinsky (1972) report that subjects will cluster items such as FLACK, PACK, SNACK, TACK and FURL, PEARL, SQUIRREL, SWIRL. On the other hand, Forrester and King (1971) and Forrester (1972) failed to find clustering of this sort.

As a final example of the kind of research done in connection with category clustering we may consider the difference between EXHAUSTIVE and NONEXHAUSTIVE CATEGORIES. When a list involves nonexhaustive categories the list does not contain *all* of the members of the categories. For example, if our list includes 15 vegetables then we have not exhausted the category of vegetables. Exhaustive categories usually involve very few members, all of which are included in our list. For example, a category of seasons may be exhaustive (summer, fall, winter, spring). The planets of our solar system could be an exhaustive category. Psychologists have asked which of these two types of categories produces (*1*) the best overall recall and (*2*) the greatest amount of clustering. Cohen (1963, 1966) presents data that suggest that both total recall and clustering are greater for exhaustive than for nonexhaustive categories. It seems we are more able to work with exhaustive categories, perhaps because we know when we are done with a category. Our organizational efforts seem to yield better retention in this instance. These few examples should provide the flavor of the research being done in connection with category clustering (see also D'Agostino, 1969 and Segal, 1969).

Associative Clustering

So far, we have been speaking of clustering that involves the recall of members of some distinct and obvious category (e.g., animals or professions). But there is still another type of clustering, which is called

ASSOCIATIVE CLUSTERING. In associative clustering the lists are composed of items that may *elicit each other in a word-association test,* but do *not* belong to some obvious category (e.g., car–wheel, tree–apple, mind–thought). Many investigators have provided evidence that suggests that we do cluster according to this type of associative relationship, as well as in terms of category membership (Jenkins & Russell, 1952; Marshall, 1967; Walker, 1971).

In a sense, it is quite difficult to maintain the distinction between category and associative clustering. The problem lies in the fact that most associatively related items may also be thought of as belonging to some common category, however obscure. For example, "car" and "wheel" may be thought of as belonging to a category of transportation items. Similarly, "tree" and "apple" are both elements of the vegetable kingdom. What we are saying is that the distinction between associative and category clustering is not as clear-cut as some would suppose.

Whatever the case, clustering of both types has been taken as evidence for the idea that organizational activities are extremely important in retention. Furthermore, there exists at least some evidence for the conclusion that clustering facilitates retention.

SUBJECTIVE ORGANIZATION

Tulving (1962) developed a technique for assessing organization in memory, which has been extremely influential. In a typical subjective organization (SO) experiment, the individual receives a long list of randomly presented items, one at a time. The items do not belong to any obvious, experimenter imposed categories. The subject is then asked to recall as many of the items as he can, in any order. Following recall, the list is again presented, usually in a new random order. A series of recall and presentation phases follow one another in this fashion. Tulving and others have found that the order in which the subject recalls these items begins to assume some consistency from recall trial to recall trial. The subject begins to recall certain words together even though they are not presented together. The subject is somehow ordering, or structuring, the material. The subject's output becomes consistent despite random input. Clearly, the subject is free to use any organizational strategy he wishes. He might build a visual image, construct a story, relate items that sound or look alike, or use some other unique, individual scheme. In any case, the constant order in which the subject recalls the items reveals that the subject is imposing some sort of structure upon the materials.

At the same time, it should be noted that the SO technique does not tell us exactly what this developing organization is (see Mandler, Worden, & Graesser, 1974). All we know is that something is happening.

This fact underlines an important difference between the clustering technique and the SO procedure. In the clustering method we *do* have some idea of the type of organizational activity which is occurring. As experimenters, we define the categories and impose them upon the subject. We observe the results of the subject's attempt to utilize these imposed categories. In SO studies, on the other hand, we may observe the development of idiosyncratic organizational strategies, unhindered by any experimenter-imposed constraints.

Subjective Organization and Overall Recall

Does increasing SO lead to greater recall? Does this sort of organization facilitate retention? This would seem to be a critical question. Unfortunately, the available data are equivocal. Several studies have reported a positive relationship between overall recall and subjective organization (Allen, 1968; Mayhew, 1967; Tulving, 1962, 1964). Others have failed to find the expected relationship (Carterette & Coleman, 1963; Postman, 1970). What do these inconsistent results imply for our notion that organization facilitates retention? There are at least two ways to view the problem (Wood, 1972). First, these results may mean that SO does not facilitate retention. Second, a true and strong relationship between this type of organization and overall recall may so far have been obscured by methodological problems.

Subjective Organization and Transfer Tests

Postman (1972) and others have argued that measures such as the SO index provide but a first step in assessing the degree and nature of organizational activities. Postman outlines a supplemental method for assessing organizational activities, which is becoming quite popular. Specifically, he argues that much greater attention should be given to tests of transfer. If a subject receives a first list, and organizes it in some particular fashion, then this organization may either facilitate or interfere with the learning of a second list, depending, of course, upon the relationship between the successive lists. By carefully controlling the relationship between successive tasks, and by noting the impact of the first tasks upon the second, Postman feels *the nature* and *extent* of first-list organization may be revealed to a degree impossible by a single-task experiment. This approach has been adopted by many experimenters and has often been assumed to be a powerful method for assessing organization (Tulving, 1966; Bower & Lesgold, 1969; Segal & Mandler, 1967).

In any case, whether or not Tulving's original formulation of SO stands the test of time, it must be recognized that the concept has had considerable impact upon our thinking and research. It is only reasonable to assume that it will be modified and supplemented by newer techniques. In a sense, Tulving's SO helped open the floodgates, and allowed the current emphasis upon organizational activities to become widespread.

STIMULUS SELECTION: ANIMALS AND HUMANS

Organizational activities take many forms, and information may be treated in many different ways. One interesting process involves not the elaboration or transformation of information, but the selection of specific, usable stimulus information from within an array of available stimulus information. What we are talking about here is the fact that individuals do not always use the entire stimulus presented to them. They may select some portion or element of the overall stimulus, and associate the response with that selected portion. This process is ofen termed STIMULUS SELECTION, and it is particularly interesting because it appears quite consistently in both animal and human learning situations. Stimulus selection, or cue selection, as it is sometimes called, provides us with one more example of the way in which animal and human capacities run parallel to one another.

Stimulus Selection in Humans

Let us begin with an example. We have all had the experience of entering a room crowded with strangers. The introductions begin. "This is Bill Sampson. And this is Terry McCarthy. And this is James Reeves . . . you know, Bill's brother? And this is Tom Winslow. Ned Turlock. Nancy Ewing. Betty Wills." And so on. By this time we have pretty much given up. But we do try to hook up a few first names with a few faces. More than likely we will concentrate upon first names and ignore second names, at least for the moment. We do not need to associate *both* names with a face (unless there are two Bills or two Terrys, etc.). First names will be sufficient for us to identify people. If a particular first name is mentioned later in the evening we will have some idea, or image, of the person. We will have connected an image of the face with the first name, but probably not with the second name. For example, if someone says, "You've met Bill?" or, "You've met Bill Sampson?" we will know who is being referred to. But if someone asks, "Have you met Sampson?" we may not remember the person, for we have not utilized second names in our early attempts to hook up names and faces. This is an example of stimulus selection. We have selected one component of a two-part stimulus and connected a response to it. We have, in a sense, ignored the second component (the last name). If the first name is presented, it will probably elicit the image of the appropriate face.

If the second name is presented we probably will not be able to come up with an image of the appropriate face.

This phenomenon has been translated into controlled experimental situations. In a typical paired-associate situation the subject first learns a list in which the responses (e.g., digits) are paired with different compound stimuli (e.g., different nonsense syllables surrounded by different colors). An example of a stimulus would be XGK surrounded by a blue rectangle. After learning the list, the subject is then tested for recall of each of the responses given each of the components of the stimuli individually (e.g., given a color by itself, or a nonsense syllable by itself). If one component is more likely to elicit the response in the recall test then we begin to suspect that some sort of selection process has been going on during the original learning phase.

The investigation of stimulus selection in paired-associate learning has led to all sorts of concerns. For example, what determines which component of a compound stimulus will be selected? As it turns out, there are many different variables that affect the selection process. Postman and Greenbloom (1967) found that if the stimuli are difficult-to-pronounce trigrams (e.g., XZC or QKX) then the subject tends to select the first letter in the syllable (i.e., X or Q). Thus the ordinal position seems to be important in stimulus selection. Other things being equal we will select the component in the left position, presumably because we read from left to right. In another example of the kind of research done in this area, Underwood, Ham, and Ekstrand (1962) used compound stimuli composed of different nonsense syllables surrounded by different colors. They found that their subjects *selected the colors over the syllables.* In some sense, this suggests that colors are more easily utilized than certain nonsense syllables in building associations. Additional variables have been investigated and discussed by Houston (1967), Merryman and Merryman (1971), Richardson (1971, 1972) and Richardson and Chisholm (1969). In a very general sense, it seems the component that becomes most effective is the one that is most easily utilized as a cue. In other words, the subject follows the path of least resistance, and utilizes whatever he perceives to be the most convenient cue in a given situation. Since subjects and situations differ enormously, it is easy to see why the selection process may vary so much.

Another controversy within this area involves the question of whether or not the various components of a compound stimulus become *directly associated with one another.* For example, suppose we associate the digit "8" with a blue rectangle enclosing the trigram "VGF." Are we also associating the color with the trigram? Some investigators have suggested that we do form direct associations between the components of a compound stimulus (Richardson, 1971), and others have argued that we do not (Wichawut & Martin, 1970).

In summary, beginning with Underwood's (1963) distinction between the NOMINAL stimulus (the stimulus as presented by the experimenter) and the FUNCTIONAL stimulus (that part of the nominal stimulus actually used by the subject), the investigation of stimulus selection in paired-associate learning has burgeoned. A complete review of this area could easily fill an entire chapter. For our purposes, it is sufficient to realize that the process of stimulus selection represents a prime example of the way in which the human is an active, complex processor of information.

Stimulus Selection in Animals

Animals display stimulus selection (Kamin, 1969a; Wagner, 1969; Wagner, Logan, Haberlundt, & Price, 1968). It appears they process information in ways roughly parallel to those of the human. For example, Kamin (1969a) demonstrated a form of stimulus selection in a classical conditioning situation. Animals experienced a series of pairings of shock (UCS) with a particular CS, which we shall designate as A. This procedure resulted in an emotional response becoming conditioned to the previously neutral CS (A). Then, after these initial pairings, an *additional* CS (X) was added to the situation. The CS became AX. AX was then paired with the shock (UCS) for a series of trials. The question was whether or not the emotional response would become associated with the new stimulus component (X). Relative to an appropriate control condition, it did not. The A component had already been associated with the emotional response produced by the shock. The introduction of an additional cue (X) was redundant.

This effect represents an organizational effort on the part of the animal. It seems to correspond to the sorts of effects which are obtained with humans. In both cases (animal and human) a response is associated with some portion of a total stimulus array.

Stimulus Selection: Attention or Association?

There are two major theroretical interpretations of stimulus selection. The first, and more traditional view, holds that stimulus selection is the result of selective attention (Lawrence, 1963; Martin, 1968). When faced with a compound stimulus, the animal or human is assumed to attend to one component, and to ignore the others. The unselected components are assumed to be relatively unavailable to the animal. For example, when learning a list in which the stimuli are something like XGQ the subject pays attention to the first letter (X) and does not even "focus" upon the remaining letters. But a new interpretation of stimulus selection has been developing (Kamin, 1969a; Rescorla & Wagner, 1972; Rudy,

1974; Wagner, 1969). According to this second view *all* of the components of the stimulus are attended to by the organism. They are all available to the organism if he needs them. But the animal does not always need all of them, hence he does not use all of them, even though they are available. For example, in the Kamin (1969a) study just mentioned, the animal first associates shock produced emotion with a CS (A). Then a new component (X) is added to the CS yielding a compound CS (AX). According to this new way of thinking X is not utilized as a cue because it is not needed to predict the coming of the shock (UCS). A is capable of doing that by itself. But X *could* be used if needed. According to this new view both A and X are attended to and available to the subject.

The distinction between these theoretical positions is a very fine one. The traditional position argues that selection is the result of differential attention to the various components of the compound stimulus at the time they are perceived. The new position argues that it is differences in the associative processes (or what one chooses to associate) that determine the selection effect, and that all components are equally attended to, or available. It seems reasonable to assume that we will eventually conclude that both positions are correct sometimes, but that neither of them is correct at all times. There are probably cases where the subject truly attends to only one component, and the remaining components become functionally unavailable (e.g., in the party situation, last names may actually be unavailable to the subject. His attention may be so riveted to the first names that he may not even register the second names; they are effectively ignored.) On the other hand, there must be cases where all of the components are equally attended to, or are equally available, and the subject chooses to use one of them while holding the others "in reserve." It would probably be premature to conclude that one of these theoretical mechanisms is more important than the other. It is probably not an "either–or" issue. It is reasonable to assume that the organism is sufficiently flexible to operate in accordance with both of these proposed mechanisms.

MNEMONICS AND "MENTAL IMAGES"

Think of a giraffe. . . . Take your time. . . . Make it a small one. About three feet tall. Pink toenails. Now put the giraffe in a fire engine. More than likely what you have been experiencing (if you have been willing to engage in this sort of nonsense) are what psychologists call visual "images." These images are of considerable interest to psychologists because they are such vivid, subjective experiences and because they seem to be an important aspect of our mental activity. They have long been of interest (see Lea, 1975) but, at the same time, they have been troublesome because they are so difficult to quantify, or to measure. For example, how would you go about comparing your image of a giraffe with someone else's image of a giraffe? We cannot observe images directly. We cannot lay them out on the table and measure or weigh them. They are such fleeting, subjective experiences that we have some trouble talking about them at all. And yet they do seem to be important components of thought. In this section we shall discuss some of the current efforts to deal with these elusive, important experiences. Specifically, we shall concern ourselves with the role these images play in the memory process. As we shall see, retention can be heavily affected by vivid mental imagery. Retention may be improved through the use of such images.

Rhymes, Images, and Retention

Let us consider some examples of the way in which images can facilitate retention. We begin with a little game, or plan, or mnemonic for remembering lists of unrelated words (Miller, Galanter, & Pribram, 1960). First, we must refresh ourselves with respect to an old children's rhyme. Rehearse the rhyme contained in Table 13.3 a couple of times. Now, once you have this rhyme firmly in mind, you are ready to move to the next step, which is to learn a list of 10 unrelated words. The first word in the list is to be associated with "One is a bun." The second word is to be associated with "Two is a shoe," and so on through the list. The first word is to be associated with "One is a bun" through the creation of some vivid, unusual, visual image containing both a *bun* and the first word. For example, if the first word were "house," you might imagine a house made of steaming hot-cross buns, or a row of tiny little green and red houses tucked neatly into a sliced bun. Each of the succes-sive words in the list is to be involved with the appropriate rhyme element

TABLE 13.3

Rhyme Used in Mnemonic Memory Plan

One is a bun.
Two is a shoe.
Three is a tree.
Four is a door.
Five is a hive.
Six is a stick.
Seven is heaven.
Eight is a gate.
Nine is wine.
Ten is a hen.

TABLE 13.4

List of Words to be Used in Mnemonic Memory Plan

CAR
FLAG
CLOCK
BOOK
KNIFE
SHIRT
DRUM
SCISSORS
PEN
SKI

through the creation of some bizarre, vivid image. Try this plan with the list of words contained in Table 13.4. Run through the list, one at a time. Give yourself enough time to establish a firm image for each word.

Now, assuming you have completed the task, we will test the effectiveness of the plan by asking a series of questions. Cover the list of words. What is the seventh word? What goes with "DOOR?" What goes with "WINE?" What is the third word? What is the fifth word? In a subjective way, you can probably sense what is occurring. The test words are so bound into your visual images that it is a simple matter to recall them. This plan for remembering has been tested experimentally. Bugelski (1968) had an experimental group learn lists of words using this plan, and control subjects learn the same lists without the plan. The experimental subjects recalled significantly more items than did the controls. In all likelihood, if you had not first learned the rhyme and been instructed in how to create images, your recall of the list would have been depressed.

Paired-Associates and Images

There is another area of research that suggests that images can improve retention. A number of investigators have shown that paired-associates are retained better if the stimuli and responses of each pair are related to one another through the use of some visual image. These images may be developed by the subject (Bower, 1972; Dempster & Rohwer, 1974; Paivio, 1971) or they may be given to the subject by the experimenter (Wollen & Lowry, 1974).

What *kinds* of images are best? There is some evidence to suggest that more unique images result in better retention (Lesgold & Goldman, 1973). In addition, there is some evidence to suggest that INTERACTIVE

IMAGES are better than NONINTERACTIVE IMAGES. For example, if you are attempting to remember the pair HORSE–ORANGE, it is probably better to imagine a horse eating an orange (or vice versa, if you prefer) than it is to imagine a horse standing in one place and an orange lying in another spot (Bower, 1970; Robbins, Bray, Irvin, & Wise, 1974). It seems interactive imagery is better than separation imagery, although *both* of these seem to be better than no imagery at all.

Visual and Verbal Coding

All this talk about visual imagery shouldn't cause us to lose sight of one important fact. We do not *always* encode information in terms of visual images. We do not *have* to use visual imagery. We can, after all, encode information verbally as well as visually. If you are trying to remember the word HORSE you do not have to cook up an image of a horse. You can obviously process this item as a word possessing auditory and semantic attributes rather than visual attributes. For example, if you wish to, you can probably encode HORSE both visually *and* verbally.

Paivio (1971) has proposed what has become known as the dual trace hypothesis. According to this hypothesis, any given stimulus (verbal or visual) can be encoded verbally and/or visually. We have the capacity to encode a given bit of information either visually or verbally. Exactly which type of coding we use depends upon the nature of the information to be coded and the demands of the task. Paivio distinguishes between CONCRETE ITEMS (horse, boat, apple) and ABSTRACT ITEMS (justice, even, obtuse). He argues that *both* concrete and abstract items are easily coded verbally. But *concrete* items are much more likely to be coded visually than are abstract items. It is easier to come up with a visual image for HORSE than for OBTUSE. Concrete items are much more likely to be encoded *both* verbally and visually. An abstract item is much more likely to be coded *only* in a verbal sense. The reader interested in pursuing this line of reasoning is referred to the large body of research (Kulhavy & Heinen, 1974; Lutz & Scheirer, 1974; Mondani & Battig, 1973; Nilsson, 1975; Paivio, 1971; Paivio & Foth, 1970; Pellegrino, Siegel, & Dhawan, 1975; Snodgrass, Wasser, & Finkelstein, 1974; Wortman & Sparling, 1974). Although Paivio's hypothesis has received considerable attention, it would be premature to conclude that the relationship between verbal and visual encoding has been clearly delineated.

One final note concerning verbal and visual encoding. Several authors (e.g., Hilgard & Bower, 1975) have suggested that verbal encoding is particularly useful in encoding information that is of a sequential nature, or distributed in time. On the other hand, the visual mode is often seen as a specialized means of encoding information that is presented simultaneously, and is distributed in space. Whether this intriguing possibility will prove to be valid remains to be seen. It is already clear that the distinction is not ironclad. For example, sequential information *may* be stored visually. We may encode sequentially presented items by placing them in ordered positions within an overall visual image (e.g., put the early items on the left and later items on the right, or put first items on the first floor of a tall building and later items on higher floors). Similarly, it seems reasonable to assume that we can encode spatially distributed items in a verbal manner. For example, we might encode the information on a map by storing "San Francisco is above Los Angeles." The point here is that the mind is flexible enough to utilize both means of coding for both types of information.

In fact, it seems reasonable to assume that much of our natural encoding efforts involve *both* verbal and visual processes. We may seldom use *pure* visual or *pure* verbal codes. For example, Underwood and Schulz (1960) had subjects learn lists of nonsense syllables paired with words. After learning the lists subjects were asked how they managed the task. Many of the subjects reported some sort of activity involving images. Some of their results are contained in Table 13.5. In looking over the

TABLE 13.5

Examples of Visual and Verbal Mediators Used by Subjects in Acquiring Trigamword Pairs[a]

Stimulus		Response	Mediating Event
CYF	—	KID	C and K similar in sound.
XBN	—	GAT	Gat is odd word, X is odd letter.
DSU	—	CAT	D to Dog to CAT.
CFY	—	DOG	C to Cat to DOG.
XBN	—	RAT	X suggested poison-poison RAT.
TPM	—	AND	T associated with symbol (&) for AND.
RZL	—	SAT	R to Rump to SAT.
RZL	—	SAT	R and S in alphabetical order.
DSU	—	BAN	U-BAN (brand of coffee).
RZL	—	KID	RZL suggested Russell; Russell is a KID.
CFY	—	THE	Remembered because first one in list.
KHQ	—	FAN	KHQ to radio to radio FAN.
IGW	—	MAN	W inverted looks like M, hence MAN.
IGW	—	MAN	IG to IGnorant to IGnorant Man.
RZL	—	BOY	RZL looks like lazy; hence, lazy BOY.
RZL	—	CAT	Z is hissing sound of CAT.

[a] Adapted from Underwood, B. J., & Schulz, R. W. *Meaningfulness and verbal learning*. New York: Lippincott, 1960, p. 299.

subjects' responses it seems clear that their efforts could easily have involved *both verbal and visual* components. Assuming we can trust subject reports we would be forced to conclude that the verbal and visual modes of encoding often go hand in hand.

ISSUES IN ORGANIZATION

So far, we have been talking about methods of detecting organization, and of simple demonstrations of organization. We now turn to some of the theoretical concerns and issues that characterize this field of investigation.

Organization and Associations

Does an organizational approach to memory preclude a consideration of the S–R associations? In one sense, an organizational approach does seem to be concerned with elements that are not easily described in terms of S–R associations (images, structures, etc.). The organizational approach seems to be concerned with "cognitive" events that might better be described in terms of some new, nonassociative language. And yet, as Postman (1972) suggests, there is no necessary disagreement between associative and organizational conceptions of memory (see also Voss, 1972). The two approaches clearly refer to two different ways of thinking and speaking about the same events. As Postman puts it, the differences between the two approaches appear to be a matter of language more than anything else. In a sense, it seems the organizational approach focuses upon the complexity and the structure of the processes and events that intervene between input and output. The organizational psychologist speaks of these intervening mental events using a certain kind of language (e.g., one that emphasizes such components as chunks, networks, and higher-order units). But these same mental events could probably be translated into S–R language. It would merely be a matter of trying to *identify extremely complex, interacting S–R relationships*.

The Locus of Organization: Storage or Retrieval?

Does organization enhance storage, retrieval, or both? This is a question that has been, and is being, asked by many investigators. The answers have varied considerably. For example, early in the study of organization it was generally assumed that organization provided a means of increasing *storage* capacity (Tulving, 1962). But it was not long before a number of psychologists began to suggest that organization facilitates *retrieval* processes (Tulving & Pearlstone, 1966; Tulving & Psotka, 1971; Weist, 1970). Postman (1972) makes the very reasonable suggestion that organization may well affect both storage and retrieval. The question, at this point, is neither well defined nor well documented.

Models of Organization

Given that we have these demonstrations of organizational activities (subjective organization, clustering, word-associations, etc.), what are the models or theories that have been developed to account for the facts? There have been many attempts to clarify and summarize the nature of organization in memory (Collins & Quillian, 1972; Freedman & Loftus, 1971; Kintsch, 1972; Mandler, 1968; Winograd, 1972). As an example we will discuss an approach taken by Lindsay and Norman (1972). The reader should be aware that the available models differ considerably and that this is but one example chosen from many. Let us begin with a simple concept, such as "TAVERN." We all have this concept stored within us, and it is not stored in isolation. It is related in many ways to many other bits of stored information. How might we characterize the relations between this bit of information (TAVERN) and the rest of the information we have stored within us? In attempting to characterize these relationships, or to define the position held by TAVERN amid an enormous amount of stored information, Lindsay and Norman (1972) distinguish among "classes," "examples," and "properties." Thus, TAVERN belongs to a certain *class*, which we may designate as ESTABLISH-MENTS. TAVERN is one *example* of an ESTABLISHMENT. TAVERN also has certain *properties*, for example, it holds BEER and WINE. BEER and WINE are *properties* we have come to associate with TAVERN. Finally, there are certain *examples* of the concept of TAVERN (e.g., LUIGI'S). Figure 13.1 contains a picture, or diagram, of a "semantic network," which might be associated with the concept of TAVERN. This network defines the relationships among TAVERN and its various classes, properties, and examples.

Hilgard and Bower (1975) discuss the network as follows:

A realistic memory, of course, contains thousands of such concepts, each with very many connections, so that the actual topographical representation would look like a huge "wiring diagram." But a fantastic amount of information is inherently encoded in such graph structures. To see just a hint of this, consider the fragment of a semantic network surrounding the concept of a *tavern* as shown in Figure [13.1]. This graph implicitly encodes the information that a tavern is a kind of business establishment (as is a drugstore), which has beer and wine, and Luigi's is an example of a tavern. It also gives some properties of beer, wine, and Luigi's. This is only a fragment, of course, and much more information could and would be in a realistic memory. But notice how very many questions one is enabled to answer with just this fragment. For example, it can answer questions that require chains of subset relations, such as that "Luigi's is an establishment" or that "A drugstore is a place." It can also read out the properties or classes that any two concepts

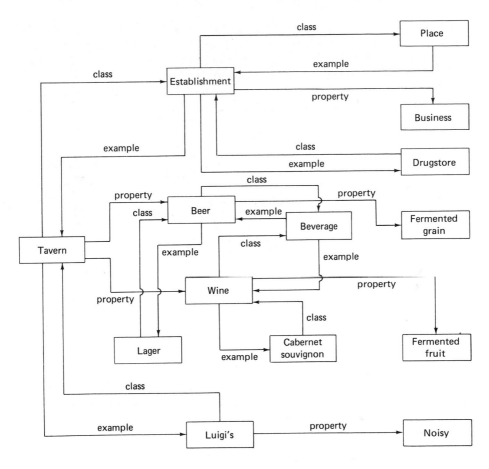

Figure 13.1. Fragment of a semantic network surrounding the concept of a *Tavern* (Adapted from Lindsay, P. H., & Norman, D. A. *Human information processing: An introduction to psychology.* New York: Academic, 1972. Fig. 10-5, p. 389.)

have in common. Thus, if we ask the system to compare the similarities and differences of *beer* and *wine*, it would quickly find that the similarities are that they are both beverages sold at taverns, but one is made from fermented grain while the other is made from fermented fruit. The number of factual relationships derivable and possible questions that can be answered increases exponentially as the number of encoded predicates or "bits of knowledge" increases [p. 594–595].

It should be obvious at this point that any attempt to characterize the existing structure or organization of memory is difficult. The preceding example seems somewhat complicated. But when one realizes that it represents nothing more than a very rough description of a very tiny segment of the total amount of information stored within each of us then one can begin to grasp the magnitude of the task before us. Modeling of this sort is in its infancy. If they are to be complete, models of this sort must, of necessity, become more and more elaborate. Can you imagine attempting to draw up blueprints, or diagrams, or networks that capture all of the overlapping and interrelated information stored within but a single individual? Putting a man on the moon was probably simple compared to this task. More than likely, models of this sort will never be complete. Rather, they will probably serve a heuristic purpose, stimulating thinking and suggesting questions. The organizational approach acknowledges the complexity of mental activity. At the same time, through this recognition, it offers new direction for our efforts to "investigate" ourselves.

SUMMARY

1. The organizational approach to the study of memory is currently very popular.

2. Organizational activities refer to what we do to information between input and output. Although there is little agreement concerning an exact definition of organization, most concepts of organization refer to the fact that we often systematize, relate, structure, order, select, elaborate, and transform information.

3. An interest in organization is not new. The issues of organization were raised by Gestalt psychologists many years ago. New methods of assessing organization have renewed interest in their issues.

4. In a WORD-ASSOCIATION TEST the subject's task is to give the first word that comes to mind in response to a set of stimulus words. Some stimulus words tend to elicit common responses (e.g., black—white). The patterns of obtained word associations suggest that words are somehow structured or organized within us.

5. Word-association tests have been used in clinical settings in attempts to reveal the patient's emotional and cognitive states.

6. The capacity of immediate memory is probably limited by the number of CHUNKS of information it can hold (7 ± 2).

7. A chunk may vary in terms of the amount of information it contains.

8. In general, so long as information can be expressed as a single response, then it represents a single chunk.

9. We may increase the capacity of our immediate memory by increasing the amount of information contained in our chunks of information.

10. CATEGORY CLUSTERING in recall refers to the fact that items drawn from various categories, and presented *randomly*, will often be recalled together.

11. Although the issue is not completely resolved, there is some evi-

dence to suggest that overall recall increases as clustering increases.

12. Although the effect is weak, it has been shown that subjects will cluster items that *sound* alike.

13. Total recall and clustering both seem to be greater for EXHAUSTIVE than for NONEXHAUSTIVE categories.

14. Category clustering provides us with a technique for examining organizational activities.

15. In ASSOCIATIVE CLUSTERING items that elicit each other in a word-association-type test (but do *not* belong to any obvious category) are recalled together.

16. The distinction between category and associative clustering is difficult to maintain for almost any two items may be thought of as belonging to some category.

17. In SUBJECTIVE ORGANIZATION experiments, lists of items are randomly presented and recalled over and over again. It is found that the order of recall takes on consistency despite random input.

18. Subjective organization experiments do not provide us with much information concerning the *nature* of the evolving organization.

19. The relationship between subjective organization and overall recall has not yet been clearly determined.

20. A supplemental method for assessing subjective organization involves the use of TRANSFER TESTS.

21. STIMULUS SELECTION refers to the fact that the organism does not always use the entire stimulus presented to him (the nominal stimulus). Sometimes he selects some portion of the presented stimulus and associates the response with that portion (the functional stimulus).

22. Many factors, including ordinal position, have been shown to influence stimulus selection.

23. Direct associations among the components of a compound stimulus may be established.

24. Animals as well as humans display stimulus selection. This represents another similarity between animal and human learning processes.

25. Some theorists feel stimulus selection is the result of selective attention. Others feel variations in the associative processes are more likely to account for selection effects. It may well turn out that both interpretations are correct some of the time.

26. MENTAL IMAGES are now being heavily investigated. Imagery may be shown to improve retention.

27. Paried-associates are retained better if the stimuli and responses are related to one another through the creation of some visual image.

28. INTERACTIVE IMAGES appear to be more effective than NONINTERACTIVE IMAGES.

29. Verbally and visually presented stimuli *may* be encoded both verbally and visually.

30. According to the DUAL TRACE HYPOTHESIS, both concrete and abstract items are likely to be coded verbally. But concrete items are more likely to be coded visually than are abstract items.

31. Although the distinction does not always hold true, some investigators have suggested that spatially distributed information is often encoded visually, whereas temporally distributed information is often encoded verbally.

32. It seems likely that our *natural* encoding efforts probably involve both verbal and visual components.

33. The organizational approach does not necessarily preclude a consideration of S–R associations. At the same time the organizational approach has stimulated many questions that had not been asked by the S–R associative approach.

34. Organization may enhance storage, or retrieval, or both.

35. Many models of organization are available. All of them represent beginnings rather than finished models. The task of mapping interrelated, stored information is formidable.

5

**EXTENSIONS AND
APPLICATIONS**

A fter having finished with 13 chapters filled with experiments, results, hypotheses, and conclusions, one might very reasonably ask where it is all leading. What is happening to the field of learning?

It is fairly obvious that the field is progressing. The last decade has seen an enormous upsurge of interest in areas such as those discussed in the preceding chapters. Much of this expansion has been in the field of human learning. This is not to say that animal studies are of no importance. To the contrary, continuing investigations of animal processes provide us with information that cannot morally or ethically be obtained from human subjects. If, as we have argued, animal and human processes have much in common, then the information we obtain from animal studies should contribute to our attempts to understand human learning.

As we have seen, many of the areas of behavioral research discussed in this text seem to be growing and developing. But there are more general questions that can be asked about the status of the field. First, are psychologists attempting to go beyond the analysis of learning on a gross behavioral level and to understand it on some more molecular, physiological level? The answer is yes. Chapter 14 will be con-

cerned with the physiological basis of learning and memory. Specifically, we shall consider some attempts to explore the relationships between the structures and functions of the brain and behavior. We shall discuss what is known of the correlations and causal relationships between activity of the brain and overt behavior. This approach to the understanding of learning is in its infancy, but it is exciting because it promises to provide new insights into the nature and behavior of man.

The second general question we can ask concerning the status of the field of learning is this: What have we been able *to do* with what we already know? Has the information presented in Chapters One through Thirteen been of any *use* to us in solving the problems of the world outside the laboratory? Has our kowledge of learning processes been applied to practical problems? It would be unreasonable to claim that everything we have learned in the laboratory has been useful in the real world. Indeed, much of what we know, or hope we know, has not yet been applied at all. But there have been some intriguing and rather important attempts to utilize laboratory-based knowledge in the solution of serious practical problems. In Chapter 15 we shall discuss some of these attempts. Specifically, we shall be concerned with BEHAVIOR MODIFICA-

TION, which is a general term referring to the modification or alteration of "natural" behaviors (normal and abnormal)) through the application of learning principles, which have been developed in the laboratory.

In summary, we shall travel in two directions in this section. First, we shall discuss attempts to understand learning on a more molecular level by discussing what is known of the relationships between brain activity and behavior. Second, we shall consider some attempts to apply the information we have already obtained in our behavioral experiments.

The Physical Basis of Learning

14

RATIONALE

Any bit of behavior may be understood on a number of different levels. For example, suppose the King of Somewhere decrees that all men shall wear the official uniform of the Kingdom. How are we to understand this action? Clearly, we can assess this behavior from several different angles. For example, we might wish to consider the *historical* aspects of this particular action. What forces led to its occurrence? What are its consequences and implications in historical terms (e.g., the possible downfall of the King)? On the other hand, we might choose to focus upon the King himself. We might wish to study the *psychology* of the King's personality (e.g., his need to dominate his subjects). Similarly, we might wish to understand this bit of behavior on a *chemical* level. We might wish to trace the chains of chemical actions and reactions that underlie the overt actions (e.g., the chemical events occurring within the brains of the participants). Or we might prefer to focus upon the *electrical* events associated with such a piece of behavior (e.g., an analysis of the electrical circuits and actions of the brains of the participants). And so on.

Exactly how many levels one chooses to define, and which level one prefers, is mostly a matter of personal preference. Knowledge obtained on one level in no way denies the validity and usefulness of information gained on another level. These levels of analysis often refer to different ways of looking at the same events and each may provide valid information about the target event.

Psychologists clearly differ in terms of their preferences for one level of analysis or another. Some (perhaps most) prefer to remain on a rather global level wherein behavior is viewed in terms of such events as bodily movements, feelings, and speech. These kinds of behavioral events are related to gross variations in the environment such as the actions of other people, printed words, colors, and temperatures. But some psychologists are not satisfied with this level of analysis. They wish to investigate the specific physiological mechanisms that produce, or account for, such gross events as talking or walking. It is a little like one person wanting to know *what* a computer will do without wanting to know exactly *how* it does it, and another person wanting to know all about the circuitry of the machine. In other words, some psychologists want to understand the actual, physical machinery that is enclosed within each of us. Psychologists who wish to investigate behavior on this more molecular, physical level are often called PHYSIOLOGICAL PSYCHOLOGISTS.

Although the concerns of physiological psychologists are many, the ones that concern us in this text are those which have to do with the functioning of the brain during learning events: What happens to the brain during learning? Which parts of the brain do what? Does a given part of the brain have only one function, or can it substitute for other brain components? What are the chemical and electrical events that accompany an overt act of learning? These are the kinds of questions that concern the physiological psychologist, and they are the kinds of questions we will consider in this chapter.

TECHNIQUES

We know there is a brain inside every skull, and we are sure it represents some kind of important control center for behavior, but how do we go about studying it, or understanding it in relation to overt behavior?

Generally speaking, there are at least three techniques for studying the relationship between brain and behavior. It is these techniques which we shall attempt to characterize in this chapter. First, there are LESION TECHNIQUES. Very bluntly, these methods attempt to delineate the functions of the brain by destroying, removing, or damaging parts of the brain. Whether or not one agrees with these methods, one must recognize that they are widely employed. The reasoning behind their use is that if the destruction or damage of a particular brain structure results in a consistent behavior change, then it is assumed that the part of the brain destroyed or damaged is intimately involved in the control of that particular piece of behavior. Examples of this technique will follow. Second, there are the ELECTRICAL TECHNIQUES. It has long been known that the brain is an electrical piece of apparatus. It is, in fact, never quiet. It is an enormous mass of incredibly complicated electrical activity. A number of different techniques have been developed to study this electrical activity. For example, using the electroencephalograph (EEG) we may read the gross electrical activity of many millions of cells by recording electrical activity from the outer surface of the skull. Changes in these recorded electrical events can then be correlated with changes in overt behavior. Another electrical technique involves the stimulation of a much smaller number of cells by implanting a tiny electrode in the actual brain of an experimental animal. A small electrical current may be fed through the tip of the electrode, thereby artificially firing the cells in the immediate vicinity of the tip. These stimulating events can also be correlated with overt behavior changes. Examples of these procedures will follow. Third, psychologists have attempted to explore the CHEMICAL nature of the brain. The general technique has been to introduce various chemicals or drugs into the brain and to observe concomitant behavior changes. Psychologists have been concerned with the effects of various drugs both within cells and between cells. We now turn to some examples of the kinds of research being done with *lesion, electrical,* and *chemical* techniques.

ANATOMICAL ASPECTS

Lesion Work

If the removal or damage of a particular part of the brain yields a consistent change in behavior (e.g., impairment of a certain type of learning ability) then the investigator feels he may have some evidence for the involvement of the lesioned structures in that particular behavior pattern. The lesion technique is not new. Despite its somewhat limited success it has been used by a great many investigators. Lashley (1950) presents an outstanding summary of much of the early work, and Lockhart and Moore (1975), Marshall and Smith (1975), Mishkin, Vest, Waxler, and Rosvold (1969), and Stein and Rosen (1974) provide more recent coverage.

The lesion techniques are not without their difficulties. For example, one problem that arises is that it has often been observed that impaired tasks may *eventually* be relearned. Even if we totally destroy a given brain structure the resulting impairment does not always seem to be permanent. This suggests that the destroyed structure was not critical, or absolutely essential, for the mastery of the task in question. It is almost as though the functions of the destroyed portions of the brain are "taken over" by other components of the brain. Another problem lies in the fact that the *same* type of lesion may produce *different* degrees of impairment in different individuals. After having had similar lesions, one individual may show marked impairment, whereas another will display only minor impairment. A third problem has been outlined by Stein, Rosen, Graziadei, Mishkin, and Brink (1969). They point out that if a given amount of damage is inflicted in a single operation then one constellation of deficits will arise. But if the *same* damage is inflicted in two or more steps (e.g., one half the damage done on Day 1 and the remaining half inflicted 30 days later) then the resulting pattern of deficits does *not* always correspond to that which appears following single-stage damage. In other words, *the order or pattern in which the damage occurs, as well as the extent and nature of the damage itself, appears to be critical in determining deficits in performance.* These three problems (i.e., eventual recovery, individual differences, and order effects) represent some of the complexities one encounters in trying to understand brain functions by using lesion techniques.

It should also be noted that lesion techniques are not totally distinct from the electrical and chemical techniques to be discussed below (see, for example, Carey, Goodall, & Lorens, 1975; Kelsey, 1975). Lesions are often accomplished electrically, or through the use of electrodes introduced into the brain. In addition, it is obvious that a lesion must produce enormous alterations in the chemical and electrical events occurring within the brain. It is a matter of focus more than anything else. Lesion studies focus upon the relationships between structural brain damage and behavior.

Split-Brains

Some very intriguing suggestions concerning brain functions come from what have been called "split-brain" preparations (Sperry, 1961). The vertebrate brain is surprisingly symmetrical. The structures on the left side of the brain seem to be perfectly duplicated on the right side of the brain. The fact that the brain is so symmetrical poses some very interesting questions concerning the location of memory "traces." Is all information processed equally on both sides of the brain? If the structures on both sides of the brain are identical is the information processed within them identical?

Interestingly, the answer seems to be in the negative. Gazzaniga (1970, 1972) and Gazzaniga and Sperry (1967) have investigated a number of humans in which the two halves of the brain had been separated surgically. Very simply, the two halves, or hemispheres, of the brain are tied together, or bridged, by an extensive bundle of fibers known as the CORPUS CALLOSUM. In order to alleviate severe epilepsy, some patients undergo an operation in which almost all of their CORPUS CALLOSUM is removed. In other words, the two halves of the brain are, in essence, "disconnected." As it turns out it is possible to deal with, or address, these disconnected halves independently. Entry into one or the other half may be accomplished by restricting visual stimuli to one half of the visual field. A stimulus flashed to the left half of the visual field of *either* eye will be relayed to the right side of the brain. A visual stimulus flashed to the right side of the visual field of either eye will be relayed to the left side of the brain. By restricting input to one half of the visual field the investigator can be sure he is dealing with but one half of the brain in a "split-brain" patient.

In testing split-brain subjects, Gazzaniga and his colleagues found that the left half of the brain tends to be relatively specialized for active speech events such as talking and writing. The left side of the brain can read words and initiate speech. If we present a printed word to the left side of the brain the split-brain subject can read it and say it aloud. The right side of the brain, on the other hand, seems to be more involved with nonverbal information, such as spatial reasoning. The right side does not do too well with verbal production. For example, if a word is flashed on the left half of the visual field (right hemisphere of the brain) the subject appears unable to say the word aloud. On the other hand, if the subject is asked to recognize the word rather than recall it, he can do so. The right half of the brain apparently has the ability to recognize verbal units but is unable to initiate verbal responses. The notion that the left and right halves of the brain are specialized for verbal and nonverbal factors, respectively, gains support from the work of other investigators (see Galin & Ornstein, 1972; Milner, 1968).

This line of research does not suggest that the two hemispheres of the brain can handle *only* certain types of information, nor does it imply that the hemispheres do not "communicate" with one another. To the contrary, in *normal* individuals one half of the brain seems capable of "taking over" the functions of the other half if the other has been damaged or incapacitated. In addition, the *corpus callosum* apparently provides a means of transferring information processed on one side of the brain into the other. But it does appear that the two sides are specialized for distinct kinds of functions.

ELECTRICAL TECHNIQUES

We now turn to research that focuses primarily upon the electrical nature of the brain. The brain is an electrical network. Electricity will activate neural tissue, or cause nerve cells to fire. Hence it is not surprising that electrical recording and stimulating techniques are quite popular in the study of the brain.

This emphasis upon the electrical nature of the brain does not deny the importance of other aspects of the brain, such as its chemical nature, it is merely an approach or focus. A complete understanding of the brain will probably require an integration of the knowledge obtained with various techniques. Such an integration is already beginning. For example, investigators are already examining the combined effects of electrical and chemical manipulations, such as those observed when the brain of an animal treated with certain chemicals is stimulated electrically.

In any case, electrical stimulation and recording techniques have received considerable attention. We shall deal with two examples; the recording of the gross electrical activity of the brain from the surface of the skull, and the electrical stimulation of relatively restricted populations of cells within the brain itself.

The Electroencephalograph

If we place electrodes upon the skull of an individual, we can record a continuous but variable state of electrical activity occurring within the brain. The brain is a living, active structure. The electroencephalograph (EEG) allows us to record the electrical activity of millions of cells operating in the vicinity of the recording electrode. Electroencephalograph records display the electrical "voice" of the brain.

The most obvious question that comes to mind is whether or not overt learning events are associated with changes in EEG records. In other words, if we master a particular task, is this learning event related to changes in the electrical activity of our brain? Some studies suggest that it is. For example John and Killam (1959) trained cats to avoid a particular light. The cats were then tested for generalization of this avoidance response by presenting a new test light, which was similar but not identical to the original training light. Generalization appeared. That is, the response to the new test stimulus was identical to the response to the original training. In addition, and more to the point, *EEG records revealed that the electrical activity of the brain in response to the new test stimulus was also identical to the activity in response to the original training stimulus.* In other words, a behavioral change correlated with an electrical change. Not all studies have been so clear-cut. The use of the EEG is fraught with difficulties which are beyond the scope of this text (see Fox & O'Brien, 1965; Stein & Rosen, 1974). On the other hand, EEG records may provide us with a unique index of the relationships between the simultaneous activity of millions of brain cells and the occurrence of overt behaviors. The final value of the EEG remains to be seen.

Brain Stimulation

There is another line of research which exemplifies the electrical approach to the understanding of the brain. These studies have to do with the rewarding and punishing effects associated with the electrical stimulation of various parts of the brain (see Olds & Milner, 1954; Valenstein, 1973). In a typical experiment an extremely small electrode is permanently implanted in the subject's brain (usually a rat, cat, etc.). The tip of the electrode is directed toward some particular portion of the brain, which is of interest to the experimenter. (Interestingly enough, the experimenter is never quite sure where the tip ends up until after the experiment is completed, the animal is killed, and its brain is sectioned, mounted on slides, and examined.) Once the electrode is in place a small electrical current may be delivered through the tip to the surrounding area. This little shock stimulates the brain cells in the immediate area and causes them to fire. (If one visits a university laboratory one may well run into a variety of animals living apparently normal lives with this sort of implantation apparatus firmly established upon their skulls.)

The experimenter may arrange the situation such that if the animal presses a bar it will receive a certain amount of brain stimulation. In other words, the rat itself determines whether or not it will receive electrical brain stimulation. If the animal learns to press the bar repeatedly, then we suspect that the area in which the electrode is implanted is a reward, or reinforcing, or "go" center. If the animal refrains from pressing the bar, we assume that the area is either neutral or punishing. If the animal will learn a particular response that terminates brain stimulation, then we assume that particular area is punishing. By implanting electrodes in various parts of the brain and testing the rats tendency to maximize or minimize stimulation we are able to map the brain in terms of its involvement with reinforcement and punishment. As it turns out, there are many reinforcing and punishing areas throughout portions of the brain lying below the cortex, and in the area of the hypothalamus in particular. Figure 14.1 should provide some idea of the location of these areas in the rat's brain.

Studies of reinforcing areas have yielded some striking results. For example, an animal pressing a bar for reinforcing brain stimulation just does not seem to want to stop. If we reinforce a hungry rat with food it will, sooner or later, satiate and stop responding. But the brain-stimulation-rewarded animal will press the bar for hours on end, sometimes stopping only when it drops from fatigue. Another interesting finding is that once the electricity is turned off the behavior (e.g., bar pressing) ceases almost immediately. This rapid cessation does not correspond to "normal" learning situations, wherein most responses extinguish quite slowly once reinforcement is removed.

Exactly what the animal is experiencing during brain stimulation is uncertain. It is often assumed that the stimulation of reinforcement centers produces positive affect, or, in some sense, pleasant sensations. This interpretation is supported by studies in which humans undergoing operations report stimulation of their brains to be joyful or relaxing (Heath & Mickle, 1960). But there are other ways to think about the situation. For example, Milner (1970), refers to RESPONSE HOLD and RESPONSE CHANGE neural systems, which determine whether the animal continues what it has been doing or changes to some new behavior. In other words, stimulation of a so-called reinforcement center might not necessarily be pleasant. It might merely initiate neural instructions to *repeat* the last response. Although it is convenient to think of REWARD

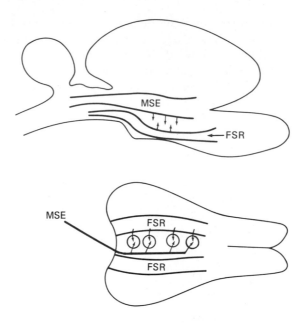

Figure 14.1. Locations of major punishment and reinforcement centers in the rat's brain. The top figure represents a brain sliced from top to bottom. The bottom figure is a horizontal section, looking down into the middle of the brain. Pure punishing effects have been obtained by stimulating the area labeled MSE (for midbrain substrate of escape). Pure positive reinforcement effects have been obtained in the areas labeled FSR (for forebrain substrate of reward). The circled areas in the lower figure yield both reinforcement and punishment effects. (Adapted from Olds, J., & Olds, M. Drives, rewards, and the brain. In F. Barron, W. C. Dement, W. Edwards, H. Lindman, L. D. Phillips, J. Olds, & M. Olds [Eds.], *New directions in psychology II.* New York: Holt, 1965. Fig. 4.20, p. 369. Copyright © 1965 by Holt, Rinehart and Winston, Inc. Reprinted by permission.)

and PUNISHMENT CENTERS we should keep in mind that their conceptions are hypotheses about what is going on, and not clearly established facts.

Deutsch and Howarth (1963) have suggested that brain stimulation does two things. First, it is assumed to reinforce the preceding response. Second, it is assumed to *motivate* the animal to respond again. The impetus for the next bar press is assumed to be provided by the brain stimulation reward. It is something like playing a pinball machine. If, with a single ball, we light up a lot of lights, ring a lot of bells, and score 1400 points, two things happen. First, we will try to shoot the next ball in *exactly* the same manner as the last one (the response was reinforced). In addition, we will be *very* interested in sending along that next ball (our success with the last ball *motivates* us to do it all over again).

Deutsch and his colleagues assume that the motivating quality of brain stimulation reward decays with time. Brain stimulation reward motivates the animal to respond again, but only momentarily. As time passes this impetus diminishes. Our motivation to shoot another pinball will be greatest immediately after our spectacular success with the preceding ball. Some studies seem to support these hypotheses (Gallistel, 1969, 1972), whereas others do not (Kent & Grossman, 1969; Sonderegger & Rose, 1970).

In summary, electrical stimulation techniques have, and are, generating a good deal of theory and research. At the same time, it should be recognized that the method is in its infancy (see Livesey & Rankine-Wilson, 1975). Stimulation techniques are generating interesting ideas about how the brain is organized but, at present, these ideas are highly speculative. (Although the ideas may have crept into a science fiction story or two we are a long way from "controlling" one another through the use of electrical techniques, and it is highly unlikely that we will all soon be pressing little buttons which automatically stimulate our "pleasure" centers.) As Valenstein (1973) puts it, stimulation techniques must be thought of as research techniques and nothing more at the present time.

CHEMICAL TECHNIQUES

We now turn to the third and final approach to the study of the brain. Although it does not deny that the brain is electrical, this approach concentrates upon the *chemical* nature of the brain. The principle concern is with the delineation of chemical changes within the brain, which accompany overt acts of learning and retention. The most obvious chemical technique is the one in which a chemical or drug is introduced into the brain and concomitant behavior changes are observed.

We shall consider two areas of research that use this technique. The first investigates chemical changes that occur, for the most part, *within* the cell. The second investigates chemical events *between* cells. But before we move to these specific areas of research one general concern should be noted. Experimenters in this area often have a problem with dosage. It is not a simple matter to say that a certain drug produces, or is correlated with, a particular behavior change, because we often observe that the behavioral effect in question appears with some doses but not with others. In fact, as Stein and Rosen (1974) point out, drugs that affect neural activity often follow *a U-shape function*. That is, high and low doses may produce the desired effect, whereas intermediate doses do not. When we consider the relationship between a particular drug and a particular neural effect we are thus forced to consider the ways in which the effect interacts with, or varies with, the amount of the drug administered.

Within–Cell Effects: DNA, RNA, Protein

If we adopt the premise that memory is somehow encoded or stored in terms of chemical events, then we may attempt to identify this chemical coding system. If memory is chemical in nature then we may wonder about the nature and action of the critical chemicals.

There have been several candidates for the role of the memory molecule, or that chemical structure which codes incoming information. The most prominent have been DNA (deoxyribonucleic acid), RNA (ribonucleic acid), and protein. Each of these refers to large, complicated, varied, and interrelated molecules. [The interested reader is referred to Gurowitz (1969) for a basic description of the makeup of these substances.] For our purposes, it is sufficient to realize that much current thinking centers around the notion that *all* of these three substances are probably involved in the memory encoding process. Although each of the three chemical structures has had its proponents (see Katz & Halstead, 1950; Caldwell & Churchill, 1967; Gaito, 1966; Hydén, 1960; Landauer, 1964), Gurowitz (1969) notes that, "theorizing about individual molecules is becoming outmoded in favor of the DNA–RNA–protein complex type of theory." Hence, in our discussion, we shall not make very much of the distinctions among these three, rather, we shall treat them as closely related and interacting.

Let us consider an example of the kind of research that has implicated the DNA–RNA–protein complex in memory. Babich, Jacobson, Bubash, and Jacobson (1965) trained hungry rats to approach a food cup in a Skinner box when a click was sounded. Each time the rats approached the food cup in response to the click they were reinforced with Purina Lab Chow. After the rats were well trained, they were killed with ether and their brains were removed. RNA was quickly extracted from the brains by a biochemical procedure described in the original article. At the same time RNA was extracted from the brains of a group of control rats (rats that had been given no click–food training). Some 8 hours after extraction, the RNA from control (untrained) and experimental (trained) rats was injected intraperitoneally into untrained receiver rats. These receiver rats were then tested in the Skinner box. (The receiver rats had never been reinforced for approaching the food cup in response to a click.) The click was sounded. The question was whether or not the rats that received "trained" RNA would approach the cup more often than rats that received "untrained" RNA. According to these authors, they did. The rats receiving "trained" RNA approached the cup more often than did the controls.

You can imagine the stir this experiment caused within the field. It was controversial, to say the least. The flow of related experiments began almost immediately. A number of investigators criticized the procedures and/or failed to replicate the finding (Barker, 1966; Branch & Viney, 1966; Carney, 1965; Halas, Bradfield, Sandlie, Theye, & Beardsley, 1966; Luttges, Johnson, Buck, Holland, & McGaugh, 1966; Worthington & Macmillan, 1966). On the other hand, there have been some replications of the transfer effect using planaria, goldfish, rats, and mice (Braud, 1970; Braud & Hoffman, 1973; Fjerdingstad, 1971; Gaito, 1966; McConnell, Bryant, Golub & Rosenblatt, 1972). Despite these studies, many investigators remain highly skeptical concerning the RNA transfer effect.

In any case, whether or not the transfer studies finally prove to be valid, there are some other sources of evidence that seem to implicate RNA–type materials in the memory process. For example, Cameron (1958, 1963) reports studies in which massive amounts of RNA were administered to aged patients in an attempt to improve their memory. The results seem to support the notion that memory may be improved by increasing the level of RNA within the system. On the other hand, it is only fair to point out that RNA may merely *stimulate* the individual (much as caffeine would) and may have little or no effect on memory per se.

Research using RNA and related substances has been promising, but it has also been confusing and equivocal. The next few years should tell whether this line of research is a dead end, or just a beginning.

Between–Cell Effects: The Synapse

As a final example of the chemical approach, we may consider the current hypothesis, which suggests that learning involves the enhancement of synaptic transmission. The emphasis here is upon chemical events that occur *between* neurons, or within the synapse. Deutsch (1968, 1971) and Deutsch and Deutsch (1973) have proposed that *learning involves the enhancement of synaptic transmission through the production of more efficient concentrations of acetylcholine* (ACh). Figure 14.2 contains a simplified version of what may be involved in the transmission of an impulse across a single synapse. An electrical impulse is presumed to travel along the presynaptic terminal. This impulse, upon reaching the end of the presynaptic cell, is presumed to release ACh from a set of vesicles. These bits of ACh drift across the synaptic gap and are taken up by ACh receptors located on the postsynaptic terminal or neuron. If enough ACh is taken up by these receptors an electrical impulse is presumed to be generated on the postsynaptic side. This impulse then travels on down the postsynaptic neuron to the next synapse. In other words, Deutsch and his colleagues suggest that a chemical mechanism mediates the transfer of an electrical impulse across the synaptic gap.

Another substance, cholinesterase, is presumed to be present in the area of the synaptic gap. This cholinesterase performs a critical function

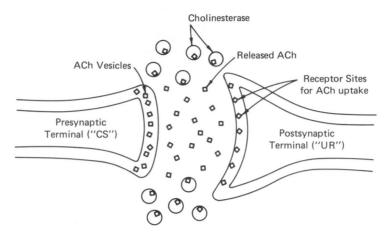

Figure 14.2. Illustration of biochemical events involved in synaptic transmission. (Adapted from Hilgard, E. R., & Bower, G. H. *Theories of learning.* Englewood Cliffs: Prentice-Hall, 1975. Fig. 14.9, p. 533.)

in the transmission process. Specifically, it neutralizes, or "devours," the ACh soon after it is released by the presynaptic terminal. If the ACh were not neutralized then the postsynaptic terminal would become "jammed" with ACh and could not fire again. For the postsynaptic cell to fire again the old ACh must be neutralized and new ACh must arrive. Hence the cholinesterase "clears away" old ACh so the transmission mechanism may operate again.

Assuming these mechanisms are responsible for synaptic transmission we might vary the effectiveness of the transmission event by introducing various drugs that affect this system. For example, if we introduce any one of several ANTICHOLINESTERASE DRUGS (drugs that reduce cholinesterase in the synaptic region) then we might expect an *increase* in ACh. In other words, ACh would not be eaten up quite so efficiently, because there would be less cholinesterase present to do the consuming. More ACh should lead to better transmission. If there is more ACh available to be taken up by the postsynaptic terminal, and if it is ACh uptake that initiates the postsynaptic impulse, then we would expect better transmission. But things are not quite that simple. This hypothesis seems to hold true when the original level of ACh is fairly *low*. But if the level of ACh is already *high* at the time of the introduction of the anticholinesterase drug then *poorer* transmission may result. By adding more ACh to an *already* high level of ACh the postsynaptic terminal becomes locked up, or jammed, and is unable to fire. Thus, when the ACh level is low the introduction of an anticholinesterase drug should lead to more efficient transmission. But if the ACh level is already high then the introduction of an anticholinesterase drug may prevent efficient transmission.

Synaptic transmission may also be affected by ANTICHOLINERGIC DRUGS such as scopolamine. These drugs are taken up by the receptor sites on the postsynaptic terminal. They block out the ACh, but they do *not* initiate an electrical impulse on the postsynaptic side. Hence the introduction of anticholinergic drugs leads to less efficient transmission.

Deutsch and his colleagues have examined the actions and interactions of these elements in some detail. The interested reader is referred to Deutsch and Deutsch (1973) and to Hilgard and Bower (1975) for reviews. For our purposes it is sufficient to realize that considerable attention is being given to the hypothesis that suggests that learning involves the enhancement of synaptic transmission. This enhancement involves an intimate relationship between the chemical and electrical properties of the nervous system. Without doubt, new and exciting developments will continue to appear within this general theoretical framework.

SUMMARY

1. Behavior may be understood on many different levels. The physiological psychologist is interested in examining the physical machinery which underlies overt behavior.

2. The most widely used methods of studying the physical basis of learning include the LESION, ELECTRICAL, and CHEMICAL TECHNIQUES.

3. In lesion work, specific parts of the brain are damaged, removed, or destroyed. The investigator then looks for specific, consistent behavior changes that are correlated with this damage.

4. There are problems with lesion work. Even if a given brain structure is totally destroyed, the resulting impairment may eventually recede. In addition, the same lesion may produce different degrees of impairment in different individuals. Finally, damage occurring in one stage may yield deficits that differ from those obtained when the same damage is inflicted in two or more stages.

5. In SPLIT-BRAIN PREPARATIONS the two halves of the brain have been separated, usually surgically. It is possible to address, or deal with each half independently. Research suggests that the left half of the brain tends to be relatively specialized for active verbal events such as talking and writing, whereas the right half tends to be more involved with nonverbal information.

6. The ELECTROENCEPHALOGRAPH may be used to record the electrical activity of the brain from the surface of the skull.

7. Some studies suggest that overt learning events will be reflected in consistent changes in EEG records.

8. By implanting a tiny electrode in the brain it is possible to stimulate and fire small groups of cells within the brain.

9. If an animal will learn to press a bar that causes a portion of

his brain to be stimulated then that area is considered a REINFORCING AREA.

10. If the animal will learn a response that terminates stimulation, then we assume that stimulation of that particular area is PUNISHING.

11. By implanting electrodes in various parts of the brain it is possible to map the punishing and reinforcing areas of the brain.

12. Animals receiving brain stimulation reward may continue to respond until they drop from fatigue.

13. When the electricity is terminated the responding stops quickly.

14. Brain stimulation reinforcement may be associated with pleasant sensations, but there are other possible interpretations of the effect.

15. It has been hypothesized that brain stimulation may REINFORCE the preceding response and, at the same time, provide the MOTIVATION for the next response.

16. The most common CHEMICAL technique involves the introduction of a chemical into the brain and the observation of concomitant behavior changes.

17. When using this technique, one must be aware that high and low doses of many chemicals may yield a particular effect, whereas intermediate doses do not.

18. RNA, DNA, and protein have all been proposed as the memory molecule. Recent thinking suggests that all three may be involved in memory.

19. Some controversial studies suggest that if RNA from a trained animal is injected into an untrained animal then the training of the original animal will be transferred to the receiver animal.

20. Other studies, equally controversial, suggest that massive doses of RNA may improve memory.

21. Recent thinking suggests that learning involves the enhancement of SYNAPTIC TRANSMISSION.

22. This enhancement may be mediated by the production of more efficient concentrations of ACETYLCHOLINE (ACh). An electrical impulse may release ACh from the presynaptic cell. This ACh is presumed to drift across the synaptic gap where it is taken up by the postsynaptic cell. If enough ACh is taken up an electrical impulse is generated on the postsynaptic side.

23. CHOLINESTERASE present in the synaptic area neutralizes ACh soon after it is released by the presynaptic cell.

24. If the ACh were not neutralized the postsynaptic cell would be "jammed" with ACh and could not fire again.

25. Synaptic transmission may be affected by ANTICHOLINESTERASE drugs. These drugs decrease cholinesterase and thereby increase ACh.

26. If the original level of ACh is fairly low then the introduction of anticholinesterase drugs may improve transmission.

27. But if the original level of ACh is already high then anticholinesterase drugs may decrease the efficiency of transmission by allowing the
postsynaptic terminal to become jammed with ACh.

28. Synaptic transmission may also be affected by ANTICHOLINERGIC
drugs such as SCOPOLAMINE. These drugs are taken up by the postsynaptic
terminal, blocking out ACh. But they do not generate an electrical impulse, thereby reducing the efficiency of transmission.

Behavior Modification

15

INTRODUCTION

In this chapter, we turn to the question of the relevance of the experimentally determined principles of learning. Of what value is all of this information we have amassed over the years? Not all of it is of much use at the present time. For that matter, much of it may never be utilized in a practical sense. But there are some areas of practical concern that do seem to draw upon, and benefit from, our experiments with rats and humans. We have chosen BEHAVIOR MODIFICATION as a prime example of the application of laboratory-based principles to the problems of the world outside the laboratory. (There are, of course, other equally important areas of application, such as those found within the field of formal education.) Behavior modification, or BEHAVIOR THERAPY as it is sometimes called, is a very general term, referring to a group of intervention techniques, or methods, for controlling behavior. The intervention techniques that we will be specifically concerned with in this chapter are those which draw heavily upon the concepts and principles of learning psychology. We shall consider the *application* of such concepts as positive and negative reinforcement, extinction, punishment, and generalization.

Behavior modification as a general method for altering, understanding, and controlling behavior differs dramatically from more traditional clinical or therapeutic approaches. Consider the following example. Suppose an 8-year-old girl is notorious for her flamboyant temper tantrums. This child truly knows how to kick and scream. Once she hits her stride there seems to be no way to stop her. She spreads out on the floor, screams, rages, kicks her feet, and turns various colors from all the exertion. The parents are upset, to say the least. They are of half a mind to punish her, and yet they are a little afraid of the strength of her tantrums. As a result they vacillate: Sometimes they punish her; sometimes they try to ignore her; sometimes they try to reason with her; sometimes they placate her.

Obviously there are a number of ways to think about this piece of behavior. On the one hand, it may be thought of as a symptom or expression of some underlying emotional problem. Depending upon one's orientation, the psychologist might want to consider such constructs as the id, the ego, early relationships, rejection, hostility, and repression. Efforts to alleviate the behavior might be directed toward a resolution of some underlying disturbance or conflict. The psychologist might try to determine how the child feels about herself and those close to her. Unconscious emotions and thoughts might be pursued. The basic causes of the tantrum behavior would be sought.

Behavior modification represents quite a different approach to the same problem behavior. Although not denying the validity and usefulness of the more traditional clinical approaches, behavior modification offers a viable alternative method for dealing with the behavior. The basic assumption the behavior modifier would make is that *the tantrum behavior is a learned behavior;* it is maintained because it is reinforced. If the child does not get what she wants she throws a tantrum. Her parents, perhaps otherwise fairly indifferent to her, become greatly concerned. They pay attention to her: They worry, shout, plead, feel angry, and feel guilty. For the girl, reactions such as these are not all bad. In fact, they probably maintain her tantrum behavior. If we assume the behavior is maintained because it is rewarded, we go about eliminating it in the same way we extinguish bar pressing in a Skinner box. We remove the reinforcement. We put the individual on an extinction schedule. We assume that the girl is being reinforced by "getting her own way" and/or by receiving attention from her parents when tantrum behaviors are shown. Eliminate these rewards and the behavior should subside.

Just such an approach was taken by Williams (1959) in a similar case. A 21-month-old boy would throw a tantrum if his parents left his room before he was asleep. The behavior was finally terminated by gently putting the child to bed, leaving the room, and closing the door. The first night the screaming and raging lasted some 45 minutes before the child finally dropped off to sleep (that amount of storming would cause all but the most carefully instructed parent to break down and enter the room). As can be seen in Figure 15.1, the length of the tantrum dropped dramatically on successive nights. The curve labeled "First extinction" represents the initial series of nights without social reinforcement or attention. After this first extinction, the child's aunt took care of the child in the absence of the parents. The tantrums began all over again, and the aunt fell into the trap of staying in the room until the child fell asleep. The tantrum behavior had to be extinguished all over again (see "Second extinction" in Figure 15.1). According to the authors, following the second extinction, no further tantrums were reported during a two-year follow up.

There is no guarantee that such children will not develop some new method for gaining their goals and obtaining attention. (Hopefully any new method would be more socially acceptable.) But this example does

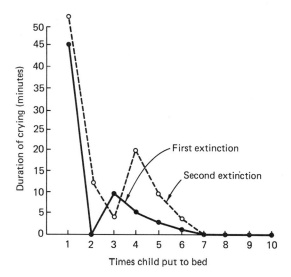

Figure 15.1. Duration of crying as a function of the number of times the child was put to bed. (Adapted from Williams, C. D. The elimination of tantrum behavior by extinction procedures. *Journal of Abnormal and Social Psychology,* 1959, *59,* 269. Fig. 1, p. 269. Copyright 1959 by the American Psychological Association. Reprinted by permission.)

illustrate the manner in which the simple principle of experimental extinction, developed in the laboratory with rats, can be used to control "natural" human action.

The behavior modification approach obviously differs from more traditional treatment methods in important ways. Williams (1973) summarizes these differences in this manner:

> Behavior therapy—or, as it is sometimes called, behavior modification—differs in many respects from the more traditional approaches to clinical problems. Behavior therapists concentrate on the analysis of specific symptoms or behaviors, termed TARGETS. The goal of the therapist is to modify or change these target symptoms by means of operant techniques and to monitor the patient's progress continuously and quantitatively. Far less attention is given by behavior therapists, as compared with other clinicians, to the early life history of the patient. Thus subjective experiences, attitudes, dreams, and insights are for the most part ignored.
>
> In line with the operant approach, the behavior therapist is concerned *only* with modifying the overt, observable aspects of behavior. He is therefore uninterested in internal hypothetical constructs such as the unconscious, the ego, and the superego. He focuses on the behavioral problem, and does not try to get at the more elusive underlying dynamics of the illness. He admits that, because of his inattention to underlying causes, "symptom substitution" may occur and realizes that he must examine the complete response repertoire of the patient for a long time after the completion of therapy. However, when the proper experimental controls are employed during therapy, symptom substitution rarely does take place (Sherman & Baer, 1969).

Another striking difference between behavior therapy and the other clinical approaches has to do with the tools or methodologies employed. Whereas the traditional clinician relies to a great extent on empathy and transference, the behaviorist does not regard a personal relationship between therapist and patient as essential for the patient's recovery. Instead, the behavioral therapist often uses electronic programming equipment and precise recording devices in attacking the target symptoms, and he employs procedures developed mainly in the laboratory [p. 171–172].

REINFORCEMENT TECHNIQUES

Positive Reinforcement

Behavior modification has been used in an enormous number of settings and has generated a great deal of research and theory. By itself, behavior modification could easily fill a text such as this. In view of the size of the field, perhaps the best we can do is provide the reader with a reasonable sample of behavior modification techniques. There are at least two ways to organize a set of behavior modification examples. One approach provides examples drawn from different settings, such as detention homes (Phillips, 1968), mental institutions (Cotter, 1967), institutions for the retarded (Redd & Birnbrauer, 1970), public schools (Schwarz & Hawkins, 1970), and home settings (Hawkins, Peterson, Schweid, & Bijou, 1966). The alternative approach, and the one adopted here, is to organize our set of examples around the principles of learning forming the basis for a given technique. Thus, we shall consider examples involving POSITIVE REINFORCEMENT, NEGATIVE REINFORCEMENT, EXTINCTION, PUNISHMENT, and GENERALIZATION.

We begin wth positive reinforcement. If you will recall, a positive reinforcer may be defined as anything that, when given to the subject, will increase the probability of a response occurring. If we follow a bar press with food, then the rat will increase his rate of bar pressing. This very basic principle has been applied in a variety of ways to the human condition.

Shaping

Shaping refers to the reinforcement of successive approximations to a desired response. The best way to train a rat to press a bar is first to reinforce approximations to the full blown bar press, and then to reinforce closer approximations, and finally to reinforce only an actual bar press. Initially we reinforce the hungry animal each time it turns toward the bar. After this response is firmly established we reinforce the animal only if it moves toward the bar. Finally we reinforce the animal only if it actually presses the bar. In other words, we slowly guide the animal toward the response we are interested in. If we were to wait for the full bar press to occur "spontaneously" before we reinforced any-thing, we might never bring the response under our control.

This same sort of shaping technique may be used in many different human situations. For example, it is often used attempting to teach autis-tic children to speak. Autistic children are, for the most part, schizo-phrenic children who do not speak. In attempting to establish verbal repertoires, these children may be deprived of one meal and then rein-forced with food (e.g., bits of sugar-coated cereal) each time they make any sound at all. At first, any sound is reinforced. Grunts, snorts, syl-lables, and squeaks are all reinforced. Then, as training progresses and the rate of sound production goes up, the experimenter becomes more selective in his reinforcing. He refrains from reinforcing just any sound, and will begin to reward only those sounds which begin to approximate some desired verbal response (e.g., a word). Gradually the child's sounds are SHAPED to conform to the desired pattern. This shaping technique appears to be quite successful in teaching previously mute children to produce distinct verbal behaviors (Hewett, 1965; Kerr, Myerson, & Michael, 1965; Lovaas, 1967; Lovaas, Berberich, Perdoff, & Schaeffer, 1966).

Social Reinforcement

Social reinforcements are probably used more widely than any other type of reinforcement in behavior modification. Factors such as PRAISE and ATTENTION are powerful reinforcers for most people. As we shall see, many other types of reinforcers have been used, but ATTENTION, PRAISE, FLATTERY, and SUPPORT all seem to be quite powerful. For exam-ple, Rekers and Lovaas (1974) report a case in which a young boy had taken on many female characteristics. He preferred feminine clothes and activities, his voice had distinctive feminine qualities, and he enjoyed feminine cosmetic articles. In attempting to change this behavior pattern (some might want to argue it should not have been changed), the mother of the child was taught to socially reinforce masculine behaviors. She was taught to praise, encourage, and support masculine activities and interests and to ignore (extinguish) feminine behaviors. Although social reinforcers were not the only reinforcers used in this study, they did form an important part of the situation and did appear to have a signifi-cant impact upon the child's behavior. The authors report that 3 years later the boy's behavior displayed most of the characteristics of traditional masculine behavior.

In another study Madsen, Madsen, and Thompson (1974) used social reinforcers (among others) to increase rural Head Start childrens' consumption of middle-class meals. Rural children, upon first entering the Head Start situation, were unfamiliar with the foods served as meals, and were hesitant to try them. The investigators found that praise and attention would serve as effective reinforcers for the consumption of the meals. (Again it should be noted that social reinforcements were used in conjuction with more concrete reinforcers such as candy and sugar-coated cereal.)

Sometimes, such as in the case of severely disturbed patients, social reinforcers are not initially effective. A disturbed child may not even register much less respond to something such as praise. He may be so withdrawn that these mild sorts of reinforcers are totally ineffective. In these cases, more basic reinforcers (such as food or the removal of shock) may have to be used initially. As training progresses the experimenter may pair social reinforcers ("Good!") with the presentation of the more primary reinforcers. Slowly, the social stimulus takes on reinforcing powers. It becomes a secondary reinforcer. It is an initially neutral stimulus that is paired repeatedly with a primary reinforcer (food). After considerable training the primary reinforcer can be dropped altogether, or faded from the situation, and the behavior brought under the control of the social reinforcer alone.

Tokens

Many institutional settings are currently employing what are known as TOKEN ECONOMIES. In a token economy, desirable behaviors are immediately reinforced with tokens, which may later be exchanged for primary reinforcers such as food, beverages, and privileges. For example, the staff of a mental hospital might reinforce desirable behaviors (positive speech, cooperation, completion of chores, neat appearance, etc.) with poker chips, gold stars, or check marks, which may later be turned in for any number of more basic rewards (clothing, personal items, games, tools, snacks, TV time, recreational privileges, etc.).

Tokens are secondary reinforcers. They are initially neutral stimuli, which acquire reinforcing properties. There are several advantages to be gained by the use of tokens. In a token economy the tokens may be presented by staff members *immediately* after the appearance of the target behavior. Thus there need be no delay of reinforcement. (If you will recall, a delay of reinforcement can lead to a drop in performance.) Second, tokens may be exchanged for a wide range of primary rewards, thereby enhancing their value and accommodating a spectrum of personal preferences. Tokens provide a convenient, efficient means of providing substantial, on-the-spot reinforcement (Ayllon & Azrin, 1965).

Tokens have been used in a number of different situations including hospitals, schools, outpatient situations, and home settings. For example, Atthowe and Krasner (1968) have successfully utilized a token economy on a closed ward of chronic psychiatric patients in a Veterans Administration Hospital. Tokens were awarded if the patients cared for their personal needs, attended their scheduled activities, helped on the ward, and/or showed increased responsibility in any way. Similarly, Schaefer and Martin (1966) report success in overcoming "apathetic" behaviors displayed by hospitalized schizophrenics through the use of token reinforcement procedures. Tokens, which could be exchanged for cereal, candy, or small toys, have also been shown to be effective in training retarded children to use sentences (Lutzker & Sherman, 1974). Tokens have been used in large scale educational systems as well as in hospitals. One need only look in a recent issue of the *Journal of Applied Behavior Analysis*, or some similar journal, to discover the widespread use of the technique.

One final study will suffice. Most of the studies we have described have involved the control of patients' or students' behavior by staff members or teachers. In an interesting turn-about, Pommer and Streedbeck (1974) applied the token technique to the *staff* of a small residential facility for disturbed children. Prompt completion of chores, such as cleaning, was rewarded with tokens. Efficient and appropriate care of the disturbed children was rewarded. For example, tokens would be awarded to the staff members if medicines were given to the children on time. The authors report a substantial upsurge in the performance of the target activities. In other words, we all respond to rewards, patient and nonpatient alike. The token method can be utilized for the control of "normal" as well as "abnormal" behaviors.

Additional Reinforcers

Social reinforcers and tokens (both secondary reinforcers) are by no means the only reinforcers used in behavior modification. To the contrary, the array of effective rewards is quite extensive. For example, Pierce and Risley (1974) have demonstrated that the opportunity for recreational activities may serve as an effective reinforcer. They set up a situation in which the young members of an urban recreational center could obtain additional recreation time if they recruited new members for the center. If a youngster brought in one new member he was allowed to enter the center an hour earlier than the other members. The technique appeared to be fairly successful in a series of recruitment drives. Knight and McKenzie (1974) have reported that bedtime thumbsucking can be eliminated through the manipulation of bedtime story reading. Several young girls, all dedicated thumbsuckers, were reinforced for nonthumbsucking by reading a bedtime story. The authors report that this method was extremely successful in eliminating thumbsucking. (Again, there are those who would probably argue that the behavior need not have been eliminated under any circumstances.)

Finally, money is often used in behavior modification studies. Chapman and Risley (1974) report that when children in high-density urban neighborhoods are paid for picking up trash and cleaning yards, clean yards increase and amount of trash in the neighborhoods decreases. This is not a surprising effect, but it does demonstrate that the systematic application of a very simple reward system can produce desired results.

In summary, positive reinforcement is a powerful tool. It produces results. Whether or not these experiments and effects correspond exactly to what occurs in a controlled laboratory situation is of limited importance to the behavior modifier. The behavior modifier is interested in results, in changed behavior, and if the manipulation of positive reinforcement yields desired results then the specific mechanisms underlying the effect are of secondary concern.

Negative Reinforcement

A negative reinforcer is anything which, when taken away from the subject, will increase the probability of a response occurring. If a rat makes a particular response and we remove, or terminate painful shock, then that response is apt to be strengthened. The shock is called a negative reinforcer.

If you will recall we have already discussed the avoidance learning situation in which a rat must leap a barrier, or make some other designated response, within a certain time limit. If it fails to respond within the time limit it will be shocked. Lovaas, Schaeffer, and Simmons (1965) used just such an avoidance training technique to instill "social behaviors" in autistic children. Severely disturbed, autistic children do not respond to normal, or mild reinforcers. Since they are so withdrawn, such factors as praise and support seem to have little or no effect upon them. Lovaas, Schaeffer, and Simmons (1965) attempted to break through this veil, or wall, by employing more intense reinforcers (i.e., the removal or avoidance of shock). Parallel lines of metallic tape were placed across the floor of an experimental room. Shock could be administered through this grid. The child was placed barefoot on the grid. The experimenter asked the child to come to him. If the child failed to approach within a short time he received a mild shock. If he did approach, no shock was given. In contrast to more mild forms of reinforcement this shock avoidance situation was extremely effective. The children learned to approach the experimenter quite rapidly. The approach response remained strong for a number of months. When it finally began to subside a single "reminder" shock was enough to reinstate the response. According to the authors the program increased genuine social behavior. The approach response was not just an instance of an isolated response being learned in an artificial situation.

The AVOIDANCE CONDITIONING procedure has also been useful with, among other behaviors, fetishism (Raymond, 1956) and transvestism (Gelder & Marks, 1969). See also Ayllon and Michael (1959) and Feldman and MacCulloch (1965).

EXTINCTION TECHNIQUES

We have focused upon the *establishment* of responses through the use of either positive or negative reinforcers. We now turn to the *elimination* of responses through extinction procedures. Because extinction refers to a decrease in response strength through repeated nonreinforcements, we are seeking examples of behaviors which may be eliminated through the removal of reinforcement.

The attenuation of human behaviors through the removal of reinforcement has been observed widely (e.g., the temper tantrum example discussed earlier). Walton (1960) treated a woman who compulsively scratched a skin condition. The investigator determined that the woman's family reinforced this behavior by showing great concern over the condition, and by talking to the woman about it. The family was simply instructed not to talk to the woman about the condition. Under this extinction schedule the compulsive scratching was eliminated within a short period of time. Similar sorts of extinction procedures have been effective with, among others, deviant sex-role behaviors (Rekers & Lovaas, 1974), passivity (Johnston, Kelley, Harris, & Wolf, 1966), and aggressive behavior (Allen, Henke, Harris, Baer, & Reynolds, 1967).

One of the best-known forms of extinction therapy is that of SYSTEMATIC DESENSITIZATION (Wolpe, 1958, 1969). Some individuals find themselves inordinately frightened by certain types of stimuli and situations (death, illness, social contacts, being alone, injections, fear of losing mind, pregnancy, medicines, fainting, etc.). These anxieties, fears, phobias, or whatever you wish to call them, can be quite incapacitating. That is, the critical stimuli elicit such a strong fear reaction that the subject is unable to function as well as he might in everyday life.

The object of desensitization is to eliminate these fears. It is assumed that the fears are the result of classical conditioning. The fear-producing stimuli are thought to be conditioned stimuli (CS). They have, sometime in the past, been paired with a UCS, which elicits a fear reaction (UCR). The fear the subject experiences in response to the CS is a conditioned response (CR), or a conditioned fear. We extinguish a CR by presenting the CS alone, over and over again, without the UCS. With one major variation, this same extinction procedure forms the basis of desensitization. In initial interviews the therapist asks the subject to list fear-producing stimuli, and to rank them in terms of the strength of the fear they produce. Thus a HIERARCHY of fear producing stimuli and situations is produced by the subject himself. The therapist then asks the subject to think about, to dwell upon, and to imagine the *weakest* of these stimuli or situations. The subject is instructed to relax and to imagine this weak fear-producing situation until it no longer elicits any fear at all. Essentially this is an extinction procedure. The CS is present without the UCS.

[This procedure has often been called COUNTERCONDITIONING, in that a *new* response (relaxation) may become conditioned to the CS.] Once the fear of the weakest stimulus has subsided, the subject goes on to the next step in the hierarchy. By gradually moving up the hierarchy of fear-producing stimuli, and by extinguishing fear at each step, the subject is able to overcome his fear of even the most frightening stimuli. Table 15.1 contains sample hierarchies for claustrophobia, death, and illness. Hierarchies, of course, will differ from individual to individual.

PUNISHMENT TECHNIQUES

Finally, we may consider PUNISHMENT TECHNIQUES. Punishment refers to the *elimination* of a response through the application of some unpleasant stimulus. If we wish to eliminate bar pressing in a rat, we may follow each bar press with a painful shock. Similar sorts of punishment effects have been obtained with humans.

In one interesting study Morosko and Baer (1970) attempted to treat alcoholics by using a punishment procedure. Subjects were presented with six cups of liquid. Four of them contained nonalcoholic beverages, whereas the other two contained alcoholic beverages. Initially, the subjects were required to drink the contents of all six cups. They were shocked as they drank the two alcoholic beverages. On subsequent trails the subjects were allowed to omit the alcoholic beverages, and thereby omit the concomitant shock. Consumption of alcohol dropped markedly. The avoidance effect persisted beyond the laboratory situation. Follow-up work indicated that many of the subjects decreased their everyday drinking.

As a further example of the punishment procedure we may note that Goldiamond (1965) reduced stuttering by following stuttering with delayed feedback of the subject's own voice. (Delayed feedback is highly aversive to most people.) In addition Pierce and Risley (1974) effectively reduced certain unwanted behaviors in an urban recreational center by following them with punishing stimuli. Each time individuals engaged in such acts as leaving trash about, leaving pool cues out, crowding in line, arguing, or breaking things they were punished by restrictions being placed upon their recreation time. Depending upon the severity of the offense, from 1 to 15 minutes of recreation time were cancelled.

The reader interested in a detailed discussion of punishment in behavior modification is referred to Lundin (1974).

THE PROBLEM OF GENERALIZATION

Each of these procedures (POSITIVE and NEGATIVE REINFORCEMENT, EXTINCTION, and PUNISHMENT) seems to be fairly effective in altering a target behavior. But, before anyone goes away with the idea that

TABLE 15.1

Anxiety Hierarchies[a]

A. Claustrophobic Series

1. Being stuck in an elevator. (The longer the time, the more disturbing.)
2. Being locked in a room. (The smaller the room and the longer the time, the more disturbing.)
3. Passing through a tunnel in a railway train. (The longer the tunnel, the more disturbing.)
4. Traveling in an elevator alone. (The greater the distance, the more disturbing.)
5. Traveling in an elevator with an operator. (The longer the distance, the more disturbing.)
6. On a journey by train. (The longer the journey, the more disturbing.)
7. Stuck in a dress with a stuck zipper.
8. Having a tight ring on her finger.
9. Visiting and unable to leave at will (for example, if engaged in a card game).
10. Being told of somebody in jail.
11. Having polish on her fingernails and no access to remover.
12. Reading of miners trapped underground.

B. Death Series

1. Being at a burial.
2. Being at a house of mourning.
3. The word *death.*
4. Seeing a funeral procession. (The nearer, the more disturbing.)
5. The sight of a dead animal (for example, a cat).
6. Driving past a cemetery. (The nearer, the more disturbing.)

C. Illness Series

1. Hearing that an acquaintance has cancer.
2. The word *cancer.*
3. Witnessing a convulsive seizure.
4. Discussions of operations. (The more prolonged the discussion, the more disturbing.)
5. Seeing a person receive an injection.
6. Seeing someoné faint.
7. The word *operation.*
8. Considerable bleeding from another person.
9. A friend points to a stranger, saying, "This man has tuberculosis."
10. The sight of a blood-stained bandage.
11. The smell of ether.
12. The sight of a friend sick in bed. (The more sick-looking, the more disturbing.)
13. The smell of methylated spirits.
14. Driving past a hospital.

---

behavior modification is the answer to our our problems, certain points should be noted. One question that constantly crops up in this sort of work is whether or not behavior trained in the laboratory will *generalize* to everyday life. If we put an alcoholic through avoidance conditioning will he, as soon as we release him from the experimental situation, head for the nearest bar? Will a mute child, trained to speak in a tightly controlled situation, fall mute again once he is removed from that situation?

The results bearing upon this issue are equivocal. Some studies report fairly good generalization, whereas others do not. For example, Tracey, Briddell, and Wilson (1974) awarded tokens each time psychiatric patients said positive things about other people and/or hospital activities such as dances, and the like. In the training condition, positive statements about both people and activities increased substantially. But the important question was whether or not these increases would carry over into the real world. Some of them did and some did not. Specifically, an increase in positive statements about hospital activities actually led to increased activity attendance. In other words, if patients were rewarded for saying positive things about the hospital dances then they tended to go to the actual dances more often. That is a pretty strong indication of the generalization of a learned response system. On the other hand, rewarding patients for making positive statements about people in the training situation did not appear to lead to more positive statements about people outside the training situation. This kind of equivocal patterns of results is indicative of the problems facing investigators in this area.

In a study previously mentioned, Lovaas, Schaeffer, and Simmons (1965) report that if autistic children are trained to respond socially in but one room then that social response does not seem to appear outside that room. But if the child is trained in several different rooms, then generalization does appear. The children will, in fact, display spontaneous social acts, which have no connections whatsoever with the training procedures.

In the Morosko and Baer (1970) study, alcoholics subjected to avoidance conditioning seemed to generalize the tendency to avoid alcohol, not only into their private lives, but also across alcoholic beverages. They not only decreased their drinking but decreased their consumption of different varieties of alcohol.

Stevens-Long and Rasmussen (1974) report that autistic children trained in the use of simple and compound sentences sometimes produce novel sentences on their own. In other words, language training may generalize in some complex manner, allowing the children to use the acquired rules and information in the construction of new sentences.

In summary, many behavior modification studies show good generalization beyond the experimental setting. On the other hand, generalization often fails to materialize. The importance of generalization, and its elusiveness, suggests that it should be made one of the critical concerns in any behavior modification study. If a behavior change is limited to the experimental setting then it is, in a practical sense, of little interest or value.

There are, of course, other problems associated with the behavior modification approach. For example, not all psychologists and therapists would argue that behavior modification *cures* a disorder, or deals in any significant way with the underlying causes of a behavior disturbance. In essence, it treats symptoms. In treating symptoms the hope is that the subject will be freed to deal more effectively with himself and his environment. An additional problem arises when we realize that it is often quite difficult to determine *exactly* what it is that has been learned in a behavior modification procedure. For example, if we teach a child to approach by reinforcing him with food there is some doubt about what it is that he has learned. Has he truly learned a social behavior, or has he merely learned to approach some large object for food?

Despite these sorts of difficulties, behavior modification represents a relatively new, and very encouraging approach to the treatment of behavior disorders. Used in conjunction with more traditional types of therapy and clinical analysis, it should prove to be invaluable in the future. It is just this sort of application of the basic principles of learning to the problems of the real world that justifies a continuation of the kinds of basic research described in this text. Much of what we discover in the laboratory may never be used. But the success of behavior modification indicates that the attenuation of considerable human suffering may eventually be accomplished through the pursuit of basic laboratory-based psychological experimentation.

SUMMARY

1. BEHAVIOR MODIFICATION, or behavior therapy, refers to the control of behavior through the application of laboratory-based principles such as reinforcement, extinction, and punishment.

2. Behavior modification techniques differ from more traditional clinical or therapeutic techniques in important ways. Behavior modifiers are more concerned with altering overt symptoms than they are in treating underlying causes. The behavior modifier does not regard a personal relationship with the patient as a necessary condition for the patient's recovery.

3. Behavior modification assumes that behavior disorders are learned, and therefore subject to the laws of learning as determined in the laboratory.

4. Many natural human behaviors may be brought under control through the use of POSITIVE REINFORCEMENT, or the presentation of reward following a response.

5. SHAPING refers to the reinforcement of successive approximations to a desired behavior pattern or response. Shaping is a convenient, effective method of controlling behavior in both experimental and natural settings.

6. SOCIAL REINFORCEMENTS (e.g., praise, attention, and social support) are powerful and are widely used.

7. Social reinforcers are secondary reinforcers. Sometimes they must acquire their reinforcing powers in a given situation through repeated pairings with more primary reinforcers, such as food.

8. In a TOKEN ECONOMY desired behaviors are reinforced with tokens, which may be exchanged for more primary reinforcers such as food, beverages, and privileges.

9. Tokens are secondary reinforcers. They provide an efficient means of providing *immediate*, *substantial*, on-the-spot reinforcement.

10. Tokens have been used successfully in hospitals, schools, outpatient settings, prisons, and home settings.

11. Tokens and social reinforcers may be used to alter "normal" as well as "abnormal" behaviors.

12. Social reinforcers and tokens are often supplemented through the use of additional reinforcers such as food, recreation privileges, and money.

13. NEGATIVE REINFORCEMENT involves the building of a response through the removal of unpleasant stimuli. AVOIDANCE CONDITIONING procedures have been used successfully with many behaviors including social responses, alcoholism, fetishism, and transvestism.

14. EXTINCTION refers to a decrease in response strength through repeated nonreinforcement. The removal of reinforcers has been shown to reduce many human behaviors such as compulsions, deviant sex-role behaviors, and aggressive behaviors.

15. SYSTEMATIC DESENSITIZATION refers to the extinction procedure in which conditioned fears, or phobias, may be eliminated. Patients are asked to imagine, or dwell upon, fear producing stimuli, one at a time, until the conditioned fear associated with the stimulus is eliminated. The treatment begins with the *weakest* fear-producing stimulus and progresses to the most frightening stimuli.

16. In PUNISHMENT TECHNIQUES unwanted behaviors are followed by unpleasant stimuli, such as shock.

17. The question of whether or not behaviors trained or altered in the laboratory will generalize to, or persist in, the patient's everyday life is of critical importance to this field.

18. The data with respect to the question of generalization are equivocal, although many studies do report good generalization.

19. Behavior modification represents an encouraging example of the application of our laboratory work to the "real world." It justifies a continuation of basic research.

References

Abramson, N. *Information theory and coding.* New York: McGraw-Hill, 1963.

Adams, J. A. *Human memory.* New York: McGraw-Hill, 1967.

Allen, K. E., Henke, L. B., Harris, F. R., Baer, D. M., & Reynolds, N. J. Control of hyperactivity by social reinforcement of attending behavior. *Journal of Educational Psychology,* 1967, *58,* 231–237.

Allen, M. M. Rehearsal strategies and response cueing as determinants of organization in free recall. *Journal of Verbal Learning and Verbal Behavior,* 1968, *7,* 58–63.

Anderson, C. M. B., & Craik, F. I. M. The effect of a concurrent task on recall from primary memory. *Journal of Verbal Learning and Verbal Behavior,* 1974, *13,* 107–113.

Anderson, J. A. A theory for the recognition of items from short memorized lists. *Psychological Review,* 1973, *80,* 417–438.

Anderson, J. R. FRAN: A simulation model of free recall. In G. H. Bower (Ed.), *The psychology of learning and motivation: Advances in research and theory,* Vol. 5. New York: Academic Press, 1972.

Anderson, J. R. Item-specific and relation-specific interference in sentence memory. *Journal of Experimental Psychology: Human Learning and Memory,* 1975, *104,* 249–260.

Anderson, J. R., & Bower, G. H. Recognition and retrieval processes in free recall. *Psychological Review,* 1972, *79,* 97–123.

Anderson, J. R., & Bower, G. H. *Human associative memory.* New York: Wiley, 1973.

Anderson, J. R., & Bower, G. H. A propositional theory of recognition memory. *Memory and Cognition,* 1974, *2,* 406–412.

Anrep, G. V. Pitch discrimination in the dog. *Journal of Physiology,* 1920, *53,* 367–385.

Archer, E. J. Postrest performance in motor learning as a function of prerest degree of distribution of practice. *Journal of Experimental Psychology,* 1954, *47,* 47–51.

Asch, S. E., & Ebenholtz, S. M. The principle of associative symmetry. *Proceedings of the American Philosophical Society,* 1962, *106,* 135–163.

Atkinson, R. C., Bower, G. H., & Crothers, E. J. *Introduction to mathematical learning theory.* New York: Wiley, 1965.

Atkinson, R. C., Brelsford, J. W., & Shiffrin, R. M., Multiprocess models for memory with applications to a continuous presentation task. *Journal of Mathematical Psychology,* 1967, *4,* 277–300.

Atkinson, R. C., & Estes, W. K. Stimulus sampling theory. In R. D. Luce, R. R. Bush, & E. Galanter (Eds.), *Handbook of mathematical psychology,* Vol. II. New York: Wiley, 1963.

Atkinson, R. C., & Shiffrin, R. M. Mathematical models for memory and learning. Technical Report Number 79, Institute for Mathematical Studies in the Social Sciences, Stanford University, 1965.

Atkinson, R. C., & Shiffrin, R. M. Human memory: A proposed system and its control processes. In K. W. Spence & J. T. Spence (Eds.), *The psychology of learning and motivation: Advances in research and theory*, Vol. 2, New York: Academic Press, 1968.

Atkinson, R. C., & Shiffrin, R. M. The control of short-term memory. *Scientific American*, August, 1971, 82–90.

Atthowe, J. M., & Krasner, L. Preliminary report on the application of contingent reinforcement procedures (token economy) on a "chronic" psychiatric ward. *Journal of Abnormal Psychology*, 1968, *73*, 37–43.

Atwater, S. K. Proactive inhibition and associative facilitation as affected by degree of prior learning. *Journal of Experimental Psychology*, 1953, *46*, 400–404.

Averbach, E., & Coriell, A. S. Short-term memory in vision. *Bell System Technical Journal*, 1961, *40*, 309–328.

Ayllon, T., & Azrin, N. H. The measurement and reinforcement of behavior of psychotics. *Journal of the Experimental Analysis of Behavior*, 1965, *8*, 357–383.

Ayllon, T., & Michael, J. The psychiatric nurse as a behavioral engineer. *Journal of the Experimental Analysis of Behavior*, 1959, *2*, 323–334.

Ayres, J. J. B. Conditioned suppression and the information hypothesis. *Journal of Comparative and Physiological Psychology*, 1966, *62*, 21–25.

Azrin, N. J. Some notes on punishment and avoidance. *Journal of the Experimental Analysis of Behavior*, 1959, *2*, 260.

Babich, F. R., Jacobson, A. L., Bubash, S., & Jacobson, A. Transfer of a response to naive rats by injection of ribonucleic acid extracted from trained rats. *Science*, 1965, *144*, 656–657.

Baddeley, A. D. Short-term memory for word sequences as a function of acoustic, semantic, and formal similarity. *Quarterly Journal of Experimental Psychology*, 1966, *18*, 362–365. (a)

Baddeley, A. D. The influence of accoustic and semantic similarity on long-term memory for wõrd sequences. *Quarterly Journal of Experimental Psychology*, 1966, *18*, 302–309. (b)

Baddeley, A. D., & Patterson, K. E. The relation between long-term and short-term memory. *British Medical Bulletin*, 1971, *27*, 237–242.

Baddeley, A. D., & Warrington, E. K. Amnesia and the distinction between long- and short-term memory. *Journal of Verbal Learning and Verbal Behavior*, 1970, *9*, 176–189.

Baer, D. M., & Gray, P. H. Imprinting to a different species without overt following. *Perceptual and Motor Skills*, 1960, *10*, 171–174.

Bahrick, H. P. Two-phase model for prompted recall. *Psychological Review*, 1970, *77*, 215–222.

Balagura, S., Brophy, J., & Devenport, L. D. A study of the aversion to sodium chloride learned after multiple experiences with lithium chloride. *Journal of Comparative and Physiological Psychology*, 1972, *81*, 212–219.

Balagura, S., Ralph, T., & Gold, R. Effects of electrical stimulation of diencephalic and mesencephalic structures on the generalized NaCl aversion after LiCl poisoning. *Physiologist*, 1972, *15*, 77.

Barker, D. J. Comment on Jacobson *et al., Psychonomic Science*, 1966, *4*, 314.

Barnes, J. M., & Underwood, B. J. "Fate" of first-list associations in transfer theory. *Journal of Experimental Psychology*, 1959, *58*, 97–105.

Barrett, J. E., Hoffman, H. S., Stratton, J. W., & Newby, V. Aversive control of following in imprinted ducklings. *Learning and Motivation*, 1971, *2*, 202–213.

Bartlett, J. C., & Tulving, E. Effects of temporal and semantic encoding in immediate recall upon subsequent retrieval. *Journal of Verbal Learning and Verbal Behavior,* 1974, *13,* 297–309.

Bateson, P. P. G. Effect of similarity between rearing and testing conditions on chick's following and avoidance responses. *Journal of Comparative and Physiological Psychology,* 1964, 57, 100–103.

Bateson, P. P. G. The characteristics and contexts of imprinting. *Biological Reviews of the Cambridge Philosophical Society,* 1966, *41,* 177–220.

Bateson, P. P. G. Imprinting and the development of preferences. In A. Ambrose (Ed.), *Stimulation in early infancy.* New York: Academic Press, 1969.

Battig, W. F. Paired-associate learning. In T. R. Dixon, and D. L. Horton (Eds.), *Verbal behavior and general behavior theory.* Englewood Cliffs, New Jersey: Prentice-Hall, 1968.

Baum, M. Dissociation of respondent and operant processes in avoidance learning. *Journal of Comparative and Physiological Psychology,* 1969, *67,* 83–88.

Baumeister, A. A., & Kistler, D. Study and retrieval interval effects in paired-associate learning. *Journal of Experimental Psychology,* 1974, *102,* 439–442.

Bedford, J., & Anger, D. Flight as an avoidance response in pigeons. Paper presented at Psychonomic Society meeting, St. Louis, October 1968.

Bellezza, F. S., & Walker, R. J. Storage-coding trade-off in short-term store. *Journal of Experimental Psychology,* 1974, *102,* 629–633.

Berlyne, D. E. The reward-value of indifferent stimulation. In J. T. Tapp (Ed.), *Reinforcement and behavior.* New York: Academic Press, 1969.

Bernbach, H. A. Replication processes in human memory and learning. In G. H. Bower & J. T. Spence (Eds.), *The psychology of learning and motivation: Advances in research and theory.* Vol. 3. New York: Academic Press, 1969.

Bernbach, H. A. Rate of presentation in free recall: A problem for two-stage memory theories. *Journal of Experimental Psychology: Human Learning and Memory,* 1975, *104,* 18–22.

Bersh, P. J. The influence of two variables upon the establishment of a secondary reinforcer for operant responses. *Journal of Experimental Psychology,* 1951, *41,* 62–73.

Bersh, P. J., Notterman, J. M., & Schoenfeld, W. N. Generalization to varying tone frequencies as a function of intensity of unconditioned stimulus. Air University, School of Aviation Medicine, U.S.A.F., Randolph AFB, Texas, 1956.

Best, P. J., Best, M. R., & Mickley, G. A. Conditioned aversion to distinct environmental stimuli resulting from gastrointestinal distress. *Journal of Comparative and Physiological Psychology,* 1973, *85,* 250–257.

Biederman, G. B. Continuity theory revisited: A failure in a basic assumption. *Psychological Review,* 1970, *77,* 255–256.

Bijou, S. W. Methodology for the experimental analysis of child behavior. *Psychological Reports,* 1957, *3,* 243–250.   (a)

Bijou, S. W. Patterns of reinforcement and resistance to extinction in young children. *Child Development,* 1957, *28,* 47–54.   (b)

Bilodeau, E. A., & Howell, D. C. Free association norms by discrete and continued methods. ONR Technical Report No 1, 1965, Tulane University, Contract Nonr-475 (10).

Bilodeau, I. McD. Information feedback. In E. A. Bilodeau (Ed.), *Acquisition of skill.* New York: Academic Press, 1966.

Bilodeau, I. M., & Schlosberg, H. Similarity in stimulating conditions as a variable in retroactive inhibition. *Journal of Experimental Psychology,* 1951, *41,* 199–204.

Bindra, D. A unified account of classical conditioning and operant training. In

A. H. Black & W. F. Prokasy (Eds.), *Classical conditioning II: Current research and theory*. New York: Appleton, 1972.

Bindra, D. A motivational view of learning, performance and behavior modification. *Psychological Review*, 1974, *81*, 199–213.

Birnbaum, I. Long term retention of first-list associations in the A-B, A-C paradigm. *Journal of Verbal Learning and Verbal Behavior*, 1965, *4*, 515–520.

Bjork, R. A. Positive forgetting: The noninterference of items intentionally forgotten. *Journal of Verbal Learning and Verbal Behavior*, 1970, *9*, 255–268.

Bjork, R. A. Theoretical implications of directed forgetting. In A. W. Melton & E. Martin (Eds.), *Coding processes in human memory*. Washington, D. C.: V. H. Winston, 1972.

Black, A. H. Cardiac conditioning in curarized dogs: The relationship between heart rate and skeletal behavior. In W. F. Prokasy (Ed.), *Classical conditioning: A symposium*. New York: Appleton, 1965.

Black, A. H., & Prokasy, W. F. (Eds.), *Classical conditioning II: Current theory and research*. New York: Appleton, 1972.

Blanchard, E. B., & Young, L. D. Of promises and evidence: A reply to Engel. *Psychological Bulletin*, 1974, *81*, 44–46.

Blanchard, R. J., Mast, M., & Blanchard, D. C. Stimulus control of defensive reactions in the albino rat. *Journal of Comparative and Physiological Psychology*, 1975, *88*, 81–88.

Blough, D. S. Steady state data and a quantitative model of operant generalization and discrimination. *Journal of Experimental Psychology: Animal Behavior Processes.* 1975, *104*, 3–21.

Blough, D. S., & Lipsitt, L. P. The discriminative control of behavior. In J. W. Kling & L. A. Riggs (Eds.), *Woodworth and Schlosberg's experimental psychology*. New York: Holt, 1971.

Boakes, R. A., & Halliday, M. S. Disinhibition and spontaneous recovery of response decrements produced by free reinforcement in rats. *Journal of Experimental Psychology*, 1975, *88*, 436–446.

Bolles, R. C. Species-specific defense reactions and avoidance learning. *Psychological Review*, 1970, *77*, 32–48.

Bolles, R., & Seelbach, S. Punishing and reinforcing effects of noise onset and termination for different responses. *Journal of Comparative and Physiological Psychology*, 1964, *58*, 127–132.

Bousfield, A. K., & Bousfield, W. A. Measurement of clustering and of sequential constancies in repeated free recall. *Psychological Reports*, 1966, *19*, 935–942.

Bousfield, W. A. The occurrence of clustering in the recall of randomly arranged associates. *Journal of General Psychology*, 1953, *49*, 229–240.

Bousfield, W. A., Puff, C. R., & Cowen, T. M. The development of constancies in sequential organization during repeated free recall. *Journal of Verbal Learning and Verbal Behavior*, 1964, *3*, 489–495.

Bousfield, W. A., & Sedgewick, C. H. An analysis of sequences of restricted associative responses. *Journal of General Psychology*, 1944, *30*, 149–165.

Bousfield, W. A., & Wicklund, D. A. Rhyme as a determinant of clustering. *Psychonomic Science*, 1969, *16*, 183–184.

Bower, G. H. Application of a model to paired-associate learning. *Psychometrika*, 1961, *26*, 255–280.

Bower, G. H. An association model for response and training variables in paired-associate learning. *Psychological Review*, 1962, *69*, 34–53.

Bower, G. H. A multicomponent theory of the memory trace. In K. W. Spence & J. T. Spence (Eds.), *The psychology of learning and motivation: Advances in research and theory*. Vol. 1. New York: Academic Press, 1967.

Bower, G. H. Imagery as a relational organizer in associative learning. *Journal of Verbal Learning and Verbal Behavior*, 1970, *9*, 529–533.

Bower, G. H. Mental imagery and associative learning. In L. W. Gregg (Ed.), *Cognition in learning and memory*, New York: Wiley, 1972.

Bower, G. H., & Bostrom, A. Absence of within-list PI and RI in short-term recognition memory. *Psychonomic Science*, 1968, *10*, 211–212.

Bower, G. H., & Lesgold, A. M. Organization as a determinant of part-to-whole transfer in free recall. *Journal of Verbal Learning and Verbal Behavior*, 1969, *8*, 501–506.

Bower, G. H., & Theios, J. A learning model for discrete performance levels. In R. C. Atkinson, (Ed.), *Studies in mathematical psychology*. Stanford: Stanford University Press, 1964.

Bowlby, J. *Attachment and Loss.* Vol. 1 *Attachment.* New York: Basic Books, 1969.

Brackbill, Y. Extinction of the smiling response in infants as a function of reinforcement schedules. *Child Development*, 1958, *29*, 115–124.

Brackbill, Y., Adams, G., & Reaney, T. P. A parametric study of the delay-retention effect. *Psychological Reports*, 1967, *20*, 433–434.

Branch, J. C., & Viney, W. An attempt to transfer a position discrimination habit via RNA extracts. *Psychological Reports*, 1966, *19*, 923–926.

Braud, W. G. Extinction in goldfish: Facilitation by intracranial injection of RNA from brains of extinguished donors. *Science*, 1970, *168*, 1234–1236.

Braud, W. G., & Hoffman, R. B. Response facilitation and response inhibition produced by intracranial injections of brain extracts from trained donor goldfish. *Physiological Psychology*, 1973, *1*, 169–173.

Bregman, A. S., & Wiener, J. R. Effects of test trials in paired-associate and free-recall learning. *Journal of Verbal Learning and Verbal Behavior*, 1970, *9*, 689–698.

Breland, K., & Breland, M. The misbehavior of organisms. *American Psychologist*, 1961, *16*, 681–684.

Breland, K., & Breland, M. *Animal behavior.* New York: Macmillan, 1966.

Broadbent, D. E. *Perception and communication.* London: Pergamon Press, 1958.

Broadbent, D. E. *Decision and stress.* New York: Academic Press, 1971.

Brogden, W. J., Lipman, E. A., & Culler, E. The role of incentive in conditioning and extinction. *American Journal of Psychology*, 1938, *51*, 109–117.

Brown, J. L. The effect of drive on learning with secondary reinforcement. *Journal of Comparative and Physiological Psychology*, 1956, *51*, 254–260.

Brown, J. S. Factors determining conflict reactions in different discriminations. *Journal of Experimental Psychology*, 1942, *31*, 272–292.

Brown, P., & Jenkins, H. M. Autoshaping of the pigeon's key-peck. *Journal of the Experimental Analysis of Behavior*, 1968, *11*, 1–8.

Brown, R. *A first language.* Cambridge, Massachusetts: Harvard University Press, 1973.

Buerger, A. A., & Gross, C. G. Effects of ventral putamen lesions on discrimination learning in monkeys. *Journal of Comparative and Physiological Psychology*, 1974, *86*, 440–446.

Bugelski, B. R. Extinction with and without sub-goal reinforcement. *Journal of Comparative Psychology*, 1938, *26*, 121–133.

Bugelski, B. R. Presentation time, total time, and mediation in paired-associate learning. *Journal of Experimental Psychology*, 1962, *63*, 409–412.

Bugelski, B. R. In defense of remote associations. *Psychological Review*, 1965, *72*, 169–174.

Bugelski, B. R. Images as mediators in one-trial paired-associate learning. II: Self-timing in successive lists. *Journal of Experimental Psychology*, 1968, *77*, 328–334.

Bugelski, B. R., & Cadwallader, T. C. A reappraisal of the transfer and retro-action surface. *Journal of Experimental Psychology*, 1956, *52*, 360–366.

Butler, R. A. Discrimination by Rhesus monkeys to visual-exploration motivation. *Journal of Comparative and Physiological Psychology*, 1953, *46*, 95–98.

Butler, R. A. Investigative behavior. In A. M. Schrier, H. F. Harlow, & F. Stollnitz (Eds.), *Behavior of nonhuman primates*. Vol. II. New York: Academic Press, 1965.

Butter, C. M., & Thomas, D. R. Secondary reinforcement as a function of the amount of primary reinforcement. *Journal of Comparative and Physiological Psychology*, 1958, *51*, 346–348.

Caldwell, D. F., & Churchill, J. A. Learning ability in the progeny of rats administered a protein-deficient diet during the second half of gestation. *Neurology*, 1967, *17*, 95–99.

Calfee, R. C. Interpresentation effects in paired-associate learning. *Journal of Verbal Learning and Verbal Behavior*, 1968, *7*, 1030–1036.

Cameron, D. E. The use of nucleic acid in aged patients with memory impairment. *American Journal of Psychiatry*, 1958, *114*, 943.

Cameron, D. E. The process of remembering. *British Journal of Psychiatry*, 1963, *109*, 325–340.

Campbell, B. A., & Spear, N. E. Ontogeny of memory. *Psychological Review*, 1972, *79*, 215–236.

Carey, R. J., Goodall, E., & Lorens, S. A. Differential effects of amphetamine and food deprivation on self-stimulation of the lateral hypothalamus and medial frontal cortex. *Journal of Comparative and Physiological Psychology*, 1975, *88*, 224–230.

Carney, R. E. Transfer of learned response by RNA injection. *Science*, 1965, *150*, 228.

Carterette, E. C., & Coleman, E. A. Organization in free recall. Paper presented at meeting of Psychonomic Society, Bryn Mawr, Pennsylvania, August, 1963.

Ceraso, J., & Henderson, A. Unavailability and associative loss in RI and PI. *Journal of Experimental Psychology*, 1965, *70*, 300–303.

Chapman, C., & Risley, T. R. Anti-litter procedures in an urban high-density area. *Journal of Applied Behavior Analysis*, 1974, *7*, 377–383.

Cherry, E. C. Some experiments on the recognition of speech. *Journal of the Acoustical Society of America*, 1953, *25*, 975–979.

Chizar, D. A., & Spear, N. E. Proactive interference in a T-maze brightness-discrimination task. *Psychonomic Science*, 1968, *11*, 107–108.

Chizar, D. A., & Spear, N. E. Stimulus change, reversal learning, and retention in the rat. *Journal of Comparative and Physiological Psychology* 1969, *69*, 190–195.

Cofer, C. N. Does conceptual organization influence the amount retained in immediate free recall? In B. Kleinmuntz (Ed.), *Concepts and the Structure of Memory*. New York: Wiley, 1967.

Cofer, C. N., & Appley, M. H. *Motivation: Theory and research.* New York: Wiley, 1964.

Cofer, C. N., Failie, N. F., & Horton, D. L. Retroactive inhibition following reinstatement or maintenance of first-list responses by means of free recall. *Journal of Experimental Psychology*, 1971, *90*, 197–205.

Cohen, B. H. An investigation of recoding in free recall. *Journal of Experimental Psychology*, 1963, *65*, 368–376.

Cohen, B. H. Some-or-none characteristics of coding behavior. *Journal of Verbal Learning and Verbal Behavior*, 1966, *5*, 182–187.

Cohen, R. L. Recency effects in long-term recall and recognition. *Journal of Verbal Learning and Verbal Behavior*, 1970, *9*, 672–678.

Cole, L. E., & Kanak, N. J. Overt versus covert pronunciational and rehearsal responses in verbal-discrimination learning and recall. *American Journal of Psychology*, 1972, *85*, 57–62.

Collier, G. Some properties of saccharin as a reinforcer. *Journal of Experimental Psychology*, 1962, *64*, 184–191.

Collier, G., & Marx, M. H. Changes in performance as a function of shifts in the magnitude of reinforcement. *Journal of Experimental Psychology*, 1959, 57, 305–309.

Collins, A. M., & Quillian, M. R. How to make a language user. In E. Tulving and W. Donaldson (Eds.), *Organization and memory*. New York: Academic Press, 1972.

Conrad, R. Acoustic confusions in immediate memory. *British Journal of Psychology*, 1964, *55*, 75–84.

Cooper, E. H., & Pantle, A. J. The total-time hypothesis in verbal learning. *Psychological Bulletin*, 1967, *68*, 221–234.

Cotter, L. H. Operant conditioning in a Vietnamese mental hospital. *American Journal of Psychiatry*, 1967, *124*, 23–28.

Craik, F. I. M. The fate of primary memory items in free recall. *Journal of Verbal Learning and Verbal Behavior*, 1970, *9*, 143–148.

Craik, F. I. M., & Lockhart, R. S. Levels of processing: A framework for memory research. *Journal of Verbal Learning and Verbal Behavior*, 1972, *11*, 671–684.

Craik, F. I. M., & Watkins, M. J. The role of rehearsal in short-term memory. *Journal of Verbal Learning and Verbal Behavior*, 1973, *12*, 599–607.

Cramer, P. Mediated transfer via natural language association. *Journal of Verbal Learning and Verbal Behavior*, 1967, *6*, 512–519.

Crespi, L. P. Quantitative variation of incentive and performance in the white rat. *American Journal of Psychology*, 1942, 55, 467–517.

Crowder, R. G. Proactive and retroactive inhibition in the retention of a T-maze habit in rats. *Journal of Experimental Psychology*, 1967, *74*, 167–171.

Culbertson, J. L. Effects of brief reinforcement delays on acquisition and extinction of brightness discriminations in rats. *Journal of Comparative and Physiological Psychology*, 1970, *70*, 317–325.

D'Agostino, P. R. The blocked-random effect in recall and recognition. *Journal of Verbal Learning and Verbal Behavior*, 1969, *8*, 815–820.

D'Agostino, P. R., & DeRemer, P. Repetition effects as a function of rehearsal and encoding variability. *Journal of Verbal Learning and Verbal Behavior*, 1973, *12*, 108–113.

Dale, H. C. A., & McGlaughlin, A. Evidence for acoustic coding in long-term memory. *Quarterly Journal of Experimental Psychology*, 1971, *23*, 1–7.

Dallett, K. M. The transfer surface re-examined. *Journal of Verbal Learning and Verbal Behavior*, 1962, *1*, 91–94.

Dallett, K. M. A transfer surface for paradigms in which second-list S–R pairings do not correspond to first-list pairings. *Journal of Verbal Learning and Verbal Behavior*, 1965, *4*, 528–534.   (a)

Dallett, K. M. In defense of remote associations. *Psychological Review*, 1965, *72*, 164–168.   (b)

Dalton, A. J., Rubino, C. A., & Hislop, M. W. Some effects of token rewards on school achievement of children with Down's syndrome. *Journal of Applied Behavior Analysis*, 1973, *6*, 251–259.

D'Amato, M. R. Secondary reinforcement and magnitude of primary reinforcement. *Journal of Comparative and Physiological Psychology*, 1955, *48*, 378–380.

D'Amato, M. R., & Fazzaro, J. Discriminated lever-press avoidance learning as a function of type and intensity of shock. *Journal of Comparative and Physiological Psychology* 1966, *61*, 313–315.

D'Amato, M. R., Fazzaro, J., & Etkins, M. Anticipatory responding and avoidance discrimination as factors in avoidance conditioning. *Journal of Experimental Psychology*, 1968, *77*, 41–47.

Davidson, M. C. A functional analysis of chained fixed-interval schedule performance. *Journal of the Experimental Analysis of Behavior*, 1974, *21*, 323–330.

Davidson, N. A., & Grayson Osborne, J. Fixed-ratio and fixed-interval schedule control of matching-to-sample errors by children. *Journal of the Experimental Analysis of Behavior*, 1974, *21*, 27–36.

Dean, M. G., & Kausler, D. H. Degree of first-list learning and stimulus meaningfulness as related to transfer in the A–B, C–B paradigm. *Journal of Verbal Learning and Verbal Behavior*, 1964, *3*, 330–334.

Dempster, F. N., & Rohwer, W. D. Component analysis of the elaborative encoding effect in paired-associate learning. *Journal of Experimental Pscyhology*, 1974, *103*, 400–408.

Deutsch, J. A. The neural basis of memory. *Psychology Today*, 1968, *1*, 56–61.

Deutsch, J. A. The cholinergic synapse and the site of memory. *Science*, 1971, *174*, 788–794.

Deutsch, J. A., & Deutsch, D. *Physiological psychology*, Homewood, Illinois: Dorsey, 1973.

Deutsch, J. A., & Howarth, C. I. Some tests of a theory of intracranial self-stimulation. *Psychological Review*, 1963, *70*, 444–460.

Devietti, T. L., & Larson, R. C. ECS effects: Evidence supporting state dependent learning in rats. *Journal of Comparative and Physiological Psychology*, 1971, *74*, 407–415.

Dillon, R. F. Locus of proactive interference effects in short-term memory. *Journal of Experimental Psychology*, 1973, *99*, 75–81.

Dinsmoor, J. A. A quantitative comparison of the discriminative and reinforcing functions of a stimulus. *Journal of Experimental Psychology*, 1950, *40*, 458–472.

Dobrzecka, C., & Konorski, J. Qualitative versus directional cues in differential conditioning. I. Left leg–right leg differentiation to cues of a mixed character. *Acta Biologiae Experimentale*, 1967, *27*, 163–168.

Dobrzecka, C., & Konorski, J. Qualitative versus directional cues in differential conditioning. *Acta Biologiae Experimentale*, 1968, *28*, 61–69.

Dolinsky, R. Clustering and free recall with alternative organizational cues. *Journal of Experimental Psychology*, 1972, *95*, 159–163.

Drachman, D. A., & Arbit, J. Memory and the hippocampal complex. *Archives of Neurology*, 1966, *15*, 52–61.

Dunham, P. J. Contrasted conditions of reinforcement: A selective critique. *Psychological Bulletin*, 1968, *69*, 295–315.

Dunham, P. J., & Kilps, B. Shifts in magnitude of reinforcement: Confounded factors or contrast effects? *Journal of Experimental Psychology*, 1969, *79*, 373–374.

Ebbinghaus, H. *Über das gedächtnis: Untersuchungen zur experimentellen psychologie.* Leipzig: Duncker and Humbolt, 1885.

Egger, M. D., & Miller, N. E. Secondary reinforcement in rats as a function of information value and reliability of the stimulus. *Journal of Experimental Psychology*, 1962, *64*, 97–104.

Egger, M. D., & Miller, N. E. When is a reward reinforcing? An experimental study of the information hypothesis. *Journal of Comparative and Physiological Psychology*, 1963, *56*, 132–137.

Eisenberger, R. Explanation of rewards that do not reduce tissue needs. *Psychological Bulletin*, 1972, *77*, 319–339.

Eisenberger, R., Karpman, M., & Trattner, J. What is the necessary and sufficient condition for reinforcement in the contingency situation? *Journal of Experimental Psychology*, 1967, *74*, 342–350.

Ekstrand, B. R. Backward associations. *Psychological Bulletin*, 1966, *65*, 50–64.

Ekstrand, B. R. Effect of sleep on memory. *Journal of Experimental Psychology*, 1967, *75*, 64–72.

Ekstrand, B. R., Wallace, W. P., & Underwood, B. J. A frequency theory of verbal-discrimination learning. *Psychological Review*, 1966, *73*, 566–578.

Ellis, H. C. *Fundamentals of human learning and cognition.* Dubuque, Iowa: Wm. C. Brown, 1972.

Ellis, H. C. Stimulus encoding processes in human learning and memory. In G. H. Bower (Ed.), *The psychology of learning and motivation*, Vol. 7. New York: Academic Press, 1973.

Elmes, D. G., Greener, W. I., & Wilkinson, W. C. Free recall of items presented after massed- and distributed-practice items. *American Journal of Psychology*, 1972, *85*, 237–240.

Entwisle, D. R. *Word associations of young children.* Baltimore, Maryland: Johns Hopkins Press, 1966.

Entwisle, D. R. To dispel fantasies about fantasy-based measures of achievement motivation. *Psychological Bulletin*, 1972, *77*, 377–391.

Estes, W. K. The statistical approach to learning theory. In S. Koch (Ed.), *Psychology: A study of a science*, Vol. II. New York: McGraw-Hill, 1959.

Estes, W. K. Learning theory and the new "mental chemistry." *Psychological Review*, 1960, *67*, 207–223.

Estes, W. K. Probability learning. In A. W. Melton (Ed.), *Categories of human learning.* New York: Academic Press, 1964.

Estes, W. K. New perspectives on some old issue in association theory. In N. J. MacKintosh & W. K. Honig (Eds.), *Fundamental issues in associative learning.* Halifax: Dalhousie University Press, 1969.

Estes, W. K. An associative basis for coding and organization in memory. In A. W. Melton & E. Martin (Eds.), *Coding processes in human memory.* New York: Wiley, 1972.

Estes, W. K., & DaPolito, F. Independent variation of information storage and retrieval processes in paired-associate learning. *Journal of Experimental Psychology*, 1967, *75*, 18–26.

Estes, W. K., & Suppes, P. Foundations of linear models. In R. R. Bush & W. K. Estes (Eds.), *Studies in mathematical learning theory.* Stanford: Stanford University Press, 1959.

Everett, P. B., Hayward, S. C., & Meyers, A. W. The effects of a token reinforcement procedure on bus ridership. *Journal of Applied Behavior Analysis*, 1974, *7*, 1–9.

Fabricius, E. Zur Ethologie junger Anatiden. *Acta Zoologica Fennica*, 1951, *68*, 1–175.

Fabricius, E. Experiments on the following response of Mallard ducklings. *British Journal of Animal Behavior*, 1955, *3*, 122.

Fabricius, E. Some aspects of imprinting in birds. *Symposium of the Zoological Society of London*, 1962, *8*, 139–148.

Fabricius, E., & Boyd, H. Experiments on the following reactions of ducklings. *Wildfowl Trust Annual Report*, 1954, *6*, 84–89.

Fantino, E., & Herrnstein, R. J. Secondary reinforcement and number of primary reinforcements. *Journal of the Experimental Analysis of Behavior*, 1968, *11*, 9–14.

Fantino, E., Sharp, D., & Cole, M. Factors facilitating lever press avoidance. *Journal of Comparative and Physiological Psychology*, 1966, *63*, 214–217.

Feigenbaum, E. A. Information processing and memory. In D. A. Norman (Ed.), *Models of human memory.* New York: Academic Press, 1970.

Feldman, M. P., & MacCulloch, M. J. The application of anticipatory avoidance learning to the treatment of homosexuality: I. Theory, technique, and preliminary results. *Behavior Research and Therapy*, 1965, *2*, 165–183.

Ferster, C. S., & Skinner, B. F. *Schedules of reinforcement.* New York: Appleton, 1957.

Findley, J. D., & Brady, J. V. Facilitation of large ratio performances by use of a conditioned reinforcement. *Journal of the Experimental Analysis of Behavior,* 1965, *8,* 125–129.

Fiske, D. W., & Maddi, S. R. *Functions of varied experience.* Homewood, Illinois: Dorsey, 1961.

Fitts, P. M., & Posner, M. I. *Human performance.* Monterey, California: Brooks/Cole 1967.

Fjerdingstad, E. J. *Chemical transfer of learned information.* New York: American Elsevier, 1971.

Foree, D. D., & LoLordo, V. M. Stimulus-reinforcer interactions in the pigeon: The role of electric shock and the avoidance contingency. *Journal of Experimental Psychology: Animal Behavior Processes,* 1975, *104,* 39–46.

Forrester, W. E. Retroactive inhibition and spontaneous recovery in the A–B, D–C paradigm. *Journal of Verbal Learning and Verbal Behavior.* 1970, *9,* 525–528.

Forrester, W. E. Effects of semantic and acoustic relatedness on free recall in a between-subjects design. *Psychological Reports,* 1972, *30,* 637–638.

Forrester, W. E., & King, D. J. Effects of semantic and acoustic relatedness on free recall and clustering. *Journal of Experimental Psychology,* 1971, *88,* 16–19.

Fowler, H. *Curiosity and exploratory behavior.* New York: Macmillan, 1965.

Fox, P. W. Patterns of stability and change in behaviors of free associations. *Journal of Verbal Learning and Verbal Behavior,* 1970, *9,* 30–36.

Fox, S. S., & O'Brien, J. H. Duplication of evoked potential waveform by curve of probability of firing of a single cell. *Science,* 1965, *147,* 888–890.

Freedman, J. L., & Loftus, E. F. Retrieval of words from long-term memory. *Journal of Verbal Learning and Verbal Behavior,* 1971, *10,* 107–115.

Friedman, M. J., & Reynolds, J. H. Retroactive inhibition as a function of response-class similarity. *Journal of Experimental Psychology,* 1967, *74,* 351–355.

Froeberg, S. Simultaneous vs. successive association. *Psychological Review,* 1918, *25,* 156–163.

Gaito, J. *Molecular psychobiology.* Springfield, Illinois: Thomas, 1966.

Galin, D., & Ornstein, R. Lateral specialization of cognitive mode: An EEG study. *Psychophysiology,* 1972, *9,* 412–418.

Gallistel, C. R. The incentive of brain-stimulation reward. *Journal of Comparative and Physiological Psychology,* 1969, *69,* 713–721.

Gallistel, C. R. Self-stimulation: The neurophysiology of reward and motivation. In J. A. Deutsch (Ed.), *The physiological basis of memory.* New York: Academic Press, 1972.

Gamzu, E., & Schwam, E. Autoshaping and automaintenance of a key-press response in squirrel monkeys. *Journal of the Experimental Analysis of Behavior,* 1974, *21,* 361–371.

Ganz, L. Hue generalization and hue discriminability in *Macaca mulatta. Journal of Experimental Psychology,* 1962, *64,* 142–150.

Ganz, L., & Riesen, A. H. Stimulus generalization to hue in the dark-reared *Macaque. Journal of Comparative and Physiological Psychology,* 1962, *55,* 92–99.

Garcia, J., Ervin, F., & Koelling, R. Learning with prolonged delay of reinforcement. *Psychonomic Science,* 1966, *5,* 121–122.

Garcia, J., Ervin, F., & Koelling, R. Conditioning with delayed vitamin injections. *Science,* 1967, *155,* 716–718.

Garcia, J., Hankins, W. G., & Rusiniak, K. W. Behavioral regulation of the milieu interne in man and rat. *Science,* 1974, *185,* 824–831.

Garcia, J., & Koelling, R. Relation of cue to consequence in avoidance learning. *Psychonomic Science*, 1966, *4*, 123–124.

Garcia, J., McGowan, B. K., & Green, K. F. Biological constraints on conditioning. In A. H. Black and W. F. Prokasy (Eds.), *Classical conditioning II: Current theory and research*. New York: Appelton, 1972.

Gardiner, J. M., Craik, F. I. M., & Birtwistle, J. Retrieval cues and release from proactive inhibition. *Journal of Verbal Learning and Verbal Behavior*, 1972, *11*, 778–783.

Gartman, L. M., & Johnson, N. F. Massed versus distributed repetition of homographs: A test of the differential-encoding hypothesis. *Journal of Verbal Learning and Verbal Behavior*, 1972, *11*, 801–808.

Gazzaniga, M. S. *The bisected brain*. NewYork: Appleton, 1970.

Gazzaniga, M. S. One brain—two minds? *American Science*, 1972, *60*, 311–317.

Gazzaniga, M. S., & Sperry, R. W. Language after section of the cerebral commisures. *Brain*, 1967, *90*, 131–148.

Gelder, M. G., & Marks, I. M. Aversion treatment in transvestism and transexualism. In R. Green (Ed.), *Transvestism and sex management*. Baltimore: Johns Hopkins Press, 1969.

Gerall, A. A., Sampson, P. B., & Boslov, G. L. Classical conditioning of human pupillary dilation. *Journal of Experimental Psychology*, 1957, *54*, 457–474.

Gibson, E. J. A systematic application of the concepts of generalization and differentiation to verbal learning. *Psychological Review*, 1940, *47*, 196–229.

Gibson, E. J. Retroactive inhibition as a function of degree of generalization between tasks. *Journal of Experimental Psychology*, 1941, *28*, 93–115.

Glanzer, M. Storage mechanisms in recall. In G. H. Bower (Ed.), *The psychology of learning and motivation*, Vol. 5. New York: Academic Press, 1972.

Glanzer, M., & Razel, M. The size of the unit in short-term storage. *Journal of Verbal Learning and Verbal Behavior*, 1974, *13*, 114–131.

Glanzer, M., & Schwartz, A. Mnemonic structure in free recall: Differential effects on STS and LTS. *Journal of Verbal Learning and Verbal Behavior*, 1971, *10*, 194–198.

Glassman, W. E. Subvocal activity and acoustic confusions in short-term memory. *Journal of Experimental Psychology*, 1972, *96*, 164–169.

Gleitman, H. Forgetting of long-term memories in animals. In W. K. Honig & P. H. R. James (Eds.), *Animal memory*. New York: Academic Press, 1971.

Gleitman, H., & Jung, L. Retention in rats: The effect of proactive interference. *Science*, 1963, *142*, 1683–1684.

Glickman, S. E., & Schiff, B. B. A biological theory of reinforcement. *Psychological Review*, 1967, *74*, 81–109.

Goggin, J. First-list recall as a function of second-list learning method. *Journal of Verbal Learning and Verbal Behavior*, 1967, *6*, 423–427.

Goggin, J., & Martin, E. Forced stimulus encoding and retroactive interference. *Journal of Experimental Psychology*, 1970, *84*, 131–136.

Gold, P. E., & King, R. A. Retrograde amnesia: Storage failure versus retrieval failure. *Psychological Review*, 1974, *81*, 465–469.

Goldiamond, I. Stuttering and fluency as manipulatable operant response classes. In L. Krasner & L. P. Ullman (Eds.), *Research in behavior modification*. New York: Holt, 1965.

Gorfein, D. S., & Jacobson, D. E. Proactive effects in short-term recognition memory. *Journal of Experimental Psychology*, 1972, *95*, 211–214.

Grant, D. A. Classical and operant conditioning. In A. W. Melton (Ed.), *Categories of human learning*. New York: Academic Press, 1964.

Green, E. Biofeedback for mind-body self-regulation: Healing and creativity. In D. Shapiro, T. X. Barber, L. V. DiCara, J. Kamiya, N. E. Miller, & J. Stoyva (Eds.) *Biofeedback and self-control 1972*. Chicago; Aldine, 1973.

Green, L., & Rachlin, H. Economic and biological influences on a pigeon's key peck. *Journal of the Experimental Analysis of Behavior*, 1975, *23*, 55–62.

Greeno, J. G. Conservation of information-processing capacity in paired-associate memorizing. *Journal of Verbal Learning and Verbal Behavior*, 1970, *9*, 581–586.

Greeno, J. G., James, C. T., & DaPolito, F. J. A cognitive interpretation of negative transfer and forgetting of paired associates. *Journal of Verbal Learning and Verbal Behavior*, 1971, *10*, 331–345.

Greenspoon, J. The reinforcing effect of two spoken sounds on the frequency of two responses. *American Journal of Psychology*, 1955, *68*, 409–416.

Greenspoon, J., & Ranyard, R. Stimulus conditions and retroactive inhibition. *Journal of Experimental Psychology*, 1957, *53*, 55–59.

Grice, G. R. The relation of secondary reinforcement to delayed reward in visual discrimination learning. *Journal of Experimental Psychology*, 1948, *38*, 1–16.

Griffith, D. Comparison of control processes for recognition and recall. *Journal of Experimental Psychology: Human Learning and Memory*, 1975, *104*, 223–228.

Gross, C. G. Visual functions of inferotemporal cortex. In R. Jung (Ed.), *Handbook of sensory physiology*, Vol. 7. Berlin: Springer-Verlag, 1973.

Grover, D. E., Horton, D. L., & Cunningham, M., Jr. Mediated facilitation and interference in a four-stage paradigm. *Journal of Verbal Learning and Verbal Behavior*, 1967, *6*, 42–46.

Gurowitz, E. M. *The molecular basis of memory*. Englewood Cliffs, New Jersey: Prentice-Hall, 1969.

Gustavson, C. R., Garcia, J., Hankins, W. G., & Rusiniak, K. W. Coyote predation control by aversive conditioning. *Science*, 1974, *184*, 581–583.

Guthrie, E. R. Association as a function of time interval. *Psychological Review*, 1933, *40*, 355–367.

Guthrie, E. R. *The psychology of learning*. New York: Harper, 1935.

Guthrie, E. R. *The psychology of learning*. (Rev. ed.) New York: Harper, 1952.

Guttman, N., & Kalish, H. I. Discriminability and stimulus generalization. *Journal of Experimental Psychology*, 1956, *51*, 79–88.

Gynther, M. D. Differential eyelid conditioning as a function of stimulus similarity and strength of response to the CS. *Journal of Experimental Psychology*, 1957, *53*, 408–416.

Hakes, D. T., James, C. T., & Young, R. K. A re-examination of the Ebbinghaus derived-list paradigm. *Journal of Experimental Psychology*, 1964, *68*, 508–514.

Halas, E. S., Bradfield, K., Sandlie, M. E., Theye, F., & Beardsley, J. Changes in rat behavior due to RNA injection. *Physiology and Behavior*, 1966, *1*, 281–283.

Hall, J. F. Studies in secondary reinforcement: II. Secondary reinforcement as a function of the strength of the drive during primary reinforcement. *Journal of Comparative and Physiological Psychology*, 1951, *44*, 462–466.

Hall, R. D., & Kling, J. W. Amount of consumatory activity and performance in a modified T maze. *Journal of Comparative and Physiological Psychology*, 1960, *53*, 165–168.

Hamilton, R. J. Retroactive facilitation as a function of degree of generalization between tasks. *Journal of Experimental Psychology*, 1943, *32*, 363–376.

Hanley, M. J., & Scheirer, C. J. Proactive inhibition in memory scanning. *Journal of Experimental Psychology: Human Learning and Memory*, 1975, *104*, 81–83.

Hansen, G., Tomie, A., Thomas, D. R., & Thomas, D. H. Effect of test stimulus range on stimulus generalization in human subjects. *Journal of Experimental Psychology*, 1974, *102*, 634–639.

Harlow, H. F. Forward conditioning, backward conditioning and pseudoconditioning in the goldfish. *Journal of Genetic Psychology*, 1939, *55*, 49–58.

Harlow, H. F. Learning by rhesus monkeys on the basis of manipulation–exploration motives. *Science*, 1953, *117*, 466–467.

Harlow, H. F., & Toltzien, F. Formation of pseudo-conditioned responses in cats. *Journal of General Psychology*, 1940, *23*, 367–375.

Hawkin, H. L., Pardo, V. J., & Cox, R. D. Proactive interference in short-term recognition: Trace interaction or competition? *Journal of Experimental Psychology*, 1972, *92*, 43–48.

Hawkins, R. P., Peterson, R. F., Schweid, E., & Bijou, S. W. Behavior therapy in the home: Amelioration of problem parent–child relations with the parent in a therapeutic role. *Journal of Experimental Child Psychology*, 1966, *4*, 99–107.

Hayes, K. J. The backward learning curve: A method for the study of learning. *Psychological Review*, 1953, *60*, 269–275.

Heath, R. G., & Mickle, W. A. Evaluation of seven years' experience with depth electrode studies in human patients. In E. R. Ramey & D. S. O'Doherty (Eds.), *Electrical studies on the unanesthetized brain*. New York: Harper & Row, 1960.

Hebert, J. A., Bullock, M., Levitt, L., Woodward, K. G., & McGuirk, F. D. Context and frequency effects in the generalization of a human voluntary response. *Journal of Experimental Psychology*, 1974, *102*, 456–462.

Heinroth, O. Beiträge zur Biologie, namentlich Ethologie und Physiologie der Anatiden. *Verhandlungen 5 Internationalen Ornithologisch Kongress*, 1911, 589–702.

Hellige, J. B., & Grant, D. A. Eyelid conditioning performance when the mode of reinforcement is changed from classical to instrumental avoidance and vice versa. *Journal of Experimental Psychology*, 1974, *102*, 710–719.   (a)

Hellige, J. B., & Grant, D. A. Response rate and development of response topography in eyelid conditioning under different conditions of reinforcement. *Journal of Experimental Psychology*, 1974, *103*, 574–582.   (b)

Hess, E. H. "Imprinting" in animals. *Scientific American*, 1958, *199*, 81–90.

Hess, E. H. Imprinting. *Science*, 1959, *130*, 133–141.

Hess, E. H. Imprinting in birds. *Science*, 1964, *146*, 1128–1139.

Hess, E. H. Ethology and developmental psychology. In P. Mussen (Ed.), *Carmichael's manual of child psychology*, New York: Wiley, 1970.

Hess, E. H. "Imprinting" in a natural laboratory. *Scientific American*, 1972, *227*, 24–31.

Hess, E. H., & Schaefer, H. H. Innate behavior patterns as indications of the "critical period." *Zeitschrift für tierpsychologie*, 1959, *16*, 155–160.

Hewett, F. M. Teaching speech to an autistic child through operant conditioning. *American Journal of Orthopsychiatry*, 1965, *35*, 927–936.

Hilgard, E. R., & Bower, G. H. *Theories of learning* (3rd ed.). New York: Appleton, 1966.

Hilgard, E. R., & Bower, G. H. *Theories of learning* (4th ed.). Englewood Cliffs, New Jersey: Prentice-Hall, 1975.

Hilgard, E. R., & Marquis, D. G. *Conditioning and learning*. New York: Appleton, 1940.

Hill, F. A., & Wickens, D. D. The effect of stimulus compounding in paired-associate learning. *Journal of Verbal Learning and Verbal Behavior*, 1962, *1*, 144–151.

Hill, W. F. *Learning: A survey of psychological interpretations*. Scranton: Chandler, 1971.

Hinrichs, J. V., & Grunke, M. E. Control processes in short-term memory: Use of retention interval information. *Journal of Experimental Psychology: Human Learning and Memory*, 1975, *104*, 229–237.

Hintzman, D. L. On testing the independence of associations. *Psychological Review,* 1972, *79,* 261–264.

Hobson, S. L. Discriminability of fixed-ratio schedules for pigeons: Effects of absolute ratio size. *Journal of the Experimental Analysis of Behavior,* 1975, *23,* 25–35.

Hoffman, H. S., & Ratner, A. M. A reinforcement model of imprinting: Implications for socialization in monkeys and men. *Psychological Review,* 1973, *80,* 527–544.

Hoffman, H. S., Ratner, A. M., & Eiserer, L. A. Role of visual imprinting in the emergence of specific filial attachments in ducklings. *Journal of Comparative and Physiological Psychology,* 1972, *81,* 399–409.

Holland, P. C., & Rescorla, R. A. Second-order conditioning with food unconditioned stimulus. *Journal of Comparative and Physiological Psychology,* 1975, *88,* 459–467.

Hollingworth, H. C. Characteristic differences between recall and recognition. *American Journal of Psychology,* 1913, *24,* 533–544.

Honig, W. K. Discrimination, generalization, and transfer on the basis of stimulus differences. In D. I. Mostofsky (Ed.), *Stimulus generalization.* Stanford: Stanford University Press, 1965.

Honig, W. K. *Operant behavior: Areas of research and application.* New York: Appleton, 1966.

Honig, W. K., & James, P. H. R. (Eds.), *Animal memory.* New York: Academic Press, 1971.

Hopkins, C. O. Effectiveness of secondary reinforcing stimuli as a function of the quantity and quality of food reinforcement. *Journal of Experimental Psychology,* 1955, *50,* 339–342.

Hopkins, R. H. Retrieval problems in successive short-term retention trials. *Journal of Verbal Learning and Verbal Behavior,* 1974, *13,* 424–429.

Hopkins, R. H., Boylan, R. J., & Lincoln, G. L. Pronunciation and apparent frequency. *Journal of Verbal Learning and Verbal Behavior,* 1972, *11,* 105–113.

Hopkins, R. H., & Epling, W. F. Pronunciation and the length of the study interval in verbal discrimination. *Journal of Experimental Psychology,* 1971, *88,* 145–146.

Horton, D. L., & Hartman, R. Verbal mediation as a function of associative directionality and exposure frequency. *Journal of Verbal Learning and Verbal Behavior,* 1963, *1,* 361–364.

Horton, D. L., & Kjeldergaard, P. M. An experimental analysis of associative factors in mediated generalization. *Psychological Monographs,* 1961, *75,* No. 11 (Whole No. 515).

Houston, J. P. S–R stimulus selection and strength of R–S association. *Journal of Experimental Psychology,* 1964, *68,* 563–566. (a)

Houston, J. P. Verbal transfer and interlist similarities. *Psychological Review,* 1964, *71,* 412–414. (b)

Houston, J. P. Verbal transfer as a function of S_1–R_2 and S_2–R_1 interlist similarity. *Journal of Experimental Psychology,* 1966, *71,* 232–235. (a)

Houston, J. P. First-list retention and time and method of recall. *Journal of Experimental Psychology,* 1966, *71,* 839–843. (b)

Houston, J. P. Stimulus selection as influenced by degrees of learning, attention, prior associations, and experience with the stimulus components. *Journal of Experimental Psychology,* 1967, *73,* 509–516.

Houston, J. P. Proactive inhibition and undetected rehearsal: A replication. *Journal of Experimental Psychology,* 1971, *90,* 156–157.

Houston, J. P., & Mednick, S. A. Creativity and the need for novelty. *Journal of Abnormal and Social Psychology,* 1963, *66,* 137–141.

Hovland, C. I. The generalization of conditioned responses. IV. The effects of varying amounts of reinforcement upon the degree of generalization of conditioned responses. *Journal of Experimental Psychology,* 1937, *21,* 261–276.

Howell, W. C. Effects of organization on discrimination of word frequency within and between categories. *Journal of Experimental Psychology*, 1973, *99*, 255–260.

Hull, C. L. *Principles of behavior*. New York: Appleton, 1943.

Hull, C. L. *Essentials of behavior*. New Haven: Yale University Press, 1951.

Hull, C. L. *A behavior system*. New Haven: Yale University Press, 1952.

Hulse, S. H. A precision liquid feeding system controlled by licking behavior. *Journal of the Experimental Analysis of Behavior*, 1960, *3*, 1.

Hulse, S. H. Reinforcement contrast effects in rats following experimental definition of a dimension of reinforcement magnitude. *Journal of Comparative and Physiological Psychology*, 1973, *85*, 160–170.

Hulse, S. H., Deese, J., & Egeth, H. *The psychology of learning*. New York: McGraw-Hill, 1975.

Humphreys, L. G. Generalization as a function of method of reinforcement. *Journal of Experimental Psychology*, 1939, *25*, 361–372.

Hunt, E. L. Establishment of conditioned responses in chick embryos. *Journal of Comparative and Physiological Psychology*, 1949, *42*, 107–117.

Hursh, S. R., Navarick, D. J., & Fantino, E. "Automaintenance": The role of the reinforcement. *Journal of the Experimental Analysis of Behavior*, 1974, *21*, 117–124.

Hutt, P. J. Rate of bar press as a function of quality and quantity of food reward. *Journal of Comparative and Physiological Psychology*, 1954, *47*, 235–239.

Hyde, T. S. Differential effects of effort and type of orienting task on recall and organization of highly associated words. *Journal of Experimental Psychology*, 1973, *79*, 111–113.

Hydén, H. The neuron. In J. Brachet & A. E. Mirsky (Eds.), *The Cell*. New York: Academic Press, 1960.

Jacoby, L. L. Encoding processes, rehearsal, and recall requirements. *Journal of Verbal Learning and Verbal Behavior*, 1973, *12*, 302–312.

Jacoby, L. L., & Bartz, W. H. Rehearsal and transfer to LTS. *Journal of Verbal Learning and Verbal Behavior*, 1972, *11*, 561–565.

Jacoby, L. L., & Goolkasian, P. Semantic versus acoustic coding: Retention and conditions of organization. *Journal of Verbal Learning and Verbal Behavior*, 1973, *12*, 324–333.

James, H. Flicker: An unconditioned stimulus for imprinting. *Canadian Journal of Psychology*, 1959, *13*, 59–67.

James, H. Imprinting with visual flicker: Evidence for a critical period. *Canadian Journal of Psychology*, 1960, *14*, 13–20.

James, W. *Principles of psychology*. New York: Holt, 1890.

Jeffrey, W. E. The effects of verbal and non-verbal responses in mediating an instrumental act. *Journal of Experimental Psychology*, 1953, *45*, 327–333.

Jenkins, H. M., & Harrison, R. H. Effect of discrimination training on auditory generalization. *Journal of Experimental Psychology*, 1960, *59*, 246–253.

Jenkins, H. M., & Moore, B. R. The form of the auto-shaped response with food or water reinforcers. *Journal of the Experimental Analysis of Behavior*, 1973, *20*, 163–181.

Jenkins, J. J. Mediated associations: Paradigms and situations. In C. N. Cofer & B. S. Musgrave (Eds.), *Verbal behavior and learning: Problems and processes*. New York: McGraw-Hill, 1963.

Jenkins, J. J., & Russell, W. A. Associative clustering during recall. *Journal of Abnormal and Social Psychology*, 1952, *47*, 818–821.

Jenkins, J. J., & Russell, W. A. Systematic changes in word association norms, 1910–1952. *Journal of Abnormal and Social Psychology*, 1960, *60*, 293–303.

Jenkins, W. O., Pascal, G. R., & Walker, R. W. Deprivation and generalization. *Journal of Experimental Psychology*, 1958, *56*, 274–277.

John, E. R., & Killam, K. F. Electrophysiological correlates of avoidance conditioning in the cat. *Journal of Pharmacology and Experimental Therapeutics*, 1959, *125*, 252–274.

Johnston, C. D., & Jenkins, J. J. Two more incidental tasks that differentially affect associative clustering in recall. *Journal of Experimental Psychology*, 1971, *89*, 92–95.

Johnston, M. K., Kelley, C. S., Harris, F. R., & Wolf, M. M. An application of reinforcement principles to development of motor skills of a young child. *Child Development*, 1966, *37*, 379–387.

Jones, J. E. All-or-none versus incremental learning. *Psychological Review*, 1962, *69*, 156–160.

Jung, J. Effects of response meaningfulness (*m*) on transfer of training under two different paradigms. *Journal of Experimental Psychology*, 1963, *65*, 377–384.

Jung, J., & Bailey, J. *Contemporary psychology experiments: Adaptations for laboratory*. New York: Wiley, 1966.

Kamin, L. J. Predictability, surprise, attention, and conditioning. In R. Church & B. Campbell (Eds.), *Punishment and aversive behavior*. New York: Appleton, 1969. (a)

Kamin, L. J. Selective association and conditioning. In N. J. MacKintosh & W. K. Honig (Eds.), *Fundamental issues in associative learning*. Halifax: Dalhousie University Press, 1969. (b)

Kanak, N. J., Cole, L. E., & Eckert, E. Implicit associative responses in verbal discrimination acquisition. *Journal of Experimental Psychology*, 1972, *93*, 309–319.

Kanak, N. J., & Neuner, S. D. Associative symmetry and item availability as a function of five methods of paired-associate acquisition. *Journal of Experimental Psychology*, 1970, *86*, 288–295.

Kanungo, R. Meaning mediation in verbal transfer. *British Journal of Psychology*, 1967, *58*, 205–212.

Karen, R. L. *An introduction to behavior theory and its applications*. New York: Harper & Row, 1974.

Katz, J. J., & Halstead, W. C. Protein organization and mental function. *Comparative Psychological Monograph*, 1950, *20*, 1–38.

Kausler, D. H. *The psychology of verbal learning and memory*. New York: Academic Press, 1974.

Kausler, D. H., & Kanoti, G. A. R–S learning and negative transfer effects with a mixed list. *Journal of Experimental Psychology*, 1963, *65*, 201–205.

Keesey, R. E. Intracranial reward delay and the acquisition rate of a brightness discrimination. *Science*, 1964, *143*, 700–701.

Keith-Lucas, T., & Guttman, N. Robust-single-trial delayed backward conditioning. *Journal of Comparative and Physiological Psychology*, 1975, *88*, 468–476.

Kelleher, R. T. Chaining and conditioned reinforcement. In W. K. Honig (Ed.), *Operant behavior: Areas of research and application*. New York: Appleton, 1966.

Keller, K. The role of elicited responding in behavioral control. *Journal of the Experimental Analysis of Behavior*, 1974, *21*, 237–248.

Kelsey, J. E. Role of pituitary-adrenocortical system in mediating avoidance behavior of rats with septal lesions. *Journal of Comparative and Physiological Psychology*, 1975, *88*, 271–280.

Kennedy, T. D. Reinforcement frequency, task characteristics, and interval of awareness assessment as factors in verbal conditioning without awareness. *Journal of Experimental Psychology*, 1971, *88*, 103–112.

Kent, E., & Grossman, S. P. Evidence for a conflict interpretation of anomalous effects of rewarding brain stimulation. *Journal of Comparative and Physiological Psychology*, 1969, *69*, 381–390.

Kent, G. H., & Rosanoff, A. J. A study of association in insanity. *American Journal of Insanity*, 1910, *67*, 37–96, 317–390.

Keppel, G. Retroactive and proactive inhibition. In T. R. Dixon and D. Horton (Eds.), *Verbal behavior and general behavior theory*. Englewood Cliffs, New Jersey: Prentice-Hall, 1968.

Keppel, G., & Rauch, D. S. Unlearning as a function of second-list error instructions. *Journal of Verbal Learning and Verbal Behavior*, 1966, *5*, 50–58.

Keppel, G., & Underwood, B. J. Proactive inhibition in short-term retention of single items. *Journal of Verbal Learning and Verbal Behavior*, 1962, *1*, 153–161.

Keppel, G., Zavortink, B., & Shiff, B. B. Unlearning in the A–B, A–C paradigm as a function of percentage occurrence of response members. *Journal of Experimental Psychology*, 1967, *74*, 172–177.

Kerr, N., Myerson, L., & Michael, J. A procedure for shaping vocalizations in a mute child. In L. P. Ullman & L. Krasner (Eds.), *Case studies in behavior modification*. New York: Holt, 1965.

Kimble, G. A. Performance and reminiscence in motor learning as a function of the degree of distribution of practice. *Journal of Experimental Psychology*, 1949, *39*, 500–510.

Kimble, G. A. *Hilgard and Marquis' conditioning and learning*. New York: Appleton, 1961.

Kimble, G. A. *Foundations of conditioning and learning*. New York: Appleton, 1967.

Kimble, G. A., & Reynolds, B. Eyelid conditioning as a function of the interval between conditioned and unconditioned stimuli. In G. A. Kimble (Ed.), *Foundations of conditioning and learning*. New York: Appleton, 1967.

Kimmel, H. D. Instrumental inhibitory factors in classical conditioning. In W. F. Prokasy (Ed.), *Classical conditioning: A symposium*. New York: Appleton, 1965.

Kinsbourne, M., & George, J. The mechanism of the word-frequency effect on recognition memory. *Journal of Verbal Learning and Verbal Behavior*, 1974, *13*, 63–69.

Kintsch, W. Habituation of the GSR component of the orienting reflex during paired associate learning before and after learning has taken place. *Journal of Mathematical Psychology*, 1964, *2*, 330–341.

Kintsch, W. *Learning, memory, and conceptual processes*. New York: Wiley, 1970.

Kintsch, W. Notes on the structure of sematic memory. In E. Tulving & W. Donaldson (Eds.), *Organization of memory*. New York: Academic Press, 1972.

Kintsch, W., & Buschke, H. Homophones and synonyms in short-term memory. *Journal of Experimental Psychology*, 1969, *80*, 403–407.

Kish, G. B. Learning when the onset of illumination is used as reinforcing stimulus. *Journal of Comparative and Physiological Psychology*, 1955, 48, 261–264.

Kling, J. W. Learning: An introductory survey. In J. W. Kling & L. A. Riggs (Eds.), *Woodworth and Schlosberg's experimental psychology*. New York: Holt, 1971.

Kling, J. W., & Schrier, A. M. Positive reinforcement. In J. W. Kling & L. A. Riggs, (Eds.), *Woodworth and Schlosberg's experimental psychology*. New York: Holt, 1971.

Klinger, E. Consequences of commitment to and disengagement from incentives. *Psychological Review*, 1975, *82*, 1–25.

Knight, M. F., & McKenzie, H. S. Elimination of bedtime thumbsucking in home settings through contingent reading. *Journal of Applied Behavior Analysis*, 1974, *7*, 33–38.

Kolvin, I. Aversive imagery treatment in adolescents. *Behavior Research and Therapy*, 1967, *5*, 245–248.

Konorski, J. *Integrative activity of the brain*. Chicago: University of Chicago Press, 1967.

Koppenaal, R. J., & Jagoda, E. Proactive inhibition of a maze position habit. *Journal of Experimental Psychology*, 1968, *76*, 664–668.

Koteskey, R. L. A stimulus-sampling model of the partial reinforcement effect. *Psychological Review*, 1972, *79*, 161–171.

Koteskey, R. L., & Hendrix, M. M. Increased resistance to extinction as a function of a double and single alternation and of subsequent continuous reinforcement. *Journal of Experimental Psychology*, 1971, *88*, 423–428.

Kovach, J. K., & Hess, E. H. Imprinting: Effects of painful stimulation upon the following response. *Journal of Comparative and Physiological Psychology*, 1963, *56*, 461–464.

Krechevsky, I. "Hypotheses" in rats. *Psychological Review*, 1932, *39*, 516–532.

Kulhavy, R. W., & Heinen, J. R. K. Mnemonic transformations and verbal coding processes. *Journal of Experimental Psychology*, 1974, *102*, 173–175.

Lacey, J. I., & Smith, R. L. Conditioning and generalization of unconscious anxiety. *Science*, 1954, *120*, 1045–1052.

Lacey, J. I., Smith, R. L., & Green, A. Use of conditioned autonomic responses in the study of anxiety. *Psychosomatic Medicine*, *XVII*, 1955, 208–217.

Lachman, R., & Laughery, K. R. Is a test trial a training trial in free recall learning? *Journal of Experimental Psychology*, 1968, *76*, 40–50.

Landauer, T. K. Two hypotheses concerning the biochemical basis of memory. *Psychological Review*, 1964, *71*, 167–179.

Landauer, T. K. Reinforcement as consolidation. *Psychological Review*, 1969, *76*, 82–96.

Landauer, T. K. Consolidation in human memory: Retrograde amnestic effects of confusable items in paired-associate learning. *Journal of Verbal Learning and Verbal Behavior*, 1974, *13*, 45–53.

Lang, P. J., Geer, J., & Hnatiow, M. Semantic generalization of conditioned autonomic responses. *Journal of Experimental Psychology*, 1963, *65*, 552–558.

Lashley, K. S. In search of the engram. *Society of Experimental Biology Symposium*, 1950, *4*, 454–482.

Lashley, K. S., & Wade, M. The Pavlovian theory of generalization. *Psychological Review*, 1946, *53*, 72–87.

Lawicka, W. The role of stimulus modality in successive discrimination and differentiation learning. *Bulletin of the Polish Academy of Sciences*, 1964, *12*, 35–38.

Lawrence, D. H. The nature of a stimulus: Some relationships between learning and perception. In S. Koch (Ed.), *Psychology: A study of a science*, Vol. 5. New York: McGraw-Hill, 1963.

Lazarus, A. A. The elimination of children's phobias by deconditioning. In H. J. Eysenck (Ed.), *Behaviour therapy and the neuroses*. London: Pergamon, 1960.

Lea, G. Chronometric analysis of the method of loci. *Journal of Experimental Psychology: Human Perception and Performance*, 1975, *104*, 95–104.

Lehr, D. J., Frank, R. C., & Mattison, D. W. Retroactive inhibition, spontaneous recovery, and type of interpolated learning. *Journal of Experimental Psychology*, 1972, *92*, 232–236.

Lenneberg, E. *The biological foundations of language*. New York: Wiley, 1967.

Lesgold, A. M., & Goldman, S. R. Encoding uniqueness and the imagery mnemonic in associative learning. *Journal of Verbal Learning and Verbal Behavior*, 1973, *12*, 193–202.

Lett, B. T. Delayed reward learning: Disproof of the traditional theory. *Learning and Motivation*, 1973, *4*, 237–246.

Levin, J. R., Ghatala, E. S., & Wilder, L. Picture-word differences in discrimination learning: I. Apparent frequency manipulations. *Journal of Experimental Psychology*, 1974, *102*, 691–695.

Lewis, D. J. Acquisition, extinction, and spontaneous recovery as a function of percentage of reinforcement and intertrial intervals. *Journal of Experimental Psychology*, 1956, *51*, 45–53.

Lewis, D. J. Partial reinforcement: A selective review of the literature since 1950. *Psychological Bulletin*, 1960, *57*, 1–28.

Light, L. L., Kimble, G. A., & Pellegrino, J. W. Comments on *Episodic memory: When recognition fails*, by Watkins and Tulving. *Journal of Experimental Psychology*, 1975, *104*, 30–36.

Lindsay, P. H., & Norman, D. A. *Human information processing: An introduction to psychology*. New York: Academic Press, 1972.

Livesey, P. J., & Rankine-Wilson, J. Delayed alternation learning under electrical (blocking) stimulation of the caudate nucleus in the cat. *Journal of Comparative and Physiological Psychology*, 1975, *88*, 342–354.

Lockhard, R. B. Several tests of stimulus-change and preference theory in relation to light-controlled behavior in rats. *Journal of Comparative and Physiological Psychology*, 1966, *62*, 415–426.

Lockhard, R. B. Reflections on the fall of comparative psychology: Is there a message for us all. *American Psychologist*, 1971, *25*, 168–179.

Lockhart, M., & Moore, J. W. Classical differential and operant conditioning in rabbits (*Oryctolagus cuniculus*) with septal lesions. *Journal of Comparative and Physiological Psychology*, 1975, *88*, 147–154.

Loess, H. Proactive inhibition in short-term memory. *Journal of Verbal Learning and Verbal Behavior*, 1964, *3*, 362–368.

Loftus, G. R. A comparison of recognition and recall in a continuous memory task. *Journal of Experimental Psychology*, 1971, *91*, 220–226.

Logan, F. A. A comparison of avoidance and nonavoidance eyelid conditioning. *Journal of Experimental Psychology*, 1951, *42*, 390–393.

Logan, F. A. *Fundamentals of learning and motivation*. Dubuque, Iowa: Wm. C. Brown, 1970.

Lopez, M., Hicks, R. E., & Young, R. K. Retroactive inhibition in a bilingual A–B, A–B′ paradigm. *Journal of Experimental Psychology*, 1974, *103*, 85–90.

Lorenz, K. Der Kumpan in der Umwelt des Vogels. *Journal of Ornithology*, 1935, *83*, 137–213, 289–413.

Lorenz, K. The companion in the bird's world. *Auk*, 1937, *54*, 245–273.

Lovaas, O. I. A behavior therapy approach to the treatment of childhood schizophrenia. In J. P. Hill (Ed.), *Minnesota symposia on child psychology*, Vol. 1. Minneapolis: University of Minnesota Press, 1967.

Lovaas, O. I., Berberich, J. P., Perdoff, B. F., & Schaeffer, B. Acquisition of imitative speech by schizophrenic children. *Science*, 1966, *151*, 705–706.

Lovaas, O. I., Schaeffer, B., & Simmons, J. Experimental studies in childhood schizophrenia: Building social behaviors using electric shock. *Journal of Experimental Studies in Personality*, 1965, *1*, 99–109.

Lundin, R. W. *Personality: A behavioral analysis*. New York: Macmillan, 1974.

Luttges, J., Johnson, T., Buck, C., Holland, J., & McGaugh, J. An examination of "transfer of learning" by nucleic acid. *Science*, 1966, *151*, 834–837.

Lutz, W. J., & Scheirer, C. J. Coding processes for pictures and words. *Journal of Verbal Learning and Verbal Behavior*, 1974, *13*, 316–320.

Lutzker, J. R., & Sherman, J. A. Producing generative sentence usage by imitation and reinforcement procedures. *Journal of Applied Behavior Analysis*, 1974, *7*, 447–460.

MacDonald, A. The effect of adaptation to the unconditioned stimulus upon the formation of conditioned avoidance responses. *Journal of Experimental Psychology*, 1946, *36*, 1–12.

MacKenzie, B. D. Measuring the strength, structure and reliability of free associations. *Psychological Bulletin*, 1972, *77*, 438–445.

Madigan, S. W. Intraserial repetition and coding processes in free recall. *Journal of Verbal Learning and Verbal Behavior*, 1969, *8*, 828–835.

Madsen, C. H., Madsen, C., & Thompson, F. Increasing rural Head Start children's consumption of middle-class meals. *Journal of Applied Behavior Analysis*, 1974, *7*, 257–262.

Maier, N. R. F. *Frustration: The study of behavior without a goal.* New York: McGraw-Hill, 1949.

Maier, N. R. F., Glazer, N. M., & Klee, J. B. Studies of abnormal behavior in the rat: III. The development of behavior fixations through frustration. *Journal of Experimental Psychology*, 1940, *26*, 521–546.

Maier, N. R. F., & Klee, J. B. Studies of abnormal behavior in the rat: XVII. Guidance versus trial and error in the alteration of habits and fixations. *Journal of Psychology*, 1945, *19*, 133–163.

Maier, S. F. Failure to escape traumatic electric shock: Incompatible skeletal–motor responses or learned helplessness? *Learning and Motivation*, 1970, *1*, 157–169.

Maier, S. F., Allaway, T. A., & Gleitman, H. Proactive inhibition in rats after prior partial reversal: A critique of the spontaneous recovery hypothesis. *Psychonomic Science*, 1967, *9*, 63–64.

Maier, S. F., Seligman, M. E., & Solomon, R. L. Pavlovian fear conditioning and learned helplessness. In B. A. Campbell & R. M. Church (Eds.), *Punishment and aversive behavior*. New York: Appleton, 1969.

Mandler, G. Association and organization: Facts, fancies, and theories. In T. R. Dixon & D. L. Horton (Eds.), *Verbal behavior and general behavior theory*. Englewood Cliffs, New Jersey: Prentice-Hall, 1968.

Mandler, G. Organization and recognition. In E. Tulving & W. Donaldson (Eds.), *Organization of memory*. New York: Academic Press, 1972.

Mandler, G., & Dean, P. J. Seriation: Development of serial order in free recall. *Journal of Experimental Psychology*, 1969, *81*, 207–215.

Mandler, G., & Heinemann, S. H. Effect of overlearning of a verbal response on transfer of training. *Journal of Experimental Psychology*, 1956, *57*, 39–46.

Mandler, G., Worden, P. E., & Graesser, A. C. Subjective disorganization: Search for the locus of list organization. *Journal of Verbal Learning and Verbal Behavior*, 1974, *13*, 220–235.

Margolius, G. Stimulus generalization of an instrumental response as a function of the number of reinforced trials. *Journal of Experimental Psychology*, 1955, *49*, 105–111.

Marr, M. J., & Zeiler, M. D. Schedules of response-independent conditioned reinforcement. *Journal of the Experimental Analysis of Behavior*, 1974, *21*, 433–444.

Marshall, G. R. Stimulus characteristics contributing to organization in free recall. *Journal of Verbal Learning and Verbal Behavior*, 1967, *6*, 364–374.

Marshall, L. B., & Smith, O. A. Prefrontal control of conditioned suppression and associated cardiovascular variables in the monkey (*Macaca mulatta*). *Journal of Comparative and Physiological Psychology*, 1975, *88*, 21–35.

Marston, A. R. Effectiveness of external feedback on the role of positive self reinforcement. *Journal of Experimental Psychology*, 1969, *80*, 175–179.

Martin, E. Transfer of verbal paired associates. *Psychological Review*, 1965, *72*, 327–343.

Martin, E. Stimulus pronunciability in aural paired-associate learning. *Journal of Verbal Learning and Verbal Behavior*, 1966, *5*, 18–22.

Martin, E. Stimulus meaningfulness and paired-associate transfer: An encoding variability hypothesis. *Psychological Review*, 1968, *75*, 421–441.

Martin, E. Verbal learning theory and independent retrieval phenomena. *Psychological Review*, 1971, *78*, 314–332.

Martin, E. Stimulus encoding in learning and transfer. In A. W. Melton & E. Martin (Eds.), *Coding processes in human memory*. New York: Wiley, 1972.

Martin, E. Generation–recognition theory and the encoding specificity principle. *Psychological Review*, 1975, *82*, 150–153.

Martin, E. & Greeno, J. G. Independence of associations tested: A reply to D. L. Hintzman. *Psychological Review*, 1972, *79*, 265–267.

Martin, E., & MacKay, S. A test of the list-differentiation hypothesis. *American Journal of Psychology*, 1970, *83*, 311–321.

Martin, E., & Schultz, R. W. Aural paired-associate learning: Pronunciability and the interval between stimulus and response. *Journal of Verbal Learning and Verbal Behavior*, 1963, *1*, 389–391.

Marx, M. H., & Knarr, F. A. Long-term development of reinforcing properties of a stimulus as a function of temporal relationship to food reinforcement. *Journal of Comparative and Physiological Psychology*, 1963, *56*, 546–550.

Massaro, D. W. Preperceptual auditory images. *Journal of Experimental Psychology*, 1970, *85*, 411–417.

Massaro, D. W. Preperceptual images, processing time, and perceptual units in auditory perception. *Psychological Review*, 1972, *79*, 124–145.

Mayhew, A. J. Interlist changes in subjective organization during free-recall learning. *Journal of Experimental Psychology*, 1967, *74*, 425–430.

McCall, R. B. Initial-consequent-change surface in light contingent bar pressing. *Journal of Comparative and Physiological Psychology*, 1966, *62*, 35–42.

McCarthy, S. V. Verbal discrimination learning as a function of associative strength between noun pair members. *Journal of Experimental Psychology*, 1973, *97*, 270–271.

McConnell, J. V., Bryant, R. C., Golub, A. M., & Rosenblatt, F. Nonspecific behavioral effects of substances from mammalian brain. *Science*, 1972, *178*, 521–523.

McCormack, P. D., & Swenson, A. L. Recognition memory for common and rare words. *Journal of Experimental Psychology*, 1972, *95*, 72–77.

McCrystal, T. J. List differentiation as a function of time and test order. *Journal of Experimental Psychology*, 1970, *83*, 220–223.

McDougall, R. Recognition and recall. *Journal of Philosophical Psychology and Scientific Methods*, 1904, *1*, 229–233.

McGaugh, J. L. Time-dependent processes in memory storage. *Science*, 1966, *153*, 1351–1358.

McGaugh, J. L., & Dawson, R. G. Modification of memory storage processes. In W. K. Honig & P. H. R. James. *Animal memory*. New York: Academic Press, 1971.

McGeoch, G. O. Whole-part problem. *Psychological Bulletin*, 1931, *28*, 713–739.

McGeoch, J. A., & Irion, A. L. *The psychology of human learning*. New York: Longmans, Green, 1952.

McGlaughlin, A., & Dale, H. C. A. Stimulus similarity and transfer in long-term paired-associate learning. *British Journal of Psychology*, 1971, *62*, 37–40.

McGovern, J. B. Extinction of associations in four transfer paradigms. *Psychological Monographs*, 1964, *78*, 16 (Whole No. 593).

McGuire, W. J. A multiprocess model for paired-associate learning. *Journal of Experimental Psychology*, 1961, *62*, 335–347.

Melton, A. W. The end-spurt in memorization curves as an artifact of the averaging of individual curves. *Psychological Monographs*, 1936, *47*, 119–134.

Melton, A. W. Implications of short-term for a general theory of memory. *Journal of Verbal Learning and Verbal Behavior*, 1963, *2*, 1–21.

Melton, A. W. The situation with respect to the spacing of repetitions and memory. *Journal of Verbal Learning and Verbal Behavior*, 1970, *9*, 596–606.

Melton, A. W., & Irwin, J. M. The influence of degree of interpolated learning on retroactive inhibition and the overt transfer of specific responses. *American Journal of Psychology*, 1940, *53*, 173–203.

Melton, A. W., & Martin, E. (Eds.), *Coding processes in human memory*. New York: Wiley, 1972.

Melvin, K. B., Cloar, F. T., & Massingill, L. S. Imprinting of Bobwhite quail to a hawk. *Psychological Record*, 1967, *17*, 235–238.

Merikle, P. M. Paired-associate transfer as a function of stimulus and response meaningfulness. *Psychological Reports*, 1968, *22*, 131–138.

Merryman, C. T., & Merryman, S. S. Stimulus encoding in the A–B', Ax–B and the A–B'$_r$, Ax–B paradigms. *Journal of Verbal Learning and Verbal Behavior*, 1971, *10*, 681–685.

Miles, R. C. The relative effectiveness of secondary reinforcers throughout deprivation and habit-strength parameters. *Journal of Comparative and Physiological Psychology*, 1956, *49*, 126–130.

Miller, G. A. The magical number seven plus or minus two: Some limits on our capacity for processing information. *Psychological Review*, 1956, *63*, 81–97.

Miller, G. A., Galanter, E., & Pribram, K. H. *Plans and the structure of behavior*. New York: Holt, 1960.

Miller, L. Compounding of discriminative stimuli correlated with chained and multiple schedules. *Journal of the Experimental Analysis of Behavior*, 1975, *23*, 95–102.

Miller, N. E. Learnable drives and rewards. In S. S. Stevens (Ed.), *Handbook of experimental psychology*. New York: Wiley, 1951.

Miller, N. E. Liberalization of basic S–R concepts: Extensions to conflict behavior, motivation, and social learning. In S. Koch (Ed.), *Psychology: A study of a science*, Vol. II. New York: McGraw-Hill, 1959.

Miller, N. E. Interactions between learned and physical factors in mental illness. *Seminars in Psychiatry*, 1972, *4*, 239–254.

Miller, N. E. Interactions between learned and physical factors in mental illness. In D. Shapiro, T. X. Barber, L. V. DiCara, J. Kamiya, N. E. Miller, & J. Stoyva (Eds.), *Biofeedback and self-control: 1972*. Chicago: Aldine, 1973.

Miller, N. E., & Banuazizi, A. Instrumental learning by curarized rats of a specific visceral response, intestinal or cardiac. *Journal of Comparative and Physiological Psychology*, 1968, *65*, 1–17.

Miller, R. R., Ott, C. A., Berk, A. M., & Springer, A. D. Appetitive memory restoration after electroconvulsive shock in the rat. *Journal of Comparative and Physiological Psychology*, 1974, *87*, 717–723.

Miller, R. R., & Springer, A. D. Amnesia, consolidation, and retrieval. *Psychological Review*, 1973, *80*, 69–79.

Miller, R. R., & Springer, A. D. Implications of recovery from experimental amnesia. *Psychological Review*, 1974, *81*, 470–473.

Millward, R. B. Theoretical and experimental approaches to human learning. In J. W. Kling & L. A. Riggs (Eds.), *Woodworth and Schlosberg's experimental psychology*. New York: Holt, 1971.

Milner, B. R. Amnesia following operation on temporal lobes. In C. W. N. Whitty & O. L. Zangwill (Eds.), *Amnesia*. London: Butterworths, 1966.

Milner, B. R. Visual recognition and recall after right temporal-lobe excision in man. *Neuropsychologia*, 1968, *6*, 191–209.

Milner, P. *Physiological psychology*. New York: Holt, 1970.

Mishkin, M., Vest, B., Waxler, M., & Rosvold, H. E. A re-examination of the effects of frontal lesions on object alternation. *Neuropsychologia*, 1969, *7*, 357–363.

Mitchell, D., Kirschbaum, E. H., & Perry, R. L. Effects of nephobia and habituation on the poison-induced avoidance of exteroceptive stimuli in the rat. *Journal of Experimental Psychology: Animal Behavior Processes*, 1975, *104*, 47–55.

Moltz, H. Imprinting: Empirical basis and theoretical significance. *Psychological Bulletin*, 1960, *57*, 291–314.

Moltz, H. Imprinting: An epigenetic approach. *Psychological Review*, 1963, *70*, 123–138.

Mondani, M. S., & Battig, W. F. Imaginal and verbal mnemonics as related to paired-associate learning and directionality of associations. *Journal of Verbal Learning and Verbal Behavior*, 1973, *12*, 401–408.

Montgomery, K. C. The relations between fear induced by novel stimuli and exploratory behavior. *Journal of Comparative and Physiological Psychology*, 1955, *48*, 254–260.

Mook, D. G. Oral and postingestional determinants of the intake of various solutions in rats with esophogeal fistulas. *Journal of Comparative and Physiological Psychology*, 1963, *56*, 645–659.

Moore, J. W. Stimulus control: Studies of auditory generalization in rabbits. In A. H. Black & W. F. Prokasy (Eds.), *Classical conditioning II: Current theory and research*. New York: Appleton, 1972.

Morosko, T. E., & Baer, P. E. Avoidance conditioning of alcoholics. In R. Ulrich, T. Stachnik, & J. Mabry (Eds.), *Control of human behavior*, Vol. 2. Glenview, Illinois: Scott, Foresman, 1970.

Mostofsky, D. *Stimulus generalization*. Stanford: Stanford University Press, 1965.

Mowrer, O. H. *Learning theory and behavior*. New York: Wiley, 1960.

Mowrer, O. H., & Jones, H. M. Habit strength as a function of the pattern of reinforcement. *Journal of Experimental Psychology*, 1945, *35*, 293–311.

Mowrer, O. H., & Lamoreaux, R. R. Avoidance conditioning and signal duration—a study of secondary motivation and reward. *Psychological Monographs*, 1942, *54*, No. 247.

Mowrer, O. H., & Lamoreaux, R. R. Fear as an intervening variable in avoidance conditioning. *Journal of Comparative Psychology*, 1946, *39*, 29–50.

Mueller, J. H., & Flanagan, J. L. Total time in verbal-discrimination learning. *American Journal of Psychology*, 1972, *85*, 69–79.

Mueller, J. H., Gautt, P., & Evans, J. H. Stimulus encoding in A–Br transfer. *Journal of Experimental Psychology*, 1974, *103*, 54–61.

Mueller, J. H., Kausler, D. H., Yadrick, R. M., & Pavur, E. J. Encoding strategies in double-function verbal discrimination learning. *Journal of Experimental Psychology: Human Learning and Memory*, 1975, *104*, 55–59.

Munn, N. L. *Handbook of psychological research on the rat*. Boston: Houghton Mifflin, 1950.

Murdock, B. B., Jr. The immediate retention of unrelated words. *Journal of Experimental Psychology*, 1960, *60*, 222–234.

Murdock, B. B., Jr. The retention of individual items. *Journal of Experimental Psychology*, 1961, *62*, 618–625.

Murdock, B. B., Jr. The serial position effect of free recall. *Journal of Experimental Psychology*, 1962, *64*, 482–488.

Murdock, B. B., Jr. Short-term memory. In G. H. Bower (Ed.), *The psychology of learning and motivation: Advances in research and therapy*, Vol. 5. New York: Academic Press, 1972.

Murdock, B. B. *Human memory: Theory and data*. New York: Wiley, 1974.

Murdock, B. B., & Wells, J. E. Parameter invariance in short-term associative memory. *Journal of Experimental Psychology*, 1974, *103*, 475–488.

Myers, G. C. A. A comparative study of recognition and recall. *Psychological Review*, 1914, *21*, 442–456.

Nachman, M. Learned taste and temperature aversions due to lithium chloride sickness after temporal delays. *Journal of Comparative and Physiological Psychology*, 1970, *73*, 22–30.

Neisser, U. *Cognitive psychology*. New York: Appleton, 1967.

Nelson, D. L., Rowe, F. A., Engel, J. E., Wheeler, J., & Garland, R. M. Backward relative to forward recall as a function of stimulus meaningfulness and formal interstimulus similarity. *Journal of Experimental Psychology*, 1970, *83*, 323–328.

Nelson, T. O., & Rothbart, R. Acoustic savings for items forgotten from long-term memory. *Journal of Experimental Psychology*, 1972, *93*, 357–360.

Nevin, J. A. On the form of the relation between response rates in a multiple schedule. *Journal of the Experimental Analysis of Behavior*, 1974, *21*, 237–248.   (a)

Nevin, J. A. Response strength in multiple schedules. *Journal of the Experimental Analysis of Behavior*, 1974, *21*, 389–408.   (b)

Newman, S. E., & Campbell, R. T. A–B and B–A performance as functions of test instructions and reading order. *Journal of Experimental Psychology*, 1971, *88*, 57–59.

Newman, S. E., Suggs, R. E., & Averitt, C. H. Use of Rule 1 and Rule 2 in verbal discrimination training. *Journal of Experimental Psychology*, 1974, *102*, 531–533.

Newton, J. M., & Wickens, D. D. Retroactive inhibition as a function of the temporal position of interpolated learning. *Journal of Experimental Psychology*, 1956, *51*, 149–154.

Nilsson, L. Locus of the modality effect in free recall: A reply to Watkins. *Journal of Experimental Psychology: Human Learning and Memory*, 1975, *104*, 13–17.

Nodine, C. F. Temporal variables in paired-associate learning: The law of contiguity revisited. *Psychological Review*, 1969, *76*, 351–362.

Norman, D. A. (Ed.), *Models of human memory*. New York: Academic Press, 1970.

Norman, D. A., & Wickelgren, W. A. Strength theory of decision rules and latency in short-term memory. *Journal of Mathematical Psychology*, 1969, *6*, 192–208.

Nowaczyk, R. H., Shaughnessy, J. J., & Zimmerman, J. Proactive interference in short-term retention and the measurement of degree of learning: A new technique. *Journal of Experimental Psychology*, 1974, *103*, 45–53.

Olds, J. Pleasure centers in the brain. *Scientific American*, 1956, *195*, 105–116.

Olds, J., & Milner, P. Positive reinforcement produced by electrical stimulation of septal area and other regions of rat brain. *Journal of Comparative and Physiological Psychology*, 1954, *47*, 419–427.

Olds, J., & Olds, M. Drives, rewards, and the brain. In F. Barron, W. C. Dement, W. Edwards, H. Lindman, L. D. Phillips, J. Olds, & M. Olds (Eds.), *New directions in psychology II*. New York: Holt, 1965.

O'Leary, K. D., & Drabman, R. Token reinforcement programs in the classroom: A review. *Psychological Bulletin*, 1971, *75*, 379–398.

Orlando, R., & Bijou, S. W. Single and multiple schedules of reinforcement in developmentally retarded children. *Journal of the Experimental Analysis of Behavior*, 1960, *3*, 339–348.

Osgood, C. E. Meaningful similarity and interference in learning. *Journal of Experimental Psychology*, 1946, *36*, 277–301.

Osgood, C. E. The similarity paradox in human learning: A resolution. *Psychological Review*, 1949, *56*, 132–143.

Osgood, C. E. *Method and theory in experimental psychology*. London and New York: Oxford University Press, 1953.

Pagel, J. C. A markov analysis of transfer in paired-associate learning with high intralist similarity. *Journal of Verbal Learning and Verbal Behavior*, 1973, *12*, 456–470.

Paivio, A. *Imagery and verbal processes*. New York: Holt, 1971.

Paivio, A., & Foth, D. Imaginal and verbal mediators and noun concreteness in paired-associate learning: The elusive interaction. *Journal of Verbal Learning and Verbal Behavior*, 1970, *9*, 384–390.

Palermo, D. S., & Jenkins, J. J. *Word association norms: Grade school through college.* Minneapolis: University of Minnesota Press, 1964.

Palermo, D. S., & Ullrich, J. R. Verbal discrimination as a function of associative strength between the word-pair members. *Journal of Verbal Learning and Verbal Behavior*, 1968, *7*, 945–952.

Pasko, S. J., & Zechmeister, E. B. Temporal separation in verbal discrimination transfer. *Journal of Experimental Psychology*, 1974, *102*, 525–528.

Patterson, K. E., Meltzer, R. H., & Mandler, G. Inter-response times in categorized free recall. *Journal of Verbal Learning and Verbal Behavior*, 1971, *10*, 417–426.

Pavlov, I. P. *Conditioned reflexes* (translated by G. V. Anrep). London and New York: Oxford University Press, 1927.

Pavlov, I. P. *Lectures on conditioned reflexes.* New York: International Publishers, 1928.

Pellegrino, J. W. A general measure of organization in free recall for variable unit size and internal sequential consistency. *Behavior Research Methods and Instrumentation*, 1971, *3*, 241–246.

Pellegrino, J. W., Siegel, A. W., & Dhawan, M. Short-term retention of pictures and words: Evidence for dual coding systems. *Journal of Experimental Psychology: Human Learning and Memory*, 1975, *104*, 95–102.

Perin, C. T. A quantitative investigation of the delay-of-reinforcement gradient. *Journal of Experimental Psychology*, 1943, *32*, 37–51.

Perkins, C. C. The relation of secondary reward to gradients of reinforcement. *Journal of Experimental Psychology*, 1947, *37*, 377–392.

Peters, D. P., & McHose, J. H. Effects of varied preshift reward magnitude on successive negative contrast effects in rats. *Journal of Comparative and Physiological Psychology*, 1974, *86*, 85–95.

Peterson, L. R. Immediate memory: Data and theory. In C. N. Cofer & B. S. Musgrave (Eds.), *Verbal behavior and learning.* New York: McGraw-Hill, 1963.

Peterson, L. R. *Learning.* Glenview, Illinois: Scott, Foresman, 1975.

Peterson, L. R., & Peterson, M. J. Short-term retention of individual verbal items. *Journal of Experimental Psychology*, 1959, *58*, 193–198.

Peterson, L. R., Wampler, R., Kirkpatrick, M., & Saltzman, D. Effect of spacing presentations on retention of a paired-associate over short intervals. *Journal of Experimental Psychology*, 1963, *66*, 206–209.

Peterson, N. Effect of monochromatic rearing on the control of responding by wavelength. *Science*, 1962, *136*, 774–775.

Petrusic, W. M., & Dillon, R. F. Proactive interference in short-term recognition and recall. *Journal of Experimental Psychology*, 1972, *95*, 412–418.

Pfaffmann, C. Taste preference and reinforcement. In J. T. Tapp (Ed.), *Reinforcement and behavior.* New York: Academic Press, 1969.

Phillips, E. L. Achievement place: Token reinforcement procedures in a home-style rehabilitation setting for "pre-delinquent" boys. *Journal of Applied Behavior Analysis*, 1968, *1*, 213–223.

Phillips, J. L., Shiffrin, R. M., & Atkinson, R. C. The effects of list length on short-term memory. *Journal of Verbal Learning and Verbal Behavior*, 1967, *6*, 303–311.

Pierce, C. H., & Risley, T. R. Recreation as a reinforcer: Increasing membership and decreasing disruptions in an urban recreation center. *Journal of Applied Behavior Analysis*, 1974, *7*, 403–411.

Pitz, G. F., & Ross, R. B. Imprinting as a function of arousal. *Journal of Comparative and Physiological Psychology*, 1961, *54*, 602–604.

Pommer, D. A., & Streedbeck, D. Motivating staff performance in an operant learning program for children. *Journal of Applied Behavior Analysis,* 1974, *7,* 217–221.

Posner, M. I., & Konick, A. On the role of interference in short-term retention. *Journal of Experimental Psychology,* 1966, *72,* 221–231.

Posner, M. I., & Rossman, E. Effect of size and location of informational transforms upon short-term retention. *Journal of Experimental Psychology,* 1965, *70,* 496–505.

Postman, L. Repetition and paired-associate learning. *American Journal of Psychology,* 1962, *75,* 372–389.   (a)

Postman, L. Transfer of training as a function of experimental paradigm and degree of first-list learning. *Journal of Verbal Learning and Verbal Behavior,* 1962, *1,* 109–118.   (b)

Postman, L. Experimental analysis of learning to learn. In G. H. Bower & J. T. Spence (Eds.), *The psychology of learning and motivation,* Vol. 3. New York: Academic Press, 1969.

Postman, L. Effects of word frequency on acquisition and retention under conditions of free-recall learning. *Quarterly Journal of Experimental Psychology,* 1970, *22,* 185–195.

Postman, L. Transfer, interference and forgetting. In J. W. Kling & L. A. Riggs (Eds.), *Woodworth and Schlosberg's experimental psychology.* New York: Holt, 1971.

Postman, L. A pragmatic view of organization theory. In E. Tulving & W. Donaldson (Eds.), *Organization of memory.* New York: Academic Press, 1972.

Postman, L., Burns, S., & Hasher, L. Studies of learning to learn: X. Nonspecific transfer effects in free-recall learning. *Journal of Verbal Learning and Verbal Behavior,* 1970, *9,* 707–715.

Postman, L., & Goggin, J. Whole versus part learning of paired-associate lists. *Journal of Experimental Psychology,* 1966, *71,* 867–877.

Postman, L., & Greenbloom, R. Conditions of cue selection in the acquisition of paired-associate lists. *Journal of Experimental Psychology,* 1967, *73,* 91–100.

Postman, L., Keppel, G., & Stark, K. Unlearning as a function of the relationship between successive response classes. *Journal of Experimental Psychology,* 1965, *69,* 111–118.

Postman, L., & Riley, D. Degree of learning and interserial interference in retention. *University of California Publications in Psychology,* 1959, *8,* 271–396.

Postman, L., & Schwartz, M. Studies of learning to learn: I. Transfer as a function of method of practice and class of verbal materials. *Journal of Verbal Learning and Verbal Behavior,* 1964, *3,* 37–49.

Postman, L., & Stark, K. Role of response availability in transfer and interference. *Journal of Experimental Psychology,* 1969, *79,* 168–177.

Postman, L., Stark, K., & Burns, S. Sources of proactive inhibition on unpaced tests of retention. *American Journal of Psychology,* 1974, *87,* 33–56.

Postman, L., Stark, K., & Fraser, J. Temporal changes in interference. *Journal of Verbal Learning and Verbal Behavior,* 1968, *7,* 672–694.

Postman, L., & Underwood, B. J. Critical issues in interference theory. *Memory and Cognition,* 1973, *1,* 19–40.

Premack, D. Toward empirical behavioral laws: I. Positive reinforcement. *Psychological Review,* 1959, *66,* 219–233.

Premack, D. Reinforcement theory. In D. Levine (Ed.), *Nebraska symposium on motivation.* Lincoln, Nebraska: University of Nebraska Press, 1965.

Premack, D. Language in chimpanzees? *Science,* 1971, *172,* 808–822.

Prokasy, W. F., Hall, J. F., & Fawcett, J. T. Adaptation, sensitization, forward and backward conditioning, and pseudo-conditioning of the GSR. *Psychological Reports,* 1962, *10,* 103–106.

Puff, C. R. Role of clustering in free recall. *Journal of Experimental Psychology*, 1970, *86*, 384–386.

Quartermain, D., & Botwinick, C. Y. Role of the biogenic amines in the reversal of cycloheximide-induced amnesia. *Journal of Comparative and Physiological Psychology*, 1975, *88*, 386–401.

Rachlin, H. C., & Hineline, P. N. Training and maintenance of key pecking in the pigeon by negative reinforcement. *Science*, 1967, *157*, 954–955.

Rajecki, D. W. Imprinting in precocial birds: Interpretation, evidence, and evaluation. *Psychological Review*, 1973, *79*, 48–58.

Ralph, T. L., & Balagura, S. Effect of intracranial electrical stimulation on the primary learned aversion to LiCl and the generalized aversion to NaCl. *Journal of Comparative and Physiological Psychology*, 1974, *86*, 664–669.

Ramsay, A. O. Familial recognition in domestic birds. *Auk*, 1951, *68*, 1–16.

Raser, G. A. Recording of semantic and acoustic information in short-term memory. *Journal of Verbal Learning and Verbal Behavior*, 1969, *8*, 567–574.

Raymond, M. S. Case of fetishism treated by aversion therapy. *British Medical Journal*, 1956, *2*, 854–857.

Razran, G. Stimulus generalization of conditioned responses. *Psychological Bulletin*, 1949, *46*, 337–365.

Redd, W. H., & Birnbrauer, J. S. Adults as discriminative stimuli for different reinforcement contingencies with retarded children. In R. Ulrich, T. Stachnik, & J. Mabry (Eds.), *Control of behavior*. Glenview, Illinois: Scott, Foresman, 1970.

Redford, M. E. & Perkins, C. C. The role of autopecking in behavioral contrast. *Journal of the Experimental Analysis of Behavior*, 1974, *21*, 145–150.

Reese, H. W. *The perception of stimulus relations*. New York: Academic Press, 1968.

Reitman, J. S. Without surreptitious rehearsal, information in short-term memory decays. *Journal of Verbal Learning and Verbal Behavior*, 1974, *13*, 365–377.

Rekers, G. A., & Lovaas, O. I. Behavioral treatment of deviant sex-role behaviors in a male child. *Journal of Applied Behavior Analysis*, 1974, *7*, 173–190.

Rescorla, R. A., & Solomon, R. L. Two-process learning theory: Relationships between Pavlovian conditioning and instrumental learning. *Psychological Review*, 1967, *74*, 151–182.

Rescorla, R. A., & Wagner, A. R. A theory of Pavlovian conditioning: Variations in the effectiveness of reinforcement and nonreinforcement. In A. Black & W. F. Prokasy (Eds.), *Classical conditioning: II. Current research and theory*. New York: Appleton, 1972.

Revusky, S. H. Aversion to sucrose produced by contingent x-irradiation–temporal and dosage parameters. *Journal of Comparative and Physiological Psychology*, 1968, *65*, 17–22.

Revusky, S. H. The role of interference in association over a delay. In W. K. Honig & H. James (Eds.), *Animal memory*. New York: Academic Press, 1971.

Revusky, S. H., & Garcia, J. Learned associations over long delays. In G. H. Bower (Ed.), *The psychology of learning and motivation: Advances in theory and research*, Vol. 4. New York: Academic Press, 1970.

Reynolds, G. S. Behavioral contrast. *Journal of the Experimental Analysis of Behavior*, 1961, 4, 57–61.   (a)

Reynolds, G. S. Relativity of response rate and reinforcement in a multiple schedule. *Journal of the Experimental Analysis of Behavior*, 1961, 4, 179–184.   (b)

Reynolds, W. F., Pavlik, W. B., & Goldstein, E. Secondary reinforcement effects as a function of reward magnitude training methods. *Psychological Reports*, 1964, *15*, 7–10.

Richards, R. W. Inhibitory stimulus control and the magnitude of delayed reinforcement. *Journal of the Experimental Analysis of Behavior*, 1974, *21*, 501–509.

Richardson, J. Cue effectiveness and abstraction in paired-associate learning. *Psychological Bulletin*, 1971, *75*, 73–91.

Richardson, J. Encoding and stimulus selection in paired-associate verbal learning. In A. W. Melton & E. Martin (Eds.), *Coding processes in human memory*. New York: Wiley, 1972.

Richardson, J., & Brown, B. L. Mediated transfer in paired-associate learning as a function of presentation rate and stimulus meaningfulness. *Journal of Experimental Psychology*, 1966, *72*, 820–828.

Richardson, J., & Chisholm, D. C. Transfer of cue selection based on letter position. *Journal of Experimental Psychology*, 1969, *80*, 299–303.

Riley, D. A. *Discrimination learning*. Boston: Allyn and Bacon, 1968.

Rilling, M., & Caplan, H. J. Frequency of reinforcement as a determinant of extinction-induced aggression during errorless discrimination learning. *Journal of the Experimental Analysis of Behavior*, 1975, *23*, 121–129.

Robbins, D., Bray, J. F., Irvin, J. R., & Wise, P. S. Memorial strategy and imagery: An interaction between instructions and rated imagery. *Journal of Experimental Psychology*, 1974, *102*, 706–709.

Robinson, E. S. *Association theory to-day*. New York: Hafner, 1964.

Rock, I. The role of repetition in associative learning. *American Journal of Psychology*, 1957, *70*, 186–193.

Rosenfeld, H. M., & Baer, D. M. Unnoticed verbal conditioning of an aware experimenter by a more aware subject: The double-agent effect. *Psychological Review*, 1969, *76*, 425–432.

Ross, L. E., & Ross, S. M. Conditioned stimulus parameters and the interstimulus interval: The processing of CS information in differential conditioning. In A. H. Black and W. F. Prokasy (Eds.), *Classical conditioning II: Current theory and research*. New York: Appleton, 1972.

Routtenberg, A. The two arousal hypothesis: Reticular formation and limbic system. *Psychological Review*, 1968, *75*, 51–80.

Rowe, E. Discrimination learning of pictures and words: A replication of picture superiority. *Journal of Experimental Child Psychology*, 1972, *14*, 303–312.

Rozin, P. Specific aversions as a component in specific hungers. *Journal of Comparative and Physiological Psychology*, 1967, *63*, 421–428.

Rozin, P. Specific aversions and neophobia resulting from vitamin deficiency or poisoning in half wild and domestic rats. *Journal of Comparative and Physiological Psychology*, 1968, *66*, 82–88.

Rozin, P. Central or peripheral mediation of learning with long CS-UCS intervals in the feeding system. *Journal of Comparative and Physiological Psychology*, 1969, *67*, 421–429.

Rozin, P., & Kalat, J. W. Specific hungers and poison avoidance as adaptive specializations of learning. *Psychological Review*, 1971, *78*, 459–486.

Rudy, J. W. Stimulus selection in animal conditioning and paired-associate learning: Variations in the associative process. *Journal of Verbal Learning and Verbal Behavior*, 1974, *13*, 282–296.

Rundus, D. Analysis of rehearsal processes in free recall. *Journal of Experimental Psychology*, 1971, *89*, 63–77.

Rundus, D. Negative effects of using list items as recall cues. *Journal of Verbal Learning and Verbal Behavior*, 1973, *12*, 43–50.

Russell, I. S. Animal learning and memory. In D. Richter (Ed.), *Aspects of learning and memory*. New York: Basic Books, 1966.

Russell, W. A., & Jenkins, J. J. The complete Minnesota norms for responses to 100 words from the Kent-Rosanoff Word Association Test. Technical Report No. 11, Contract No. 8, ONR-66216 (1954).

Saltz, E. Spontaneous recovery of letter-sequence habits. *Journal of Experimental Psychology*, 1965, *69*, 304–307.

Saltzman, I. J. Maze learning in the absence of primary reinforcement: A study of secondary reinforcement. *Journal of Comparative and Physiological Psychology*, 1949, *42*, 161–173.

Salzen, E. A. Imprinting and environmental learning. In L. R. Aronson, E. Tobach, D. S. Lehrman, & J. S. Rosenblatt (Eds.), *Development and evolution of behavior*. San Francisco: W. H. Freeman, 1970.

Salzen, E. A., & Sluckin, W. The incidence of the following response and the duration of responsiveness in domestic fowl. *Animal Behavior*, 1959, 7, 172–179.

Schaefer, H. H., & Martin, P. L. Behavioral therapy for "apathy" of hospitalized schizophrenics. *Psychological Reports*, 1966, *19*, 1147–1158.

Schmitt, D. R. Effects of reinforcement rate and reinforcer magnitude on choice behavior in humans. *Journal of the Experimental Analysis of Behavior*, 1974, *21*, 409–419.

Schoenfeld, W. N., Antonitis, J. J., & Bersh, P. J. A preliminary study of training conditions necessary for secondary reinforcement. *Journal of Experimental Psychology*, 1950, *40*, 40–45.

Schwartz, M. Verbal discrimination as a concept-attainment task using the evaluative dimension. *Journal of Experimental Psychology*, 1974, *102*, 415–422.

Schwarz, M. L., & Hawkins, R. P. Application of delayed conditioning procedures to the behavior problems of an elementary school child. In R. Ulrich, T. Stachnik, & J. Mabry (Eds.), *Control of behavior*. Glenview, Illinois: Scott, Foresman, 1970.

Seagoe, M. V. Qualitative wholes: A re-evaluation of the whole–part problem. *Journal of Educational Psychology*, 1936, *27*, 537–545.

Segal, E. M. Hierarchical structure in free recall. *Journal of Experimental Psychology*, 1969, *80*, 59–63.

Segal, M. A., & Mandler, G. Directionality and organizational processes in paired-associate learning. *Journal of Experimental Psychology*, 1967, *74*, 305–312.

Seligman, M. E. P. CS redundancy and secondary punishment. *Journal of Experimental Psychology*, 1966, *4*, 546–550.

Seligman, M. E. P. On the generality of the laws of learning. *Psychological Review*, 1970, *77*, 406–418.

Seward, J. P. An experimental study of Guthrie's theory of reinforcement. *Journal of Experimental Psychology*, 1942, *30*, 247–256.

Shallice, T., & Warrington, E. K. Independent functioning of verbal memory stores: A neuro-psychological study. *Quarterly Journal of Experimental Psychology*, 1970, *22*, 261–273.

Shanmugam, A. V., & Miron, M. S. Semantic effects in mediated transfer. *Journal of Verbal Learning and Verbal Behavior*, 1966, *5*, 361–368.

Shannon, C. E. A mathematical theory of communication. *Bell System Technical Journal*, 1948, *27*, 379–423.

Shapiro, D., Barber, T. X., DiCara, L. V., Kamiya, J., Miller, N. E., & Stoyva, J. (Eds.), *Biofeedback and self-control 1972*. Chicago: Aldine, 1973.

Shapiro, D., & Schwartz, G. E. Biofeedback and visceral learning: Clinical applications. *Seminars in Psychiatry*, 1972, *4*, 171–184.

Sheffield, F. D. A drive induction theory of reinforcement. In R. N. Haber (Ed.), *Current research in motivation*. New York: Holt, 1966.

Shepard, R. N. Recognition memory for words, sentences, and pictures. *Journal of Verbal Learning and Verbal Behavior*, 1967, *6*, 156–163.

Sherman, J. A., & Baer, D. M. Appraisal of operant therapy techniques with children and adults. In C. M. Franks (Ed.), *Behavior therapy: Appraisal and Status.* New York: McGraw-Hill, 1969.

Sherman, R. A. *Behavior modification: Theory and practice.* Monterey, California: Brooks/Cole, 1973.

Shiffrin, R. M. Memory search. In D. A. Norman (Ed.), *Models of human memory.* New York: Academic Press, 1970.   (a)

Shiffrin, R. M. Forgetting: Trace erosion or retrieval failure? *Science,* 1970, *168,* 1601–1603.   (b)

Shuell, T. J. Clustering and organization in free recall. *Psychological Bulletin,* 1969, *72,* 353–374.

Shulman, H. G. Similarity effects in short-term memory. *Psychological Bulletin,* 1971, *75,* 399–415.

Shulman, H. G. Semantic confusion errors in short-term memory. *Journal of Verbal Learning and Verbal Behavior,* 1972, *11,* 221–227.

Shulman, H. G., & Martin, E. Effects of response-set similarity on unlearning and spontaneous recovery. *Journal of Experimental Psychology,* 1970, *86,* 230–235.

Sidman, M. A note on functional relations obtained from group data. *Psychological Bulletin,* 1952, *49,* 263–269.

Silverstein, A. Unlearning, spontaneous recovery, and the partial reinforcement effect in paired-associate learning. *Journal of Experimental Psychology,* 1967, *73,* 15–21.

Sisqueland, E. R. Basic learning processes: Instrumental conditioning in infants. In H. W. Reese & L. P. Lipsitt (Eds.), *Experimental child psychology: The scientific study of child behavior and development.* New York: Academic Press, 1970.

Skinner, B. F. *The behavior of organisms; an experimental analysis.* New York: Appleton, 1938.

Skinner, B. F. *Science and human behavior.* New York: Macmillan, 1953.

Slamecka, N. J. Retroactive inhibition of connected discourse as a function of practice level. *Journal of Experimental Psychology,* 1960, *59,* 104–108.

Slamecka, N. J. Proactive inhibition of connected discourse. *Journal of Experimental Psychology,* 1961, *62,* 295–301.

Slamecka, N. J. An inquiry into the doctrine of remote associations. *Psychological Review,* 1964, *71,* 61–76.

Slamecka, N. J. In defense of a new approach to old phenomena. *Psychological Review,* 1965, *72,* 242–246.

Slamecka, N. J. Supplementary report: A search for spontaneous recovery of verbal associations. *Journal of Verbal Learning and Verbal Behavior,* 1966, *5,* 205–207.

Slamecka, N. J. A temporal interpretation of some recall phenomena. *Psychological Review,* 1969, *76,* 492–503.

Sluckin, W. *Imprinting and early learning.* Chicago: Aldine, 1965.

Sluckin, W., & Salzen, E. A. Imprinting and perceptual learning. *Quarterly Journal of Experimental Psychology,* 1961, *13,* 65–77.

Smith, E. E., Barresi, J., & Gross, A. E. Imaginal versus verbal coding and the primary–secondary memory distinction. *Journal of Verbal Learning and Verbal Behavior,* 1971, *10,* 597–603.

Smith, D. F., & Balagura, S. The role of oropharyngeal factors in LiCl aversion. *Journal of Comparative and Physiological Psychology,* 1969, *69,* 308–310.

Smith, F. V., & Hoyes, P. A. Properties of the visual stimuli for the approach response in the domestic chick. *Animal Behavior,* 1961, *9,* 159–166.

Smith, J. C., & Roll, D. L. Trace conditioning with x-rays as the aversive stimulus. *Psychonomic Science,* 1967, *9,* 11–12.

Snodgrass, J. G., Wasser, B., & Finkelstein, M. On the fate of visual and verbal memory codes for pictures and words: Evidence for a dual coding mechanism in recognition memory. *Journal of Verbal Learning and Verbal Behavior*, 1974, *13*, 27–37.

Solomon, R. L. Punishment. *American Psychologist*, 1964, *19*, 239–253.

Solomon, R. L., & Corbit, J. P. An opponent-process theory of motivation. *Psychological Review*, 1974, *81*, 119–145.

Solomon, R. L., & Wynne, L. C. Traumatic avoidance learning: Acquisition in normal dogs. *Psychological Monographs*, 1953, *67*, (Whole No. 354).

Sonderegger, T. B., & Rose, G. H. Approach gradients obtained through intracranial stimulation of the medial forebrain bundle in rats. *Journal of Comparative and Physiological Psychology*, 1970, *71*, 52–58.

Spalding, D. A. Instinct, with original observations on young animals. *MacMillan's Magazine*, 1873, *27*, 283–293. [Reprinted; *British Journal of Animal Behavior*, 1954, *2*, 2–11.]

Spear, N. E. Forgetting as retrieval failure. In W. K. Honig. & P. H. R. James (Eds.), *Animal memory*. New York: Academic Press, 1971.

Spear, N. E. Retrieval of memory in animals. *Psychological Review*, 1973, *80*, 163–194.

Spear, N. E., Ekstrand, B. R., & Underwood, B. J. Association by contiguity. *Journal of Experimental Psychology*, 1964, *67*, 151–161.

Speidel, G. E. Motivating effect of contingent self-reward. *Journal of Experimental Psychology*, 1974, *102*, 528–530.

Spelt, D. K. The conditioning of the human fetus *in utero*. *Journal of Experimental Psychology*, 1948, *38*, 338–346.

Spence, K. W. The nature of discrimination learning in animals. *Psychological Review*, 1936, *43*, 427–449.

Spence, K. W. The differential response in animals to stimuli varying within a single dimension. *Psychological Review*, 1937, *44*, 430–444.

Spence, K. W. The role of secondary reinforcement in delayed reward learning. *Psychological Review*, 1947, *54*, 1–8.

Spence, K. W. *Behavior theory and conditioning*. New Haven: Yale University Press, 1956.

Spence, K. W. *Behavior theory and learning: Selected papers*. Englewood Cliffs, New Jersey: Prentice-Hall, 1960.

Sperling, G. The information available in brief visual presentations. *Psychological Monographs*, 1960, *74* (11, Whole No. 498).

Sperling, G. A model for visual memory tasks. *Human Factors*, 1963, *5*, 19–31.

Sperry, R. W. Cerebral organization and behavior. *Science*, 1961, *133*, 1749–1757.

Spielberger, C. D. Theoretical and epistemological issues in verbal conditioning. In S. Rosenberg (Ed.), *Directions in psycholinguistics*. New York: Macmillan, 1965.

Spooner, A., & Kellogg, W. N. The backward conditioning curve. *American Journal of Psychology*, 1947, *60*, 321–334.

Stein, D. G., & Rosen, J. J. *Learning and memory*. New York: Macmillan, 1974.

Stein, D. G., Rosen, J. J., Graziadei, J., & Brink, J. J. Central nervous system: Recovery of function. *Science*, 1969, *166*, 528–530.

Stevens-Long, J., & Rasmussen, M. The acquisition of simple and compound sentence structure in an autistic child. *Journal of Applied Behavior Analysis*, 1974, *7*, 473–479.

Strand, B. Z. Change of context and retroactive inhibition. *Journal of Verbal Learning and Verbal Behavior*, 1970, *9*, 202–206.

Strassman, H. D., Thaler, M. B., & Schein, E. H. A prisoner of war syndrome: Apathy as a reaction to severe stress. *American Journal of Psychiatry*, 1956, *112*, 998–1003.

Stubbs, D. A. Second-order schedules and the problem of conditioned reinforcement. *Journal of the Experimental Analysis of Behavior*, 1971, *16*, 289–313.

Sumby, W. H. Word frequency and serial position effects. *Journal of Verbal Learning and Verbal Behavior*, 1963, *1*, 443–450.

Suppes, P., & Ginsberg, R. Application of a stimulus sampling model to children's concept formation with and without an overt correction response. *Journal of Experimental Psychology*, 1962, *63*, 330–336.

Szwejkowska, G. Qualitative versus directional cues in differential conditioning. II. Go–no go differentiation to cues of a mixed character. *Acta Biologiae Experimentale*, 1967, *27*, 169–175.

Taffel, C. Anxiety and the conditioning of verbal behavior. *Journal of Abnormal and Social Psychology*, 1955, *51*, 496–501.

Talland, G. A. *Deranged memory: A psychonomic study of the amnesic syndrome.* New York: Academic Press, 1965.

Tapp, J. T. Current status and future directions. In J. T. Tapp (Ed.), *Reinforcement and behavior.* New York: Academic Press, 1969.

Tarpy, R. M. *Basic principles of learning.* Glenview, Illinois: Scott, Foresman, 1975.

Taylor, A. B., & Irion, A. L. Continuity hypothesis and transfer of training in paired-associate learning. *Journal of Experimental Psychology*, 1964, *68*, 573–577.

Tell, P. M. The role of certain acoustic and semantic factors at short and long retention intervals. *Journal of Verbal Learning and Verbal Behavior*, 1972, *11*, 455–464.

Terrace, H. S. Discrimination learning with and without "errors." Unpublished doctoral dissertation, Harvard University, 1961.

Terrace, H. S. Discrimination learning with and without "errors." *Journal of the Experimental Analysis of Behavior*, 1963, *6*, 1–27.   (a)

Terrace, H. S. Errorless transfer of a discrimination across two continua. *Journal of the Experimental Analysis of Behavior*, 1963, *6*, 223–232.   (b)

Terrace, H. S. Wavelength generalization after discrimination learning with and without errors. *Science*, 1964, *144*, 78–80.

Thomas, D. R., Mariner, R. W., & Sherry, G. Role of pre-experimental experience in the development of stimulus control. *Journal of Experimental Psychology*, 1969, *79*, 375–376.

Thomas, D. R., & Mitchell, K. Instructions and stimulus categorizing in a measure of stimulus generalization. *Journal of the Experimental Analysis of Behavior*, 1962, *5*, 375–381.

Thomas, D. R., Svinicki, M. D., & Vogt, J. Adaptation level as a factor in human discrimination learning and stimulus generalization. *Journal of Experimental Psychology*, 1973, *97*, 210–219.

Thompson, C. P. On the incompatibility of the Houston and Osgood transfer surfaces. *Psychological Review*, 1966, *73*, 586–588.

Thompson, C. P., Hamlin, V. J., & Roenker, D. L. A comment on the role of clustering in free recall. *Journal of Experimental Psychology*, 1972, *94*, 108–109.

Thompson, R., & McConnell, J. Classical conditioning in the planarian, *dugesia dorotocephala*. *Journal of Comparative and Physiological Psychology*, 1955, *48*, 65–68.

Thorndike, E. L. *The psychology of learning.* New York: Teachers College, 1913.

Thorndike, E. L. *Animal intelligence.* New York: Hafner, 1964.

Thorpe, W. H. *Learning and instinct in animals.* Cambridge, Massachusetts: Harvard University, 1956.

Thune, L. E. Warm-up effect as a function of level of practice in verbal learning. *Journal of Experimental Psychology*, 1951, *42*, 250–256.

Thurlow, W. R. Audition. In J. W. Kling & L. A. Riggs (Eds.), *Woodworth and Schlosberg's experimental psychology.* New York: Holt, 1971.

Timberlake, W., & Allison, J. Response deprivation: An empricial approach to instrumental performance. *Psychological Review*, 1974, *81*, 146–164.

Tinbergen, N. *The study of instinct.* Oxford: Clarendon Press, 1951.

Tinbergen, N. The curious behavior of the stickleback. *Scientific American,* 1952, *187,* 22–26.

Tracey, D. A., Briddell, D. W., & Wilson, G. T. Generalization of verbal conditioning to verbal and nonverbal behaviors: Group therapy with chronic psychiatric patients. *Journal of Applied Behavior Analysis,* 1974, *7,* 391–402.

Tracy, W. K. Wavelength generalization and preference in monochromatically reared ducklings. *Journal of the Experimental Analysis of Behavior,* 1970, *13,* 163–178.

Tragash, H. J., & Newman, S. E. Effects of pairing- and test-order constancy on performance during and after paired-associate training. *Journal of Verbal Learning and Verbal Behavior,* 1967, *6,* 762–765.

Trapold, M. A., & Overmier, J. B. The second learning process in instrumental learning. In A. H. Black & W. F. Prokasy (Eds.), *Classical conditioning II: Current theory and research.* New York: Appleton, 1972.

Tulving, E. Subjective organization in free recall of "unrelated" words. *Psychological Review,* 1962, *69,* 344–354.

Tulving, E. Intratrial and intertrial retention: Notes towards a theory of free recall verbal learning. *Psychological Review,* 1964, *71,* 219–237.

Tulving, E. Subjective organization and effects of repetition in multitrial free-recall learning. *Journal of Verbal Learning and Verbal Behavior,* 1966, *5,* 193–197.

Tulving, E. Retrograde amnesia in free recall. *Science,* 1969, *164,* 88–90.

Tulving, E. Episodic and semantic memory. In E. Tulving & W. Donaldson (Eds.), *Organization of memory.* New York: Academic Press, 1972.

Tulving, E., & Arbuckle, T. Y. Sources of intratrial interference in immediate recall of paired associates. *Journal of Verbal Learning and Verbal Behavior,* 1963, *1,* 321–334.

Tulving, E., & Donaldson, W. (Eds.), *Organization of memory.* New York: Academic Press, 1972.

Tulving, E., & Pearlstone, Z. Availability versus accessibility of information in memory for words. *Journal of Verbal Learning and Verbal Behavior,* 1966, *5,* 381–391.

Tulving, E., & Psotka, J. Retroactive inhibition in free recall: Inaccessibility of information available in the memory store. *Journal of Experimental Psychology,* 1971, *87,* 1–8.

Tulving, E., & Thomson, D. M. Retrieval processes in recognition memory: Effects of associative context. *Journal of Experimental Psychology,* 1971, *87,* 116–124.

Tulving, E., & Thomson, D. M. Encoding specificity and retrieval processes in episodic memory. *Psychological Review,* 1973, *80,* 352–373.

Twedt, H. M., & Underwood, B. J. Mixed versus unmixed lists in transfer studies. *Journal of Experimental Psychology,* 1959, *48,* 111–116.

Underwood, B. J. Interference and forgetting. *Psychological Review,* 1957, *64,* 49–60.

Underwood, B. J. Ten years of massed practice on distributed practice. *Psychological Review,* 1961, *68,* 229–247.

Underwood, B. J. Stimulus selection in verbal learning. In C. N. Cofer & B. S. Musgrave (Eds.), *Verbal behavior and learning: Problems and processes.* New York: McGraw-Hill, 1963.

Underwood, B. J. A breakdown of the Total-Time Law in free-recall learning. *Journal of Verbal Learning and Verbal Behavior,* 1970, *9,* 573–580.

Underwood, B. J. Are we overloading memory? In A. W. Melton & E. Martin (Eds.), *Coding processes in human memory.* New York: Wiley, 1972.

Underwood, B. J., & Ekstrand, B. R. An analysis of some shortcomings in the interference theory of forgetting. *Psychological Review,* 1966, *73,* 540–549.

Underwood, B. J., Ham, M., & Ekstrand, B. Cue selection in paired-associate learning. *Journal of Experimental Psychology,* 1962, *64,* 405–409.

Underwood, B. J., Jesse, F., & Ekstrand, B. R. Knowledge of rights and wrongs in verbal-discrimination. *Journal of Verbal Learning and Verbal Behavior*, 1964, *3*, 183–186.

Underwood, B. J., & Keppel, G. One trial learning? *Journal of Verbal Learning and Verbal Behavior*, 1962, *1*, 1–13.

Underwood, B. J., Runquist, W. N., & Schulz, R. W. Response learning in paired-associate lists as a function of intralist similarity. *Journal of Experimental Psychology*, 1959, *58*, 70–78.

Underwood, B. J., & Schulz, R. W. *Meaningfulness and verbal learning*. Philadelphia: Lippincott, 1960.

Valenstein, E. S. *Brain stimulation and motivation: Research and commentary*. Glenview, Illinois: Scott, Foresman, 1973.

Veroff, J., & Veroff, J. B. Reconsideration of a measure of power motivation. *Psychological Bulletin*, 1972, *78*, 279–291.

Verplanck, W. S. The operant conditioning of human motor behavior. *Psychological Bulletin*, 1956, *53*, 70–83.

Vincent, S. B. The function of the vibrissae in the behavior of the white rat. *Behavioral Monographs*, 1912, *5*.

Voeks, V. W. Acquisition of S–R connections: A test of Hull's and Guthrie's theories. *Journal of Experimental Psychology*, 1954, *47*, 137–147.

Voss, J. F. On the relationship of associative and organizational processes. In E. Tulving & W. Donaldson (Eds.), *Organization of memory*. New York: Academic Press, 1972.

Wagner, A. R. Stimulus selection and a "modified continuity theory." In G. H. Bower & J. T. Spence (Eds.), *The psychology of learning and motivation*, Vol. 3. New York: Academic Press, 1969.

Wagner, A. R., Logan, R. A., Haberlundt, K., & Price, T. Stimulus selection in animal discrimination learning. *Journal of Experimental Psychology*, 1968, *76*, 171–180.

Wahlsten, D. L., & Cole, M. Classical and avoidance training of leg flexion in the dog. In A. H. Black & W. F. Prokasy (Eds.), *Classical conditioning II: Current theory and research*. New York: Appleton, 1972.

Walk, R. D., & Walters, C. P. Effect of visual deprivation on depth discrimination of hooded rats. *Journal of Comparative and Physiological Psychology*, 1973, *85*, 559–563.

Walker, H. J. Interaction of imagery, associative overlap, and category membership in multitrial free recall. *Journal of Experimental Psychology*, 1971, *88*, 333–339.

Wallace, R. K., & Benson, H. The physiology of meditation. *Scientific American*, 1972, *226*, 84–90.

Wallace, W. P. Clustering in free recall based upon input contiguity. *Psychonomic Science*, 1969, *14*, 290–292.

Wallace, W. P. Consistency of emission order in free recall. *Journal of Verbal Learning and Verbal Behavior*, 1970, *9*, 58–68.

Walton, D. The relevance of learning theory to the treatment of an obsessive–compulsive state. In E. J. Eysenck (Ed.), *Behavior therapy and the neuroses*. London: Pergamon, 1960.

Warren, L. An analysis of proactive inhibition in a cued recall task. *Journal of Experimental Psychology*, 1974, *103*, 131–138.

Warrington, E. K., & Shallice, T. The selective impairment of auditory verbal short-term memory. *Brain*, 1969, *92*, 885–896.

Warrington, E. K., & Weiskrantz, L. New method of testing long-term retention with special reference to amnesic patients. *Nature*, 1968, *217*, 972–974.

Warrington, E. K., & Weiskrantz, L. Amnesic syndrome: Consolidation or retrieval? *Nature*, 1970, *228*, 628–630.

Wasserman, E. A., & Molina, E. J. Explicitly unpaired key light and food-presentations: Interference with subsequent auto-shaped key pecking in pigeons. *Journal of Experimental Psychology: Animal Behavior Processes*, 1975, *104*, 30–38.

Watkins, M. J. Locus of the modality effect in free recall. *Journal of Verbal Learning and Verbal Behavior*, 1972, *11*, 644–648.

Watkins, M. J. Concept and measurement of primary memory. *Psychological Bulletin*, 1974, *81*, 695–711.

Watkins, M. J., & Tulving, E. Episodic memory: When recognition fails. *Journal of Experimental Psychology: General*, 1975, *104*, 5–29.

Watson, J. B. The effect of delayed feeding upon learning *Psychobiology*, 1917, *1*, 51–60.

Waugh, N. C. Presentation time and free recall. *Journal of Experimental Psychology*, 1967, *73*, 39–44.

Waugh, N. C. On the effective duration of a repeated word. *Journal of Verbal Learning and Verbal Behavior*, 1970, *9*, 587–595.

Waugh, N. C., & Norman, D. A. Primary memory. *Psychological Review*, 1965, *72*, 89–104.

Weaver, G. E. Stimulus encoding as a determinant of retroactive inhibition. *Journal of Verbal Learning and Verbal Behavior*, 1969, *8*, 807–814.

Weiner, B. Motivation and memory. *Psychological Monographs*, 1966, *80*, No. 18 (Whole No. 626).

Weisberg, P., & Waldrop, P. B. Fixed interval work habits of Congress. *Journal of Applied Behavior Analysis*, 1972, *5*, 93–97.

Weisman, R. G., & Davis, E. R. Response-dependent shock in second-order fixed-ratio schedules of food presentation. *Journal of the Experimental Analysis of Behavior*, 1975, *23*, 103–109.

Weist, R. M. Optimal versus nonoptimal conditions for retrieval. *Journal of Verbal Learning and Verbal Behavior*, 1970, *9*, 311–316.

Weist, R. M. Associative structure and free recall. *Journal of Experimental Psychology*, 1972, *94*, 110–112.

Wessells, M. G. The effects of reinforcement upon the prepecking behaviors of pigeons in the autoshaping experiment. *Journal of the Experimental Analysis of Behavior*, 1974, *21*, 125–144.

Wichawut, C., & Martin, E. Selective stimulus encoding and overlearning in paired-associate learning. *Journal of Experimental Psychology*, 1970, *85*, 383–388.

Wichawut, C., & Martin, E. Independence of A–B and A–C associations in retroaction. *Journal of Verbal Learning and Verbal Behavior*, 1971, *10*, 316–321.

Wickelgren, W. A. Acoustic similarity and intrusions in short-term memory. *Journal of Experimental Psychology*, 1965, *70*, 102–108.

Wickelgren, W. A. Context-sensitive coding, associative memory, and serial order in (speech) behavior. *Psychological Review*, 1969, *76*, 1–15.

Wickelgren, W. A. Multitrace strength theory. In D. A. Norman (Ed.), *Models of human memory*. New York: Academic Press, 1970.

Wickelgren, W. A. The long and the short of memory. *Psychological Bulletin*, 1973, *80*, 425–438.

Wickens, D. D. Encoding categories of words: An empirical approach to meaning. *Psychological Review*, 1970, *77*, 1–15.

Wickens, D. D., Schroder, H. M., & Snide, J. D. Primary stimulus generalization of the GSR under two conditions. *Journal of Experimental Psychology*, 1954, *47*, 52–56.

Wickens, D. D., & Wickens, C. D. Some factors related to pseudo-conditioning. *Journal of Experimental Psychology*, 1942, *31*, 518–526.

Wike, E. L. *Secondary reinforcement*. New York: Harper, 1966.

Wilder, L., & Levin, J. R. A developmental study of pronouncing responses in the discrimination learning of words and pictures. *Journal of Experimental Child Psychology*, 1973, *15*, 278–286.

Williams, C. D. The elimination of tantrum behavior by extinction procedures. *Journal of Abnormal and Social Psychology*, 1959, *59*, 269.

Williams, D. R., & Williams, H. Automaintenance in the pigeon: Sustained pecking despite contingent non-reinforcement. *Journal of the Experimental Analysis of Behavior*, 1969, *12*, 511–520.

Williams, J. L. Effects of the duration of a secondary reinforcer on subsequent instrumental responses. *Journal of Experimental Psychology*, 1970, *83*, 348–351.

Williams, J. L. *Operant learning: Procedures for changing behavior*. Monterey, California: Brooks/Cole, 1973.

Williams, J. P. A selection artifact in Rock's study of the role of repetition. *Journal of Experimental Psychology*, 1961, *62*, 627–628.

Williams, R. F., & Underwood, B. J. Encoding variability: Tests of the Martin hypothesis. *Journal of Experimental Psychology*, 1970, *86*, 317–324.

Winnick, W. A., & Hunt, J. McV. The effect of an extra stimulus upon strength of response during acquisition and extinction. *Journal of Experimental Psychology*, 1951, *41*, 205–215.

Winograd, E. List differentiation as a function of frequency and retention interval. *Journal of Experimental Psychology*, 1968, 76, Monograph Supplement No. 2.

Winograd, E. Some issues relating animal memory to human memory. In W. K. Honig & P. H. R. James (Eds.), *Animal memory*. New York: Academic Press, 1971.

Winograd, T. Understanding natural language. *Cognitive Psychology*, 1972, *3*, 1–191.

Wolfe, J. B. The effect of delayed reward upon learning in the white rat. *Journal of Comparative Psychology*, 1934, *17*, 1–21.

Wolfle, H. M. Time factors in conditioned finger-withdrawal. *Journal of General Psychology*, 1930, *4*, 372–378.

Wolfle, H. M. Conditioning as a function of the interval between the conditioned and original stimulus. *Journal of General Psychology*, 1931, *7*, 80–103.

Wolford, G., & Bower, G. H. Continuity theory revisited: Rejected for the wrong reasons? *Psychological Review*, 1969, *76*, 515–518.

Wollen, K. A. Effects of instructional set and materials upon forward and backward learning. *Journal of Experimental Psychology*, 1970, *85*, 275–277.

Wollen, K. A., & Lowry, D. H. Conditions that determine effectiveness of picture-mediated paired-associate learning. *Journal of Experimental Psychology*, 1974, *102*, 181–183.

Wolpe, J. *Psychotherapy by reciprocal inhibition*. Stanford, California: Stanford University Press, 1958.

Wolpe, J. The systematic desensitization treatment of neuroses. *Journal of Nervous and Mental Disease*, 1961, *132*, 189–203.

Wolpe, J. *The practice of behavior therapy*. New York: Pergamon, 1969.

Wolpe, J., & Lazarus, A. A. *Behavior therapy techniques: A guide to the treatment of neuroses*. New York: Pergamon, 1966.

Wood, G. Organizational processes and free recall. In E. Tulving & W. Donaldson (Eds.), *Organization of memory*. New York: Academic Press, 1972.

Woodward, A. E., & Bjork, R. A. Recall and recognition as a function of primary rehearsal. *Journal of Verbal Learning and Verbal Behavior*, 1973, *12*, 608–617.

Worthington, A. G., & MacMillan, M. B. Maze preferences in naive rats produced by injection of ribonucleic acid from trained rats: A further comment. *Psychonomic Science*, 1966, *5*, 298.

Wortman, P. M., & Sparling, P. B. Acquisition and retention of mnemonic information in long-term memory. *Journal of Experimental Psychology*, 1974, *102*, 22–26.

Yerkes, R. M., & Morgulis, S. The method of Pavlov in animal psychology. *Psychological Bulletin*, 1909, *6*, 257–273.

Young, J. L. Effects of intervals between reinforcement and test trials in paired-associate learning. Institute of Mathematical Studies in the Social Sciences Technical Report No. 101, 1966, Stanford University.

Young, P. T. Hedonic organization and regulation of behavior. *Psychological Review*, 1966, *73*, 59–86.

Young, R. K. Serial learning. In T. R. Dixon & D. L. Horton (Eds.), *Verbal behavior and general behavior theory*. Englewood Cliffs, New Jersey: Prentice-Hall, 1968.

Young, R. K., Hakes, D. T., & Hicks, R. Y. Effects of list length in the Ebbinghaus derived-list paradigm. *Journal of Experimental Psychology*, 1965, *70*, 338–341.

Yukl, G., Wexley, K. N., & Seymore, J. Effectiveness of pay incentives under variable ratio and continuous reinforcement schedules. *Journal of Applied Psychology*, 1972, *56*, 10–13.

Yum, K. S. An experimental test of the law of assimilation. *Journal of Experimental Psychology*, 1931, *14*, 68–82.

Zacks, R. T. Invariance of total learning time under different conditions of practice. *Journal of Experimental Psychology*, 1969, *82*, 441–447.

Zeaman, D. Response latency as a function of the amount of reinforcement. *Journal of Experimental Psychology*, 1949, *39*, 466–483.

Zeiler, M. D. Stimulus definition and choice. In L. P. Lipsitt & C. C. Spiker (Eds.), *Advances in child development and behavior*. Vol. III. New York: Academic Press, 1967.

Zentall, T. R. Effects of context change on forgetting in rats. *Journal of Experimental Psychology*, 1970, *86*, 440–448.

Zimmerman, D. W. Durable secondary reinforcement. *Psychological Review*, 1957, *64*, 373–383.

Index